PRAISE FOR *INVENTING DESTINY*

"Readers hoping to learn more about the culture of US expansion need look no further than this compelling interdisciplinary collection. The essays in *Inventing Destiny* offer fresh perspectives on the contested nature of territorial conquests across the North American continent."
   Amy S. Greenberg, author of *A Wicked War: Polk, Clay, Lincoln, and the 1846 U.S. Invasion of Mexico*

"In the most important rethinking of US imperialism and expansionism since Amy Kaplan and Donald Pease's *Cultures of United States Imperialism* in 1993, *Inventing Destiny* provides a complex, multifaceted, multidimensional reconsideration of manifest destiny. Moving readers beyond the simplistic narrative of expansionism, the essays in this collection challenge the notion that there is anything simple about manifest destiny or American imperialism. Instead, they compellingly demonstrate that seemingly simple rhetorical devices like manifest destiny emerge from a complicated network of cultural contexts and represent competing agendas, ideals, and goals."
   Gregory Eiselein, professor and University Distinguished Teaching Scholar, Department of English, Kansas State University

"Taking a creative, multidisciplinary approach to the study of American westward expansion, *Inventing Destiny* challenges scholars to think about the cultural driving forces—including art, literature, gender, and religion—behind the rapid transformation of the nation's nineteenth-century frontier."
   William S. Kiser, author of *Coast-to-Coast Empire: Manifest Destiny and the New Mexico Borderlands*

"These eclectic, indeed kaleidoscopic, essays take the story of America's territorial growth from the early republic to the Gilded Age in fresh directions. They reveal we can learn as much about the impulses *and limits* of US expansion from capsule biographies and microscopic and interdisciplinary analyses of obscure texts, maps, artistic renderings and incidents, as we can learn from the machinations of political leaders and diplomats and the victories and setbacks of national armies. Editor Jimmy Bryan Jr. and his fellow authors collectively provide a fascinating cultural take not only on the saga of America's 'manifest destiny' on its western and southern borderlands, but also on the particular roles of women and marginalized peoples—especially Native Americans, African Americans, and Mormons—within that process.

This volume should appeal to anyone tempted to delve beyond commonplace narratives of nineteenth-century America's thrust westward and southward."

Robert E. May, author of *Slavery, Race, and Conquest in the Tropics: Lincoln, Douglas, and the Future of Latin America*

"The disciplinary range on display in these essays is impressive, and the collection shows that while manifest destiny was an expression of domination, no one group dominated the creation of the discourse. This book makes a significant contribution to our understanding of the American West and the American nation."

Jon T. Coleman, author of *Vicious: Wolves and Men in America*

Inventing Destiny

Inventing Destiny

Cultural Explorations
of US Expansion

Edited by Jimmy L. Bryan Jr.

University Press of Kansas

Published by the University Press of Kansas (Lawrence, Kansas 66045),
which was organized by the Kansas Board of Regents and is operated
and funded by Emporia State University, Fort Hays State University,
Kansas State University, Pittsburg State University, the University of Kansas,
and Wichita State University.

Library of Congress Cataloging-in-Publication Data
Names: Bryan, Jimmy L., Jr., editor.
Title: Inventing destiny : cultural explorations of US expansion /
edited by Jimmy L. Bryan Jr.
Description: Lawrence : University Press of Kansas, [2019] |
Includes bibliographical references and index.
Identifiers: LCCN 2019004077
ISBN 9780700628179 (cloth : alk. paper)
ISBN 9780700628186 (pbk. : alk. paper)
ISBN 9780700628193 (ebook)
Subjects: LCSH: United States—Territorial expansion—Social aspects.
Classification: LCC E179.5 .I68 2019 | DDC 973.2—dc23
LC record available at https://lccn.loc.gov/2019004077.

British Library Cataloguing-in-Publication Data is available.

Printed in the United States of America

10 9 8 7 6 5 4 3 2 1

Editor's dedication
For my brothers, Gene and Shane

Contents

A photo gallery follows page 130.

Acknowledgments

In many ways, this project originated in a class on US expansion that I took at the University of Texas at Arlington with Sam W. Haynes. I still own my dog-eared, battered copies of Norman Graebner, Frederick Merk, Reginal Horsman, and Thomas Hietala, but the book that stood out for me was Robert Johannsen's *To the Halls of the Montezumas* (1985). When I decided to become a historian, I was attracted to stories told in the past, and here, Johannsen took seriously both the stories and the imagination that empowered them. Narratives and emotions stirred by romanticism revealed how communities and nations made sense of their world, how they sublimated the ugly things about themselves, and how they constructed the artifices of national belonging and exceptionalism. Those lessons have influenced my studies ever since.

The other key moment for this project occurred much more recently when I not so inadvertently mentioned the idea to Kim Hogeland, my editor at the University Press of Kansas. I am grateful for her sustaining encouragement, support, and patience. Thank you, Kim, Kelly Chrisman Jacques, Michael Kehoe, Susan Ecklund, and the entire team at Kansas. I am delighted by the spirit of collaboration that I have enjoyed with my fellow contributors to the volume, and I thank them for their hard work and their generosity in sharing their research. Jon Coleman, Gregory Eiselein, and Robert May reviewed the original proposal and offered sage and welcome comments. Eiselein and an anonymous reviewer read the entire manuscript, and their suggestions significantly enhanced the final product. I owe a special thanks to Sam Haynes and Andy Doolen, who read and commented on the introduction. Their frank assessment and collegial support helped me avoid some obvious pitfalls, although I no doubt stepped into others against which they warned me. My colleagues at Lamar University also read portions of the manuscript during our departmental brown bag seminar. Thank you, Rebecca Boone, Miguel Chavez, Jeff Forret, Brendan Gillis, Tina Kibbe, Mark Mengerink, Gwinyai Muzorewa, and Yasuko Sato. As always, I owe the most gratitude to my wife, Lisa Castillo Bryan.

Inventing Destiny

"Everybody Needs Some Elbow Room": Culture and Contradiction in the Study of US Expansion

Jimmy L. Bryan Jr.

In the 1970s during Saturday morning programming, the ABC television net-work broadcast *Schoolhouse Rock*, a series of animated musical shorts intended to educate children on math, grammar, and science. Beginning in late 1975, marking the bicentennial celebration of the American Revolution, the produc-ers turned to US history. The episode "Elbow Room," released on March 6, 1976, offered an elementary-school explanation of US territorial conquest. The upbeat lyrics matched the campy images and catchy melody. As the title suggests, the song taught its cartoon aficionados that Thomas Jefferson ac-quired Louisiana in 1803 in order to accommodate the population surge in the United States. The only Native American who lived within that new territory, Sacagawea, merrily guided the explorers Meriwether Lewis and William Clark across the continent. The animators show their canoe meandering through a blank, white space, revealing in its wake a psychedelic landscape that abounds in the promise of future prosperity. The songwriter Lynn Ahrens included an oblique reference to conflicts, yet insisted, "But the West was meant to be; / It was our Manifest Destiny!" The singsong simplicity of the message lionized US expansion as a national achievement that made everyone happy.[1]

Mindful of its Scooby-Doo-watching demographic, "Elbow Room" did not attempt to explain the era's complexities and dissonance that scholars had already established. To be sure, a number of triumphalist historians bought into the "winning of the West" school inherited from Theodore Roosevelt and Frederick Jackson Turner, but a small group of intellectual and diplomatic historians offered a much more critical assessment.[2] In *Manifest Destiny* (1935), the earliest professional book-length examination of the topic, Albert K. Weinberg delved into the contradictions of a people who claimed to occupy a moral and humanist high ground yet consistently sacrificed those principles for the pragmatic advantages afforded by the pursuit of more land. He equated expansionists to "the energetic individual who decides upon, plans, and carries out the robbery of a bank" (273). Norman Graebner agreed in *Empire on the Pacific* (1955). He argued that a commercial impulse drove US policy makers to secure Pacific ports for the Asian trade. Similarly, with *Manifest Destiny and Mission in American History* (1963), Frederick Merk affirmed that US diplomatic leaders in the 1840s resorted to propaganda in order to manipulate a public that was largely resistant to territorial conquest. Although traditional in approach, these scholars' insights laid the groundwork for critically examining US expansion.[3]

If "manifest destiny" defined a process of US territorial acquisition, it was a messy one. If it described an era in history, its boundaries were fuzzy. Although the drive across North America in the early nineteenth century represented a unique period with its own peculiarities and consequences, it nevertheless figured within a long continuum of empire that predated, and continued after, the creation of the United States. In its own moment, opponents within and without the nation loudly contested the assumptions of expansion at every point along its timeline. Its outcome was not inevitable. Its implementation was often uncoordinated, accidental, and fraught with alternative contingencies, but the proponents of expansion worked deliberately and aggressively to achieve their dreams. In so doing, they often contradicted their professed virtuousness. As historian Amy S. Greenberg later summarized, "It was a self-serving ideology that achieved a variety of purposes, few of which were noble."[4]

But "Elbow Room" serves as an interesting marker not for its simplistic message but for its timing. It appeared at the moment during which scholars began a fundamental reassessment of the past. The social and counterculture movements that crescendoed in the late 1960s roused students of history, American studies, literature, art, and other disciplines to recover the experiences and thoughts of women and ethnic minorities, as well as the less wealthy and less powerful. This awakening led to a grand dispersion of traditional academic fields that many celebrated for its diversity and fresh perspectives, while others lamented its fracturing of a cherished consensus and the blurring of once precise boundaries. It led to the rise of class, ethnic, and feminist perspectives in history and literature.[5] American studies jettisoned its reliance on the old assumptions that a unanimous "American Mind" originated from its representation in "high culture," inviting scholars to seek out underrepresented pasts and recover alternative texts to get at those stories unspoken in the traditional record.[6] This "cultural turn" also inspired a cadre of historians who drew upon fresh social perspectives and adopted the methodologies of American studies, literary criticism, anthropology, and others. As an amorphous group that existed within and without established disciplines, they deconstructed the scaffolding—the symbologies, the metaphors, and the narratives—that reinforced cultural fictions.[7]

Significantly for empire studies, the 1960s social upheavals also included an active and determined antiwar movement. The US intervention in Vietnam provoked a generation to question the old narratives that positioned the United States as the world's champion for democracy and human rights. The long Cold War and the 1970s scandals of Richard Nixon's presidency compounded a growing disenchantment with, and distrust of, the nation's political leaders. Coupled with the rising interest in the histories of women, ethnic groups, and the less wealthy, the critique of US policies led scholars to re-examine that period so often referred to as "manifest destiny."

From the early 1970s to the early 1990s, multidisciplinary approaches produced the foundational corpus in the cultural study of US expansion and empire more generally. This work established that racism and ethnic stereotyping significantly informed the justifications for continental acquisitions, debunking arguments that Mexicans were lazy and unworthy of the lands they occupied, that Native Americans were nobly yet inevitably destined for vanishing, or that new territory would assuage the anxieties stirred by African American slavery and European immigration.[8] Feminist scholars recovered the experiences of women in the US West and the expansionist enterprise or deciphered the female metaphors encoded in colonial rhetoric.[9] The cultural historical approach further demonstrated the crucial role that narrative, imagination, and metaphor played in conveying the justifications of empire, such as rendering extranational territory as a blank canvas that invited new representations—to naturalize exotic lands and sublimate the evil of its conquest. As Edward W. Said summarized in *Culture and Imperialism* (1991), "The main battle in imperialism is over land, of course; but when it came to who owned the land, who had the right to settle and work on it . . . these issues were reflected, contested, and even for a time decided in narrative" (xii).[10]

During this time, historians studying North American frontiers, the US West, and Native American history renovated the old term "borderlands" and revitalized a field that recognized the fluidity and impact of arbitrarily drawn boundaries, culture change within contact zones, the continuum of conquest, and the agency and persistence of marginalized communities.[11] They also benefited from works that reoriented and transected national and imperial borders, rejecting an Anglo- or Eurocentric view of the world and focusing on peoples on the outside of empire.[12] Chicana/o historians, furthermore, reminded scholars that the process of colonization did not end with the American Revolution. Instead, the mechanisms of "internal colonialism" continue to exploit peoples oppressed by expansionism.[13]

By 1993, the publication of Amy Kaplan and Donald E. Pease's *Cultures of United States Imperialism* confirmed that scholars had established the thematic foundations of the field. Following the close of the Cold War and the Gulf War, the anthology brought a focus to the underappreciated lessons that American studies, literary history, and cultural history taught about the US imperial experience. It offered a glimpse of the scholarship that would follow, showcasing essays that asked questions about colonialism, transnationalism, race, and gender. The volume reinforced the value of the multidisciplinary, cultural historical approach to the study of empire but privileged topics that focused on the late nineteenth and twentieth centuries. Of the twenty-four essays, only two dealt with the early nineteenth century. Nevertheless, *Cultures of United States Imperialism* heightened the visibility of the field and demonstrated the wide range of untapped topics for study. Since its appearance, scholars of the cultural history of US expansion and empire have engaged in a vigorous discourse, building upon the established themes and introducing new ones.

After coediting the anthology, Kaplan published her influential essay "Manifest Domesticity" (1998). Applying deconstruction methodologies from gender and culture studies, she finds that when female authors expressed their views about US empire, many assembled an externalized version of domesticity. Kaplan contends that the idea supported imperial projects by developing narratives that shaped conquest as a force that civilized racial and religious others. Adrienne Caughfield and Laurel Clark Shire followed with studies on women who participated in the physical settlement of contested regions. With *True Women and Westward Expansion* (2005), Caughfield argues that Anglo-American female settlers in Texas willingly and crucially supported their husbands and fathers in transforming the frontier into a domestic garden. Shire, writing in *The Threshold of Manifest Destiny* (2016), also finds women who actively shaped land policy as well as formulated the stories that justified the taking of Seminole homes.[14]

About the same time that Kaplan's essay appeared, Gail Bederman, in *Manliness and Civilization* (1995), and Kristin L. Hoganson, in *Fighting for American Manhood* (1998), applied similar gender analyses but focused on how manliness impacted US culture and policy at the time of the Spanish-American War, discovering the intricate connections between gender and race, and gender and empire. With *Manifest Manhood and the Antebellum American Empire* (2005), Amy S. Greenberg recovers an antidomestic impulse within the filibuster and expansionist literature of the 1850s. Advocates of a martial manhood defined themselves against restraint and found opportunities for attaining dominion, or a "personal annexation," in unsanctioned invasions of Latin American nations. By closely examining the western tours of Scottish noble William Drummond Stewart in *Men in Eden* (2012), William Benemann argues that the world of the Rocky Mountain fur trade permitted, if not welcomed, male-male sexuality. Monica Rico's *Nature's Noblemen* (2013) portrays Stewart and his fellow aristocrats—British and US—playing out their "fantasies of mastery" in the West. In so doing, they reinforced each other's class standing. In my book *The American Elsewhere* (2017), I find similar tensions between differing concepts of manliness within a reckless generation of the early nineteenth century. These men rejected the industrious male of their fathers' generation to reconstruct the adventurous male as a paragon of US exceptionalism and empire.[15]

Race also continues to serve as a category of analysis for US expansion. Shelley Streeby, in *American Sensations* (2002), and Jaime Javier Rodríguez, in *Literatures of the US-Mexican War* (2010), explore texts produced during the US-Mexican War and agree that the writers at the time attempted to generate sympathies between US soldiers and the Mexican aristocracy, presumed European, but they ultimately failed because their narratives and imagination refused to accommodate the presence of mestizo peoples. With *Fugitive Empire* (2005), Andy Doolen confirms the "historical trinity of US imperialism—war, slavery, and territorial expansion" (xv), locating the origins of that union of exigencies in the mid-eighteenth century. Eric T. L. Love, however, questions these assumptions. In *Race over Empire* (2004), he finds that although racism informed US policies in many different arenas, it also motivated antiexpansionists, who expressed concerns about incorporating nonwhites into the national domain.[16]

Scholars interested in the constructions of the imaginary Indian have made significant contributions since the early 1990s. Jill Lepore's *The Name of War* (1998) describes how Native Americans suffered a disadvantage relative to their literate European American foes, who could preserve and transmit their words to future generations. She shows how nineteenth-century representations of King Philip's War (1675–1676) abetted the removal of Native Americans and reinforced their consignment to the past. Joshua David Bellin, with *The Demon of the Continent* (2001), reinserts Native American perspectives in early nineteenth-century US literature that sought to banish it to an inevitable disappearing. In *Firsting and Lasting* (2010), Jean M. O'Brien explores the process of "firsting" by which New Englanders wrote Natives out of their historical narratives and thereby naturalized their dominion over the land. Examining the works of George Catlin, John Hausdoerffer's *Catlin's Lament* (2009) depicts the artist as moderately antiexpansionist, especially as a critic of American avarice. Hausdoerffer concedes, however, that Catlin's unintended reframing of Native American culture enabled the conquest of Natives' lands. William H. Truettner, in *Painting Indians and Building Empires in North America* (2010), compares British and US empires through Native American portraiture, finding that the former emphasized the potential improvement of the "noble savage," while the latter depicted its subjects as laudably yet hopelessly primitive and doomed to extinction.[17]

Expanding on the foundational works of Myra Jehlen, Mary Louise Pratt, Angela Miller, and others, recent scholarship has uncovered new ways to understand the crucial role that the geographic imaginary plays in conceiving empires and its connections to national identity. Beth L. Lueck's *American Writers and the Picturesque Tour* (1997) demonstrates that US travel writers used the western landscape and the language of the picturesque to empower US exceptionalism and title to new lands. In *From the Fallen Tree* (2003), Thomas Hallock focuses on how artists and other culture makers privileged the pastoral over the wilderness, and he finds similar processes of naturalization that occurred when these influential groups projected Indian lands into the future as rural and cultivated. Gretchen Murphy, with *Hemispheric Imaginings* (2005), examines how the Monroe Doctrine influenced US cultural production to create an expansive sense of entitlement and exceptionalism, and in *The Geographic Revolution in Early America* (2006), Martin Brückner attests that "geographic literacy" in the early republic was crucial to the formation of national identity. The geographic imagination included a predatorial gaze, according to Kenneth Haltman. In *Looking Close and Seeing Far* (2008) and "Flight and Predation" (2014), he sees this recurrent theme within the landscapes and hunting scenes of Samuel Seymour, Titian R. Peale, and Alfred Jacob Miller, where "predatory looking" activated the viewer's desires for consumption. In presenting landscapes and Indians via print culture, the medium by which most Americans visually encountered the West, Matthew N. Johnston (*Narrating the Landscape*, 2016) argues that artists created a sense of immediacy with viewers that divorced their subjects from their history and thus enabled the seizure of their lands.[18]

In contrast, when Anne Farrar Hyde published *An American Vision* in 1990, she challenged the foundational views that US observers sought to inscribe nationalist meaning upon the landscape. She argued that the physical West mystified early nineteenth-century US travel writers because they lacked a textual and visual vocabulary to explain its alienness. Anne Baker, Richard V. Francaviglia, and Rachel St. John sympathize with this perspective. Baker, with *Heartless Immensity* (2006), contends that the unsettled bounds of the United States contributed to deep anxieties over its formlessness. In *Go East, Young Man* (2011), Francaviglia suggests that US travel writers attempted to exoticize the land through a process of Orientalism in order to make something new, while St. John, in "Contingent Continent" (2017), observes that both pro-expansionists and antiexpansionists used geographic determinism to support their arguments.[19]

Since the turn of the twenty-first century, borderlands scholars have produced a body of work that provides in-depth explorations of how many groups of people have confronted, challenged, and compromised with US empire. Native Americans and Mexicans were not passive victims, and they found ways to work within and without to forestall or find a place within geopolitical shifts. Deena J. González (*Refusing the Favor*, 1999), Andrés Resendéz (*Changing National Identities at the Frontier*, 2005), Raúl Ramos (*Beyond the Alamo*, 2008), and Karen Roybal (*Archives of Dispossession*, 2017) chart how *nuevomexicano* and Tejano communities endured the influx of Anglo-American capital, settlers, and authority, struggling to preserve their distinct identities and adapting to their new realities. Ned Blackhawk's *Violence over the Land* (2006) recenters the violence of US colonial practices around the perspective of Native groups who inhabited the Great Basin, while Pekka Hämäläinen (*The Comanche Empire*, 2008) and Brian DeLay (*War of a Thousand Deserts*, 2008) study how Comanches influenced the imperial currents on the southern Great Plains and beyond. In *Empires, Nations, and Families* (2011), Anne Farrar Hyde combines this scholarship with her own extensive research to show how the interior of North America teemed with trade and multiethnic interactions in the early decades of the nineteenth century. Kinship and fluid identity defined imperial relationships between diverse peoples, but the arrival of the United States, with its economic might and a racial hierarchy intolerant of the mixed ancestries, realigned these commercial networks. Hyde, however, refuses to tell the story of inevitable failure but instead portrays a complex world of families and traders who demonstrated the fallacies of peripheries and preordained destinies.[20]

As Hyde suggests, families served at the vanguard of US colonial projects. Bethel Saler, Laurel Clark Shire, and Dawn Peterson focus on this settler experience and especially on how women and the family function as crucial nexuses of conquest. In *The Settlers' Empire* (2014), Saler follows the cultural and legal processes of state making in early Wisconsin, while Shire reveals how the construction of households served the Anglo-American conquest of Seminole Florida. Where Saler and Shire emphasize the struggles over meanings and policies regarding land and community, Peterson, with *Indians in the Family* (2017), reveals the reinscriptions of Native bodies through metaphor as well as physical adoption into white families.[21]

As befits the term, transnational studies cross the boundaries that have defined the fields investigating settler colonialism, borderlands, and the geographic imaginary. Those who embrace the approach explore communities that extend beyond artificial demarcations of nations and empires—communities that have created globalized, hemispheric, or diasporic cultures. In *Writing to Cuba* (2005), Rodrigo Lazo shows how Cuban nationals influenced US designs on their homeland, while Aims McGuinness (*Path of Empire*, 2008) and Michel Gobat (*Empire by Invitation*, 2018) illustrate that Panamanians and Nicaraguans faced US interlopers with attitudes that ranged from resistance to welcoming. With *Territories of Empire* (2014), Andy Doolen draws upon this field and argues that for a brief period after Mexico gained independence in 1821, many commentators in the United States were sympathetic to the idea of sharing the hemisphere with like-minded, anticolonial republics. Doolen also examines how "cartographic texts" shaped conceptions of territoriality.[22]

As Eric T. L. Love's work on racism as a hindrance to empire illustrates, expansionist culture and policies incited equally powerful antiexpansionist sentiments that have attracted scholarly interest in recent years. Etsuko Taketani's *U.S. Women Writers and the Discourses of Colonialism* (2003) finds that many female authors intended their utopian and reformist themes as a subversion of US colonialism. With *A Wicked War* (2012), Amy S. Greenberg takes a personal approach to the opposition against the US invasion of Mexico by focusing on the impact of the war on individual leaders, soldiers, and their female family members. During the presidential election of 1844, Whigs were tepid in the face of broad enthusiasm for conquest, but as news of excesses committed against Mexicans reached the public, opposition to the war deepened. In *Global West, American Frontier* (2013), David M. Wrobel counters those scholars who have argued that travel writers encouraged imperial projects. He does not deny that many travelers were sympathetic, but he finds a select number who wrote from a globalist perspective and who have consistently offered sharp criticisms of empire and its costs to indigenous peoples. Love, Taketani, Greenberg, and Wrobel contribute meaningful correctives to the assumption that US expansion was an uncontested, universally accepted idea, but as Ian Tyrrell and Jay Sexton observe in the introduction to their anthology *Empire's Twin* (2015), the scholarship on anti-imperialism wanes in comparison to works that examine the forces of conquest.[23]

The antiexpansionist position suggests that a clear division existed between those who advocated territorial conquest and those who protested, but such boundaries are rarely so clear. Scholars interested in these indistinctions have uncovered numerous literary interventions of empire—texts that expressed trepidation and questioned the fictions created by those who clamored for expansion. In *Literary Culture and U.S. Imperialism* (2000), John Carlos Rowe interrogates canonical texts from Charles Brockden Brown to Herman Melville for their awareness of and commentary on empire and discovers the contradictions that they reveal. He observes, "American interpretations of themselves as a people are shaped by a powerful imperial desire and a profound anti-colonial temper" (3). Peter J. Kastor's *The Nation's Crucible* (2004) offers less ambiguity. After the Louisiana Purchase, administrators of the new territory lacked enthusiasm for empire because they had to deal with unruly mixed populations of squatters with dubious loyalties, rebellious African American slaves, and enduring Indians. In *William Clark's World* (2011), Kastor reminds his readers that during the early decades of the nineteenth century, explorers like Clark were cautious and advocated a sober and orderly process of acquisition and settlement. Stephanie LeMenager's *Manifest and Other Destinies* (2004) finds that during the "lawless interval" between the Louisiana Purchase and Texas annexation, the terrain beyond the Mississippi River and the people who occupied it created transnational "counter-sites" that resisted US expansionist narratives during this period. Doolen also examines this era of abeyance and discusses how US cultural leaders considered alternative destinies by joining Mexico and other potential republics to preserve the Western Hemisphere from European domination.[24]

When conceived of as an interdisciplinary enterprise and viewed within flexible periodization, the study of US expansion has produced a robust and diverse corpus since the 1970s. The numbers and common thematic approaches suggest that these authors have engaged in intensive conversations with each other, but that is not always the case. Too often these scholars restrict their readings to their individual fields, and although they deliver important and meaningful studies, their work could have benefited and reached a wider audience had they incorporated findings or borrowed methodologies from each other.

In some ways, *Inventing Destiny* exhibits these same issues. Within the confines of their chapters, many of the contributors work primarily within their own disciplines. By presenting these perspectives within a single volume, this anthology seeks to inspire a dialogue between the authors and their specializations, thereby demonstrating the value of multidisciplinary explorations of US expansion. With contributors who represent fields in American studies, history, literary criticism, art history, and religious studies, and who examine a wide variety of source material such as artwork, literature, and geospatial analysis, as well as novel readings of traditional historical texts, *Inventing Destiny* strives to illuminate the complexities rather than simplify—to transgress borders rather than redraw them—to amplify the undertold stories rather than repeat the old ones.

In evoking the phrase "cultural explorations" in the subtitle, this collection embraces the freedoms of broadly conceived parameters and definitions. Scholars who venture into this field understand that contradictions and ambiguities exist within any given historical moment, supplying the fodder for their studies as they investigate the varied ways in which humans attempt to resolve these gray areas through narrative, metaphor, sublimation, and other sleight-of-hand techniques. This mode of inquiry also encourages works that provide understudied perspectives, presenting history from the point of view of those who enacted expansion, those who resisted, and those who attempted to shape it for their own advantage.

This flexibility also defies strict chronological boundaries. The anthology includes essays that range from the late eighteenth century to the late nineteenth century, in contrast to the traditional demarcation of US expansion occurring between the Louisiana Purchase (1803) and the Treaty of Guadalupe Hidalgo (1848). This broader view underscores the conclusions of Albert K. Weinberg and others that the compulsion for empire existed before the creation of the United States and continues into the twenty-first century.[25] Periodization, however, can be as helpful as restrictive. Centering the discussion on the first half of the nineteenth century provides an organizational focus from which to work, inviting comparisons to, and departures from, the history of the expansionist era.

I open the anthology with a chapter on pro-expansionists' brash and often extravagant prophecies. I borrow strategies that cultural scholars have employed to reveal how empire building functioned as an act of imagination and how its advocates cultivated emotional appeals in order to generate sympathies with the broadest possible audience. I examine the future as envisioned by early nineteenth-century expansionists, parsing a variety of texts, including essays, fiction, speeches, poetry, and visual representations. By including a wide range of authors and artists, I demonstrate the preponderance of their techniques and themes, concluding that the prophets of empire stoked the conceits of their audiences by playing upon their dreams of ethnic superiority, technological innovation, and national chauvinism. In so doing, these future-seers employed a romantic tool kit, inciting an emotional reaction in order to connect the individual personally to the otherwise impersonal schemes of empire.

By contrast, the religious commentators who populate Daniel J. Burge's chapter used similar future-seeing tactics, but instead of technological and prosperous futures, they foretold of doom in consequence of national avarice. Burge finds that from the time of the 1830s Indian Removal to the 1870s project of Caribbean annexation, antiexpansionists persistently drew upon a biblical fable to protest the immorality of expansion. They evoked the story of King Ahab, who swindled a vineyard away from his neighbor Naboth. The prophet Elijah had cautioned the king that if he proceeded with his scheme, he would suffer a humiliating death. Ahab ignored the warning, seized the vineyard, and died at the hands of his enemies. The allegory reminded professed Christians that their god not only frowned upon those who coveted their neighbors' lands but would punish them for doing so. In confirming the persistent use of this religious critique, Burge offers an important counterpoint to long-held assumptions that US Christianity uniformly empowered the belief in a providentially sanctioned "manifest destiny."[26]

Where I focus on pro-expansionist and Burge on antiexpansionist sentiments, Kenneth Haltman locates a more ambiguous position in Charles Bird King's painting *Keokuk, the Watchful Fox* (1829). Using the techniques of object analysis, he demonstrates that scholars still have much to discover about how Anglo-Americans deliberately shaped Native American imagery. In preparing portraits of Native dignitaries for the superintendent of Indian affairs and the secretary of war, King ostensibly served as an agent of US empire. By interrogating the visual language of a single text, Haltman reveals that the painting transcends its position as an example of ethnographic portraiture. Instead, the choices the artist made in framing his subject and the symbols that he encoded within it reflect the imperial equivocations of the 1820s. Although King predicted the ultimate demise of Keokuk and his people, he positions the Native leader standing proudly against that lamentable yet inevitable vanishing.

In the early-nineteenth century, living Natives often contradicted the images that Anglo-Americans created about them. In many different communities throughout North America, they contended with the forces of expansion in acts of defiance as well as accommodation. Elana Krischer takes the reader back to one of the first spaces into which the early United States attempted to extend its dominion—western New York in the late eighteenth century. She describes a territory over which numerous private, public, and corporate interests wrangled. Senecas, the state of New York, the Holland Land Company, Quakers, and various individuals within each group worked with, as often as they vied against, one another in attempts to preserve or remake the region to best fit their specific self-interests. In so doing, Krischer establishes the contested quality of national, state, and private boundaries and demonstrates that the processes of settler colonialism continued well after the American Revolution.

In her monograph *The Threshold of Manifest Destiny* (2016), Laurel Clark Shire recovers the colonial enterprise in 1840s Florida. She resituates women, families, and African American slaves as agents—willing and not-so-willing—seizing territory from Native Americans. In her chapter for this volume, Shire returns to Florida but employs a new analytical tool. By using geospatial computing techniques, she visually maps the settlement patterns of the lands designated in the Armed Occupation Act (1842), showing that the Anglo-American families who moved into the region were not the pioneers that later generations celebrated. Many of them constructed communities and farms in the very same locations established previously by removed Seminoles. Further, the mapping confirms the central role that women, slaves, and family played in Florida and, by extension, other lands that US colonizers took from Native groups.

As Shire investigates the impact of women as settlers, Susan L. Roberson explores their travel writing. Caroline Kirkland, Margaret Fuller, Catharine Maria Sedgwick, and Constance Fenimore Woolson wrote about their journeys through the Old Northwest. Initially they may have supported the US settlement of the region and the domesticity it established, but their works also exhibited caution and criticism. Taken together, their writings function as a literary intervention that deplored the treatment of Native Americans and decried the environmental consequences of empire.

As Chad A. Barbour finds, the literati could intervene when those domestication narratives went awry. Such was the case of Hannah Duston. Cotton Mather first related the account of her ordeal as a Puritan woman who was taken from her home by Abenakis and managed to escape by hacking her abductors to death. Barbour charts the evolution of Duston's story through several nineteenth-century retellings. Situating them within the intersections of domesticity and empire, he illustrates how authors like Nathaniel Hawthorne paternally reoriented their versions by focusing on the husband, Thomas Duston. These iterations celebrated the father's rescue of his children as an act of defending and extending the domestic space and condemning Hannah's brutality as a caution against the descent into savagery.

The title of John Dunn Hunter's *Memoirs of a Captivity among the Indians of North America, from Childhood to the Age of Nineteen* (1823) suggests that it belongs to the same genre as the Duston narrative, but Andy Doolen shows that the author instead presented himself as an adopted son who grew up among the Kaws and Osages. Instead of comparing different retellings of a story like Barbour, Doolen considers Hunter's own words. He finds that Hunter's *Memoirs* functioned as a literary borderland. The author used his ability to cross between cultures to generate sympathy for the plight of Native Americans as well as championing the idea of pan-Indian resistance to US imperial policies.

Hunter grew up among peoples who struggled against the disorientations created by expansion, but some citizens within the United States chose to expatriate themselves in order to take advantage of those conditions. Many like Lansford Hastings sought opportunities that did not always align with national goals. He occupies a dubious place within historical memory as the man whose information led the Donner Party toward its tragic end. Thomas Richards Jr., however, focuses on Hastings as a visionary whose loyalties drifted between systems that offered him the best chance to realize his personal dreams. Richards identifies a consistent ambition in Hastings's writing. He wanted to establish a society based on what Richards describes as a "democratic patriarchy"—an agrarian ideal in which landed elites shared power and lorded over estates farmed by poor white and nonwhite laborers. Hastings made several attempts to establish this kind of society in California, the Confederate West, and the Brazilian Amazon before he died in the Caribbean.

Gerrit Dirkmaat also explores this expatriate aspect of US expansion—not through an individual—but in the experiences of thousands of Mormons.[27] By the mid-1840s, at the height of US territorial acquisition and the debates it stirred, Mormons struggled to find their place within the national domain. Dirkmaat recovers how members of this religious group professed their patriotism and advocated expansion yet suffered harsh persecution from their neighbors, which included the 1844 murder of Joseph Smith, one of their leaders. At a time when US nationalism reached a crescendo, the Mormon perspective exposed its failures of exclusivity and violence. The Mormons sought escape from the country of their birth within the extranational spaces of the Great Basin to outrun US expansion. Dirkmaat further explains that when they considered a new homeland in the Great Basin, they relied on a geographic imaginary that conceived of that space as lying outside the jurisdiction of the United States, nominally within Mexican territory and largely absent of Native American inhabitants.

According to Maria Angela Diaz, different regions of the United States entertained different geographies of expansion. Along with Dirkmaat, she joins a discourse that decenters the conception of empires and borders away from the nation-state to encompass larger spheres of racial, cultural, economic, and other interactions. Focusing on the rhetoric generated by pro-slavery advocates of the Gulf South, Diaz contrasts their dreams of an empire that encompassed Latin and Caribbean America with the more familiar continental visions. Supporting conflicts in Texas, Mexico, and Cuba, these southerners employed racial arguments in the service of noncontiguous expansions.

Matthew N. Johnston closes the anthology with an exploration of the print culture produced by early archaeologists in the southwestern United States. He demonstrates that although the military resolution of expansion occurred by 1848, the cultural enterprise continued for decades longer. The conquered space required a reinterpretation of the geographic imaginary. In 1854 and 1879, John Russell Bartlett and Frederic Ward Putnam published extensive reports that included surveys of the material and built cultures of Native American groups and Spanish colonizers of the early Southwest. With their authorial and interpretative privileges, Bartlett and Putnam usurped the textual and visual representations of those who originally inhabited contested lands and wrote them out of history. In so doing, Johnston contends, they left the region vulnerable to imperial reinscription.

Together, the contributors to *Inventing Destiny* hope to inspire and inform scholarly debates about the meaning and consequences of US expansion. They each lend the expertise and perspectives of their individual fields, participating in a conversation that confirms the value of cross-discipline analyses. The fictions employed to justify US territorial conquest in the early nineteenth century yet resonate within the later narratives of world war and Cold War victories, the Moon landing, and the twenty-first-century wars on terror. By studying these processes, students of history expose the agendas that lay hidden beneath the allure of fantasies like "manifest destiny," "the new frontier," "the evil empire," or "make America great again."

In its own moment, *Inventing Destiny* appears at a time when the study of US expansion flourishes and when those lessons provide illumination in understanding the past, present, and future of US imperialism. The contributors do not pretend to offer solutions to modern-day problems, but the times suggest a need to better understand the mechanisms of cultural production. Whether demystifying, reverse engineering, or reinforcing the value of multiple perspectives, these authors recover the many ways in which groups and individuals experienced, internalized, and rendered meaningful US territorial acquisition. Some US citizens may not have perceived their own culpability and bought into the fictions of "manifest destiny" that assuaged their misgivings. Tens of thousands, however, volunteered in the wars for expansion, colonized Native American spaces, or took advantage of the disorientations for their own gain. Yet like the Senecas or John Dunn Hunter or Keokuk or the Mormons, many others resisted physically, politically, and culturally. As targets of displacement, they stood up to conquest. Others reminded their friends about the immorality of coveting their neighbor's land, while still others sought alternatives to the American mantra of progress, entitlement, and divine privilege.

NOTES

1. Lynn Ahrens, "Elbow Room," *Schoolhouse Rock* (schoolhouserock.tv); *Schoolhouse Rock*, Internet Movie Database (imdb.com).

2. For the "winning of the West" school, see Theodore Roosevelt, *The Winning of the West*, 4 vols. (New York: G. P. Putnam's Sons, 1889–1896); Frederick Jackson Turner, "The Significance of the Frontier in American History," *Annual Report of the American Historical Association for the Year 1893* (1894): 199–227; Bernard DeVoto, *Across the Wide Missouri* (Boston: Houghton Mifflin, 1947); Ray Allen Billington, *Westward Expansion: A History of the American Frontier* (New York: Macmillan, 1949); Thomas D. Clark, *Frontier America: The Story of the Westward Movement* (New York: Charles Scribner's Sons, 1959).

3. Albert K. Weinberg, *Manifest Destiny: A Study of Nationalist Expansionism in American History* (Baltimore: John Hopkins University Press, 1935); Norman Graebner, *Empire on the Pacific: A Study in American Continental Expansion* (New York: Ronald Press, 1955); Frederick Merk, *Manifest Destiny and Mission in American History: A Reinterpretation* (New York: Alfred A. Knopf, 1963). See also R. W. Van Alstyne, *The Rising American Empire* (New York: Oxford University Press, 1960); Merk, *The Oregon Question: Essays in Anglo-American Diplomacy and Politics* (Cambridge, MA: Belknap Press of Harvard University Press, 1967); Merk, *Slavery and the Annexation of Texas* (New York: Alfred A. Knopf, 1972); David M. Pletcher, *The Diplomacy of Annexation: Texas, Oregon, and the Mexican War* (Columbia: University of Missouri Press, 1973). For later studies, see Anders Stephanson, *Manifest Destiny: American Expansion and the Empire of Right* (New York: Hill and Wang, 1995); Walter Nugent, *Habits of Empire: A History of American Expansion* (New York: Alfred A. Knopf, 2008). For a historiographical review of the literature, see Sam W. Haynes, "Manifest Destiny and the American Southwest," in *A Companion to the Era of Andrew Jackson*, ed. Sean Patrick Adams (Malden, MA: Wiley-Blackwell, 2009), 549–567. For a discussion of Weinberg, see Walter A. McDougall, *Promised Land, Crusader State: The American Encounter with the World since 1776* (Boston: Houghton Mifflin, 1997), 82–84. For the historiography before 1968, see Norman A. Graebner, *Manifest Destiny* (Indianapolis: Bobbs-Merrill, 1968), lxxiv–lxxxii.

4. Amy S. Greenberg, *Manifest Destiny and American Territorial Expansion: A Brief History with Documents* (Boston: Bedford/St. Martin, 2011), 15.

5. Eric Foner, "Preface to the Revised and Expanded Edition" and "Introduction to the First Edition," in *The New American History*, ed. Eric Foner, rev. ed. (Philadelphia: Temple University Press, 1997), vii–xiii.

6. For a lament on the changes in 1970s scholarship, see Gene Wise, "'Paradigm Dramas' in American Studies: A Cultural and Institutional History of the Movement," *American Quarterly* 31 (1979): 293–337. For a discussion of Wise and an assessment of the field, see Donald E. Pease and Robyn Wiegman, "Futures," in *The Futures of American Studies*, ed. Donald E. Pease and Robyn Wiegman (Durham, NC: Duke University Press, 2002), 1–42. See also Amy Kaplan, "'Left Alone in America': The Absence of Empire in the Study of American Culture," in *Cultures of United States Imperialism*, ed. Amy Kaplan and Donald E. Pease (Durham, NC: Duke University Press, 1993), 3–21.

Before and during the 1960s, major works on the US West by American studies and literary scholars reveal crucial intersections between the mythologies of the frontier and the fictions of empire. See Henry Nash Smith, *Virgin Land: The American West as Symbol and Myth* (Cambridge, MA: Harvard University Press, 1950); Roy Harvey Pearce, *Savagism and Civilization: A Study of the Indian in the American Mind* (Baltimore: Johns Hopkins University Press, 1953); R. W. B. Lewis, *The American Adam: Innocence, Tragedy, and Tradition in the Nineteenth Century* (Chicago: University of Chicago Press, 1955); Perry Miller, *Errand into the Wilderness* (Cambridge, MA: Belknap Press of Harvard University Press, 1956); Leo Marx, *The Machine in the Garden: Technology and the Pastoral Ideal in America* (New York: Oxford University Press, 1964); Roderick Nash, *The Wilderness in the American Mind* (New Haven, CT: Yale University Press, 1967).

7. Wise, "'Paradigm Dramas,'" 322–325; Lynn Hunt, ed., *The New Cultural History* (Berkeley: University of California Press, 1989); Alun Munslow, *Deconstructing History* (New York: Routledge, 1997); James W. Cook and Lawrence B. Glickman, "Twelve Propositions for a History of US Cultural History," in *The Cultural Turn in US History: Past, Present and Future*, ed. James W. Cook, Lawrence B. Glickman, and Michael O'Malley (Chicago: University of Chicago Press, 2008), 3–57.

8. For Anglo-American attitudes toward Mexicans, see Raymund A. Paredes, "The Mexican Image in American Travel Literature, 1831–1869," *New Mexico Historical Review* 52 (January 1977): 5–29; David J. Weber, "'Scarce More Than Apes': Historical Roots of Anglo-American Stereotypes of Mexicans," in *New Spain's Far Northern Frontier: Essays on Spain in the American West, 1540–1821*, ed. David J. Weber (Albuquerque: University of New Mexico Press, 1979), 293–307; Antonia Castañeda, "The Political Economy of Nineteenth-Century Stereotypes of Californianas," in *Between Borders: Essays on Mexicana/Chicana History*, ed. Adelaida del Castillo (Encino, CA: Floricanto Press, 1990). For the persistence of the noble savage and disappearing-Indian motifs, see Robert F. Berkhofer Jr., *The White Man's Indian: Images of the American Indian from Columbus to the Present* (New York: Alfred A. Knopf, 1978); Richard Drinnon, *Facing West: The Metaphysics of Indian-Hating and Empire-Building* (Minneapolis: University of Minnesota Press, 1980); Lee Clark Mitchell, *Witness to a Vanishing America: The Nineteenth-Century Response* (Princeton, NJ: Princeton University Press, 1981); Brian W. Dippie, *The Vanishing American: White Attitudes and U.S. Indian Policy* (Middletown, CT: Wesleyan University Press, 1982); Lucy Maddox, *Removals: Nineteenth-Century American Literature and the Politics of Indian Affairs* (New York: Oxford University Press, 1991). For an examination of race and the anxieties generated by slavery, see Reginald Horsman, *Race and Manifest Destiny: The Origins of American Racial Anglo-Saxonism* (Cambridge, MA: Harvard University Press, 1981); Thomas R. Hietala, *Manifest Design: Anxious Aggrandizement in Late Jacksonian America* (Ithaca, NY: Cornell University Press, 1985).

9. Annette Kolodny, including *The Lay of the Land: Metaphors as Experience and History in American Life and Letters* (Chapel Hill: University of North Carolina Press, 1975) and *The Land before Her: Fantasy and Experience of the American Frontiers, 1630–1860* (Chapel Hill: University of North Carolina Press, 1984); Julie Roy Jeffrey, *Frontier Women: The Trans-Mississippi West, 1840–1880* (New York: Hill and Wang, 1979); John Mack Fara-

gher, *Women and Men on the Overland Trail* (New Haven, CT: Yale University Press, 1979); Sandra L. Myres, *Westering Women and the Frontier Experience, 1800–1915* (Albuquerque: University of New Mexico Press, 1982).

10. Edward W. Said, *Culture and Imperialism* (New York: Alfred A. Knopf, 1991); Myra Jehlen, *American Incarnation: The Individual, the Nation, and the Continent* (Cambridge, MA: Harvard University Press, 1986); Robert W. Johannsen, *To the Halls of the Montezumas: The Mexican War in the American Imagination* (New York: Oxford University Press, 1985); Martin Green, including *Dreams of Adventure, Deeds of Empire* (New York: Basic Books, 1979) and *The Great American Adventure* (Boston: Beacon Press, 1984); Peter Antelyes, *Tales of Adventurous Enterprise: Washington Irving and the Poetics of Western Expansion* (New York: Columbia University Press, 1990); Anne Farrar Hyde, *An American Vision: Far Western Landscape and National Culture, 1820–1920* (New York: New York University Press, 1990); Stephen Greenblatt, *Marvelous Possessions: The Wonder of the New World* (Chicago: University of Chicago Press, 1991); Bruce Greenfield, *Narrating Discovery: The Romantic Explorer in American Literature, 1790–1855* (New York: Columbia University Press, 1992); Mary Louise Pratt, *Imperial Eyes: Travel Writing and Transculturation* (New York: Routledge, 1992); Angela Miller, *The Empire of the Eye: Representations and American Cultural Politics* (Ithaca, NY: Cornell University Press, 1993); W. J. T. Mitchell, "Imperial Landscape," in *Landscape and Power*, ed. W. J. T. Mitchell (Chicago: University of Chicago Press, 1994), 5–17.

11. David J. Weber, including *The Mexican Frontier, 1821–1846: The American Southwest under Mexico* (Albuquerque: University of New Mexico Press, 1982) and *The Spanish Frontier in North America* (New Haven, CT: Yale University Press, 1992); Patricia Nelson Limerick, *The Legacy of Conquest: The Unbroken Past of the American West* (New York: W. W. Norton, 1987); Richard White, *The Middle Ground: Indians, Empires, and Republics in the Great Lakes Region, 1650–1815* (New York: Cambridge University Press, 1991).

12. Edward W. Said, *Orientalism* (New York: Pantheon, 1978); Paul Gilroy, *The Black Atlantic: Modernity and Double Consciousness* (Cambridge, MA: Harvard University Press, 1993). For a discussion of origins and definitions, see Paul Jay, *Global Matters: The Transnational Turn in Literary Studies* (Ithaca, NY: Cornell University Press, 2010), 15–32.

13. Rodolfo Acuña, *Occupied America: The Chicano's Struggle toward Liberation* (San Francisco: Canfield Press, 1972); Mario Barrera, *Race and Class in the Southwest: A Theory of Racial Inequality* (Notre Dame, IN: University of Notre Dame Press, 1979).

14. Amy Kaplan, "Manifest Domesticity," *American Literature* 70 (September 1998): 581–606; Adrienne Caughfield, *True Women and Westward Expansion* (College Station: Texas A&M University Press, 2005); Laurel Clark Shire, *The Threshold of Manifest Destiny: Gender and National Expansion in Florida* (Philadelphia: University of Pennsylvania Press, 2016). Amy Kaplan expands on her article with case studies that move her analyses to the early twentieth century. Kaplan, *The Anarchy of Empire in the Making of US Culture* (Cambridge, MA: Harvard University Press, 2002). See also Linda S. Hudson, *Mistress of Manifest Destiny: A Biography of Jane McManus Storm Cazneau, 1807–1878* (Austin: Texas State Historical Association, 2001); Mark M. Carroll, *Homesteads Ungovernable: Families, Sex, Race, and the Law in Frontier Texas, 1823–1860* (Austin: University of

Texas Press, 2001); Nina Baym, *Women Writers of the American West, 1833–1927* (Urbana: University of Illinois Press, 2011); Amy S. Greenberg, *A Wicked War: Polk, Clay, Lincoln, and the 1846 US Invasion of Mexico* (New York: Alfred A. Knopf, 2012).

15. Gail Bederman, *Manliness and Civilization: A Cultural History of Gender and Race in the United States, 1880–1917* (Chicago: University of Chicago Press, 1995); Kristin L. Hoganson, *Fighting for American Manhood: How Gender Politics Provoked the Spanish-American and Philippine-American Wars* (New Haven, CT: Yale University Press, 1998); Amy S. Greenberg, *Manifest Manhood and the Antebellum American Empire* (New York: Cambridge University Press, 2005); William Benemann, *Men in Eden: William Drummond Stewart and Same-Sex Desire in the Rocky Mountain Fur Trade* (Lincoln: University of Nebraska Press, 2012); Monica Rico, *Nature's Noblemen: Transatlantic Masculinities and the Nineteenth-Century American West* (New Haven, CT: Yale University Press, 2013); Jimmy L. Bryan Jr., *The American Elsewhere: Adventure and Manliness in the Age of Expansion* (Lawrence: University Press of Kansas, 2017). Dana D. Nelson includes a discussion on the Lewis and Clark Expedition as an example of how the fraternal connections of whiteness, manliness, and economics defined a national identity. Nelson, *National Manhood: Capitalist Citizenship and the Imagined Fraternity of White Men* (Durham, NC: Duke University Press, 1998). See also Brian Rouleau, *With Sails Whitening Every Sea: Mariners and the Making of an American Maritime Empire* (Ithaca, NY: Cornell University Press, 2014).

16. Shelley Streeby, *American Sensations: Class, Empire, and the Production of Popular Culture* (Berkeley: University of California Press, 2002); Jaime Javier Rodríguez, *Literatures of the US-Mexican War: Narrative, Time, and Identity* (Austin: University of Texas Press, 2010); Andy Doolen, *Fugitive Empire: Locating Early American Imperialism* (Minneapolis: University of Minnesota Press, 2005); Eric T. L. Love, *Race over Empire: Racism and US Imperialism, 1865–1900* (Chapel Hill: University of North Carolina Press, 2004).

17. Jill Lepore, *The Name of War: King Philip's War and the Origins of American Identity* (New York: Alfred A. Knopf, 1998); Joshua David Bellin, *The Demon of the Continent: Indians and the Shaping of American Literature* (Philadelphia: University of Pennsylvania Press, 2001); Jean M. O'Brien, *Firsting and Lasting: Writing Indians Out of Existence in New England* (Minneapolis: University of Minnesota Press, 2010); John Hausdoerffer, *Catlin's Lament: Indians, Manifest Destiny, and the Ethics of Nature* (Lawrence: University Press of Kansas, 2009); William H. Truettner, *Painting Indians and Building Empires in North America, 1710–1840* (Berkeley: University of California Press, 2010). See also Thomas R. Hietala, "'This Splendid Juggernaut': Westward a Nation and Its People," in *Manifest Destiny and Empire: American Antebellum Expansion*, ed. Sam W. Haynes and Christopher Morris (College Station: Texas A&M University Press, 1997), 48–67; Bryan, *American Elsewhere*, 193–203. For significant works on Anglo-American representations of Indians focused more on national identity and less on empire, see Philip J. Deloria, *Playing Indian* (New Haven, CT: Yale University Press, 1998); Susan Scheckel, *The Insistence of the Indian: Race and Nationalism in Nineteenth-Century American Culture* (Princeton, NJ: Princeton University Press, 1998); Nelson, *National Manhood*.

18. Beth L. Lueck, *American Writers and the Picturesque Tour: The Search for National Identity, 1790–1860* (New York: Garland, 1997); Thomas Hallock, *From the Fallen Tree: Fron-*

tier Narratives, Environmental Politics, and the Roots of a National Pastoral, 1749–1826 (Chapel Hill: University of North Carolina Press, 2003); Gretchen Murphy, *Hemispheric Imaginings: The Monroe Doctrine and Narratives of US Empire* (Durham, NC: Duke University Press, 2005); Martin Brückner, *The Geographic Revolution in Early America: Maps, Literacy, and National Identity* (Chapel Hill: University of North Carolina Press, 2006); Kenneth Haltman, including *Looking Close and Seeing Far: Samuel Seymour, Titan Ramsay Peale, and the Art of the Long Expedition, 1818–1823* (University Park: Pennsylvania State University Press, 2008) and "Flight and Predation: The Anti-documentary Poetics of Alfred Jacob Miller," *American Art* 28 (Spring 2014): 33–55; Matthew N. Johnston, *Narrating the Landscape: Print Culture and American Expansionism in the Nineteenth Century* (Norman: University of Oklahoma Press, 2016).

19. Hyde, *American Vision*; Anne Baker, *Heartless Immensity: Literature, Culture, and Geography in Antebellum America* (Ann Arbor: University of Michigan Press, 2006); Richard V. Francaviglia, *Go East, Young Man: Imagining the American West as the Orient* (Logan: Utah State University Press, 2011); Rachel St. John, "Contingent Continent: Spatial and Geographic Arguments in the Shaping of the Nineteenth-Century United States," *Pacific Historical Review* 86 (February 2017): 18–49. See also John Miller Morris, *El Llano Estacado: Exploration and Imagination on the High Plains of Texas and New Mexico, 1536–1860* (Austin: Texas State Historical Association, 1997); Thomas Patin, "Exhibitions of Empire: National Parks and the Performance of Manifest Destiny," *Journal of American Culture* 22 (March 2004): 41–59; Mark Rifkin, *Manifesting America: The Imperial Construction of US National Space* (New York: Oxford University Press, 2009).

20. Deena J. González, *Refusing the Favor: The Spanish-Mexican Women of Santa Fe, 1820–1880* (New York: Oxford University Press, 1999); Andrés Resendéz, *Changing National Identities at the Frontier: Texas and New Mexico, 1800–1850* (New York: Cambridge University Press, 2005); Raúl Ramos, *Beyond the Alamo: Forging Mexican Ethnicity in San Antonio, 1821–1861* (Chapel Hill: University of North Carolina Press, 2008); Karen Roybal, *Archives of Dispossession: Recovering the Testimonies of Mexican American Herederas, 1848–1960* (Chapel Hill: University of North Carolina Press, 2017); Ned Blackhawk, *Violence over the Land: Indians and Empires in the Early American West* (New York: Cambridge University Press, 2006); Pekka Hämäläinen, *The Comanche Empire* (New Haven, CT: Yale University Press, 2008); Brian DeLay, *War of a Thousand Deserts: Indian Raids and the U.S.-Mexican War* (New Haven, CT: Yale University Press, 2008); Anne F. Hyde, *Empires, Nations, and Families: A History of the North American West, 1800–1860* (Lincoln: University of Nebraska Press, 2011).

21. Bethel Saler, *The Settlers' Empire: Colonialism and State Formation in America's Old Northwest* (Philadelphia: University of Pennsylvania Press, 2014); Shire, *Threshold of Manifest Destiny*; Dawn Peterson, *Indians in the Family: Adoption and the Politics of Antebellum Expansion* (Cambridge, MA: Harvard University Press, 2017). For reflections on the field, see Frederick E. Hoxie, "Retrieving the Red Continent: Settler Colonialism and the History of American Indians in the US," *Ethnic and Racial Studies* 31 (September 2008): 1153–1167; Alyosha Goldstein, "Where the Nation Takes Place: Propriety Regimes, Antistatism, and US Settler Colonialism," *South Atlantic Quarterly* 107 (Fall 2008): 833–861.

22. Rodrigo Lazo, *Writing to Cuba: Filibustering and Cuban Exiles in the United States* (Chapel Hill: University of North Carolina Press, 2005); Aims McGuinness, *Path of Empire: Panama and the California Gold Rush* (Ithaca, NY: Cornell University Press, 2008); Michel Gobat, *Empire by Invitation: William Walker and Manifest Destiny in Central America* (Cambridge, MA: Harvard University Press, 2018); Andy Doolen, *Territories of Empire: U.S. Writing from the Louisiana Purchase to Mexican Independence* (New York: Oxford University Press, 2014). Since its inception, transnational scholarship has multiplied exponentially, straining to contain many different modes of analysis. Steven Vertovec, "Conceiving and Researching Transnationalism," *Ethnic and Racial Studies* 22 (January 1999): 447–462. For territoriality, see Charles S. Maier, *Once within Borders: Territories of Power, Wealth, and Belonging since 1500* (Cambridge, MA: Belknap Press of Harvard University Press, 2016). For the emerging literature on Native American territoriality, see Juliana Barr, "Geographies of Power: Mapping Indian Borders in the 'Borderlands' of the Early Southwest," *William and Mary Quarterly* 68 (January 2011): 5–46; Matthew Babcock, "Territoriality and the Historiography of Early North America," *Journal of American Studies* 50 (August 2016): 515–536; David Bernstein, *How the West Was Drawn: Mapping, Indians, and the Construction of the Trans-Mississippi West* (Lincoln: University of Nebraska Press, 2018).

23. Love, *Race over Empire*; Etsuko Taketani, *U.S. Women Writers and the Discourses of Colonialism, 1825–1861* (Knoxville: University of Tennessee Press, 2003); Greenberg, *Wicked War*; David M. Wrobel, *Global West, American Frontier: Travel, Empire, and Exceptionalism from Manifest Destiny to the Great Depression* (Albuquerque: University of New Mexico Press, 2013); Ian Tyrrell and Jay Sexton, eds., *Empire's Twin: US Anti-imperialism from the Founding Era to the Age of Terrorism* (Ithaca, NY: Cornell University Press, 2015).

24. John Carlos Rowe, *Literary Culture and U.S. Imperialism: From the Revolution to World War II* (New York: Oxford University Press, 2000); Peter J. Kastor, including *The Nation's Crucible: The Louisiana Purchase and the Creation of America* (New Haven, CT: Yale University Press, 2004) and *William Clark's World: Describing America in an Age of Unknowns* (New Haven, CT: Yale University Press, 2011); Stephanie LeMenager, *Manifest and Other Destinies: Territorial Fictions of the Nineteenth-Century United States* (Lincoln: University of Nebraska Press, 2004). See also Doolen, *Territories of Empire*; Paul Foos, *A Short, Offhand, Killing Affair: Soldiers and Social Conflict during the Mexican-American War* (Chapel Hill: University of North Carolina Press, 2002); Kris Fresonke, *West of Emerson: The Design of Manifest Destiny* (Berkeley: University of California Press, 2003); Amy Kaplan, "Imperial Melancholy in America," *Raritan* 28 (Winter 2009): 13–31; Jon T. Coleman, *Here Lies Hugh Glass: A Mountain Man, a Bear, and the Rise of the American Nation* (New York: Hill and Wang, 2012); Samuel J. Watson, *Peacekeepers and Conquerors: The Army Officer Corps on the American Frontier, 1821–1846* (Lawrence: University Press of Kansas, 2013); Amy S. Greenberg, "'Time's Noblest Empire Is the Last': Texas Annexation and the Presumed Course of American Empire," in *Contested Empire: Rethinking the Texas Revolution*, ed. Sam W. Haynes and Gerald D. Saxon (College Station: Texas A&M University Press, 2015), 139–164.

25. Weinberg, *Manifest Destiny*; Alstyne, *Rising American Empire*; Marc Egnal, *A Mighty Empire: The Origins of the American Revolution* (Ithaca, NY: Cornell University Press, 1988);

Charles S. Maier, *Among Empires: American Ascendancy and Its Predecessors* (Cambridge, MA: Harvard University Press, 2006); Nugent, *Habits of Empire*; Wrobel, *Global West*.

26. For works on the interconnection between religion and US national identity as well as empire, see Ernest Lee Tuveson, *Redeemer Nation: The Idea of America's Millennial Role* (Chicago: University of Chicago Press, 1968); Sacvan Bercovitch, including *The Puritan Origins of the American Self* (Chicago: University of Chicago Press, 1975) and *Rites of Assent: Transformations in the Symbolic Construction of America* (New York: Routledge, 1993); Horsman, *Race and Manifest Destiny*; Stephanson, *Manifest Destiny*; McDougall, *Promised Land, Crusader State*; John C. Pinheiro, *Missionaries of Republicanism: A Religious History of the Mexican-American War* (New York: Oxford University Press, 2014).

27. For work on the connections between expatriates and US expansion, see Eric R. Schlereth, including "Privileges of Locomotion: Expatriation and the Politics of Southwestern Border Crossing," *Journal of American History* 100 (March 2014): 995–1020, and "Voluntary Mexicans: Allegiance and the Origins of the Texas Revolution," in Haynes and Saxon, *Contested Empire*, 11–41; Sarah K. M. Rodriguez, "'The Greatest Nation on Earth': The Politics and Patriotism of the First Anglo American Immigrants to Mexican Texas, 1820–1824," *Pacific Historical Review* 86 (February 2017): 50–83; Thomas Richards Jr., "'Farewell to America': The Expatriation Politics of Overland Migration, 1841–1846," *Pacific Historical Review* 86 (February 2017): 114–152.

CHAPTER 1

"A Destiny in the Womb of Time": US Expansion and Its Prophets

Jimmy L. Bryan Jr.

Territorial expansion was an imaginative act. It incorporated the visionary elsewhere of both space and time by charting futures both plausible and extravagant. Prophesying about the transcontinental nation not only granted US imperialists of the early nineteenth century the latitude to stretch their visions and astonish their readers, but also afforded the flexibility to create the narratives and metaphors they used to cloak their guilt over conquest. They predicted that their endeavors would clear the land for farms and towns and inspire technological innovation, and they understood that this future would not accommodate the peoples of Native America or Mexico. When filibuster Thomas J. Green spoke of "a destiny in the womb of time" in describing the prospects of Texas annexation, he evoked the fiction of natural inevitability that empowered the rhetoric of expansion.[1] He shared in a vision of national greatness that confirmed the optimism and chauvinism that many Americans felt about their abilities to realize grand enterprise and fulfill the will of providence. Expansionists employed the tools of the romantic, marshaling their imaginations to evoke an emotional response that would link territorial acquisition to a proud nationalist mission.

The most familiar expression of expansion and the document that introduced it to the world originated in an act of fortune-telling. The July 1845 number of the *United States Magazine and Democratic Review* published an unsigned essay that supported the US acquisition of the Republic of Texas. Most often attributed to the journal's editor, John L. O'Sullivan, the article famously proclaimed that annexation represented the first step toward the "fulfillment of our manifest destiny to overspread the continent allotted by Providence." At its heart, "manifest destiny" was prophecy. After arguing that the United States and Texas had already completed negotiations and that slavery had little relevance to the project, O'Sullivan spent the bulk of the essay looking to the future, predicting that California and Canada would naturally follow the Texas example. He concluded with a clairvoyant's flourish, foreseeing that in the next century Europe could not hope to contain "the three hundred millions—and American millions—destined to gather beneath the flutter of the stripes and stars, in that fast hastening year of the Lord 1945!"[2]

In the conceptions of state and empire, envisioning the future was commonplace, but cultural and political leaders of the United States saw themselves and their institutions as unique. In their classic works, Merle Curti and Henry Nash Smith identify forward-looking as a key feature of US nationalism and myth creation. The Declaration of Independence was in many ways a document of prophecy that established the basis of American dreams as "the pursuit" of some future "happiness." The conceit of destiny instilled a sense of entitlement that some higher power had selected the American people as the chosen few, reinforced by Protestant fears and hopes of the hereafter and by their holy book filled with future-seers. In a previous essay attributed to O'Sullivan, "The Great Nation of Futurity" (1839), the writer assumed the role of a modern-day Ezekiel. With an earlier iteration of the famous phrase, he proselytized, "The far-reaching, the boundless future will be the era of American greatness. In its magnificent domain of space and time, the nation of many nations is destined to manifest to mankind the excellence of divine principles."[3]

Celebrations of the past often undergirded nationalism, but a group of US expansionists rejected this looking backward. Writing in 1819, geographer William Darby might shed "a tear of bitter regret" when he contemplated the ashes of past societies, but he much preferred to peer ahead. He declared, "I would rather indulge my fancy in following the future progress, than in surveying the wreck of human happiness." In 1843, Lewis Cass—the former governor of Michigan and an aspirant to the presidency—evoked a similar temporal divorce when he spoke at the opening of the Wabash and Erie Canal that coincided with the Fourth of July. He declared, "Onward, is the great word of our age and country," but he would not obtain his party's nomination. A new and brash generation of Democrats led by O'Sullivan blocked his ambitions, but the editor nonetheless shared Cass's rhetoric. Four years earlier, in the 1839 essay, he argued that the United States existed only for new tomorrows, free of ancient constraints, suggesting that "our national birth was the beginning of a new history . . . which separates us from the past and connects us with the future only. . . . We may confidently assume that our country is destined to be *the great nation of futurity.*" Although less bellicose, Ralph Waldo Emerson spoke to this new generation, naming their type "the Young American" and echoing Darby, Cass, and O'Sullivan when he submitted that the United States "has no past: all has an onward and prospective look."[4]

Historian Jason Phillips, however, argues that the study of the future requires more than just switching the perspective from the past. Building on the work of German scholar Reinhart Koselleck, he contends that when a people prophesy, they impact their present. As such, historians should examine the ways communities look forward. Focusing on the Civil War era, Phillips delves into moments of intense crises in which doomsayers projected their visions of the Apocalypse. Angela Miller identifies similar prognostications in the early nineteenth-century landscape painters such as Thomas Cole who prepared their audiences for visions of empire by incorporating wilderness scenes to evoke a sense of anticipation about regions to quell in the future. Thomas Hallock, furthermore, underscores the power of prophecy in preparing those contested spaces for a pastoral nationalism that required narrative leaps to explain away the territorial claims of Native groups.[5]

Although a few prophets of expansion warned of overextended empires, most peddled in the optimism and chauvinism of prosperity and security. In both cases, however, the seers used their auguries to incite sensation, building emotional bridges that invested the individual with larger nationalist endeavors. The ability to successfully marshal and shape the anticipations of a nation represented critical acts of power, creating fictive bonds of belonging for one group to the exclusion of others.

Scholars as early as Curti and Smith have documented that expansionists had recognized the persuasive power of fortune-telling even before the creation of the United States. In 1760, Benjamin Franklin proclaimed that "*the future grandeur and stability of the British empire lie in America.*" By 1771, however, Philip Freneau and Hugh Henry Brackenridge shifted the emphasis away from the Old World and bestowed that imperial destiny upon "Britain's sons." In an ode to "the rising glory of America," they foresaw "Dominion to the north and south and west / Far from th' Atlantic to Pacific shores."[6]

After the United States achieved independence, such grand speculations would become ubiquitous fixtures in nationalist publications and celebrations. In his book *The American Geography* (1789), Jedidiah Morse included the essay "The Western Territory," referring to the region north and west of the Ohio River. Guided by his confidence in American genius and the god of nature, he predicted an internal empire populated by a refined humankind. He assured,

"Elevated with these prospects, which are not merely the visions of fancy, we cannot but anticipate the period, as not far distant, when the American Empire will comprehend millions of souls, west of the Mississippi." At a Fourth of July ceremony in 1793, New Jersey congressman Elias Boudinot gave a speech mostly about future generations of leaders coming from the common classes, but he continued, prophesying a commercial empire. Employing a common tactic, he invited his listeners to cast their gazes ahead in time. Anticipating Cole, he guides them through a once-wild country tamed by farming and community building. He encouraged, "Take into view the pleasing shores of our immense lakes, united to the Atlantic States, by a thousand winding canals, and beautified with rising cities, crowded with innumerable, peaceful fleets, transporting the rich produce from one coast to another." Here, Boudinot cataloged the benefits that an expansionist future promised—bountiful agriculture, flourishing commerce, and innovative technology. By doing so, he established a narrative strategy that the prophets of expansion would use for decades.[7]

When these visionaries peered past the curtain, they promised bounty, prosperity, and security. In 1813, for example, Daniel Bryan, a lawyer in Harrisonburg, Virginia, published *The Mountain Muse*, an epic poem that celebrated American progress in the West. After he chose Daniel Boone as his specially trained hero, the Angel of Enterprise gazed over the West, "from th' Alleganean Mountain's base; Westward to the Pacific deeps," and witnessed the distant hereafter:

[The Angel] bid the cheerless forest-glooms disperse,
And o'er the wastes the polish'd Arts extend. . . .
Young Agriculture smiling o'er the west;
While Labor's healthful sons around him flock,
And wait his mild commands. I see rich fields,
Green-waving Meads, and flosculous Gardens spread . . .
The Virtues vivify, illume, refine,
Exalt, and sublimate, the new-born World![8]

This was the same impulse that Thomas Cole experienced when he thought about the wilderness. The artist suggested that "in looking over the yet uncultivated scene, the mind's eye may see far into futurity. Where the wolf roams, the plough shall glisten." The unspoiled territory seemed to enjoy no other prospect than to become tilled over and cultivated for its superabundant harvests.[9]

The taming that agriculture imposed upon the wilderness also fostered the security that came with the development of towns. In 1819, when William

Darby wrote about his travels across the prairies and woodlands of North America, he explicitly drew these connections. Later travelers over the Great Plains anticipated how the plow would upturn the desolate landscape and transform it into blossoming fields and buzzing communities. Where many prophets saw visions of such progress, a soldier in the US Dragoons heard it, declaring that "the sound of the hammer of the artizan shall ring across the prairie, and the woodman's axe shall resound through the forest." Together with other visionaries, they foresaw macadamized turnpikes connecting towns and farms, peopled with like-minded yeoman farmers and industrious mechanics.[10]

Those prophets who imagined the commercial prospects of territorial expansion made little effort to repress their hyperbole. In 1845, for example, New York magazine editor George Wilkes wrote *The History of Oregon*, advocating US possession of that region. After describing the geographic advantages, he crowed, "The view that this opens to the mind . . . staggers speculation with its immensity, and stretches beyond all ordinary rules of calculation." Even when he claimed to have moderated his visions, Wilkes nevertheless predicted, "The riches of the most unlimited market in the world would be thrown open to our enterprise. . . . We should become the common carrier of the world for the India trade."[11]

In evoking the symbols of the plow, the hammer, and the ax, these visionaries understood that such progress required the destruction of the natural world. Even as they reposed "under the glances of the swan of Leda, the gleams of Sirius," and ached over "the fairy picture of the distant prairie" as Darby had, they perceived that the untouched state of the wilderness invited its domestication. "I have thus often in the awful solitude . . . ," Darby explained, "contemplated the rapid march of active industry. . . . I have beheld the deep gloom around me dispelled, the majestic but dreary forest disappeared, the savage was turned into civilized man; schools, colleges, churches, and legislative halls arose."[12]

As Darby's reference to the "savage" indicated, the plight of Indian cultures also figured into expansionist visions. Many candidly accepted the destruction of Native Americans as necessary and inevitable in order to realize their grand dreams. Advocates like fur trapper Zenas Leonard took a more aggressive stance toward the original Americans. He rhetorically asked his readers, could the United States possibly subdue "the thousands of savages now roaming over these plains" and replace them with a "hardy freeborn population [and] here plant their homes . . . and flourish?" Leonard answered, "Yes, here, even in this remote part of the great west." Travel writer and novelist John T. Irving Jr. exhibited little sympathy when he predicted, "It is probable, that [before] two centuries shall elapse, there will be but a very remnant of their race; a few retched beings, lingering about the then abodes of civilization, unheeded, unnoticed; strangers in the land of their fathers." If any survived, they would become severely diminished and serve only as relics of a curious past, as a writer for the *Seneca Observer* foresaw. That author predicted the extinction of Native peoples in the year 2000, but museums would preserve representative specimens under glass.[13]

Indians also disappeared in Mary Griffith's "Three Hundred Years Hence." In this story, Edward Hastings fell asleep on a snowbank and dreamed that he visited the year 2135. His host eagerly informed him about the humanizing influence of women in power, technological wonders, commercial prosperity, and emancipated slaves happily transported to Africa, but in this utopia, the Native American had no place. "They have gone from their 'hunting ground,'" Hastings's guide explained, but although he had access to *The Record of Self-Inflicted Miseries*, he would not talk about who currently inhabited those lands. He exclaimed, "What demon closed up the springs of tender mercy when Indian rights were in question I know not!—but I must not speak of it!" Griffith's story illustrated how the romantic lamented the vanishing Indian yet failed to reconcile that sympathy to the reality of conquest. The savage who nobly faced his inevitable doom represented one of the most popular narratives of early nineteenth-century US literature because it permitted American readers to assuage their guilty feelings by celebrating the very thing that they destroyed.[14]

Critics of the aggressiveness and avarice evident in US expansionist rhetoric engaged in their own versions of prophecy. Opened to public viewing in 1836, Thomas Cole's *The Course of Empire* (1833–1836) series offered a dramatic warning. In five separate canvases, the artist depicts the progression of human societies from the savage state, peaking at the height of empire, and falling back into ruin. Based on Mediterranean aesthetics, *The Consummation of Empire* (1835–1836; plate 1) depicts the riches that vast overseas trade brings into a busy port metropolis. White, marble architecture gleams with golden statues draped in silks. Viewing the panels separately, pro-expansionists might perceive their own dreams realized in this abject decadence, but the next panel alerts them to the inevitable fall of empires. Cole connects *Destruction* (1836; plate 2) to the same caution evident in many of his wilderness landscapes, with similar swirling storm clouds and smoke. An army ransacks the city portrayed in *Consummation*. More than toppling statues and burning buildings, Cole details the orgy of bloodshed in every corner of the image as the conquerors commit outrages upon women and children. It is a harsh prophecy that defeat will follow hubris.[15]

Doomsaying also permitted expansionists to draw a contrast that rendered their visions more appealing. During a Fourth of July oration in Boston in 1835, George S. Hilliard, author and law partner of Charles Sumner, reviewed the American Revolution and the present prosperity of US institutions. He concluded with a view of the future that first brought "gloomy pictures" of despots and civil war, but he dismissed them on this occasion of celebration, declaring, "I would not invite your imaginations to dwell upon" these dreary prospects. Instead, Hilliard focused on empire building to gladden the mood of his audience, boasting, "The loud burst of joy and gratitude, which is on this day breaking from the full hearts of a mighty people, will never cease to be heard. . . . The farthest West shall hear it and rejoice."[16]

As Hilliard exemplified, focusing on the pleasant visions of the expansionist future was a crucial narrative strategy. When Boudinot cataloged the "pleasing shores" and beautified cities of tomorrow, he demonstrated that he and the seers who followed him were less interested in appealing to logic than to irrational sentimentality. By conjuring temporal elsewheres, expansionists awakened individual imaginations in order to build emotional, personal connections that invested their neighbors with their own dreams for empire.[17]

In the same way that they built upon the established rhetorical technique of forecasting, expansionists also took advantage of the romantic movement that swept over from Europe to the United States during the late eighteenth and early nineteenth centuries. In one of the earliest and often-quoted expressions of romanticism, Scottish philosopher Dugald Stewart celebrated the capacity of individuals to imagine and feel something larger than themselves. He concluded his *Elements of the Philosophy of the Human Mind* (1792) with a discussion about how envisioning tomorrow inspired pleasant optimism. The "common bias of the mind," he wrote, tends "to think favourably of the future. . . . It invites the imagination beyond the dark and troubled horizon . . . to wander unconfined in the regions of futurity." He used such phrasing as "cheers and animates," "double relish," "agreeable anticipation," and others to describe the sensations incited by looking ahead. Stewart admitted that such indulgences might seduce less disciplined thinkers toward dissipation, but reasoned contemplation could "have a favourable effect on the character, by inspiring that ardour and enthusiasm which both prompt to great enterprises."[18]

The prophets of expansion understood that emotion was the key to their arguments and often stressed the enjoyable sensations of their visions. Darby identified himself with the French romantic François-René de Chateaubriand and revealed how his fortune-telling stoked "a pleasing sentiment of poetic enthusiasm." A writer for an 1836 number of the *Knickerbocker* crowed, "It is impossible to contemplate, without exulting hopes and throbbing expectations, the destiny of this great portion of the North American continent." In 1844, after the US Congress passed a canal bill for his region, Sam Ryan Jr., the editor of the *Green Bay Republican*, could not contain his excitement, looking into the future as "visions of glory—scenes redundant with eloquence—flit rapidly through the enraptured imagination."[19]

The authors of these "peeps into futurity" evoked emotional responses when they deliberately played upon the ethnic conceits of their readers. In their visions, they did not include the peoples of Native America and Mexico, and the achievements they imagined were exclusively Anglo-American. The contributor to the *Knickerbocker* expressed these sentiments when he anticipated a North America "possessed by the Anglo-Saxon race . . . [who] gives the quickening impulse to civilization, and soul to enterprise." J. Henry Carleton, an officer in the US dragoons stationed at Fort Leavenworth, agreed when he remarked, "One can hardly ride over these widely extended plains, which in the hands of the whites, would be made to produce *so much*." Reflecting these same attitudes, the writer of the "Annexation" essay viewed the peoples of Mexico as unworthy or incapable of extracting the bounty from the lands that they inhabited. He described Mexicans as "imbecile and distracted," and like the natural wilderness, they invited their own conquest by an "irresistible army of Anglo-Saxon emigration . . . armed with the plough and the rifle."[20]

If ethnic chauvinisms failed to stir an emotional response, these seers could resort to sensationalizing by claiming a mystical privilege that elevated the incredibility of their visions yet, in the same moment, invited their audiences to participate. Darby assured, "It is when the mind's eye is sweeping over this magnificent canvass that we are forced to exclaim, 'What mighty series of events are in the womb of futurity,'" while Ryan of the *Green Bay Republican* encouraged, "Draw aside the veil of Futurity." Others beguiled their readers and listeners with opportunities to peer "through the horoscope" or share in "the magic work." Crossing over the Great Plains, a soldier followed this cue. With the flourish of a thespian, the anonymous author of *Dragoon Campaigns* (1836) asked his audience, "Let me draw aside the curtain—fifty years hath flown away . . . what seest thou?" He paused in his contemplation and requested patience, realizing that he risked betraying the credulity of his readers. "Indulge me, if not with me," promising that he would reveal "what is now hidden behind the curtain of futurity."[21]

In the same way they called upon the mystical, the prophets could astonish with wonders of future technology. The Texas filibuster Thomas J. Green foresaw a system of steamboat navigation, railroads, and canals that would connect the mouth of the Rio Grande with the Gulf of California. He and his contemporaries predicted innovations in transportation that would carry the Asian trade and western bounty across the continent, enticing those who dreamed of grand commerce. Imagining these extravagant opportunities, a writer for the *Buffalo Gazette* exclaimed, "What fields for enterprise—What wealth would be floated down these channels!"[22]

The article in the *Buffalo Gazette* further illustrated how the Erie Canal inspired a number of commentators to imagine technologically driven futures. In 1817, construction of the project to connect Albany and Buffalo with an artificial waterway began, and soon the nation was abuzz with overwrought prognostications. New York lawyer Charles G. Haines published *Considerations on the Great Western Canal* (1818) and predicted that the waterway would eventually connect with the Mississippi River. He crowed about how the prosperity that followed would "carry us along to that height of glory which breaks upon our gaze through the vista of futurity, and beckens [*sic*] us to its cloudless summit." Pennsylvania state senator Samuel Breck promoted Philadelphia as the crossroads of a future canal traffic, but he allowed a moment's indulgence to peer even farther. He suggested that engineers could construct a canal across the Rocky Mountains to connect the Missouri with the Columbia. Although he indulged in the "astonishment at the contemplation of the immensity of the scene," he nevertheless reassured his readers that the prospect of linking the Pacific and the Atlantic was not an example of "soaring into the regions of fancy to suppose that at a future day."[23]

The glowing predictions of canal construction, however, paled in comparison to the excitement over the railroad. In 1833, a correspondent to the *American Railroad Journal* proclaimed, "The steam engine is the most important modern invention. . . . This portable elastic power is now felt, or soon will be, throughout the land . . . from the Atlantic to the Rocky Mountains and the Pacific." Long before Asa Whitney presented his famous petition to Congress in 1845 and even before the opening of the first rail lines in the United States, visionaries confidently predicted the construction of railroads to the Pacific. As early as 1820, Baltimore architect Robert Mills suggested a portage railroad across the Rocky Mountains. Nine years later, Caleb Atwater traveled to Prairie du Chien as US agent to the Winnebagos, and he published an account of his travels in which he marveled about the prospects for continental trade. He wrote, "When locomotive engines are brought to . . . perfection . . . , goods and passengers could pass between the two seas, in ten days." Fellow traveler Rufus Sage also foresaw this wondrous project and argued that a "continuous rail-road" to the Pacific would carry freight "to every part of the Union, and thus unite their aid in the magic work of up-building the Great West."[24]

The vision of the puffing and hissing machines carrying commerce and conquering vast distances with human ingenuity lit imaginations. "Railroad iron is a magician's rod," Ralph Waldo Emerson declared in his 1844 "Young American" speech. He suggested that the technology catalyzed the future. It "has given a new celerity to *time*." Inspired by Whitney's petition, John L. O'Sullivan hinged his prediction that California would eventually join the United States upon the completion of a transcontinental railroad. In the "Annexation" essay attributed to him, he declared, "But that great work, colossal as appears the plan on its first suggestion, cannot remain long unbuilt. . . . The day cannot be distant which shall witness the conveyance of the representatives from Oregon and California to Washington."[25] In 1839, the *Knickerbocker* published a comic story that claimed that a New Englander had invented a steam-powered carriage with which he had disappeared. In the next issue, Washington Irving wrote a letter under the pseudonym Hiram Crackenthorpe, a trapper from St. Louis. He claimed that while traversing the Black Hills, he and his friends briefly encountered the locomotive and its inventor "shooting, like a jack-a-lantern, over the Rocky Mountains." Significantly, the contraption destroyed as it made its way west. Crackenthorpe and his companions followed the trail and found where it had "cut through a great drove of buffalo," killing two hundred as well as having plowed through a Black Feet village, killing the leader and his family. Irving as trapper concluded with a report that the locomotive had steamed its way to Astoria, demonstrating how the Rockies "are traversable with carriages, and that it is perfectly easy to have a rail-road to the Pacific."[26]

Later that year, the *Knickerbocker* published an ode to the steam-powered locomotive that positioned its place in the future and its role in empire. "Where he travels now so gloriously, / Shall his destined path in the future be," the author of the "Iron Horse" proclaimed.

On our mountain ridges his chariots gleam,
He follows the track of the winding stream;
He will carry us forth from our early homes,
To the fairy scenes of the glowing West . . .

'Tis the the Iron Horse; he hath passed the bound
Of the wild sierras that fenced him round;
He hath no more on the land to gain,
His path is free to the western main![27]

These visionaries conveyed the message that only with American genius and the project to conquer North America would these wonderful technologies reach their potential. In the future, then, the United States with its new

Figure 1.1. *An American Exhibiting to the Sovereigns of Europe the Progress of His Country.* Detail from Edward H. Ensign and Horace Thayer, *Ornamental Map of the United States and Mexico.* New York: Ensign & Thayer, 1848. The David Rumsey Map Collection, Cartography Associates, San Francisco, CA.

empire and fabulous toys would become the envy of all other nations. Upon completion of a transcontinental railroad, Sage assured, "It is then that the mighty resources of our national confederacy will begin more fully to develop themselves, and exhibit to an admiring world the giant strides of civilization and improvement." This was the message of an engraving published by Edward H. Ensign and Horace Thayer. *An American Exhibiting to the Sovereigns of Europe the Progress of His Country* (fig. 1.1) appeared as part of their *Ornamental Map of the United States and Mexico* (1848). The image celebrated the conclusion of the US-Mexican War with a graphic representation of the future. The sensibly attired American stands upon a parapet, guarded by formidable cannons, as he looks down upon a group of European military and noble elite. He holds out his hand to present the view of a busy Pacific harbor where the steamship *Union* with its unfurled Stars and Stripes puffs toward the open ocean. On the far shore, a locomotive wends its way past well-ordered agricultural fields and humming factories. In addition to the technological marvels of steamboats and railroads, an aerial balloon rises over the mountains while the passenger train crosses under them through a human-engineered, subterranean tunnel.[28]

Playing upon the vanity of their audience, future-seers presented expansion as a nationalist project. After boasting about the promised boons of a Pacific railroad, Atwater asked, "How is the heart of the patriot . . . filled with joy, unutterable, when he looks with prophetic eye, over this vast field of future happiness, grandeur and glory?" Sage, Ensign and Thayer, and Atwater deliberately equated territorial acquisition and technological innovation to national achievements and divine favor. In "My Country," which appeared in an 1836 number of the *Knickerbocker*, the narrator sat upon Jefferson's Rock at Harpers Ferry. The writer, as if reacting to a view of Cole's *Destruction*, spends the bulk of his time convincing his readers that US industries and ingenuity would prevent their country from falling into ruin like Egypt, Greece, or Rome. Instead, he concluded, "When the tide of population shall have swept beyond the mighty mountains of the Pacific, and lined its fruitful shores with the tumultuous throngs of commerce . . . , who can doubt the heaven-directed destiny of his country!"[29]

In part to tap into this optimism and give it a narrative focus, US periodicals occasionally published speculative stories that imagined distant futures when the United States achieved continental, if not world, domination. In 1817, the *New-England Galaxy and Masonic Magazine* published an article entitled "Anno Domini 2009 Anticipated." Presented in the format of future news correspondence, the story reported that the Russian emperor had transferred the east coast of Asia to the United States, which already possessed North America from the Bering Strait to a border with Venezuela, including a canal constructed across Panama. In 1832, the *Ladies' Magazine and Literary Gazette* published "A Peep through Time's Telescope" that also contained letters from the future. A writer traveling from Astoria in the year 2352 described the hundred-mile-an-hour trip in a steam-propelled airship and discussed the politics of empire on the Pacific. The correspondent confirmed the continued use of the steam railroad but viewed it as an archaic form of travel. This speculative fiction permitted writers to demonstrate the prosperity and dominion that technology and expansion promised.[30]

The audacious and fantastic qualities of expansionist prophecy attracted a fair number of naysayers. A writer for the *American Monthly Magazine and Critical Review* cautioned against Charles G. Haines's projections about canals connecting New York with the Far West, writing that "his *zeal in the cause* has led him . . . beyond the sober deductions of authorized reasonings," but allowed that "still must we view his efforts with peculiar satisfaction." The *Oregonian, and Indian's Advocate* was less forgiving. A contributor compared the nonsense of building a transcontinental railroad in 1839 to the fantasy of space travel. "The idea of a railroad to Oregon very strongly reminds us of a mode of ascent to the moon . . . , and we have about as much hope of visiting the Lunarians . . . as we have of going to Oregon in railroad cars." William J. Snelling, editor of the *New-England Magazine*, criticized Atwater's predictions, reminding his readers that the territory over which such a route would cross consisted of thousands of miles of Sahara-like desert. He wondered where the passengers would obtain their food. Where would the operators acquire the wood for fuel? He further asked, "Will the Indians have been exterminated, or will the steam-cars run over them?" For those like Zenas Leonard who predicted the achievements of an Anglo-American empire, their answer was an emphatic "yes."[31]

As clairvoyants, however, pro-expansionists often anticipated their doubters. The reactions of the *American Monthly*, the *Oregonian*, and Snelling confirmed that their attempts to astonish might stretch the credulity of their readers. When the anonymous dragoon soldier pulled back the curtain, he asked, "Is this all visionary?" He claimed that it was not because he merely extrapolated from "the signs of the times." Sage, appropriate to his name, claimed wisdom that he shared not only with the dragoon but with all Americans. As he mused about the prospects of Oregon, he affirmed, "It needs no prophetic eye to foresee all this, nor the effort of centuries to transform this rough sketch of fancy into a more than sober reality."[32]

Such moderation did not undermine the emotional appeal of these predictions. Rather, it served to bolster the confidence in their probabilities. The prophets insisted that their extravagant visions were attainable because they based their forecasts on recent memory. This emphasis on the necessity of history contrasted with the view that the United States was a "nation of futurity," divorced from its past. Lewis Cass exemplified this contradiction in his 1843 speech in which he declared, "It is better to look forward to prosperity than back to glory," but he nevertheless reassured his listeners, "The prospects of the future may be seen in the progress of the past." Based on former successes in internal improvement, steam power, and the tide of migration from across the Allegheny Mountains, he confirmed that his predictions "are not due to the magician's lamp. They have a purer origin. They spring from industry and enterprise." Earlier, in 1824, William Darby supported his predictions with tables of statistics from the US Census, advocating for more liberal laws toward internal improvements to accommodate the expected population explosion in the West. Still, after providing all those numbers, he lapsed into reverie, admitting, "The mind swells with a momentous futurity. The rapidity of change deceives the senses, mocks the legislator, and outruns the geographer."[33]

An exploration into a generation's future-seeing reveals how its members perceived themselves in their own time. It also demonstrates how prophecy represents a performance of power. This clever narrative mechanism allows authors to establish destinies that preempt any controversy in the present by predetermining outcomes, rendering any debate rhetorically moot because the future resolves current questions as unquestionable.

Early nineteenth-century expansionists deftly used this strategy. They incited the conceits and chauvinisms of their fellow citizens by astonishing them with visions of prosperous empires, boundless trade, and wondrous technologies. Tapping into this romantic appeal, these future-seers—these adept rhetoricians—shamelessly used extravagant language and imagery to inspire the individual to invest personally in the imperial endeavor. They claimed a shared racial entitlement, evoked the marvelous, and deflected alternative futures. Expansionists utilized such tactics to democratize empire for the masses— achieved in the catchphrase "manifest destiny."

NOTES

1. Thomas J. Green, *Journal of the Expedition against Mier* (New York: Harper & Brothers, 1845), 406.

2. John L. O'Sullivan (attributed), "Annexation," *United States Magazine and Democratic Review* 17 (July and August 1845): 5. After a grammatical analysis, Linda S. Hudson suggests that Jane McManus Storm Cazneau was the author of the article and phrase. Hudson, *Mistress of Manifest Destiny: A Biography of Jane McManus Storm Cazneau, 1807–1878* (Austin: Texas State Historical Association, 2001), 59–62, 209–210. Robert D. Sampson refutes the claim, arguing that one of Hudson's control samples was not written by O'Sullivan and could not be used as representative of his style. Sampson, *John L. O'Sullivan and His Times* (Kent, OH: Kent State University Press, 2003), 244–245.

3. John L. O'Sullivan (attributed), "The Great Nation of Futurity," *United States Democratic Review* 6 (November 1839): 427; Merle Curti, *The Roots of American Loyalty* (New York: Columbia University Press, 1946), 6, 32–41, 62, 140; Henry Nash Smith, *Virgin Land: The American West as Symbol and Myth* (1950; repr., Cambridge, MA: Harvard University Press, 1970), 3–12. Diplomatic historian Norman A. Graebner observed, "The belief in a national destiny was neither new nor strange; no nation or empire in history has ever been totally without it." Graebner, *Manifest Destiny* (Indianapolis: Bobbs-Merrill, 1968), xv. Anders Stephanson describes the ideology of manifest destiny as "a prefixed trajectory of spatial and temporal aims for an anointed nation" (xiv). See also his discussion of the American "consuming interest in prophecy" (8–10). Stephanson, *Manifest Destiny: American Expansion and the Empire of Right* (New York: Hill and Wang, 1995).

4. All italics are original to the source. William Darby, *A Tour from the City* (New York: Kirk & Mercein, 1819), iv; Lewis Cass, "Celebration of the Completion of the Wabash and Erie Canal, on the Fourth [of] July, 1843," *Niles' National Register*, August 12, 1843; O'Sullivan, "Great Nation of Futurity," 427; Ralph Waldo Emerson, "The Young American," *Dial* 4 (April 1844): 492; Edward L. Widmer, *Young America: The Flowering of Democracy in New York City* (New York: Oxford University Press, 1999), 40, 43, 68–69. See also W.H.R., "My Country," *Knickerbocker* 7 (June 1836): 72–77.

5. Jason Phillips, "Harpers Ferry Looming: A History of the Future," *Rethinking History* 18 (March 2014): 13–12; Angela Miller, *The Empire of the Eye: Representations and American Cultural Politics* (Ithaca, NY: Cornell University Press, 1993), 15; Thomas Hallock, *From the Fallen Tree: Frontier Narratives, Environmental Politics, and the Roots of National Pastoral, 1749–1826* (Chapel Hill: University of North Carolina Press, 2003), 4, 6, 29–31. Phillips cites Reinhart Koselleck, *Futures Past: On the Semantics of Historical Time*, trans. Keith Tribe (New York: Columbia University Press, 2004). See also Phillips, "The Prophecies of Civil War Soldiers: A History of the Future," in *The Martial Imagination: Cultural Aspects of American Warfare*, ed. Jimmy L. Bryan Jr. (College Station: Texas A&M University Press, 2013), 183–200.

6. Benjamin Franklin to Lord Kames, January 3, 1760, in *The Writings of Benjamin Franklin*, ed. Albert H. Smyth, 10 vols. (New York: Macmillan, 1905–1907), 4:4; Philip Freneau and Hugh Henry Brackenridge, "A Poem on the Rising Glory of America," in Freneau, *Poems of Philip Freneau: Poet of the American Revolution*, ed. Fred Lewis Patee, 3 vols. (Princeton, NJ: University Library, 1902–1907), 1:xxi, 75; Curti, *Roots of American Loyalty*, 6, 32–41, 62. For a discussion and quotations of Benjamin Franklin, Philip Freneau, and Hugh Henry Brackenridge, see Smith, *Virgin Land*, 8–9. See also Reginald Horsman, *Race and Manifest Destiny: The Origins of American Racial Anglo-Saxonism* (Cambridge, MA: Harvard University Press, 1981), 81–97.

7. Jedidiah Morse, *The American Geography; or, a View of the Present Situation of the United States of America* (Elizabethtown, [NJ]: Shepard Kollock, 1789), 469; Elias Boudinot, "An Oration Delivered at Elizabeth-Town (New-Jersey) Agreeably to a Resolution of the State Society of Cincinnati," July 4, 1793, *United States Magazine*, June 1794. In 1833, the British romantic Samuel T. Coleridge sympathized with the "possible destiny of the United States" for expanding English culture and institutions across the continent. "Why should we not wish to see it realized? America would then be England viewed through a solar microscope; Great Britain in a state of glorious magnification!" Coleridge, *Specimens of the Table Talk*, 2 vols. (London: John Murray, 1835), 2:150. US expansionists often quoted him. For examples, see W.H.R., "My Country," 77; Samuel Gordon, "Speech of Mr. Gordon," *Congressional Globe* (Washington, DC), January 6, 1846; Henry W. Hilliard, *Speech of Mr. Hilliard of Alabama on the Oregon Question* (Washington, DC: J. & G. S. Gideon, 1846), 14. See also Timothy Dwight, *Greenfield Hill: A Poem in Seven Parts* (New York: Childs and Swaine, 1794), pt. 7, "The Vision"; Rufus Easton to William Hunter, Washington, DC, April 30, 1816, *Niles' Weekly Register*, August 24, 1816; Henry M. Brackenridge, *Journal of a Voyage Up the River Missouri*, 2nd ed. (Baltimore: Coale & Maxwell, 1816), 92, 105; review of Brackenridge in *North-American Review and Miscellaneous Journal*, 3rd ed., 4 (November 1816): 113; John S. Tyson, "Speech," *American and Daily Commercial Advertiser* (Baltimore), July 10, 1821; George S. Hilliard, *An Oration* (Boston: John H. Eastburn, 1835); Cass, "Celebration of the Completion of the Wabash and Erie Canal."

8. Daniel Bryan, *The Mountain Muse* (Harrisonburg, VA: Davidson and Bourne, 1813), bk. 1, lines 812–820.

9. Thomas Cole, "Essay on American Scenery," *American Monthly* 7 (January 1836):

12. See also Edwin Bryant, *What I Saw in California* (New York: Appleton, 1848), 67; Easton to Hunter, April 30, 1816; review of Brackenridge, 113; A Dragoon, *Dragoon Campaigns to the Rocky Mountains* (New York: Wiley & Long, 1836), 192. For the "Garden of the World" mythology, see Smith, *Virgin Land*, 123–230.

10. Darby, *Tour from the City*, v; Dragoon, *Dragoon Campaigns*, 192–194. See also Bryant, *What I Saw in California*, 67.

11. George Wilkes, *The History of Oregon* (New York: William H. Colyer, 1845), 53.

12. Darby, *Tour from the City*, iv–v; Dragoon, *Dragoon Campaigns*, 33. In 1843, Texas filibuster Steward A. Miller sat on the banks of the Brazos River and contemplated the day when steamboats might ply that stream. Steward A. Miller diary, entry April 27, 1843, Briscoe Center for American History, University of Texas at Austin. Leo Marx terms this the "technological sublime" that preserved nature as pastoral in the face of American progress. Marx, *Machine and the Garden: Technology and the Pastoral Ideal in America* (New York: Oxford University Press, 1964), 194–197, 214–215. For the tension and accommodation of romantic nature and the technological aesthetic, see John Seelye, *Beautiful Machine: Rivers and the Republican Plan, 1755–1825* (New York: Oxford University Press, 1991), 351–361. Cecelia Tichi terms the mission of transfiguring nature into usable space a "New Earth" mentality and traces it back to the Puritans of New England. Tichi, *New World, New Earth: Environmental Reform in American Literature from the Puritans through Whitman* (New Haven, CT: Yale University Press, 1979), 1–36.

13. Zenas Leonard, *Narrative of Adventures of Zenas Leonard* (Clearfield, PA: D. W. Moore, 1839), 49–50; John T. Irving Jr., *Indian Sketches, Taken during an Expedition to the Pawnee Tribes*, 2 vols. (Philadelphia: Carey, Lea & Blanchard, 1835), 1:41; Dragoon, *Dragoon Campaigns*, 192, 195; Anonymous, "A Vision of the Year 2000," *Seneca Observer*, reprinted in *Indiana Democrat* (Indianapolis), March 23, 1838; see also Green, *Journal of the Expedition against Mier*, 414–415.

14. Mary Griffith, "Three Hundred Years Hence," in *Camperdown* (Philadelphia: Carey, Lea & Blanchard, 1836), 16–18, 30–34, 47–48, 90–92. Griffith does not directly address the issue of empire, but as literary historian Etsuko Taketani reveals, she hinted at outlines of a surreptitious US version of colonialism that operated on "cultural exploitation." Taketani, *U.S. Women Writers and the Discourses of Colonialism, 1825–1861* (Knoxville: University of Tennessee Press, 2003), 1–3. For discussions of the "vanishing-Indian" narrative, see Richard Drinnon, *Facing West: The Metaphysics of Indian-Hating and Empire-Building* (Minneapolis: University of Minnesota Press, 1980), 119–351; Lee Clark Mitchell, *Witness to a Vanishing America: The Nineteenth-Century Response* (Princeton, NJ: Princeton University Press, 1981), 3–21, 115–164; Brian W. Dippie, *The Vanishing American: White Attitudes and US Indian Policy* (Middletown, CT: Wesleyan University Press, 1982), 3–31; Lucy Maddox, *Removals: Nineteenth-Century American Literature and the Politics of Indian Affairs* (New York: Oxford University Press, 1991), 6–11, 19–49, 134–168; Andy Doolen *Territories of Empire: US Writing from the Louisiana Purchase to Mexican Independence* (New York: Oxford University Press, 2014), 154–161; Chad A. Barbour, *From David Boone to Captain America: Playing Indian in American Popular Culture* (Jackson: University Press of Mississippi, 2016), 4–5. For a discussion of what Renato

Rosaldo terms "imperial nostalgia," see Rosaldo, *Culture and Truth: The Remaking of Social Analysis* (Boston: Beacon Press, 1989), 68–72.

15. Miller, *Empire of the Eye*, 29–33; Amy Kaplan, "Imperial Melancholy in America," *Raritan* 28 (Winter 2009): 13–31; Amy S. Greenberg, "'Time's Noblest Empire Is the Last': Texas Annexation and the Presumed Course of American Empire," in *Contested Empire: Rethinking the Texas Revolution*, ed. Sam W. Haynes and Gerald D. Saxon (College Station: Texas A&M University Press, 2015), 139–164.

16. Hilliard, *An Oration*, 29–30. Caleb Atwater also worried about the future that "some miserable nullifier" might bring, but he focused on expansion. Atwater, *Remarks Made on a Tour to Prairie du Chien; thence to Washington City, in 1829* (Columbus, OH: Isaac N. Whiting, 1831), 31.

17. Boudinot, "Oration Delivered at Elizabeth-Town."

18. Dugald Stewart, *Elements of the Philosophy of the Human Mind* (London: A Strahan and T. Cadell, 1792), 525–526. See also Anonymous, "The Future," *Knickerbocker* 3 (April 1834): 278–279; Timothy Flint, "The Past—the Present—and the Future," *Knickerbocker* 3 (September 1834): 165–175.

19. Darby, *Tour from the City*, iv–v; Anonymous, "The Spirit of the Age," *Knickerbocker* 8 (August 1836): 190; Sam Ryan Jr., "Apologetical," *Republican* (Green Bay, WI), June 18, 1844. Upon departing the Mandan village on April 7, 1805, Meriwether Lewis looked forward to the journey ahead, writing in his journal that "when the immagination [*sic*] is suffered to wander into futurity, the picture which now presented itself to me was a most pleasing one." Meriwether Lewis and William Clark, *Original Journals of the Lewis and Clark Expedition, 1804–1806*, ed. Reuben Gold Thwaites, 7 vols. (New York: Dodd, Mead, 1904–1905), 1:285. A young Walt Whitman (attributed) enjoyed the emotional allure, writing, "We love to indulge in thoughts of the future extent and power of this republic." Whitman, "Our Territory on the Pacific," *Brooklyn Eagle*, July 7, 1846. See also Brackenridge, *Journal of a Voyage*, 104; Columbus, "The Great Canal," *Buffalo Gazette*, as reprinted in *New York Weekly Museum*, February 1, 1817; A Traveller [William Darby?] to Gales and Seaton, July 10, 1839, *Niles' National Intelligencer*, July 23, 1839.

20. J. Henry Carleton, "Prairie Log Book: or Rough Notes of a Dragoon Campaign to the Pawnee Villages in '44," *Spirit of the Times*, December 28, 1844; Anonymous, "Spirit of the Age," 190; O'Sullivan, "Annexation," 9. See also Cass, "Celebration of the Completion of the Wabash and Erie Canal"; Rufus B. Sage, *Scenes in the Rocky Mountains* (Philadelphia: Carey & Hart, 1846), 191.

21. Traveller [Darby?] to Gales and Seaton, July 10, 1839; Ryan, "Apologetical"; Dragoon, *Dragoon Campaigns*, 194.

22. Green, *Journal of the Expedition against Mier*, 402, 412–413; Columbus, "Great Canal." See also Sage, *Scenes in the Rocky Mountains*, 226; *Plough Boy* 1 (June 19, 1819): 23; P. F., "Internal Improvements," *Commercial Bulletin* (New Orleans), as reprinted in *American Railroad Journal* 3 (August 30, 1834): 530–531.

23. Charles G. Haines, *Considerations on the Great Western Canal*, 2nd ed. (Brooklyn: Spooner & Worthington, 1818), 7, 14, 43.

24. J. McC. to Editor, Nashville, January 28, 1833, *American Railroad Journal* 2 (February 16, 1833): 101; Robert Mills, *A Treatise on Inland Navigation* (Baltimore: F. Lucas Jr., 1820), 52–59; Atwater, *Remarks Made on a Tour*, 31–33; Sage, *Scenes in the Rocky Mountains*, 226; Richard V. Francaviglia and Jimmy L. Bryan Jr., "'Are We Chimerical in This Opinion?': Visions of the Pacific Railroad and Westward Expansion before 1845," *Pacific Historical Review* 71 (May 2002): 179–202. See also Anonymous, "A Vision of the Year 2000."

25. Sullivan also predicted the telegraph would connect the Pacific coast with the Atlantic. O'Sullivan, "Annexation," 9.

26. Emerson, "Young American," 488; D., "The First Locomotive," *Knickerbocker* 13 (April 1839): 343–348; Hiram Crackenthorpe (Washington Irving) to Sir, *Knickerbocker* 13 (May 1839): 445–446. The *Washington Globe* (June 6, 1839) identified Irving as the author of the Crackenthorpe letter.

27. Anonymous, "The Iron Horse," *Knickerbocker* 14 (November 1839): 415.

28. Sage, *Scenes in the Rocky Mountains*, 226. The map also shows the proposed route of a Pacific railroad. Edward H. Ensign and Horace Thayer, *Ornamental Map of the United States and Mexico* (New York: Ensign & Thayer, 1848).

29. Atwater, *Remarks on a Tour*, 38; W.H.R., "My Country," 72–77. See also Flint, "The Past—the Present—and the Future," 165–175; Anonymous, "Spirit of the Age," 190; Cass, "Celebration of the Completion of the Wabash and Erie Canal."

30. Anonymous, "Anno Domini 2009," *New-England Galaxy and Masonic Magazine* 1 (March 27, 1818): 2; Robertine, "A Peep through Time's Telescope," *Ladies' Magazine and Literary Gazette* 5 (November 1832): 494–513; Griffith, "Three Hundred Years Hence," 30–34. In another story, the narrator wakes up in the year 2000 to find a railroad to China via the Bering Strait, cotton planters on the Pacific coast, the United States at war with Persia, and technologies like balloon travel, diverting electricity from a thunderstorm, and a wood-chopping mechanical man. Anonymous, "A Vision of the Year 2000."

31. C.A.B., review of Haines's *Considerations on the Great Western Canal*, *American Monthly Magazine and Critical Review* 3 (October 1818): 421; Anonymous, "Railroad to Oregon," *Oregonian, and Indian's Advocate* 1 (1839): 331; William J. Snelling review of Atwater, *New-England Magazine*, September 1832, 249; Francaviglia and Bryan, "Are We Chimerical in This Opinion?," 198.

32. Dragoon, *Dragoon Campaigns*, 194, 195; Sage, *Scenes in the Rocky Mountains*, 226.

33. Dragoon, *Dragoon Campaigns*, 192, 195; Cass, "Celebration of the Completion of the Wabash and Erie Canal"; Anonymous, *Life and Public Service of Lewis Cass* (1848), 29; William Darby, *Geographical, Historical, and Statistical Repository* (Philadelphia: William Brown, 1824), 1:52.

CHAPTER 2

Stealing Naboth's Vineyard: The Religious Critique of Expansion, 1830–1855

Daniel J. Burge

In December 1870, Charles Sumner delivered a speech in the US Senate, expressing his opposition to the annexation of Santo Domingo. President Ulysses S. Grant hoped to acquire the Caribbean nation but ran into strident congressional opposition. Sumner was the chairman of the Senate Foreign Relations Committee, and as such, his support for the treaty was crucial. The first sentence set the tone for the rest of the speech: "The resolution before the Senate commits Congress to a dance of blood." What followed was equally inflammatory. Sumner recognized the importance of his speech, and a short time later he printed it for public consumption. In the printed version, however, he made a few subtle changes. He called his speech "Naboth's Vineyard" and appended three verses from the Bible to the title page.[1]

Sumner culled the verses from the first book of Kings. The twenty-first chapter tells the story of Ahab and Naboth. King Ahab rules over Israel and desires the vineyard of a man named Naboth. Ahab wants Naboth's land because it is contiguous to his palace, and he wants to plant a vegetable garden. The king offers to purchase the land, but Naboth informs him that the land is his inheritance from his ancestors and that he will not sell at any price. Learning of Ahab's distress, his wife, Jezebel, concocts an elaborate scheme whereby Naboth is accused of blasphemy while at a feast, leading to his execution and allowing the king to seize the vineyard. A short time later, the prophet Elijah approaches Ahab and informs him that he will be punished for his behavior. In the ensuing chapter, King Ahab is killed in battle with the Assyrians. When his chariot is washed, the dogs lick up the blood, thus fulfilling the prophecy of Elijah, who had foretold that the dogs would drink Ahab's blood.

By indirectly comparing Grant to Ahab, Sumner alleged that the annexation of Santo Domingo was a morally reprehensible plot to steal land. Sumner was not the only nineteenth-century American to oppose expansion by using the story of Naboth. Although historians have examined resistance to expansion through the lenses of race, gender, and region, they have scarcely analyzed religious opposition. This chapter, then, examines the ways in which nineteenth-century Americans utilized one biblical story to challenge expansionist projects from the removal of the Cherokees in the 1830s to the acquisition of Santo Domingo four decades later.[2]

Although religious leaders expressed their opposition to expansion in many other forms, this focus on a single argument demonstrates two overriding points. In the first place, the Bible provided them with ammunition to advance their arguments. Scholars such as Sacvan Bercovitch, Ernest Lee Tuveson, Reginald Horsman, and John C. Pinheiro have traced the ways in which religious language, especially the idea of the United States as a chosen nation, led many expansionists to justify their conquests in the nineteenth century. Walter A. McDougall in his *Promised Land, Crusader State* traced these ideas from John Winthrop through the Cold War, an approach similar to that taken by Anders Stephanson in his *Manifest Destiny: American Expansion and the Empire of Right* (1995). These volumes leave out those who derived a different message from their reading of the Bible. This chapter places back into the historical narrative the voices of those who took seriously the biblical command not to covet the goods and lands of their neighbors. Second, it demonstrates that opponents of expansion constructed a comprehensive critique that they deployed consistently for almost a century. By drawing upon a single story, they crafted a common narrative that they deployed against projects that sought to enlarge the boundaries of the United States.[3]

The story of Naboth's vineyard first took prominence in the midst of debates over Indian Removal. In 1829, Jeremiah Evarts began penning a series of letters entitled "Present Crisis in the Condition of the American Indians," under the pseudonym William Penn. A prominent New England reformer and graduate of Yale, Evarts had worked within a variety of organizations, including the New England Tract Society, the Massachusetts Bible Society, and the American Board of Commissioners for Foreign Missions. Angered at the treatment the Cherokees endured at the hands of the US government, Evarts defended them. In doing so, he drew upon the character of Naboth.

"If the people of the United States will imitate the ruler who coveted Naboth's vineyard," he wrote, referring to Ahab, "the world will assuredly place them by the side of Naboth's oppressor." Evarts tried to impress upon his readers that the United States would be judged if it took advantage of the Cherokees. While the Cherokees might not be able to defeat the United States, God would ultimately intervene and humble the American nation.[4]

Evarts's essay paved the way for a veritable deluge of Naboth-related arguments about the removal of the Cherokees. The *New York Daily Advertiser* ran a poem called "The Indians" in October 1829 that reflected this same theme. Beginning with "I saw the Red man o'er the unconquer'd West / Reigning supreme. Thro' the deep forest shade," the poem traced the sanguinary history of settler colonialism. As Evarts had done previously, this author highlighted the biblical story: "Have ye never read / Of that bad king whom Jezebel stirr'd up / To covet Naboth's vineyard. . . . Oh, take heed! Earth hath a tale for the high Judge's ear." A mere year later, as the debate over removal continued, Hugh Maxwell, a prominent New York County district attorney, spoke to a group of citizens gathered in New York to protest the government's treatment of Native Americans. He discussed the long history of the US government's involvement with Native Americans and then turned to 1 Kings and retold the story. "So it is with the poor Indians at the present day," Maxwell intoned, "if the lands which they now possess are not wanted for a garden of herbs, they are wanted for cotton fields." However, he trusted that justice would be done: "If . . . the Indians shall be driven from the lands, let those who shall be guilty of the deed, consider the fate of Ahab." Like Evarts, Maxwell did not believe that the Cherokees could defend their homelands. He portrayed them dying heroic deaths on the tombs of their fathers, but he nonetheless believed that those who committed such a flagrant act of injustice would receive divine retribution.[5]

Soon parodies of the story of Naboth's vineyard began to appear in popular newspapers alongside serious articles. The *Cherokee Phoenix, and Indians' Advocate*, for example, reprinted one such burlesque from the *New York Observer*. The editorial, purportedly written by "A Persian Mullah," defended the conduct of Ahab and his treatment of Naboth. The author posited that the king was a "kind and generous master" and that his neighbor was a "foolish, obstinate, ungrateful rascal." Moreover, "Ahab had a perfect title to the vineyard on another ground. He wanted it for a 'garden.' Naboth used it merely for the purpose of raising grapes. Grapes, it is well known, contain very little nutriment." A similar story appeared in the *Connecticut Courant* a year later and was also reprinted in the *Cherokee Phoenix, and Indians' Advocate*, in which King Ahab wrote an editorial. "The Senate and House of Representatives," he wrote, "in

Israel ought to be apprized, that before the murder of Naboth, I made him a very generous offer,—I proposed to give him a lot in exchange for his, in the wilderness of Lebanon." Editorials such as these used the story of Naboth to lampoon the US government and its claim to Cherokee land.[6]

Naboth's story provided ammunition to both whites and Native Americans to challenge the rapidly expanding American nation. For writers such as Jeremiah Evarts, this story allowed them to put forth a clear religious critique, one that stripped down and exposed the language of benevolence relied upon by Andrew Jackson and his supporters. This rhetoric of dissent, however, was not merely utilized by his opponents clustered in New York and New England. As seen in the case of the *Cherokee Phoenix*, native voices also deployed the parable, casting themselves in the role of Naboth.[7]

This is most clearly seen in a speech delivered by a man directly impacted by removal. Daniel Bread was a leader of the Oneida nation who helped to oversee the movement of his people from New York to Wisconsin. Calvin Colton included one of Bread's speeches in his travelogue *Tour of the American Lakes, and among the Indians of the North-West Territory* (1833). In it, Bread mentions the fact that President James Monroe promised his people protection, yet again, whites clamored for more land. "But, brothers," Bread noted, "we remember it is written in your Bible, which is our Bible: 'And there arose another king in the land, which knew not Joseph.'" Bread made it clear to his audience that he, and presumably his people, knew the Bible as well as those who were anxious to take their lands. He then punctuated his speech with the story: "Ahab said to Naboth: 'I will give thee for it a better vineyard.' So said our father the President . . . and he promised to defend it for us and for our children forever. Now, we do not complain of the vineyard. . . . But Ahab wants this also; and we are more exposed to the cruelties and depredations of his people." Unlike Evarts, Bread did not threaten the United States with doom if it carried out the destruction of his people. Instead, he employed the story to impugn the morality of the United States and its treatment of other nations.[8]

From 1829 to 1838, opponents of expansion utilized the story of Naboth's vineyard to challenge Indian Removal. To these critics, the United States was pursuing an immoral policy of aggression against the original inhabitants of the land, who were completely justified in their refusal to accommodate the whims of a capricious government. As historians have observed, these protests proved inefficacious. Nonetheless, the parable of Naboth aptly demonstrated that some Americans were uncomfortable with the continuing expansion of the nation. Using the story allowed them to challenge the benevolent facade of Jackson's Indian policy and to hope that some form of retribution would be swift. Perhaps it was John Keen who best summed up this point of view. At a banquet given by the recently formed Whig Party in the city of Philadelphia in 1838, Keen toasted, "The Cherokees: victims to a faithless government, betrayed by their protectors, who have added insult to injury by pretended show of kindness, but, Ahab like, have seized upon the spoils. May Naboth's vengeance be theirs." With the Democrats firmly ensconced in power, and with an economic panic increasingly turning attention away from the issue of Indian Removal, this was the only form of retribution imaginable.[9]

A strange transformation began to take place as the decade progressed, however. In the early 1830s, critics routinely applied the story of Naboth to the case of the Cherokee Nation, but by the middle part of the decade, the narrative had shifted. Article after article appeared that linked the story not to Indian Removal but to the attempted annexation of Texas. In July 1837, the *Emancipator*, an abolition paper, ran an article that used 1 Kings 21:7 as its "text." "The application of our text is very plain," the editor confidently noted. "The slaveholders set their heart on Texas more than ten years ago. The sum of $10,000 was offered for it by Mr. [Joel] Poinsett, our minister to Mexico." In this rendition of the story, Jezebel represented the seductive voice of the slave power, which was plotting to take over Texas. A short time later, the *Emancipator* again tried to rally antislavery forces to block the possibility of annexation: "Let every possible exertion be made to speak the sentiments of freemen on this subject . . . and it may be that the nation will be too deeply roused to suffer the Naboth's vineyard of the slaveholders to answer the purpose for which it was coveted." Gone was the concern over the plight of Native Americans. The slave power had become the enemy.[10]

This argument continued into the 1840s, when the United States and Texas reopened the issue of annexation. In 1845, David Lee Child published *The Taking of Naboth's Vineyard, Or History of the Texas Conspiracy*, in which he portrayed the potential acquisition as a vast southern conspiracy, one that had been conjured by men such as Thomas Hart Benton and Andrew Jackson. Child casts southerners as the villains, men who were committed to expanding the institution of slavery, in spite of morality and human decency. Yet Child, like the generation of antiremoval activists before him, used Naboth as his chief example. In his concluding paragraph, he observed, "The people of the United States cannot be said to have contrived and premeditated this great crime, yet by accepting the booty, they are partakers of the iniquity. . . . King Ahab did not contrive nor execute the murder of Naboth, but he coveted." Child concluded his pamphlet by reminding his readers that the crime of Ahab and Jezebel did not go unnoticed. Though it seemed as if they had gotten away with it, "the avenging prophecy was at length fulfilled," and the blood of Ahab was licked up by the dogs.[11]

The point of narratives such as Child's was not difficult to miss. In the *Broadway Journal*, Edgar Allan Poe confirmed, "The name of the author of this pamphlet will remove all doubts as to the meaning of Naboth's Vineyard. Every body will understand that Naboth is Mexico, and the Vineyard Texas." Even if his meaning was clear, Child failed to convince enough of his readers that the annexation of Texas was not in the best interest of the United States. On December 29, 1845, Texas became the twenty-eighth state. As had happened more than a decade earlier, the opponents could not block expansion. Men like Child could only warn about the possible retribution of God upon the nation for its willingness to covet and possess its neighbor's territory.[12]

But the critique of expansion did not stop after the annexation of Texas. Following the outbreak of the US-Mexican War, opponents reworked the story of Naboth to object to the invasion of their southern neighbor. In the summer of 1846, shortly after the commencement of hostilities, William Lloyd Garrison reprinted a story in the *Liberator* called simply "Twenty First Chapter of the First Book of Kings." In this version of the story the vineyard of Naboth is the territory "between the River Nueces and the Rio Grande" that is owned by Mariano Paredes y Arrillaga, the president of Mexico. As the story progresses, US president James K. Polk, like the character Ahab, tries to convince Paredes to sell his land. When he refuses, Polk is comforted by "Slavery," a character who enters the narrative in the guise of Jezebel. Not surprisingly, she encourages him to start a war with Mexico, which she promises Polk will enable him to claim even more territory than his heart can desire. Joshua, "whose surname is Giddings," warns Polk that God will punish him for his aggression against Mexico. The final verse of this mock scripture concludes, "But there was none like unto Polk, which did sell himself to work wickedness in the sight of the Lord, whom Slavery, his wife, stirred up."[13]

Opponents of the US-Mexican War used the narrative to warn that God would punish the aggressor. As they had cautioned about the dangers of Cherokee removal and the annexation of Texas, they admonished their listeners that God would not long suffer any nation that willingly coveted the land of its neighbors. One writer to the Whig *Daily National Intelligencer* made that precise argument. Writing under the pseudonym "An Old Farmer," he began his missive by asking President Polk "and his advisors" to heed the story of the Israelites. After retelling the familiar story of Ahab and Naboth, he warned Polk that he needed to listen to the words "recorded by the pen of Eternal Truth and Wisdom" and further noted, "If we 'annex' Mexico, we must annex with it an unmeasurable degree of suspicion, disgust, hatred, and a spirit of never-dying revenge." In essence, the acquisition of Mexican territory would be a "curse" upon the American people. Letters such as this evinced little concern about the plight of the Mexican people, but they did guarantee that the United States would suffer for its sin.[14]

The letter of the Old Farmer to the *National Intelligencer* struck a nerve. Less than a week later the *Union*, the Democratic organ of the Polk administration, printed its own letter. "I saw with surprise, in a late National Intelligencer," the author noted, "the whole history of Ahab and Naboth, and seizure of his vineyard . . . followed by a pretended application." This writer, who merely used his initials, then recounted the entire story of Naboth and Ahab and the manner in which the Old Farmer had applied it to the Polk administration. Instead of offering a scriptural defense of the invasion of Mexico, the author fell back upon patriotism. He labeled the Whig position as "moral treason" and openly equated it to that held by the Federalist Party during the War of 1812. In his conclusion, the author could do little more than castigate the Old Farmer for being a traitor. "How can a peace be negotiated," the author bewailed, "when Mexico is openly addressed and encouraged in this way from the great organ of whigism at Washington? Whigism seems to have become so reckless as to be quite unconscious of the unpatriotic position she is taking." Whether or not the war was morally upright did not seem to matter to this particular writer.[15]

Apparently, the editors at the *Union* were not satisfied with this response. A mere three days later, they produced a slightly more learned rebuttal. In yet another column, this one signed by "A Democrat," the *Union* blasted the Old Farmer for his misuse of scripture. The similarities between Ahab and Polk did not hold up, the author alleged, because Ahab and Jezebel went on the attack, whereas Mexico attacked the United States. "The Intelligencer does not read the Bible carefully, or applies it badly," the author then noted. Not content to point out the letter's flawed exegesis, the author countered with a different passage, recommending that the *Intelligencer* read the fifth chapter of the book of Judges, where the prophet Deborah denounced those who had not supported her military actions and called down curses upon their heads. "But those who now join with Mexico against their own country are even more inexcusable," the author opined, "than those ancient Jews, upon whose guilty heads the prophetess invoked the bitter curses of Heaven." The author concluded by stating that the United States was winning the war against Mexico; hence, God had to be pleased with the behavior of the Polk administration.[16]

Whether or not the *Intelligencer* or the *Union* won this debate, the exchange demonstrates two overriding points. First, political opponents of expansion often turned to religion. The story of Naboth, in this case, was deployed not by a prominent nineteenth-century minister but rather by an ordinary individual who believed in the authority of the Bible. It found expression not in a published sermon but in a partisan Whig newspaper published in the nation's capital. Second, this exchange illustrates the fact that the religious critique of expansion was national in scope. The few historians who have studied the antiwar movement have tended to downplay its significance and have delimited it to New England abolitionists and preachers. The *Intelligencer*, however, was the most influential paper of the Whig Party and was hardly a mouthpiece for abolitionist sentiment. A fairer conclusion, then, would be that the majority of Whigs, north and south, did not approve of Polk's war aims and they did not hesitate to use the story of Naboth to illustrate their dissatisfaction.[17]

What is intriguing about the story of Naboth is the manner in which both politicians—predominantly those who had adopted the Whig principle of "no territory" from Mexico—and religious leaders deployed it. At the outbreak of the war, Reverend E. Edwin Hall, a minister at the First Church of Christ in Guilford, Connecticut, used 1 Kings 21:2. In the preface to his book, Hall rebuked those who put party above religion and who supported the US-Mexican War. "If the government turn aside from the way of righteousness," he noted, "it is no want of patriotism to refuse to follow." He then retold the story of Ahab and Naboth. The United States was at fault for coveting the territory of its neighbors, and therefore Hall had no difficulty in declaring the conflict "a stench in the nostrils of every true-hearted American." He further asserted, "We first coveted those fair fields, and then in the spirit of robbery seized them because our arms were longer and stronger than the arms of Mexico." Famed minister Theodore Parker put forth a similar argument in his 1848 sermon at the Melodeon in Boston, when he chose the same passage from the Old Testament to read aloud to his parishioners.[18]

The story of Naboth also allowed individuals to call out ministers who supported the US-Mexican War. The *Louisville Morning Courier*, for instance, printed a lengthy response to a lecture delivered by Reverend J. N. Maffitt, who had justified the conflict using biblical arguments. The editor of the *Courier* complained, "It is bad enough to hear unscrupulous politicians talk of blotting empires from existence, and sweeping millions of human beings into oblivion. But when a 'minister of the cross' casts the eye of an Ahab upon the vineyards of Naboth, and talks of dispossessing eight millions of people, . . . we feel bound to rebuke the transgressor, and to lash him into repentance." What clearly irked this editor was that Maffitt used his pulpit to preach war, but he did not wish Naboth's vengeance upon the reverend. "Bro. Maffitt should commit his Mexican lectures to the flames," the author concluded, "he should bow himself before the Lord, and pray in sackcloth and ashes, and obtain forgiveness of the King of Kings, for having preached pillage, rapine, violence and every evil thing in his name, as a minister of the cross."[19]

This critique of the US-Mexican War only increased as it became clear that Polk sought territory in peace negotiations with Mexico. Reverend Asa Brainerd delivered a Thanksgiving Day sermon in which he blamed the president for his unjust demands. "We have battered down her fortresses and her cities, . . . and our victorious army now revels in her capital. True, we have offered her peace; but it is such peace as Ahab offered to Naboth—such peace, I had almost said, as the vulture offers to the lamb." Others agreed with Brainerd's assessment. "Naboth and Mexico seem to be in much the same predicament," one northern newspaper editorialized. "Mr Polk may perhaps be considered more merciful than Ahab, in that he offers life and existence to Mexico, on condition that she will consent to yield the 'vineyard.'" The fact that Polk and his administration came to speak openly of acquiring a large portion of Mexico as "indemnity" confirmed to many critics that had been his endgame from the outset. Even after the signing of the Treaty of Guadalupe Hidalgo, many complained about the legality of the transaction. "We announce our determination to keep a portion of the Mexican territory," one magazine noted, "which we have conquered and which is as conveniently contiguous to our own as Naboth's vineyard was to Ahab's palace ground."[20]

But how effective was this argument? A sceptic could argue that the US-Mexican War represented yet another failure for the antiexpansionists. Opponents had failed in the case of Cherokee removal, could not prevent the annexation of Texas, and did not stop Polk from grabbing a third of Mexico. Seemingly, all they could do was warn of an impending judgment for the crimes of the nation. However, such a view overlooks the strength of the antiwar movement. As Amy Greenberg recently argued, "Polk got California, but it was the antiwar movement that conquered a peace." Greenberg attributed the strength of the antiwar movement to several factors: its racism, for one, convinced Americans not to expand farther into Mexico; second, its fear of slaveholders led many to feel uncomfortable with the creation of additional slave states; third, many grew tired of the loss of life and expenditure of money as the war progressed. Doubtless, these all played an important role, but so too did religion. Many Americans remained uncomfortable with expansion because they felt it was wrong to covet and claim the land of one's neighbors. The story of Naboth provided ministers, abolitionists, newspaper editors, and politicians with a clear reason that heaven was not pleased with the US-Mexican War. At the very least, the religious critique forced Polk and his fellow expansionists to be more explicit in their war aims.[21]

Opponents of expansion did not cease using the story of Naboth after the signing of the Treaty of Guadalupe Hidalgo. As had occurred in the past, they merely applied the story to a new annexation project, when the United States turned its Ahab gaze upon Cuba. In 1854, Abraham Watkins Venable, a Democrat who represented the state of North Carolina in the House of Representatives, spoke against its acquisition. "I commend those who are so full of our destiny," he opined, "and see its fulfillment in the absorption of Canada and Cuba, the continent, and the adjacent islands, to an instructive lesson found in the history of a certain king of Israel." He then retold the story of Ahab and Naboth before stating that Cuba had become the Naboth's vineyard of the United States. Others joined Venable in linking Cuba and Naboth. "As to the itching desire for Cuba," one writer intoned, "which now rages as a monomania . . . it is the depraved thirst of the inebriate. . . . It is Ahab coveting Naboth's vineyard, and there will be some Jezebel, in the shape of filibusters, to devise a way to consummate the deed." Writers such as this felt confident that the United States merely waited for its opportunity to pounce upon Cuba. They thus dug up the familiar argument that coveting territory was a violation of God's word and that divine judgment would fall upon the nation that carried out violent attacks upon its neighbors.[22]

This criticism intensified after the public release of the Ostend Manifesto. President Franklin Pierce had made it clear in his inaugural address that he was interested in acquiring additional territory, but up until the winter of 1854, he had made very little progress. Then, in December, word leaked out of a secret gathering of US ministers at Ostend, Belgium. A short time later, Secretary of State William Marcy released the document penned by James Buchanan, John Y. Mason, and Pierre Soulé. These three men reasoned that circumstances could force the nation to act. They argued that Spain's refusal to sell Cuba at a fair price would justify the US seizure of the island. The public reaction to the release of the communication was swift and savage.[23]

Not surprisingly, the Ostend Manifesto triggered several Naboth-related critiques of the administration. Reverend George B. Cheever delivered one in an article appropriately titled "Ahab in Naboth's Vineyard." He argued that the United States copied Ahab's policies in its pursuit of Cuba. "A large sum of money will be offered; and the refusal to sell will be considered an insult and a crime against Ahab's kingdom and rights," he predicted. "A new nondescript race of warriors will appear upon the stage, called Filibusters, who, by their incursions into Naboth's possessions, will annoy and provoke Naboth." The meeting at Ostend proved to the critics such as Cheever that the United States merely looked for an excuse to seize the island of Cuba. Others agreed. A writer in the *Christian Advocate and Journal* made similar points. "We see no difference between our covetousness of Cuba, and the proposed mode of obtaining it, and the case of Ahab toward Naboth," this author opined as part of a lengthy denunciation of US policy. Indeed, the similarities between the Ostend Manifesto and King Ahab were difficult to ignore.[24]

In this instance, however, King Ahab did not represent the president of the United States. Instead, critics blamed James Buchanan and not Franklin Pierce for the Ostend Manifesto. After all, Pierce had not penned the Ostend Manifesto, and he worked to separate himself from that document upon its publication. Moreover, most critics recognized that by 1855, he had little political capital and was unlikely to make another attempt to acquire Cuba. Buchanan was different. As he became the Democratic nominee for the presidency in 1856, opponents linked his name with King Ahab. The *Boston Daily Atlas* put it bluntly in an article entitled "The Political Morality of James Buchanan." After quoting from the Ostend Manifesto, the author turned to 1 Kings, chapter 21, but did not quote from it because the narrative was "familiar to all." The author then observed, "James Buchanan, the political Ahab, would have the United States offer the money for the vineyard, and if refused, would have them destroy Naboth and enter upon the inheritance."

Critics repeatedly utilized the argument during the election season. At the New York Republican State Convention, the chairman delivered a speech in which he observed that the Ostend Manifesto was "unequalled in villany since the first Cain" and then equated the behavior of Buchanan with what was done to Naboth. After quoting from the biblical passage, an author in the *Lowell Daily Citizen and News* bluntly concluded, "Now Ahab finding Naboth indisposed to trade, anticipated Buchanan's doctrines as set forth at Ostend, and 'pitching in' to Naboth killed him and 're-annexed' the vineyard to his kitchen garden." All of these individuals warned that the illegal acquisition of Cuba would lead to the United States being punished by God. Although Buchanan did win the election of 1856, all his attempts to establish a protectorate over northern Mexico and his subsequent requests for appropriations from Congress to purchase Cuba failed. When rebuffed for funding, however, Buchanan eschewed his own ideas as put forth in the Ostend Manifesto and refused to use force to acquire additional territory.[25]

The story of Naboth thus had a remarkably long life during the nineteenth century. During the US Civil War, Horace Greeley turned to the story when he characterized American foreign policy in the 1850s as that of a "pirate" and "bully." After the war, William Lloyd Garrison, having helped vanquish slavery, turned his wrath upon expansionism and the attempted purchase of Santo Domingo. Shortly after Sumner delivered his speech in the US Senate, Garrison published an article that bore the same title as Sumner's speech, "Naboth's Vineyard," in which he attacked Grant for his covetousness. Furthermore, as had happened in the 1830s, 1840s, and 1850s, those who were targets of appropriation also turned to the familiar story. After the passage of the Dawes Act that, among other provisions, led to the allotment of Native American lands, articles featuring Naboth appeared with frequency in the *Cherokee Advocate*. Queen Liliuokalani of Hawaii, to cite one final example, turned to Naboth in her autobiography, which she penned after being ousted from the throne in 1893. In her penultimate paragraph, she pleaded with her readers, "Do not covet the little vineyard of Naboth's, so far from your shores, lest the punishment of Ahab fall upon you, if not in your day, in that of your children."[26]

The invocation of this single story demonstrates that those troubled by expansion in the nineteenth century often turned to religious critiques. They did not bow to the overwhelming expansionist sentiment. Indeed, when compiled, the list of individuals who embraced this particular argument is impressive: George Cheever, Charles Sumner, William Lloyd Garrison, Queen Liliuokalani, and Jeremiah Evarts. Certainly, nineteenth-century Americans like Albert Beveridge believed that God's blessings allowed the nation to conquer its neighbors and seize their territory. But historians would do well to remember that in 1898, the same year that Beveridge delivered his much-ballyhooed "March of the Flag" speech, William Jennings Bryan delivered one entitled "Naboth's Vineyard." Although Bryan's speech is rarely read today, he invoked the story to demonstrate that expansion was a violation of biblical precepts. Bryan observed, "Wars of conquest have their origin in covetousness, and the history of the human race has been written in characters of blood because rulers have looked with longing eyes upon the lands of others."[27] For every Beveridge there was a Bryan.

The effectiveness of the Naboth argument waxed and waned over the course of a century, but it is one that should not be overlooked. As historians like Reginald Horsman and Eric T. L. Love have demonstrated, race often served as a double-edged sword during the nineteenth century. It led many to support the idea of a massive, ever-expanding Anglo-Saxon empire, but it also led others to reject expansion for fear of incorporating unwanted populations into the United States. Religion functioned in a similar way. Many missionaries and ministers saw the spread of the Protestant faith as a good thing and thus looked favorably upon events such as the US-Mexican War. Others disagreed. If the United States expanded for purely economic motives, they argued, if it merely coveted the vineyards of its neighbors and sought to dispossess them, then that expansion was morally wrong. The United States, these critics warned, should never allow itself to become the King Ahab of the nineteenth-century world.

NOTES

I thank Rachel St. John, Derek Everett, and Amy Greenberg for their helpful comments on an earlier version of this chapter presented at the meeting of the Society for Historians of the Early Republic. I also thank Conrad Wright, Katheryn Viens, Peter Drummey, Sara Georgini, and Daniel Hinchen for their insightful guidance at the Massachusetts Historical Society. In addition to the MHS, the Kentucky Historical Society, the New England Regional Fellowship Consortium, and the Redd Center for Western Studies at Brigham Young University have also supported this research. This chapter is dedicated to Terry Bouton, historian and mentor, who set me on the path of becoming a historian.

1. *Appendix to Cong. Globe*, 41st Cong., 3rd Sess. (pt. 1), 227; "Naboth's Vineyard: Speech of Hon. Charles Sumner, of Massachusetts, On the Proposed Annexation of 'The Island of San Domingo,' Delivered in the Senate of the United States, December 21, 1870" (Washington, DC: F. & J. Rivers & Geo. A. Bailey, 1870).

2. For racial opposition to expansion, see Eric T. L. Love, *Race over Empire: Racism and U.S. Imperialism, 1865–1900* (Chapel Hill: University of North Carolina Press, 2004), 26. For gendered resistance to expansion, see Amy S. Greenberg, *Manifest Manhood and the Antebellum American Empire* (Cambridge: Cambridge University Press, 2005), 14. For constitutional and limited-government critiques of expansion, see essays in Ian Tyrrell and Jay Sexton, eds., *Empire's Twin: U.S. Anti-imperialism from the Founding Era to the Age of Terrorism* (Ithaca, NY: Cornell University Press, 2015), and Michael Patrick Cullinane, *Liberty and American Anti-imperialism, 1898–1909* (New York: Palgrave Macmillan, 2012). For religious attitudes toward expansion in the early Republic, see Emily Conroy-Krutz, *Christian Imperialism: Converting the World in the Early American Republic* (Ithaca, NY: Cornell University Press, 2015), 9.

3. Sacvan Bercovitch, *The Puritan Origins of the American Self* (New Haven, CT: Yale University Press, 1975), 185; Bercovitch, *Rites of Assent: Transformations in the Symbolic Construction of America* (New York: Routledge, 1993), 185; Ernest Lee Tuveson, *Redeemer Nation: The Idea of America's Millennial Role* (Chicago: University of Chicago Press, 1968), 91–96; Reginald Horsman, *Race and Manifest Destiny: The Origins of Racial Anglo-Saxonism* (Cambridge, MA: Harvard University Press, 1981); John C. Pinheiro, *Missionaries of Republicanism: A Religious History of the Mexican-American War* (New York: Oxford University Press, 2014); Walter A. McDougall, *Promised Land, Crusader State: The American Encounter with the World since 1776* (Boston: Houghton Mifflin, 1997); Anders Stephanson, *Manifest Destiny: American Expansion and the Empire of Right* (New York: Hill & Wang, 1995).

4. Jeremiah Evarts, *Essays on the Present Crisis in the Condition of the American Indians: First Published in the National Intelligencer* (Boston: Perkins & Marvin, 1829), 6. Evarts was not the only writer to turn to the figure of Naboth in 1829. See also "Naboth's Vineyard," *Baltimore American*, reprinted in *Western Intelligencer, Religious, Literary and Political* (Hudson, OH), May 15, 1829. For an examination of arguments used in this debate, see Ronald M. Satz, *American Indian Policy in the Jacksonian Era* (1974; repr., Norman: University of

Oklahoma Press, 2001), 20–48; John A. Andrew III, *From Revivals to Removal: Jeremiah Evarts, the Cherokee Nation, and the Search for the Soul of America* (1992; repr., Athens: University of Georgia Press, 2007), 151; John M. Coward, *The Newspaper Indian: Native American Identity in the Press, 1820–90* (Urbana: University of Illinois Press, 1999), 79–84; Jason Edward Black, *American Indians and the Rhetoric of Removal and Allotment* (Jackson: University Press of Mississippi, 2015), 49–57.

5. "The Indians," *New York Daily Advertiser*, reprinted in *New-Hampshire Statesman and Concord Register*, October 31, 1829; "Georgia and the Indian," *New York Spectator*, reprinted in *Observer and Telegraph* (Hudson, OH), March 19, 1830.

6. A Persian Mullah, "Ahab & Jezebel Vindicated," *New York Observer*, reprinted in *Cherokee Phoenix, and Indians' Advocate*, October 21, 1829; "For the Courant," *Connecticut Courant*, December 28, 1830, reprinted as "Indians," *Cherokee Phoenix*, January 29, 1831. For a more serious critique of American practices, see Naboth, "Cherokee Nation Jan. 1832," *Cherokee Phoenix*, February 4, 1832. For other examples, see David Vann, "The Cherokees," *Niles' Weekly Register*, July 16, 1831; "Journal of a Southern Tour," *New York Evangelist*, August 9, 1834.

7. "The Better Vineyard," *New York Observer*, reprinted in *Western Recorder*, December 1, 1829.

8. Calvin Colton, *Tour of the American Lakes, and among the Indians of the North-West Territory, in 1830, Disclosing the Character and Prospects of the Indian Race*, vol. 1 (London: Westley and Davis, 1833), 262–263.

9. "The Whig Celebration of the Fourth of July, 1838," *Pennsylvania Inquirer and Daily Courier*, July 13, 1838.

10. "Texas," *Christian Register and Boston Observer*, September 10, 1836; "The Annexation of Texas," *Emancipator* (New York), June 22, 1837; "Texas-Texas!," *Emancipator*, July 27, 1837. This argument was frequently made in Britain by abolitionists. See the *London Patriot* reprinted in Benjamin Lundy, *The War in Texas* (Philadelphia: Merrihew & Gunn, 1836), 49; Thompson's speech is reprinted in "Texas," *Vermont Phoenix*, August 25, 1837.

11. David Lee Child, *The Taking of Naboth's Vineyard, Or History of the Texas Conspiracy* (New York: S. W. Benedict & Co., 1845), 29. Nicholas Guyatt argues that Indian Removal led many Americans to embrace "judicial providentialism," the idea that God would judge the United States for its mistreatment of others. He demonstrates that this argument was later used by those opposed to African colonialism and slavery. It appears that it became a staple argument of those who opposed expansionism as well. Guyatt, *Providence and the Invention of the United States, 1607–1876* (New York: Cambridge University Press, 2007), 174.

12. Edgar Allan Poe, "Book Reviews," *Broadway Journal*, April 5, 1845.

13. "Twenty First Chapter of the First Book of Kings," *True Democrat*, reprinted in the *Liberator*, July 31, 1846. In this story, Joshua Giddings, a fierce congressional opponent of slavery and the war, takes the place of the prophet Elijah.

14. An Old Farmer, "The Old Farmer, Once More," *Daily National Intelligencer*, November 19, 1847.

15. W.H.S. "'Moral Treason'—National Intelligencer of the War of 1812," *Union* (Washington, DC), November 27, 1847.

16. A Democrat, "Ahab and Naboth—The Intelligencer Wrong as Usual—A Quotation for Its Benefit," *Union*, November 30, 1847.

17. John H. Schroeder, *Mr. Polk's War: American Opposition and Dissent, 1846–1848* (Madison: University of Wisconsin Press, 1973), 34; Pinheiro, *Missionaries of Republicanism*, 86; Robert W. Johannsen, *To the Halls of the Montezumas: The Mexican War in the American Imagination* (New York: Oxford University Press, 1985), 214–215; Stephanson, *Manifest Destiny*, 49.

18. E. Edwin Hall, *Ahab and Naboth* (New Haven, CT: A. H. Maltby, 1847), 4, 14; Theodore Parker, *A Sermon of the Mexican War: Preached at the Melodeon, on Sunday, June 25th, 1848* (Boston: Coolidge and Wiley, 1848), 3.

19. "Professor Maffitt's Lecture on the Mexican War," *Louisville Morning Courier*, November 1, 1847. See also "Communications," *Marshall Statesman*, February 22, 1848. In this editorial, the author condemned Senator Ambrose Sevier for a speech he delivered. This author used Ahab and Naboth as his story. "There are some, I know, among the Locofocos, who believe less in 'manifest destiny,' which is another phrase for 'undoubting atheism,' than they do in an overruling Providence. If dogs eat the flesh of Jezebel, for her iniquity, in an age of little light, what shall be the punishment of those who copy her example . . . in a period of far greater light."

20. "True Patriotism," *New York Evangelist*, December 23, 1847; "President's Message," *Vermont Phoenix*, December 24, 1847; "Peace—And What Next?," *New Englander* 6 (April 1848): 292.

21. As Amy S. Greenberg later stated, "Although Polk never mentioned Lincoln or his attacks directly, the cumulative effect of national antiwar agitation generally, and congressional antiwar agitation in particular, was to limit both the duration of the war and Polk's demands for Mexican territory." Greenberg, *A Wicked War: Polk, Clay, Lincoln, and the 1846 U.S. Invasion of Mexico* (New York: Alfred A. Knopf, 2012), 263.

22. *Cong. Globe*, 32nd Cong., 2nd Sess., 190; "Ethics of Filibusterism," *New York National Democrat*, reprinted in *National Intelligencer*, February 4, 1854; "Letters from the South," *National Intelligencer*, June 24, 1854.

23. For early reactions to the meeting, see "The Ostend Conference—Attempt of the Cabinet to Suppress Inquiry," *New York Herald*, December 9, 1854; "The Meeting at Ostend," *North American and United States Gazette*, December 7, 1854. For the text of the document, see James Buchanan, John Y. Mason, and Pierre Soulé to William L. Marcy in *The Diplomatic Correspondence of the United States: Inter-American Affairs, 1831–1860*, ed. William R. Manning, 12 vols. (Washington, DC: Carnegie Endowment for International Peace, 1932–1939), 7:579–585.

24. George B. Cheever, "Ahab in Naboth's Vineyard," *Independent* (New York), April 5, 1855; "Cuba the Vineyard of Naboth," *Christian Advocate and Journal*, May 3, 1855.

25. "The Political Morality of James Buchanan," *Boston Daily Atlas*, August 12, 1856; "The Political Campaign," *Weekly Herald*, September 20, 1856; "No Title," *Lowell Daily Citizen and News*, November 1, 1856. For Buchanan's imperial ideas during his

presidency, see Frederick Moore Binder, *James Buchanan and the American Empire* (Selinsgrove, PA: Susquehanna University Press, 1994), 217–258.

26. Horace Greeley, "Dark and Bright Hours," *Independent*, May 14, 1863; William Lloyd Garrison, "Naboth's Vineyard," *Independent*, December 22, 1870; Pocahontas, "Naboth's Vineyard," *Cherokee Advocate*, October 9, 1895; W. A. Duncan, "Statehood," *Cherokee Advocate*, October 14, 1893; Liliuokalani, *Hawaii's Story by Hawaii's Queen* (Boston: Lothrop, Lee & Shephard, 1898), 373.

27. Albert Jeremiah Beveridge, "The March of the Flag," in *The Meaning of the Times and Other Speeches* (Indianapolis: Bobbs-Merrill, 1908); 47; "Naboth's Vineyard," in William Jennings Bryan, *Speeches of William Jennings Bryan*, 2 vols. (New York: Funk & Wagnalls Company, 1909), 2:6–7.

CHAPTER 3

The Art of Indian Affairs:
Land and Sky in Charles Bird King's
Keokuk, the Watchful Fox

Kenneth Haltman

Widespread ambivalence in the 1820s and 1830s among eastern elites caught up in a collective enthusiasm for territorial expansion yet appalled at the prospect of state-sponsored Indian Removal found abundant expression in the documentary archive, in texts ranging from personal correspondence to speeches and sermons to treaty documents.[1] Few historians have concerned themselves with the visual imaginary, which remains virtually unexamined for its possible contribution to historical understanding, at best providing illustrations that embellish a historical account, unanalyzed as primary evidence. That such evidence abounds in the visual record would come as little surprise to art historians, who attempt to make sense of images (or objects) understood as responses to historical circumstance.

The neglect by historians—and, to be fair, most art historians—of the impressive series of Native American portraits, among them an image of the Sauk chief Keokuk (plate 3) painted on the occasion of a visit to the "Seat of Government" by a delegation that he led, is, however, still hard to understand given its proximity to the heart of that imperial enterprise, executed in the 1820s for the War Department by among the finest American painters of his generation, Charles Bird King.[2]

Commissioned by Superintendent of Indian Affairs Thomas L. McKenney to decorate the outer office of Secretary of War John C. Calhoun, the image was one among 111 identically sized effigies of Native leaders that literally lined the improvised gallery's walls above glass-case and tabletop displays of aboriginal artifacts culminating in an imposing "war canoe" suspended from the ceiling. Designed to be viewed by army officers, members of Congress, journalists, and foreign dignitaries, this ensemble, an elaborate trophy room featuring the removed heads (or heads of soon-to-be-removed) Native dignitaries, would have induced in these visitors, in the words of cultural historian Susan Stewart, feelings of "infinite reverie" in response to a display of hegemonic power thinly disguised at once as ethnographic record and diplomatic archive.[3] Like the assembled artifacts, the portraits served in their ensemble to authenticate the ideology of dispossession informing their selection and display.

This effect was, of course, in keeping with the tradition of ethnographic portraiture itself, a genre developed in late eighteenth-century Europe to represent indigenous peoples first encountered and then subjugated in pursuit of the colonial enterprise. Because the military officers and expeditionary scientists responsible had sought to frame these earlier depictions in a manner comprehensible to period viewers likely otherwise to find their strangeness disconcerting, these representations were informed by an amalgam of pictorial conventions familiar from other contexts, based on compositional arrangements drawn, to varying degrees, from zoological specimen drawing, plein air landscape, and a style of aristocratic studio portraiture designed to put a sitter's dignity as well as status prominently on display.

The result was an ambitious genre torn by contradictory impulses as the oxymoron "ethnographic portraiture" surely suggests, informed at once by concern to convey generalized information germane to an entire culture and far more particular concern with recording individuality and specificity. *Kee-o-Kuck, First War Chief of the Sauks*, for example, represents that tribe in one of scores of similarly metonymic gestures, yet his features and accoutrements suggest a moment of authentic encounter with one man in particular, recording a visit to King's studio, whose radical decontextualization—armless and legless, afloat in a sea of faces—reconfigured that encountered in such a way as to invite both sympathy born of recognition of a shared humanity and a viewer's sense of cultural superiority.

The easy political symbolism of the rows of heads in which such works as King's bust of Keokuk found its place achieved greater nuance in a small handful of full-length portraits by the same artist that served to frame the larger display, including a second version of Keokuk (plate 4) painted several years later, this time only partially from life, in which the themes and representational strategies of the ensemble achieved their most distilled and accomplished expression.[4] This later image, *Keokuk, the Watchful Fox*, represents not the fragment of a man but, magisterially accoutred and adorned, placed in an expressively specific landscape, his entire self, a powerful dramatic depiction of what might be termed his ethnographic situation.[5]

Keokuk stands facing to our right in three-quarter profile, his expression meditative, even melancholy. In his right hand he grips a decorated war club, its triangular tip glinting with reflected light, visual metaphor for an acuity of intellect and force of character here held in check. A red deer hair "roach" has been fastened to his scalp lock. All these elements at least are familiar ones, borrowed from King's earlier portrait. Here, however, a vigorous man in his thirties or forties, barely clad by European standards but nonetheless impressively arrayed and juxtaposed against a view of distant mountains, Keokuk appears to emanate from those environs, a celebration of wildness however framed and contained.

Much else in the full-length portrait, however, derives from another work, a lost watercolor painted from life at the treaty council of Prairie du Chien held on the Upper Mississippi in the summer of 1825, also at the behest of the War Department, by another artist, itinerant scene painter, engraver, and stage actor James Otto Lewis.[6] We have some sense of that lost watercolor from a hand-colored lithograph (plate 5) Lewis later published in his *Aboriginal Port-Folio* (1835–1836) issued in Philadelphia in ten eight-image folios based on his earlier fieldwork.[7] From Lewis, King adopted the notion if not the details of his more explicitly delineated background setting. He borrowed the details of Keokuk's costume as well: the red breechcloth and red and tan embroidered moccasins; the long white foxtail that depends from his behind; the bundle of horsehair hanging from his arm; the fur and feathers at his calves; his silver ornaments (headband, choker, armlets above the elbows); the peace medal suspended on a leather thong around his neck; the white hands painted on his chest. Finally, King incorporated into his composition the strong vertical of the ceremonial lance lined with alternating black and white feathers that Keokuk holds upright in his extended left hand, linking earth to sky.

All these seem ethnographic elements in the true sense—an accurate record of how a Sauk or Fox chief might well have chosen to appear on a formal occasion in August 1825. But in King's full-length version, important changes are in evidence as well. Keokuk's other hand, resting passively in Lewis on a rounded thigh, now bears the glinting tomahawk held ready at the level of his groin, a gesture of assertion, combined with an air of psychological detachment, here suggestive of prerogative and dignity, effeminacy masculinized.[8] (We might further note in this regard the conventionally feminine divided waterfall rhymed with chubby thighs in Lewis replaced by King with rugged mountains.) There seems little doubt this effeminizing in the former instance was in keeping with official policy—Lewis was well connected, socially and politically, with Prairie du Chien treaty commissioner and territorial governor Lewis Cass, a factor in his employ in the first place—just as celebrating the dignity of an American ally was King's later tactical response to state interests. Indeed, King's modifications to the landscape in Lewis are, if possible, of greater significance still. The topographic realism of a midground from which cascading water flows in the direction of the picture plane has been rescripted as a radical discontinuity between the narrow ledge of reddish earth where Keokuk now stands and cooler tonal harmonies beyond, a distance of water and picturesque mountains from which the foreground has been radically divided by a sheer drop into the valley below.[9]

That is to say, the painting belongs to a hybrid genre, landscape portraiture, animated by contradictory pictorial impulses and effects. Where landscape invites one into picture space, portraiture confronts and interrupts. In beholding *Keokuk, the Watchful Fox*, the eye trained by convention to seek resolution in a mountain distance, deep in picture space, is thus drawn into dramatic confrontation with the figure of a man whose stance, weaponry, and seeming self-assurance take their force from other pictorial conventions entirely, those of aristocratic portraiture.[10] Nicholas Hilliard's late sixteenth-century miniature of George Clifford, third Earl of Cumberland (plate 6), for instance, represents Clifford as enjoying full possession of the land before which he stands, access to which he bodily denies the viewer. King lends this conceit a fuller, far more lush articulation, representing western wilderness as a locus of desire that lures the viewer's gaze yet challenges the very desire that that wilderness invites, our visual claims to midground territory prepossessed, as it were already framed, by the imposing body of the man who stands before it gazing back.

This echo, as present in the portrait of Keokuk by Lewis as in that by King, had a long lineage as a structuring component of at least a century of simpler ethnographic portraits in which Indians were figured as natural aristocracy. John Verelst's portrait of an Iroquois king at Queen Anne's court painted in England in 1710, seen here in a period engraving by John Simon (fig. 3.1), offers a typical example as, somewhat closer to home, does Paul Revere's popular 1772 engraving of the Wampanoag chief King Philip (plate 7).[11] While King's *Keokuk* derives from this tradition—he had studied historical portraiture in London under American-born Benjamin West, painter to the king—his innovation was to place landscape, more specifically nonprivatized land, at the thematic center of his composition.[12]

In an essay not intended principally for art historians, it seems useful at this point to address the question of the evidentiary value of these observations

SA GA YEATH QUA PIETH Tow, King of the Maquas.

Printed for Ja. O'perke Print: at the Golden Horse in Litchfield London

Figure 3.1. John Simon, after John Verelst, *Sa Ga Yeath Qua Pieth Tow, King of the Maquas*. 1710. Third state. Mezzotint on paper. 13-1/2 × 10-1/16 in. Yale University Art Gallery, New Haven, CT.

and the utility of the concept of visual (or pictorial) evidence itself on which the ensuing analysis relies. What, in fact, have we accomplished thus far? For one thing, mere *ekphrasis*, the translation of visual perceptions into language, has greatly enhanced our recognition of the *means* by which King's image signifies both structurally and thematically. In the words of art historian Joseph Koerner, "Rather than saying *what* a visual image means, description tells us *how* an image has opened itself to an interpretation."[13] We cannot make sense of works of art otherwise than under the aegis of language.

But, of course, an image, understood as a historical event in its own right, signifies only in the particular historical contexts in which it was produced and to which it refers. Not surprisingly, the contest for territorial possession that underlay and animated the contemporary viewer's encounter with Keokuk was historically specific, to do with the immensely rich Galena lead fields that the Sauks and Foxes controlled and that we may imagine behind him, down along the river. In the late eighteenth century, during the years of increasing American commercial and political presence in the Old Northwest, the Sauks and Foxes had come to reside in a series of permanent villages along both banks of the Upper Mississippi, their subsistence based on a corn crop planted in the spring supplemented by men hunting and by women digging for lead.[14] The Sauks and Foxes worked shallow excavation mines and smelted what ore they could extract in crude log furnaces.[15] Whites had been aware of the existence of these rich lodes since Nicolas Perrot and Pierre-Charles Le Sueur had reported them in the late seventeenth century. John Lawson, in *A New Voyage to Carolina*, had described the lead mines in 1709 as "of great value to the Sawkee and Fox Nations."[16] In fact, by 1720, a French *directeur-général des mines*, P. François de Renault, was operating its own Ioway lead mines enjoying a very high yield. Pelts and furs on the one hand, lead ore on the other, were carried downstream to white traders. As was typical of such trade, this economy was based on credit extended each spring as a result of which the tribes were kept perpetually in debt.[17] In 1804, following the Louisiana Purchase, in a move to solidify its territorial control, the federal government agreed to take over the tribe's obligations in exchange for land. The resulting treaty, signed in St. Louis by a small delegation representing a pro-American faction generously plied with alcohol, notorious even in its day, relinquished Sauk and Fox claims to their entire range east of the Mississippi, a territory totaling some fifty million acres. Though their rights to live and hunt on the ceded land were assured, over the following decades settlers poured in and conditions worsened. Game grew so scarce that hunting parties, forced to forage farther and farther west, came into conflict with bands of Sioux. In a classic, by King, in fact, classicized difference over the proper tactical response, some, led by

Black Hawk, favored armed resistance; others, led by Keokuk, a realpolitik of accommodation.[18]

The treaty council of Prairie du Chien, called in the summer of 1825 ostensibly to adjudicate boundary disputes among the region's tribes to prevent further disruption of trade, had a larger goal. Establishing tribal boundaries laid the legal groundwork for further forced expropriations and removals.[19] But there was a more specific goal as well. Signatories to the treaty acknowledged "the general controlling power of the United States," and poor white squatters from neighboring Tennessee, Kentucky, Missouri, and southern Illinois, who had long coveted the lead mined by the Sauks and Foxes yet previously shown restraint, now understood their aspirations to enjoy the sanction of law. An immediate report of this expanding supply of lead appeared in *Niles' Weekly Register* already later that year. Historian William Peterson describes the shift in the regional economy: "From the very start, the growth in [non-Native] population in the mining region was phenomenal. On July 1, 1825, there were 100 miners at the Fever River mines. On August 31, 1826, there were 453, with the number steadily increasing."[20] By the time King conceived the composition of his portrait, the influx of white miners had taken on the proportions of a rush documented in early Galena, Illinois, settler R. W. Chandler's 1829 *Map of the United States Lead Mines on the Upper Mississippi* (fig. 3.2). Prairie du Chien appears at the upper left, with new exploitations and Indian mines recently taken over by whites indicated by the dozens of black dots just to the south and east. Timothy Flint, in his *Condensed Geography and History of the Western States* (1828), noted: "Lead ore is found in different points of this valley with more ease and in greater abundance, perhaps, than in any other part of the world." Writing years later about that time, one then hopeful white miner reported: "About the year 1826, there was a great excitement in regard to the lead mines of the Upper Mississippi. In 1827 I thought I would try my luck one season at the mines."[21]

This, I would argue, is the immediate economic and historical context in which the full-length landscape portrait of Keokuk is to be understood. King's familiarity with the practical stakes involved in this specific territorial dispute is beyond question. As a result of increased production, lead prices "on the Atlantic Coast" (including those of the domestically manufactured oil paints King himself used in his portraits) had in four years' time fallen by half—an economic consequence described by Prairie du Chien treaty commissioner Caleb Atwater, who considered "the Purchase of Mineral Country" the treaty's purpose.[22] Both the events and the tensions in the Great Lakes region were widely reported in the eastern press, with particular attention being paid to the increased production of lead, Keokuk's grudging cooperation with white

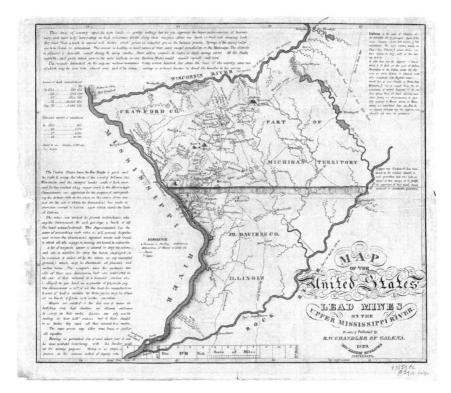

Figure 3.2. Ebenezer Martin, after R. W. Chandler, *Map of the United States' Lead Mines on the Upper Mississippi River.* 1829. Beinecke Rare Book and Manuscript Library, Yale University, New Haven, CT.

interests, and Black Hawk's increasing militancy. The peace medal worn by Keokuk signifies ambivalently as a badge of honor and token of captivity. While it seems certain that the former meaning would have outweighed the latter for Keokuk, in an image intended for an eastern audience of whites in this context the medal suggests, as I have argued elsewhere, not just political allegiance but acquiescence to a greater power.[23]

King's familiarity with the moralizing terms of liberal political debate pertaining to this issue is also beyond question. McKenney, who commissioned the painting, as superintendent of Indian affairs was deeply involved in the government's formulation of a policy response to the deterioration in Indian-White relations occasioned by the lead fields, which he had toured in 1827.[24] His own views in this period were undergoing a sea change. While his belief in the possibility of Christianizing Indians was liberal for his time, his first trip west a year earlier had shaken his commitment to assimilation.

He had been horrified to witness the corrupting effects of exposure to un-scrupulous whites on tribal culture and found himself increasingly persuaded that Indian survival (which he understood as Indian salvation) could only be ensured by so-called voluntary removals of entire populations west beyond the Mississippi. The choice seemed to him increasingly clear: "If the Indians do not emigrate, and fly the causes which have proved so destructive in the past, they must perish!" Eastern Woodland tribes, he wrote, "are perishing [both] before our presence, *and because of it*."[25]

King's portrait recapitulates the drama it celebrates, the Treaty of Prairie du Chien and its aftermath, through a manipulation of the landscape in which or rather before which Keokuk stands backed like a hunted animal to the edge of a precarious abyss. The image thus responds complexly to a complex ma-trix of economic, political, and philosophical concerns with Indian Removal, a violent process involving dislocation and disruption, yet works to naturalize and to legitimize the very process of displacement that it represents by princi-pally aesthetic means.

While Keokuk's "grounding" has been weakened by his nearness to the edge of the cliff (fig. 3.3), King makes dramatic use of that potential fall to offer reassurance of his subject's possible apotheosis, a recuperation effected through a potent visual allegory in which the presence at the line of the cliff's edge of Keokuk's winged calves, like the *talaria* associated in the ancient world with winged Hermes, rescripts the prospect of his uncontrolled descent as a possibility of flight thus of salvation. In the words of James Hall, McKenney's collaborator:

> The Indian loves his tribe, he loves his wild, free habits of life, he loves
> the wilderness; but all those feelings are personal; they travel with him in
> his wanderings, and abide with his people wherever they may happen to
> dwell. They are not attached to the soil, nor interwoven with recollections
> of place and scenery. They are not connected with the sacred and delight-
> ful associations of home and country. The wild man has no home nor
> country.[26]

This conceit too had its iconographic precedents, notably Benvenuto Cel-lini's sixteenth-century bronze *Mercury* (fig. 3.4) captured in the moment of ascent, described by French phenomenologist Gaston Bachelard as the ar-chetypal image of the dream of flight. Distinguishing images corrupted by conscious thought from unmediated products of imagination, Bachelard con-cludes: "We do not fly because we have wings; we think we have had wings because we have flown."[27] Oneiric flight occurs, as here, at the heel, point of

Figure 3.3. Detail of Charles Bird King, *Keokuk, the Watchful Fox.*
1829. Oil on canvas. 38-1/2 × 26-1/2 in. Private collection.
Image courtesy of Gerald Peters Gallery, Santa Fe, NM. For full-
color version, see plate 4.

Figure 3.4. Benvenuto Cellini,
Gruppo del Perseo: Mercurio. Ca. 1545–
1554. Bronze. 37-3/4 in. Museo
Nazionale del Bargello, Firenze.
Photograph courtesy of Alinari/Art
Resource, NY.

interrupted contact with the earth. The art historian Jean Lancri describes such imagined terrestrial connections that allow a subject to gather strength to rise as the products of a *complexe d'Antée*, invoking the plight of the giant Antaeus whom in ancient myth Hercules overcame by lifting him from his mother Gaea, the Earth.[28]

King's creative thematic response to this suggestion, a sophisticated mapping of geopolitical concerns onto the viewer's encounter with a man whose attachment to the soil is unsubtly at issue, relied less perhaps on any source in prior art than on pragmatic imagination as he sought to resolve the contradiction at the heart of a commission that would have him dramatize the violence of Indian Removal in terms the viewer could feel good about. Keokuk's feathers as well as wings evidence his tendency to spiritual uplift. In the end, significantly impelled by our—that is to say, the viewer's territorial—desire, Keokuk will rise up as the viewer enters picture space, at one with distant sky and mountains, opening the midground (and its mineral wealth) to those who would possess it, bloodlessly removed, the savage in possession of desired land transformed—or rather dematerialized—into a symbol of transcendence.[29] As Alexis de Tocqueville would express it in 1835: "Thoughts of the savage, natural grandeur that is going to come to an end become mingled with splendid anticipations of the triumphant march of civilization."[30]

Something further: to most viewers in the 1820s, symbolically armed Indians encountered in a wilderness landscape were perceived not as a natural landed aristocracy—a rhetorical usage noted earlier in the engravings of Simon and Revere—but instead as savage hunters. Roy Harvey Pearce has described in his now classic study *Savagism and Civilization* (1953), the trained unwillingness of Americans by early in the first Andrew Jackson administration to understand Native Americans as anything *but* hunters despite the traditional importance to eastern peoples especially of agriculture, not to mention mining among tribes in the Old Northwest. The "intellectual and cultural traditions and ideas of order [of whites]," Pearce concludes, "so informed their thoughts and their actions that they could see and conceive of nothing but the Indian who hunted."[31] These associations had special relevance given that the principal rhetorical device employed to justify removal was the old Jeffersonian dictum that progress relied on the displacement of primitive hunting societies by fields and farms.

Metaphoric hunting inscribes King's painting with historical significance beyond its record of physiognomy and costume, providing the thematic basis for a dramatic reversal on which the image turns. For although Keokuk's foxtail ornament and weaponry identify *him* as a hunter, the structure of predation energizing his portrait casts him less in that role than as prey, identified synecdochically with the animals he wears—his sobriquet the Watchful Fox. The conceit that progress was a kind of hunt, and Native Americans big game, informed in fact much of the period's thinking. Lewis, in captioning his own version of the portrait, sounded the conventional lament: "Desolation pursues the Indians to their mountain retreats, and, like the beasts of prey, they are hunted from the[ir] fastnesses in the woods." McKenney echoed the terms of this sentiment almost exactly in justifying the national policies that, after a fashion, he hired King to illustrate. "The poor things have land," he wrote, "and while there is a foot that we can put upon, that is worth occupying, they will, I fear, be hunted and driven off."[32] The hunt for Keokuk is the hunt for the territory on which and before which he stands, and *Keokuk, the Watchful Fox* (the painting) essentially a trophy of that hunt, a landscape portrait designed to appeal to his patron Thomas McKenney's desire to read continuity in violent change.[33]

The image works to reconcile uneasy contradictions between the realities of deportation (what occurs when Keokuk is pressed to take that last backward step) and liberal sentiment (which held that this would lead to his upliftment), and does so by associating Indian savagery with land and Indian nobility with distant sky. In the Barthean sense, the image masks its ideological commitment by naturalizing it. King's clever use of landscape serves here to inscribe his portrait with a moralizing narrative. If the viewer is imagined to enter picture space on the axis of history or progress, Keokuk's potential fall and viewer-impelled apotheosis enact a spatial, that is to say properly territorial, allegory, the inevitability of its trajectory suggested by the strong line of his lance which, planted on the ground, points up into the heavens.[34] Thus the cultural work the portrait performs: Keokuk, though savage in fact, is yet noble in spirit, and the viewer's gaze, like the nation's territorial ambitions, justified as morally redemptive. The Indian Gallery offered visitors a reassuring grid of control even as it offered many windows, as it were, on wilderness presided over by the sign, no longer by the fact, of Native wildness.

This trace of ambivalence resulted less from the ingenuity of any particular artist maker than from the nexus of competing interests—intellectual, political, cultural, aesthetic—out of which the images themselves emerged, shaped by period conventions in response to the anticipated and articulated needs, themselves ambivalent, of individuals (McKenney, perhaps Calhoun) and the establishment whose values their commission represented. That the pictorial metaphors involved were structural as well as narrative, involving flight and predation, only heightened the phenomenological effect of a hybrid, thus commensurately hyperexpressive, pictorial genre a writer in the *United States Review and Literary Gazette* in 1827 aptly termed "historical or poetic portraiture."[35]

NOTES

Versions of portions of this chapter have been delivered as conference papers and public lectures over the course of several decades. These previous iterations include talks given at the annual meeting of the College Art Association in Chicago in February 1992, at Wesleyan University in November 1993 as Scholar in Residence in the College of Letters, at the Gilcrease Symposium at the University of Tulsa in March 2008, at the annual Southwest Art History Conference in Taos in November 2012, and at the Art Gallery of Western Australia in Perth in September 2015. I first encountered the works of art discussed in this chapter at the Whitney Gallery of Western Art in Cody, Wyoming, as a fellow at the Buffalo Bill Historical Center in the summer of 1985 while a graduate student in American studies at Yale, and the following year, thanks to a summer research award in the Smithsonian's Office of American Studies, its last year in operation, I had the good fortune to discuss this material with its director, Wilcomb Washburn, a specialist in Native American history, who introduced me to Bill Sturtevant and Ives Godard at the National Museum of Natural History, allowing me access to the Anthropological Archives. During a Huntington Library summer fellowship in 1990 and yearlong predoctoral fellowship at the Smithsonian's National Museum of American Art the following year, I pursued my research in their remarkable historical and pictorial archives. An NEH Short-Term Travel to Collections grant in 1993 permitted me to consult the unpublished papers of John Francis McDermott, the first historian to consider these materials, at Southern Illinois University Edwardsville. At about that time I visited the Galena lead fields and, for me as movingly, Prairie du Chien and the site of old Fort Atkinson. I wish to thank Sarah Boehme, Peter Hassrick, and Gerald Peters for their helpful correspondence; Jean Lancri for introducing me to Bachelard; and my students at Yale, Bryn Mawr, Emory, Michigan State, the University of Oklahoma, and the University of Western Australia with whom I've had the pleasure of sharing versions of this material for their always insightful responses.

1. See, for instance, Michael Paul Rogin, "Liberal Society and the Indian Question," *Politics and Society* 1 (May 1971): 269–312; Robert F. Berkhofer Jr., *The White Man's Indian: Images of the American Indian from Columbus to the Present* (New York: Vintage, 1980), pt. 2, "From Religion to Anthropology: The Genealogy of the Scientific Image of the Indian."

2. See John Canfield Ewers, "Charles Bird King: Painter of Indian Visitors to the Nation's Capitol," *Annual Report of the Smithsonian Institution for 1953* (Washington, DC: Government Printing Office, 1953), 463–473; Herman J. Viola, "Washington's First Museum: The Indian Office Collection of Thomas L. McKenney," *Smithsonian Journal of History* 3 (Fall 1968): 1–18.

3. It may have been Richard Drinnon in *Facing West: The Metaphysics of Indian-Hating and Empire-Building* (New York: New American Library, 1980), 193, who first described McKenney as a trophy hunter who encouraged successive secretaries of war to bring delegations of Native leaders to Washington at public expense in order to enlarge his

personal holding in heads. See Susan Stewart, *On Longing: Narratives of the Miniature, the Gigantic, the Souvenir, the Collection* (Baltimore: Johns Hopkins University Press, 1984), 152.

4. For this and other biographical information I have relied principally on Andrew J. Cosentino, *The Paintings of Charles Bird King (1785–1862)* (Washington, DC: National Gallery, 1977).

5. King was paid twenty dollars for each bust and twenty-seven dollars for each full-length portrait. Of the 116 portraits completed by 1828, he received the higher price for only 5. For a basic accounting of the painting and its history, see *The Important Collection of Twenty-One Portraits of North American Indians by Charles Bird King [1785–1862], Property of the Redwood Library and Athenaeum* (New York: Parke-Bernet Galleries, 1970), cat. 15.

6. Lewis had been engaged by the territorial governor of Michigan on McKenney's behalf to take Native American likenesses for eventual inclusion in the War Department gallery. The forty (or in one account sixty) "drawings," most likely watercolors, he shipped to McKenney over the course of three years' service on the treaty circuit burned in the great Smithsonian fire of 1865. For an 1859 pre-fire inventory, see William J. Rhees, *An Account of the Smithsonian Institution, Its Founder, Building, Operations, &c.* (Washington, DC: Thomas McGill, 1859). The most authoritative biography of Lewis we have, though fragmentary and unpublished, remains the draft John Francis McDermott preserved among his papers (box 6, folder 14), Lovejoy Library, Southern Illinois University at Edwardsville. See also Philip R. St. Clair, ed., *James Otto Lewis: The American Indian Portfolio: An Eyewitness History, 1823–28* (Kent, OH: Volair Limited, 1980), and William Reese, *James Otto Lewis and His Aboriginal Port Folio* (New Haven, CT: Overland Press, 2008).

7. The image, *Kee-O-Kuck, or the Watching Fox*, appeared as the first plate in folio 2 (June 1835). On the Lewis-King "collaboration," see James D. Horan, *The McKenney-Hall Portrait Gallery of American Indians* (New York: Crown, 1972), 48–49, 64–65, 78–80, 108; see also Rowena Houghton Dasch, "'Now Exhibiting': Charles Bird King's Picture Gallery, Fashioning American Taste and Nation 1824–1861" (PhD diss., University of Texas at Austin, 2012), 144–145.

8. See Colin F. Taylor, *Native American Weapons* (Norman: University of Oklahoma Press, 2001), 26.

9. While it has been suggested that King may have borrowed his picturesque mountain backdrop from Rocky Mountain landscapes by Samuel Seymour from the Long Expedition of 1820 (Kathryn Sweeney Hight, "The Frontier Indian in White Art, 1820–1876: The Development of a Myth" [PhD diss., University of California, Los Angeles, 1987], 42]), it seems as likely that he borrowed the use *made* of the device by the *other* artist who accompanied that expedition, Titian Ramsay Peale, in his specimenscapes of creatures that, though ones Peale himself had shot, he represented as alive and free, both hunting trophy and museum group display. On Seymour and Peale, see Kenneth Haltman, *Looking Close and Seeing Far: Samuel Seymour, Titian Ramsay Peale, and the Art of the Long Expedition, 1818–1823* (College Park: Penn State University Press, 2008).

10. King did few landscapes but is known to have copied while in England from both Salvator Rosa and Claude Lorrain. His familiarity with Hilliard and the traditions of British portraiture is well documented, as well, in Cosentino (as in note 4) and elsewhere; see, for example, William Dunlap, *History of the Rise and Progress of the Arts of Design in the United States*, 3 vols. (Boston: C. E. Goodspeed & Co., 1834), 2:262.

11. See Bradford F. Swan, *An Indian's an Indian; or, The Several Sources of Paul Revere's Engraved Portrait of King Philip* (Providence, RI: Roger Williams Press, 1959); for a discussion of Revere's debt to Simon and through John Verelst, see Swan, "Prints of the American Indian, 1670–1775," *Boston Prints and Printmakers, Colonial Society of Massachusetts Collections* 46 (1973): 269–271; and Theresa Fairbanks Harris, "Paul Revere's Philip, King of Mount Hope, from Thomas Church's *The Entertaining History of King Philip's War*: A Conservator's Analysis," *Yale University Art Gallery Bulletin* (2013): 120–125.

12. See Andrew J. Cosentino, "Charles Bird King: An Appreciation," *American Art Journal* 6 (May 1974): 54–71; Cosentino, *Paintings of Charles Bird King*; Dorinda Evans, *Benjamin West and His American Students* (Washington, DC: National Portrait Gallery, 1980), exhibition catalog, 146–150; and Dasch, "'Now Exhibiting,'" 137–147. King made his living pleasing an American establishment political clientele, the most distinguished painter in the nation's capital.

13. Joseph Leo Koerner, *The Moment of Self-Portraiture in German Renaissance Art* (Chicago: University of Chicago Press, 1993), 277. For a schematic explanation of this process, see Kenneth Haltman, "Introduction," in *American Artifacts: Essays in Material Culture*, ed. Jules David Prown and Kenneth Haltman (East Lansing: Michigan State University Press, 2000), 1–10.

14. See Zachary Gussow, "An Anthropological Report on Indian Use and Occupancy of Royce Areas 69 and 120 Which Were Ceded to the United States by the Sac, Fox, and Iowa Indians Under the Treaty of August 4, 1825" (docket 135 before the Indian Claims Commission), in *Sac, Fox, and Iowa Indians*, ed. David Agee Hort, vol. 1 (New York: Garland, 1974), 29–120. See also Jacob Van Der Zee, "Early History of Lead Mining in the Iowa Country," *Iowa Journal of History and Politics* 13 (January 1915): 30.

15. On the Sauk and Fox mining operations, see John A. Walthall, *Galena and Aboriginal Trade in Eastern North America*, Illinois State Museum Publication, Scientific Papers 17; see also William H. Keating, *Narrative of an Expedition to the Source of the St. Peters River*, 2 vols. (London: George Whittaker, 1825), 1:182–186.

16. See John Lawson, *A New Voyage to Carolina* (London: for the author, 1709), 255.

17. I have relied here principally on William J. Hagan, *The Sac and Fox Indians* (Norman: University of Oklahoma Press, 1958).

18. See Benjamin Drake, *The Life and Adventures of Black Hawk with Sketches of Keokuk, the Sac and Fox Indians, and the Late Black Hawk War*, 7th ed., rev. (Cincinnati: George Conklin, 1846); Alvin M. Josephy Jr., *The Patriot Chiefs: A Chronicle of American Indian Leadership* (New York: Viking Press, 1961), 211–251; Roger L. Nichols, *Black Hawk and the Warrior's Path* (Arlington Heights, IL: Harlan Davidson, 1992).

19. See "Treaty with the Sioux and Chippewa, Sacs and Fox, Menominie, Ioway, Sioux, Winnebago, and a portion of the Ottawa, Chippewa, and Potawattomie Tribes" (August 19, 1825), in Charles J. Kappler, *Indian Affairs: Laws and Treaties* (Washington, DC: Government Printing Office, 1904), 250–255; Benjamin Freeman Comfort, *Lewis Cass and the Indian Treaties* (Detroit: Charles M. May, 1922).

20. *Niles' Weekly Register*, 5 (October 29, 1825): 130; William J. Peterson, *Steamboating on the Upper Mississippi: The Water Way to Iowa; Some River History* (Iowa City: State Historical Society of Iowa, 1937), 207; Weston Arthur Goodspeed, *History of Dubuque County, Iowa* (Chicago: Goodspeed Historical Association, 1912), 17–30; Reuben Gold Thwaites, "Notes on Early Lead Mining in the Fever (or Galena) River Region," *Wisconsin Historical Collections* 13 (1895): 271–293.

21. Timothy Flint, *A Condensed Geography and History of the Western States, or the Mississippi Valley*, 2 vols. (Cincinnati: E. H. Flint, 1828), 1:45; John W. Spencer, *Reminiscences of Pioneer Life in the Mississippi Valley* (Davenport, IA: Griggs, Watson, & Day, 1872), 14.

22. Typically, if not sold in New Orleans, Galena lead was shipped to Philadelphia or New York. Henry Rowe Schoolcraft, *A View of the Lead Mines of Missouri* (New York: Charles Wiley & Co., 1819), 44; Caleb Atwater, *Remarks Made on a Tour to Prairie du Chien: Thence to Washington City, in 1829* (Columbus, OH: Isaac N. Whiting, 1831), 199. See also William H. Pulsifer, *Notes for a History of Lead and an Inquiry into the Development of the Manufacture of White Lead and Lead Oxides* (New York: D. Van Nostrand, 1888), 322.

23. See Haltman, *Looking Close and Seeing Far*, 5. On the use and symbolism of peace medals more generally, see Herman J. Viola, *Diplomats in Buckskin: A History of Indian Delegations in Washington City* (Washington, DC: Smithsonian Institution Press, 1981); on the history of their distribution, see Esther Felt Bentley, "The Madison Medal and Chief Keokuk," *Princeton University Library Chronicle* 19 (Spring and Summer 1958): 153–158; Paul Russell Cutright, "Lewis and Clark Peace Medals," *Missouri Historical Society Bulletin* 24 (1968): 160–167; Howard Michael Madaus, "Peace and Friendship: Diplomatic Gifts to the Indians," *Lore* 22 (Spring 1972): 68–78; and Klaus Lubbers, "Strategies of Appropriating the West: The Evidence of Indian Peace Medals," *American Art* 8 (Summer/Fall 1994): 79–95.

24. See Herman J. Viola, *Thomas L. McKenney, Architect of America's Early Indian Policy, 1816–1830* (Chicago: Swallow Press, 1974), 166.

25. Francis Paul Prucha, "Thomas L. McKenney and the New York Indian Board," *Mississippi Valley Historical Review* 48 (March 1962): 637. Quotes from Thomas L. McKenney, *Memoirs, Official and Personal; with Sketches of Travel among the Northern and Southern Indians; Embracing a War Excursion, and Descriptions of Scenes along the Western Borders*, 2 vols. (New York: Paine and Burgess, 1846), 1:241; cited in Drinnon, *Facing West*, 181; "Letter from Col. McKenney to his friend in Baltimore, dated, Georgetown, May 15, 1828," *American and Commercial Daily Advertiser* (Baltimore), May 19, 1828 (emphasis in the original). See also "The Origin and Destruction of a National Indian Portrait Gallery," *Anthropological Essays Presented to William Henry Holmes in Honor of His Birthday* (Washington, DC: By Subscription, 1916), 191n.

26. James Hall, "An Essay on the History of the North American Indians," in *The Indian Tribes of North America, with Biographical Sketches and Anecdotes of the Principal Chiefs*, ed. Thomas L. McKenney and James Hall, 3 vols. (Philadelphia: I. T. Bowen, 1836–1844), 3:133.

27. See Gaston Bachelard, *L'air et les songes: Essai sur l'imagination du mouvement* (Paris: José Corti, 1943), 27–78; Bachelard, *Air and Dreams: An Essay on the Imagination of Movement*, trans. Edith R. Farrell and C. Frederick Farrell (Dallas: Dallas Institute of Humanities and Culture, 1988), 19–64. My thanks to Walter Cahn for suggesting the comparison with Cellini.

28. See Jean Lancri, *L'index montré du doigt: Huit plus un essais sur la surprise en peinture* (Paris: l'Harmattan, 2000), 139–174.

29. Typical of antebellum American landscape, King's composition, grounded in a foreground represented in warm earth tones, materially present, lures the gaze to travel deeply into picture space, seeking optical so thematic resolution in a celestially blue atmospheric distance. For a seminal discussion of the larger iconographic and thematic shift from bloodthirsty to noble savages in the United States and its continental territories in this period, see Berkhofer, *White Man's Indian*, pt. 3, "Imagery in Literature, Art, and Philosophy: The *Indian* in White Imagination and Ideology."

30. See Alexis de Tocqueville, *Journey to America* (1835), trans. George Lawrence, ed. J. P. Mayer (New York: Doubleday, 1971), 399.

31. Roy Harvey Pearce, *Savagism and Civilization: A Study of the Indian and the American Mind* (1953; repr., Baltimore: Johns Hopkins University Press, 1965), 66.

32. James Otto Lewis, *The North-American Aboriginal Port-Folio* (London: Ackermann & Co., 1838), 55; Thomas L. McKenney, *Sketches of a Tour to the Lakes* (Baltimore: Fielding Lucas, Jr., 1827), 70.

33. A similar strategy has been discerned in the Indian dramas popular in the period in which most easterners had their only live Indian encounters; see Marilyn Jeanne Anderson, "The Image of the American Indian in American Drama" (PhD diss., University of Minnesota, 1974). She writes, "Most of the Indian dramas allowed their audiences to satisfy both their idealistic and their materialistic yearnings. They were invited to indulge in sentimental admiration for the natural virtues of the red man and to feel pity for his passing into oblivion. They were not, however, really challenged to refrain from those tactics which were ruthlessly pushing the Indian from his land and snatching the last vestiges of his native culture from him" (435). Bryan Jay Wolf comments on the tendency among artists in this period to refigure imperialism redemptively, a triumph of continuity over discontinuity. Wolf, "All the World's a Code: Art and Ideology in Nineteenth-Century American Painting," *Art Journal* 44 (Spring 1984): 328–337.

34. As Bachelard states in this regard, "On ne peut se passer de l'axe vertical pour exprimer les valeurs morales." Bachelard, *L'air et les songes*, 18. "It is impossible to express moral values without reference to the vertical axis." Bachelard, *Air and Dreams*, 10.

35. *United States Review and Literary Gazette* (New York: G. and C. Carvill, 1827), 144; cited in Howard S. Merritt, ed., *Studies in Thomas Cole, an American Romanticist* (Balti-

more: Baltimore Museum of Art, 1967), 18n126. Calhoun's War Department Indian Gallery itself, the original Lewis watercolors, the *Aboriginal Port-Folio* he later based on them, and, even, for that matter, the more beautifully illustrated, bound, multivolume work by McKenney and Hall that better served a relatively narrow mass market were dominated by bust or half-length portraits that represented their subjects (including Keokuk; see plate 3) as objects: appendageless, spatially disconnected, disempowered, out of context. See Haltman, *Looking Close and Seeing Far*, 2–5. The concerns of full-length landscape portraiture, by contrast, were inevitably relational, frequently both locating figures in space and offering the viewer a fully dramatized theatrical encounter: compositions, in the case of Lewis, informed by a decade or more of professional stage performance first in Philadelphia, then with Samuel Drake's Theatrical Company in the settled West, as combination actor (or "walk-on gentleman," as one rather adulatory period biographer put it, Hastings in *She Stoops to Conquer* a typical role), set designer, and scenic painter, each occupation offering in its way ideal training for his later turn to aboriginal subjects; in King by his training in West's atelier, at the heart of the empire, where men of station paid good money to be represented in contrived performances of presence in the world.

CHAPTER 4

Expansion in the East: Seneca Sovereignty, Quaker Missionaries, and the Great Survey, 1797–1801

Elana Krischer

When tracing the origins of systematic expansion, historians have tradition-ally examined the Northwest Territory and moved west from there. Between the years 1797 and 1801, however, surveyors, missionaries, and the Senecas started these processes when they attempted to rewrite the landscape of west-ern New York. The Treaty of Big Tree (1797) was a major turning point and began the multifaceted project of expansion and state making in western New York. New York, with a fully formed political and legal system, had no blue-print for dealing with new settlements, but at the end of the eighteenth cen-tury, Holland Land Company surveyor Joseph Ellicott, a group of Quaker missionaries from the Philadelphia Yearly Meeting, and Seneca leaders con-tended with one another to defend their interests and at the same time shape the future of expansion.

In New York, land agents and missionaries altered both the physical land-scape and the meaning of settlement and expansion for white settlers and the Iroquois. Surveyors, charged with facilitating white settlement, unsettled an area already settled by the Senecas. They created state and county boundaries, property lines, and reservations through what were once continuous territories dotted by Seneca villages and Iroquois paths. The surveyors, like Joseph Ell-icott, opened the space for New York to become the edge of western expan-sion by making Lake Erie more accessible from the east. Quaker missionaries altered the physical landscape on a smaller scale, encouraging the Senecas to build houses, fences, and spaces for farm animals to graze and men to farm. The Quakers, who witnessed Seneca villages transform into reservations with specific boundaries, had visions for Native territory that intersected with and diverged from the Holland Land Company's goals. Although Ellicott and the missionaries did not see each other as a barrier to their visions, the work that they did inherently conflicted. These settler groups started to work out what western expansion would look like in New York State before the nineteenth century even began.

The Treaty of Big Tree in 1797 extinguished Seneca title to almost three million acres of land and carved ten reservations out of a once continuous territory. Robert Morris, a wealthy land speculator and financier of the American Revolution, had previously purchased the preemption right to the land, which meant he had the first right to buy when the Senecas chose to sell. This permitted Morris to extinguish Native title to this land and sell it to the Holland Land Company, which, beginning in 1798, surveyed and divided the land for white settlement, including the tract that Morris kept for himself. A few months later, five Quaker missionaries arrived to instruct the Senecas in the "civilized arts." As soon as Morris extinguished Seneca title, settler groups descended on their territory to facilitate the incorporation of that space into New York State.

Scholars who focus on the Northwest Territory have recently argued that historians should view American expansion as temporally continuous and that its work came in many forms. As settler groups worked for and against the Senecas in what is now western New York, they helped mold the processes of early expansion that drove later, more aggressive movements in the mid-nineteenth century. The ideas that drove territorial conquest were culturally embedded from the time the United States came into being, and the Quaker mission and Ellicott's survey are just two examples of how that ideology manifested itself as settler groups negotiated America's continental empire.[1]

JOSEPH ELLICOTT AND THE HOLLAND LAND COMPANY

Joseph Ellicott, who worked for the Holland Land Company at the beginning of the nineteenth century and who surveyed the lands west of the Genesee River in New York, created the western boundaries of the state. Within these new borders, settlers were subject to state law and given the protections extended to any citizen of New York and the United States. Yet he rarely considered this "political and constitutional weight" that his surveys carried in his early correspondence or reports as chief of survey. To Ellicott, transforming the land was a scientific and precise process that brought with it a profit from the sale of private property. More important, he saw the Holland Land Company's holdings on the east coast of Lake Erie as the key to western expansion through the physical movement of settlers and the potential commercial ties that would come from connecting the waterways in the east. He was one among many surveyors who created new boundaries in the early republic, but the precision he required and the profits he made shaped what land, property, and sovereignty meant in the narrative of American empire.[2]

The Holland Land Company was a group of Dutch banks that made money by investing in private property. The company had plans to invest in France, but the revolution there proved threatening to such ventures, so it turned to the frontiers of New York and Pennsylvania. Although the federal government acquired many frontier areas in the Ohio Valley and Northwest Territory, private investors found many opportunities to acquire property in the less settled areas of established states. Ellicott was American, but his work for a foreign, private company in part shaped how he envisioned land use and the purpose of surveying. Rarely in his communications about the territory west of the Genesee River did he mention that this work would ultimately lead to the land's incorporation in New York State. He focused on profit and transforming the land into very precise pieces of private property. During his survey, he did not contemplate the laws, rights, or cultural assumptions that came with converting the land into not just private property but an extension of one of the oldest states in the union.[3]

The Holland Land Company chose Joseph Ellicott to attend the negotiations for the Treaty of Big Tree in 1797 to protect the interests of the company as the Senecas and land speculator Robert Morris negotiated over land sales. Morris, who owned the preemption right to this territory, and the company both invested in land speculation, but Morris invested in the land as profit for personal gain with no intention of facilitating settlement, while the Holland Land Company divided the land into townships and created state boundaries. It is no surprise that the company chose Ellicott to survey its lands at the conclusion of the treaty, as he came from one of the most prominent surveying families in the early republic. His older brother, Andrew Ellicott, demarcated the boundaries between Pennsylvania, Maryland, and Virginia immediately after the American Revolution and the border that separated the United States from Spanish territory. Joseph previously worked for the company on its holdings in Pennsylvania, and at the time of Joseph's project in New York, Andrew was still surveying lands in the South. The Ellicott family's dedication to scientific precision made them the most desirable surveyors in the United States.[4]

Surveying was critical in the early republic because boundaries gave legit-imacy to the expanding nation. Such mapping required expertise in mathe-matics and astronomy and the use of advanced and rare surveying tools that only surveyors like the Ellicott family could provide. The creation of exact borders brought with it "a specific framework of laws, of government, and eventually of values." Measuring and dividing land to create precise bound-aries was fundamental to the creation of a successful federal republic. After the Revolution, the federal government wanted to systematically expand the nation, and land surveyors were critical to this project. Although the system-atic survey system had been used in the past all over the world, the township became the foundational building block of state formation in the United States.[5]

Ellicott and his superiors at the company were most concerned with the legal and monetary issues that came with surveying in the colonial era because they knew boundary disputes were often taken to court and expensive resur-veys were common. Ellicott frequently mentioned in his correspondence how problematic past surveys were, which measured property by "making a mark on a Tree or a Bush," and touted that his survey would be the most precise in the world, "executed with . . . Exactitude and permanency." He deemed his surveys superior to those completed during the colonial era, and in his mind, he took every step to ensure that his work would never have to be redone. He saw his own divisions as being as permanent as the land's natural features, despite the constantly changing landscape of the early republic and the insta-bility of the new nation in the 1790s. However, many of Ellicott's markings were not as permanent as he indicated they were. Most of the notes from this survey included the types of trees present in each tract, and he assumed the trees would still be there when settlers chose to purchase a tract. Timber stripping was common in western New York during this time, so that trees that would soon be gone were notable features of the landscape. Indian villages, however, were not because Ellicott believed the Senecas were not part of the state's future. A white man's division of the land was exact and permanent, but Seneca land use was not. This shows that Ellicott believed private property in the United States was meant only for white settlers. The process of survey-ing was a process of erasing Seneca settlement.[6]

At the conclusion of the Treaty of Big Tree in the fall of 1797, Ellicott immediately began his plans for the survey of the territory of more than three million acres. He estimated that the survey required 150 men, includ-ing surveyors, axmen, cooks, chainmen, boatmen, blacksmiths, and men to bring provisions between camps. Because private individuals such as Robert Morris still held large tracts in the area, Ellicott needed to locate and mark the boundaries of the Holland Land Company's claims, as well as divide the claims into townships of six square miles.

Ellicott was also tasked with surveying the boundaries of the ten remaining Seneca reservations. The Treaty of Big Tree determined the acreage of Buffalo Creek and Tonawanda, but Ellicott had to negotiate with the Senecas on the specific boundaries. For other reservations like Cattaraugus, the treaty provided vague outlines, but not the acreage. As general agent of the Holland Land Company and Ellicott's immediate superior, Theophile Cazenove instructed the surveyor to use his familiarity with the landscape to ensure that the reservations "run in certain directions in prefference [*sic*] to others." Even though the Senecas were supposed to be consulted as to the exact boundaries of their reservations, Cazenove considered it Ellicott's job to make sure they did not have too much say in the boundaries of their own lands. To maximize profit for the company, Cazenove directed Ellicott to keep the most valuable lands, particularly along the shores of Lake Erie, outside of the reservations.[7]

The Holland Land Company demanded such an orderly process because it expected an enormous and immediate influx of settlers, asking Ellicott to complete the survey of the entire area in just one year. As the work progressed, Cazenove instructed Ellicott to pick the best villages for initial settlements and consider best placement for the roads that would bring settlers in. He desired "the best specie of settlers from Pennsylvania and New England," and he wanted the surveyor to create roads so that they would not pass established white settlements on their way into the territory and decide to stop. Cazenove envisioned a steady flow of settlers to all parts of the company's lands and wanted them evenly dispersed throughout its holdings.[8]

Ellicott ensured that his measurements were accurate by using the most advanced tools available at the time, and he believed that his surveys were more accurate than earlier ones. Confident in his efforts, he provided equipment for settlers who purchased the land to check his work. He measured the boundaries with transit instruments, and based them on meridian lines that were "astronomically ascertained." Only one portable transit instrument existed in the world, and Ellicott's brother Andrew was using it in Natchez. Joseph Ellicott suggested that the Holland Land Company commission the creation of one or two for his use west of the Genesee River. He often wrote in his reports and correspondence that he wanted a survey so precise that whoever bought the land could go to the survey office, examine the map of the tract or township, and determine the accuracy of the measurements themselves. According to Ellicott, the owner of the property could check the accuracy of the measurements whether the land was newly purchased or whether fifty years had passed, the amount of time he predicted it would take for all the tracts to be

Figure 4.1. Joseph Ellicott and B. Ellicott, *Map of Morris's Purchase of West Geneseo in the State of New York*. 1804. The David Rumsey Map Collection, Cartography Associates, San Francisco, CA.

settled. He rarely mentioned settlers as citizens. Instead, he was invested in the creation and distribution of private property to individual settlers, whom he viewed more as customers. To Ellicott, western expansion was not an impulse based on shared republican ideals; it was a commercial opportunity.[9]

Aside from the transit instrument, Ellicott made sure that each chain used in the survey was exactly twelve inches long. He instructed his workers to measure it against the standard chain after every six miles and adjust compasses based on astronomical observations whenever possible. He also created a very detailed system for taking field notes, compiled an index to those field notebooks so that anyone could easily look up the boundary line, and attached brass rulers exactly twelve inches long to the backs of the field notebooks in case the land ever needed to be resurveyed. Ellicott's desire to avoid the expense of resurveying poorly measured boundaries, to avoid litigation between white settlers, and to avoid boundary disputes between the land company and the Senecas drove his obsession for accuracy.[10]

Ellicott and his team of surveyors created extremely detailed field notes that included the number of links and chains in a specific boundary, types of trees, quality of the soil, and descriptions of the "Land, Waters, Hills, Plains, Valleys, mines, [and] minerals." Although the surveyors frequently interacted with Seneca sachems, which is clear from Ellicott's correspondence, the field notes never mention these interactions. Ellicott's approach to the land as property was very scientific, although sometimes land company officials mentioned the beauty of the territory. From his office in Philadelphia, Cazenove instructed a surveyor working under Ellicott, in his leisure time, to collect information about "views of falls and other remarkable spots, also a specimen of the most rare birds, insects, plants &c. and some Indian curiosities." It is unclear by this statement whether land company officials saw the Senecas as part of the land in that they were the curiosity, or as completely absent from future interactions in the area.[11]

Ellicott believed land divided for the purpose of private property was off limits to the Senecas. In correspondence and official reports, he only referred to them as a hindrance to that process. Although the Treaty of Big Tree stipulated that the Senecas should consult on the exact boundaries of their reservations, they resisted measurements of their territories if they suspected fraud. Most of Ellicott's interactions with the Senecas during this period included reports from his team that at some reservations the Natives postponed the survey by calling councils or alerting federal agents that they had not received their annuities. Ellicott then had to reach out to US commissioners to assist him in smoothing out relations and reassuring the Senecas.[12]

Cazenove instructed that any major alterations made to the treaty terms "require some writing or other authentic proofs such alterations have been made by mutual consent." However, in the same letter, he instructed Ellicott to offer liquor to the chiefs and women, as "the expense will not be an object and may have a good effect towards the Holland Company." This use of alcohol in negotiations went directly against the Quakers' prescriptions for transforming the Senecas into yeoman farmers. The Quakers established their mission in the same year the survey began, and they believed alcohol hindered their project and urged temperance in Native communities. The Holland Land Company acted to reverse their work, and as the assertion that trees were permanent but Seneca settlement was not suggests, the land company thought the original inhabitants would disappear rather than live in Quaker-inspired communities in western New York.[13]

Ellicott mostly attributed any interruption to his survey of the reservations to people other than the Senecas. At the Allegany Reservation, he blamed the meddling of nearby Quaker missionaries, whom he believed told the Senecas that Robert Morris would not be able to pay them the money he promised for their lands. In his official report, Ellicott also blamed problems with the survey at Buffalo Creek on "some evil persons residing in the British province of Upper Canada . . . with a View to give all the trouble that lay in their power to frustrate the operation of this business." However, the Senecas themselves caused most of the delays to the survey, because for the most part they wanted to make sure they received their annuities before they signed the reservation deeds. The Treaty of Big Tree did not mention these documents, but Ellicott saw them as essential to the permanency of the survey so that the Senecas could not later dispute the boundaries he created.[14]

The boundaries of Allegany caused the most conflict. The Treaty of Big Tree provided forty-two square miles for the reservation, but the Senecas insisted on determining its exact shape. They wanted their boundary to run two miles on either side of the Allegheny River, strategic in their desire for the good lands in nonmountainous terrain. Ellicott wrote that the Allegany Senecas got what they wanted, but that much of the reservation was mountainous terrain anyway. He wanted the Senecas to own the least valuable, and therefore least fertile, land, which was necessary for the success of the Quaker mission, but he was more concerned about the amount of time that surveying both sides of the river would take. However, as a result of the final boundaries, the Allegany Senecas shaped the physical landscape of western New York on their own terms. In other examples, the Senecas also desired access to natural resources. Ellicott altered the boundaries of the Tonawanda Reservation to include a spring where the Senecas boiled salt and created a separate one-square-mile reservation to encompass an oil spring. The Treaty of Big Tree may have dictated the general location of reservations, but the Senecas determined the land and resources within those bounds.[15]

Ellicott cited Buffalo Creek as his main source of anxiety. He explained that the land nearby was "one of the Keys to the Companies lands, which if included in this reservation would be very detrimental," and it would impede "uninterrupted communication with the East end of Lake Erie at this place." Although Ellicott saw the entire region west of the Genesee River as valuable because it could be sold as private property, the lands along the east coast of Lake Erie were most valuable because of access to other waterways. The Erie Canal was just a dream for New York officials at this time, but Ellicott saw the value in that natural landscape, and his work ensured that the canal project was viable in the future with little further impediment from the Senecas. In his 1798 report to the company, he explained that he planned Buffalo Creek and Tonawanda so "as not in the least to injure that spot or place designed by nature for the grand emporium of the Western world I mean the mouth of

Buffaloe creek and the country contiguous thereto." New York did not build the Erie Canal until a few decades later, but Ellicott clearly understood that the trans-Genesee region would form a wellspring for white migration into territories farther west.[16]

The land Ellicott transformed into private property was a part of New York, but this was of little importance to Ellicott in his correspondence and reports. Although he discussed settlement in terms of villages and townships, his earliest plans for that space went beyond incorporation into the state. Rarely did Ellicott discuss the ramifications of jurisdiction or sovereignty that came with incorporation. Prior to an influx of settlers, he referred to the region as "backwoods," but as he transformed the lands into private property for white settlers and opened access to waterways into the west, he envisioned western New York as the birthplace of western expansion in the early republic.[17]

THE QUAKER MISSION TO THE ALLEGANY SENECAS

In April 1798, as Joseph Ellicott's survey was under way, five Quakers from Philadelphia left their homes and set out for an Indian village just below the border of New York in Pennsylvania. Joshua Sharpless and John Pierce accompanied Henry Simmons, Joel Swayne, and Halliday Jackson, young men in their twenties and thirties, to set up a mission among a group of Senecas led by a sachem named Cornplanter. The Friendly Association for Regaining and Preserving Peace with the Indians by Pacific Measures, which from 1795 forward was known as the Philadelphia Yearly Meeting Indian Committee, sent out a circular letter in 1796 to the Natives of New York inquiring about their interest in receiving instruction in the "civilized arts." Cornplanter was the only Seneca leader to reply.[18]

After a long and difficult journey, staying with other Friends and acquaintances along the way, the five men met Joseph Johnston, an assistant surveyor for the Holland Land Company. Johnston accompanied the Quakers on the Allegheny River to within fifteen miles of Cornplanter's settlement. Sharpless wrote in his journal that Johnston claimed he "had used no spirits in his company last summer and that several of the surveyors had come to a resolution to entirely reject this pernicious article." The five men were then led part of the way by an Indian guide and finally arrived at the village. Cornplanter served the tired Quakers "Indian dumplings" served with "Bears Oil" for dipping, which Sharpless found unpalatable. The missionaries had to wait for their supplies to arrive by boat. In the meantime, they survived on corn, potatoes, beans, seeds, venison, and fish supplied by the Senecas. The Quakers noted that Cornplanter operated a sawmill on his private tract and engaged in trade at Pittsburgh.[19]

Prior to the Quakers' arrival, efforts were in part under way to limit the Seneca consumption of liquor, Cornplanter was already profiting from the white settlement around his tract, and the Senecas were not going hungry. These Quakers could not survive without the help of the Senecas to navigate the landscape so far from Philadelphia. The two older men, Sharpless and Pierce, had previously acted as missionaries, but the three younger men had no experience at all, except Simmons, who was a teacher. Daniel Richter argues that despite direct evidence to the contrary, Quaker missionaries believed that Native Americans were starving because of their preconceived notions about Native Americans. In many ways, Cornplanter's people were already making efforts toward becoming "civilized," and these missionaries seemed unequipped to carry out the civilizing mission.[20]

Prior to the Quakers' arrival, the Senecas took steps toward solidifying their place in the early republic on their own terms. Their participation in the market economy, however, was the reason the Friends believed the Senecas were suffering. The Quakers' main focus was a fundamental societal shift for the Senecas. Yet the Quakers were very different from other missionaries who lived in Native communities in the late eighteenth and early nineteenth centuries. Emphasizing the reorganization of Seneca society into the image of the yeoman farmer, they did not deem conversion as the measure of success and wasted no time proselytizing. The Quaker focus on farming and technology, and later legal advice and defense at treaty negotiations, made Cornplanter and other Senecas open to receiving them. The missionaries saw their work as a way to participate in the growth of the early republic without violating their pacifism, while working on what historian Matthew Dennis calls "public policy" that was integral to the success of the new nation. Although they frequently disagreed about how best to make changes, the alliance between the Quakers and the Senecas endured for more than a century as the latter faced continuous threats to their land and sovereignty.[21]

Unlike Ellicott, the Quakers supported the Senecas' efforts to remain on their lands but nevertheless desired to exclude them from western expansion and the market economy. In their journals, the missionaries never mentioned that they wished the Senecas to be confined to reservations but did state that existing Seneca territory was integral to the so-called civilizing mission. The Quakers referred to Cornplanter's land as his "village" or "settlement" and rarely wrote "reservation" after "Buffalo Creek" or "Allegany," even after surveying began. Despite this recognition of Seneca territory as communities not unlike their American neighbors, they often treated Ellicott as if he were simply another settler rather than a force interfering with their mission. Ellicott believed the Quakers had interfered with his survey, but he stayed with them on one of his journeys during the survey, and Henry Simmons stayed with Ellicott on a trip to Buffalo and accepted a letter of accommodation from him for lodging elsewhere. At different times throughout the period the survey took place, the missionaries and Ellicott viewed each other's work sometimes as compatible and at other times as an interference. Ellicott viewed the Senecas as erasable, while the Quakers worked toward building a place for them in the early republic, yet the missionaries and Holland Company men often relied on each other as if their goals did not conflict. As expansion in the east continued, the lines of settler colonialism often became blurred because the ideology behind early expansion encompassed both Ellicott's and the Quakers' work even as their tasks conflicted.[22]

While, on a large scale, the Quakers did not want to physically alter Seneca territory, they did wish to alter how they used that space. By establishing a model farm at the lightly populated village of Genesinguhta, the missionaries desired to teach the men how to farm so that they could grow food and replace what they purchased through the market economy with items they made themselves. By farming instead of hunting, the Quakers believed, the Senecas would be able to isolate themselves from the forces of the market economy that were harmful to their survival, such as the alcohol they frequently obtained when trading furs. Joel Swayne noted that the women already had corn patches scattered throughout the woods and called their techniques "extraordenary." However, the Quakers believed that the Senecas could achieve progress in agriculture only when men used oxen to plow fields and when they kept those oxen, along with other farm animals, in fenced areas. The missionaries tried to divide Seneca space by gendered activities that reflected early American republican values.[23]

When the Quakers first chose the area to set up their model farm, they purchased a small cabin from a Seneca woman to live in until they could build their own house. A few months into their stay, they built "a comfortable two story Lewd log house 18 feet by 22 covered with White Pine Shingles and cellared underneath." They also built a stable, purchased horses and cows, and planned to establish a school at Cornplanter's village. Once established, they proposed to teach the Senecas the American way of farming. They agreed to provide tools and to pay for half a gristmill if the Senecas could save enough from their annuity to cover the balance, and thus, reward those who were most industrious. The Quakers vouched to pay two dollars to every man who grew twenty-five bushels of wheat or rye, and they offered to buy linen or woolen cloth from the women, even though there were no female Quaker missionaries in Cornplanter's village yet to instruct the Senecas in that craft. The Indian Committee of the Philadelphia Yearly Meeting questioned "whether it may yet be reasonable to invite Females to so material a change of life at a distance so great till the manners & customs of the Natives become more assimilated to the modes & principles of Civilized life."[24]

As Joseph Ellicott's survey of the Allegany Reservation began, the Quakers also expressed concern about how the Senecas desired to shape it. They were worried that the land on either side of the river would flood too frequently and hinder farming, causing the Natives to revert to "their usual mode of subsistence." The Senecas expressed the fears about the encroaching "Holland People," but when asked to give advice on the matter, the Quakers said they were not sufficiently acquainted with the matter. They advised the Natives to focus on the land they still had. Representatives from the Philadelphia Yearly Meeting attended many treaty councils in the eighteenth century, so it is unclear why the missionaries at Allegany were hesitant to offer guidance about the 1797 land sale.[25]

Even though these Quaker missionaries were hesitant to give advice, they still attempted to act as a barrier against western expansion despite their role in the early American republic's setter colonial project. The Philadelphia Yearly Meeting Indian Committee formed as a way for members to participate in the early republic without violating their religious beliefs. However, these beliefs often led the missionaries to give advice that was not best for Seneca livelihood. They needed more than isolation from the corruption of the market economy. The Senecas really wanted to stake their claim in an expanding nation of white settlers by participating in the market economy and creating the boundaries of their own nation.

CONCLUSION

Settler groups and the Senecas negotiated the processes of early western expansion through conflicting and intersecting projects centered on Seneca territory. Although New York's expansion required incorporation of territory into an existing state rather than the creation of a new state, early surveying and missionary work in New York State shows that the underlying ideologies of western expansion played out in the east even before settlers began to push west of the Mississippi River in large numbers. In the early republic, empire was a continuous process, proceeding from the end of the eighteenth through the nineteenth century, and the negotiations over Seneca land and society contributed to its development.

Although motivated by the same ideology, the actors in western New York carried out projects that frequently conflicted. Joseph Ellicott's survey intended to confine the Senecas to smaller pieces of land, physically erase the signs of their settlement, and replace them with white settlers. The Quaker missionaries from the Philadelphia Yearly Meeting worked to carve a space for the Senecas in the early American republic by transforming them into yeoman farmers and isolating them from the corruption of the market economy. The Senecas altered these projects by shaping the boundaries of their reservations and participating in the market economy that grew as white settlers moved into the area. These conflicting projects shaped the physical landscape of western New York and contributed to the processes of expansion as the United States pushed farther west in the nineteenth century.

NOTES

1. John P. Bowes, *Land Too Good for Indians: Northern Indian Removal* (Norman: University of Oklahoma Press, 2016); Bethel Saler, *The Settlers' Empire: Colonialism and State Formation in America's Old Northwest* (Philadelphia: University of Pennsylvania Press, 2014).

2. Andro Linklater, *The Fabric of America: How Our Borders and Boundaries Shaped the Country and Forged Our National Identity* (Ann Arbor: University of Michigan Press, 2008), 4–5. See also William Wyckoff, *The Developer's Frontier: The Making of the Western New York Landscape* (New Haven, CT: Yale University Press, 1988).

3. Brian Phillips Murphy, *Building the Empire State: Political Economy in the Early Republic* (Philadelphia: University of Pennsylvania Press, 2015), 166–167; Andro Linklater, *Measuring America: How the United States Was Shaped by the Greatest Land Sale in History* (New York: Plume, 2003).

4. Theophile Cazenove to Joseph Ellicott, Philadelphia, July 25, 1797, in *Holland Land Company's Papers, Reports of Joseph Ellicott as Chief of Survey, 1797–1800, and as Agent, 1800–1821, of the Holland Land Company's Purchase in Western New York,* ed. Robert Warwick Bingham, 2 vols. (Buffalo, NY: Buffalo Historical Society, 1937), 1:2 (hereafter cited as HLCP). Andrew Ellicott educated Meriwether Lewis in surveying methods. Joseph's younger brother, Benjamin, was also a surveyor and did surveying work in Washington, DC, Pennsylvania, and New York. Linklater, *Fabric of America,* 50.

5. Linklater, *Fabric of America,* 4–5; Wyckoff, *Developer's Frontier,* 25.

6. "Report and account of the Survey of the Genessee by Mr. Jh. Ellicott," HLCP, 1:83.

7. Cazenove to Ellicott, Philadelphia, July 24, 1797, and May 10, 1798, HLCP, 1:16; William Chazanof, *Joseph Ellicott and the Holland Land Company* (Syracuse, NY: Syracuse University Press, 1970), 25.

8. "Report and account" and Cazenove to Ellicott, Philadelphia, May 10, 1798, HLCP, 1:28.

9. "Report of Joseph Ellicott for the Year 1797 to Theophilus Cazenove Esquire," "Report of Mr. Joseph Ellicott Concerning the State of the Survey of the Genesee

Lands Made in 1798," and "Report and account," HLCP, 1:19; Linklater, *Fabric of America*, 12–13.

10. "Report and account" and Cazenove to Ellicott, Philadelphia, May 10, 1798, HLCP, 1:84.

11. "Report 1797" and Cazenove to Ellicott, Philadelphia, May 10, 1798, HLCP, 1:27.

12. "Report and account," HLCP, 1:92–93.

13. Cazenove to Ellicott, Philadelphia, May 10, 1798, HLCP, 1:17.

14. It is plausible that the Quakers really did tell the Seneca this, as in 1798 Robert Morris was bankrupt and sent to debtors' prison. Joshua Sharpless's diary indicates this was a Seneca concern. Joshua Sharpless diaries, Quaker and Special Collections, Haverford College, Haverford, PA. Although Ellicott believed this to be an issue fourteen years before the War of 1812, the British who remained in North America did influence, ally with, and arm Native Americans leading up to and during that war, and US observers often argued that such meddling represented a hindrance to western expansion. "Substance of a speech at the Council held at Buffalo Creek Reservation by Joseph Ellicott, June 28, 1798," and "Report and account," HLCP, 1:92–93.

15. "Report and account" and Ellicott to Cazenove, Buffalo Creek, August 29, 1798, HLCP, 1:74.

16. Ellicott to Cazenove, Buffalo Creek, September 25, 1798, and "Report 1798," HLCP, 1:42.

17. "Report and account," HLCP, 1:108.

18. Joel Swayne diary, Quaker and Special Collections; Henry Simmons, "A Circulatory Letter from the Committee of the Indian Institution appointed by the Yearly Meeting of Philadelphia—To the Six Nations of Indians," Henry Simmons letterbooks, Quaker and Special Collections.

19. Sharpless diaries; Swayne diary; David Swatzler and Henry Simmons, *A Friend among the Senecas: The Quaker Mission to Cornplanter's People* (Mechanicsburg, PA: Stackpole Books, 2000), 239.

20. Swatzler and Simmons, *Friend among the Senecas*, 22; Daniel K. Richter, "'Believing That Many of the Red People Suffer Much for the Want of Food': Hunting, Agriculture, and a Quaker Construction of Indianness in the Early Republic," *Journal of the Early Republic* 19 (Winter 1999): 602–603.

21. According to Matthew Dennis, the Quakers believed that all humans had an inner light and were willing to make comparisons between the Christian God and the Great Spirit. This meant that the Quakers spent more time focusing on farming and domestic work. Dennis, *Seneca Possessed: Indians, Witchcraft, and Power in the Early American Republic* (Philadelphia: University of Pennsylvania Press, 2010), 120, 125–126.

22. Henry Simmons journal, Quaker and Special Collections.

23. Swayne diary; Karim Tiro, *The People of the Standing Stone: The Oneida Nation from the Revolution through the Era of Removal* (Amherst: University of Massachusetts Press, 2011), 107.

24. Simmons, "Letter of the Committee on Indian affairs from Henry Simmons and Joel Swayne, Genesinguhtau November 16, 1798," and Thomas Wistar to Simmons, Philadelphia, June 22, 1799, Henry Simmons letterbooks, Quaker and Special Collections; Swayne diary.

25. Sharpless diaries; Dennis, *Seneca Possessed*, 125.

CHAPTER 5

Armed Occupiers and Slaveholding Pioneers: Mapping White Settler Colonialism in Florida

Laurel Clark Shire

The maps created for and analyzed in this chapter use visual and geographic data about the US settlement of Florida under the Armed Occupation Act (AOA) to challenge some of the assumptions that settler colonial origin stories have installed at the heart of many American frontier histories. These stories often use imperial actors as villains, while they cast the settlers as the humble, deserving protagonists who persevered through many hardships to find "freedom" for themselves and their families. Through this narrative frame, they justify the land and wealth that the settlers have accrued as their well-deserved reward for hard work and surviving challenging times, while omitting their role in dispossessing or enslaving other peoples. Congress enacted the AOA in 1842 to encourage white settlers to move to central Florida. Each AOA claimant attested that he or she was the "head of a family" with enough "sons and/or slaves" to make the land productive. Each promised to build a house and to plant at least five acres while residing on the land claim for five years, the model later used for the 1862 US Homestead Act.

As in Florida and other states, settler regimes rationalized imperial violence in the past and disown it in the present through cultural narratives like the Thanksgiving story that frame colonization as well-intentioned, unavoidable, or natural. In addition to the "deserving settlers," these narratives rely on the erasure of indigenous people (e.g., the founders discovered virgin land) and marginalize the labor of white women and of enslaved peoples, such that all the "founders" of importance (or invading settlers) are presumed to have been white men. This obscures the contributions that white women made, and the privileges that they accrued, in settler colonial projects, as well as the significance of enslaved labor to nation building. Such inconvenient historical facts challenge the cherished nationalist story of hearty pioneers bringing civilization, Christianity, and democracy to the wilderness.

This chapter demonstrates that white *families* (not solitary men) settled Florida, and that they settled on the sites of former Native American towns—not in empty, unsettled wilderness. Furthermore, many of them were slave owners or hoped to become slaveholders. Settlers were not innocent folk but invading colonizers from a society that awarded rights and privileges on racial, class, and gendered grounds. They understood those terms and reproduced that social structure as they exploited national expansion for their own gain. The visual data in this chapter represent three things: American families did not move into previously uninhabited land; the settlers were not all hardy, pioneer frontiersmen, but looked a lot like the Seminole extended families they replaced; and the new residents of Florida were not all white and were not all participating in colonizing the region voluntarily.

In Florida, frontier and pioneer myths continue to shape public memory. Central Florida's Sumter County represents its origins with this introduction on its official website: "From what once was an area known for its simple beauty, where Seminole Indians roamed freely, to a strong community bringing settlers in search of land to farm and raise their families, a county grew. From a portion of Marion County, Sumter County was established by legislation on January 8, 1853, and proves today to be the same small community with big dreams." While this introduction cites the existence of indigenous people in this region, it also sets 1853 as the beginning of "real" history in Sumter County. It continues with the following description of "The Early Years": "In its very early years when settlers came to Sumter County, battles arose with Seminole Indians in the Second Seminole Indian War." This description, phrased in the passive voice—"battles arose," "a county grew," "was established"—erases the violence that white Americans and their government brought to bear in order to "settle" land in Sumter County where they could "raise their families." From the 1810s through the 1840s, US invasions and Indian Removal policies unsettled and displaced the people who had lived and made history in Sumter County before whites arrived.[1] Other accounts cite Fort King (today, Ocala, in Marion County) as the "first" place established in this part of Florida, a Second US-Seminole War fort and Indian agency built in the late 1820s, and the destination of the US troops attacked in the "Dade Massacre." An April 2008 newspaper article titled "Marion County's Beginnings" in the *Ocala Star Banner* notes, "Because six military roads converged on Fort King, it became a natural meeting place and soon a store, a post office, the county's first courthouse, and a Methodist church sprang up near the fort." But why was Fort King located there in the first place? Because many Seminoles and Black Seminoles already lived there. Once again, local history uses the passive voice—"sprang up"— and frames history as something that only began once white people arrived.[2] These examples invoke "firsting," a dynamic that historian Jean O'Brien has exposed in local histories in New England, which frame white "firsts" as the real beginnings of history in ways that erase the indigenous history and people that preceded settler colonial invaders.[3]

Yet Native Americans lived in Florida long before 1853. For centuries, many different societies had occupied parts of what became "Florida" with Spain's arrival there in the 1500s. By 1800, disease, warfare, and the slave trade had wiped out most of Florida's earliest inhabitants. In the early eighteenth century, however, other Native groups came south to repopulate the peninsula, and they built towns across what is today the panhandle and northern Florida. By the late eighteenth century, Euro-Americans referred to them as the "Florida Indians" and the "Seminoles," but indigenous Floridians did not cohere into one nation or tribe at that point (in this chapter, I sometimes refer to them as Seminoles for the period before 1835 for ease and clarity, but they were not a united community until they collectively resisted US rule). Some historians believe the name Seminole derives from a Muscogee Creek word for wild plants and animals, while others suggest that the name originated from the Spanish word for runaway—*cimarron*. By 1821, at least five thousand Native American people, as well as several hundred self-emancipated or free people of African descent, lived in Florida. By 1835, the "Florida Indians" lived in four main regional centers—Apalachicola, Apalachee, Alachua, and Mikasuki—that were largely autonomous. These population centers were also separate from the Muscogee Creeks (their nearest ancestral relatives) and Europeans. They farmed a variety of crops, raised cattle and hogs, and traded with each other, other tribes, and whites. Like most Native peoples in the Southeast, they classified themselves and their relationships with others through matrilineal kinship.

The people of Native American and African heritage who migrated into Florida in the early 1810s settled in a string of towns northeast of Tampa Bay. They had moved south for several reasons: white settlers from the United States had been moving ever closer to their settlements near the Florida-Georgia border and stealing their cattle, igniting cycles of retaliatory violence.

In 1813, Georgia and Tennessee militiamen attacked their villages, set fire to their homes, and destroyed their property during the "Patriot's War," a filibustering invasion. A few years later, US soldiers under Andrew Jackson invaded the Spanish colony of East Florida and, again, burned down their towns. Most of the inhabitants abandoned their homes and villages before soldiers arrived and set them ablaze, so most had survived. Many of them, however, had no desire to continue their contact with white settlers and soldiers. Those of African descent among them had the added incentive of staying out of the hands of slave traders. So, in the early 1810s, some of them moved south, in search of fertile soil and good grazing lands, where they might start anew. They joined and expanded a group of existing towns in the region northeast of Tampa Bay (map 5.1). Some of these villages had been established at least as early as 1715, when Upper Creeks had migrated south and begun planting in the region's well-drained fertile savannas.[4]

These towns were prosperous and well known to whites and other Native peoples, and they attracted traders as well as raiders. In 1823, three decades before Sumter County was carved out of Marion County and established by Americans, American trader Horatio Dexter visited many of them. After repeated invasions into the region, Spain had ceded Florida to the United States in 1821, and the new territorial governor, William Duval, sent him shortly thereafter to invite indigenous people to a council at Moultrie Creek. There, the United States would sign its first treaty with Florida's indigenous people. Dexter reported back to the governor that he found nearly fifteen hundred people living in seventeen towns in the region. He met Seminole leader Micanopy living with his band at Okihamky, about seventy-five miles northeast of Tampa Bay. One hundred African Americans, claimed by Micanopy as slaves according to Dexter, lived in their own village, Peliklikaha, twelve miles south of Okihamky, where they were cultivating one hundred acres of corn, rice, and peanuts, and raising ponies and cattle in enclosed pastures. Twenty-eight miles farther south, he found the prosperous Indian town of Chukochatty, where Simaka and his people owned three slaves, 160 head of cattle, ninety horses, and "many" hogs. Just two years before his visit, Creeks had stolen sixty slaves from Chukochatty, its prosperity making it a target of raiding parties. Of the people he met in these villages, Dexter remarked, "They are by some represented as outlaws or runaways from the Creek Nation but they appear to have been rather a colony tempted to emigrate by the superior advantages for hunting & pasturage afforded by the fertile & beautiful savannas of the western part of the Peninsula." Indeed, Dexter noted that the land stretching from the Alachua Prairie southwest toward Tampa Bay was fertile, with rolling hills, hammocks of dark, rich soil, and piney woods.[5]

Map 5.1. Select Seminole and Black Seminole towns before 1834. This map includes the towns Dexter visited, as well as Cuscowilla (an earlier Creek town encountered by naturalist William Bertram at the site of modern-day Micanopy, Florida, named for a Seminole leader) and Fort King (location of the US Indian agency after 1821). As a reminder that the rest of Florida was not empty, Nero's Town and the Negro Fort at Prospect Bluff are also included on this map.

Unfortunately, as the modern local histories quoted here indicate, the haven that black and indigenous migrants had found in central Florida before and during the 1810s did not last very long. American soldiers invaded the towns, including Peliklikaha and Chukochatty, in the spring of 1836 and burned them to the ground. One militia volunteer from Tennessee reported that the Black Seminoles at Peliklikaha lived in thatch-roofed chickees and small pine houses with beef and other supplies stored in the rafters.[6] General

Abraham Eustis, who lead the US troops that invaded the town, reported that the residents had fled before his men arrived, but there were many horses and cattle left behind. He gave the order to burn all the fences and houses.[7] Seminole descendant Charlie Gopher related this account of wartime terror, from his own family's stories:

> Many times the white soldiers would sneak up on a village and set fire to it. When they did this, men, women and children would come running out of their little chickees. The soldiers would start shrieking and shouting at them in their English language, and our people did not understand. In less than a few minutes the villages were in black, bellowing smoke, and then there was complete dead silence, and only the smoking rooms [ruins] lay there.

As in Gopher's account, many Seminoles were displaced when American soldiers set their homes ablaze. Stories like his are supported by military and press reports, which included burning Indian villages and fields and taking Seminoles and the African Americans among them as captives.[8] Soon after the Native and African American town dwellers fled from the invaders, the US Congress passed new land laws to encourage white settlers to resettle the region. Once again, whites encroached on Seminole and Black Seminole homes and farms and took away from them the prosperity they had built in the preceding decades.

Although local historical accounts usually cite the first white inhabitants as the "first" or the "real beginning" of the history of a place, in fact the migration of the white settlers who displaced them followed the paths already established by black and indigenous migrants. For example, shortly after 1821, when Florida officially transferred from Spain to the United States, brothers John and William Mobley moved from Georgia to Hamilton County, Florida, just across the Georgia-Florida border. They joined white settlers who had been encroaching on indigenous communities in northern Florida in the 1810s. The Mobleys purchased land in Hamilton County in the 1820s and 1830s, and they lived, farmed, and remained there until the early 1840s. By 1850, however, the Mobleys and other white families had relocated farther south in Florida, near the recently burned-out Black Seminole town of Peliklikaha. Thus, they were following the earlier migration routes of indigenous families. Other white families from Hamilton County relocated a few miles farther southwest at the site of Chukochatty. White settlers migrated into previously settled places, not a barren wilderness, and they were not pioneering new territory but following on the heels of earlier Native and African American migrants. This pattern in Florida and elsewhere in North America forced many indigenous people to migrate repeatedly ahead of ever-expanding white settlements in the eighteenth and nineteenth centuries.[9] Waves of white settlers repeatedly displaced earlier residents of Florida, both indigenous people and self-emancipated enslaved people who had entered Florida in the previous centuries in search of refuge and freedom. This pattern also suggests that this was not necessarily a "natural" or inevitable process, but that white settlers observed where indigenous people found prosperous farmland and then took it from them.

In 1842 and 1843, the Armed Occupation Act drew these white American families farther south, into territory recently emptied of indigenous and free black people. Under this policy, the Mobleys and several of their kin and neighbors applied for 160 acres of "free government land" in southern Marion County (today, Sumter County), Florida, an area that had been included in lands reserved for Indians in the 1823 Treaty of Moultrie Creek (a prehistoric event for those recounting local history). In 1850, William and John Mobley and their families remained at their new homes near the former Seminole villages, now located in a place whites called Marion County. The Mobleys and others who had migrated from Hamilton County can also be found in the 1860, 1870, and 1885 censuses of Florida.[10]

These white families came in the wake of Indian Removal and war. The first new white settlers arrived in Chukochatty and Peliklikaha in February 1842, before the Second US-Seminole War ended in August of that year. Soldiers escorted them down Native American paths and military roads built for the war and moved them into blockhouses built for white families. Many, though not all, of these families filed for free land in 1842 and 1843 under the AOA. Their settlement reshaped the demographics of the region, and by 1860, in place of the black and Seminole families who had lived there before the war, 1,000 white Americans and 549 persons they claimed as slaves lived in the region around Peliklikaha.[11]

In and around these former Seminole and Black Seminole towns, and elsewhere in central and south Florida, white families eagerly took up the government's offer of free land. In all, about 34 percent of those who filed an AOA claim eventually received title, testifying to the many difficulties involved in completing all the requirements. Map 5.2 shows where the 445 successful AOA settlers staked their claims in the early 1840s, as well as where their households clustered in relation to the sites of the Seminole and Black Seminole towns that the United States destroyed during the war. As this map illustrates, many AOA settlers claimed land at or very near the sites of former indigenous towns, such as Chukochatty, Peliklikaha, and Cuscowilla.

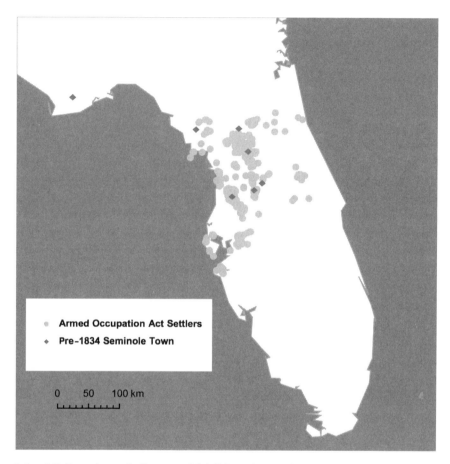

Map 5.2. Locations of all successful AOA settlers and select pre-1834 Seminole towns.

Government forms and land records often referred to landmarks of Seminole settlement and cultivation when describing the location of a particular parcel of land. "Indian old fields" and "Tiger Tail's island," for example, are among the geographic landmarks cited by white settlers in their applications for permits under Florida's Armed Occupation Act.[12] As the dense clusters of AOA settlers in the region between Chukochatty and Cuscowilla make clear, the AOA did not simply make the territory safer for whites by removing hostile inhabitants; it made desirable land "available" to white settlers by taking it directly away from people of Native and African heritage and giving it to white families willing to settle on it.

These maps of Native and free black towns in Florida, alongside the land claims of AOA settlers and Dexter's 1823 account, make it clear that the white migrants who came into the region in the 1840s colonized previously inhabited lands.[13] The region in which most AOA settlers claimed homesteads had very recently been a prosperous farming community where Seminoles and Black Seminoles grew crops and raised livestock. Importantly, the previous black and Indian residents had not been "roaming freely" or "wasting" that land by reserving it only for hunting and "gardening"—whites sometimes used this last term to differentiate planting done by Native women from what they perceived as their own "civilized farming."[14] As Horatio Dexter noted, hundreds of acres of land in this region were under cultivation in 1823. He had further remarked "They live generally in Villages, where the women plant Indian corn, rice & the men leave them during the hunting season. They have had large stocks of cattle, horses, & hogs," but, he noted, their population and livestock had recently been greatly reduced by invasions from Creek and white raiding parties. Interested in reporting back to US authorities that this land was viable for agricultural settlement, Dexter's account also exposes that it was hardly a virgin wasteland prior to the arrival of white farmers. Archaeological evidence combined with accounts like Dexter's indicate that since the eighteenth century Native and African American peoples had pastured livestock and grown crops, including melons, peaches, pumpkins, corn, and rice, in this part of Florida. They had also raised enough to sell excess meat and produce to the Spanish colonial market.[15] While they shared a culture different from that of many white Americans, they had *not* proved themselves unable to participate in an agriculturally based market economy. In fact, as with the other so-called Five Civilized Tribes in the Southeast (Cherokee, Choctaw, Chickasaw, Creeks), the problem was that they had been too successful, attracting the envy of neighboring whites and other tribes, greedy to take the land and livestock they had accumulated.[16]

Due to their prosperity in the region northeast of Tampa Bay, the people of African and Native American heritage who lived there faced white encroachment and violence in the 1830s. In the ethnic cleansing campaign that whites called the "Second Seminole War," many Seminoles died—from starvation, violence, or disease—but other Seminole people endured, and their families and clans continued.[17] For the indigenous peoples living in Florida, the threat of removal was especially disheartening. Many were refugees from previous conflicts with colonists and settlers, or the descendants of indigenous or enslaved people who had fled earlier frontier wars and slavery. Life during the three early nineteenth-century US-Seminole Wars, which Native Americans in Florida called the "White Wars," consisted of trying to survive, resist, and remain in Florida under terrible conditions while mourning those they had lost.[18] Stories from Seminole oral tradition explain the era of war and removal as a time when their ancestors fought to protect their homes and families.[19] They attest to the terror and grief that US rule and Indian Removal policies brought to Florida, but they always conclude with a reminder that their ancestors *survived*. Today there are more than four thousand Seminoles and Miccosukees in Florida, as well as a large Seminole Nation in Oklahoma.[20]

WHITE SETTLERS AND US LAND POLICY IN FLORIDA

Even before the United States sought to neutralize and relocate the Seminoles and their allies among self-emancipated blacks, white settlers had set their sights on Florida soils. White yeomen and planters quickly inundated upper Florida after 1821, while land speculators invested in the territory. The American population increased quickly, from a total of 34,730 in 1830 (the date of the first US Census in Florida) to 87,445 in 1850. By 1850, migrants from other states constituted more than half (56.1 percent) of the free, native-born population in Florida. In that same period, the indigenous population of Florida dropped dramatically, from about 5,000 to fewer than 400. As in many settler colonies, white colonization happened in tandem with Indian Removal and the expansion of slavery into Florida.[21]

Although they were vital to white colonization, there were relatively few white women in antebellum Florida until the mid-1840s.[22] As the Second US-Seminole War began, many white women fled to neighboring states, even as the population of white men swelled to fill military ranks. In 1840, there were almost twice as many white men in Florida as white women. Furthermore, the enslaved population continued to grow with nearly equal numbers of males and females, so that by 1840 enslaved black women outnumbered white women. Florida's white population skewed male, and its white female population skewed young. Aware that they needed reproductive-age wives to create families and support white colonization, US leaders enacted supportive family settlement policies—which culminated in the AOA—in the early 1840s as they ended the Second US-Seminole War. As a result, gender ratios among white adults reached 1.3 men for every white adult woman in 1850, as compared with 1.74 in 1840. By 1860, it reached 1.18. As white families arrived or formed, white women expanded the population by bearing more children. In addition to voluntary and coerced migration, reproduction boosted Florida's population: children under the age of fifteen made up 41 to 45 percent of the total population in the decades after 1821, and by 1850 Florida had more white children than the national average, and about the same proportion of enslaved children.[23]

Under the AOA, white families directly replaced American soldiers as colonizing agents in the part of Florida recently inhabited by prosperous, independent Seminoles and their black allies. President John Tyler signed the AOA bill into law on August 4, 1842. It stipulated that any "head of a family" or single man over eighteen, able to bear arms, could claim 160 acres of public land south of the "line of settlement" in Florida if he or she had enough "sons and/or slaves" to cultivate the land. The law required settlers to get a permit from the land office; build a house and reside on the claim for five consecutive years; and clear, enclose, and cultivate at least five acres of land. The occupation requirement prevented absentee slaveholders who would not populate the region with whites. Enslaved and free blacks and Native Americans were ineligible. The General Land Office specified that eligible settlers could not already own 160 acres in Florida in order to attract *new* settlers and those who could not otherwise afford to come. Further, settlers could not claim lands within two miles of US military installations, and policy makers moved the line of settlement farther south than originally planned in the final bill. Both requirements installed white settlers in parts of Florida that Americans did not control at the close of the Second US-Seminole war. Although the war was "over," the United States loaned AOA settlers weapons and ammunition if they could not acquire them, as the law required them to defend themselves rather than expecting US forces to come to their aid.[24] Lawmakers thus created a policy in the AOA that would entice white settlers into central and southern Florida and ensure that they brought families and a labor force with them. The law's stipulations aimed to draw permanent settler families rather than absentee planters or temporary soldiers.[25]

In spite of the fact that many women were present and vital to colonization, they are often sidelined in histories of pioneers and frontiers. In part, this is due to the fact that many settler colonial origin myths rely on gender, for example, to establish the "innocence" of women and children targeted by Native violence, or the chivalry of the men who torched Indian homes and families in the name of protecting "peaceful" settler families. Those frames paint women as victims rather than agents, and as dependents rather than members of an invading force. Histories of early frontiers also marginalize white women because leaders in the past explicitly recruited men to settle on frontiers, but could only tacitly recruit women due to the gender conventions of the time. As the dependents of white men, women were supposed to be protected, not recruited to be members of an occupying force. Those who championed the AOA, therefore, focused the policy on armed male settlers, de-emphasizing the role of white women and children. The ideal male settler was, however, definitively a family man with a wife and children.[26]

In order to visually represent the fact that the white colonists on these maps were not all adult white men, I created maps based on the shared surnames among the AOA settlers. These maps illustrate that *families*—households in which women and children often outnumbered adult white men—were present and essential to colonization. They provided domestic and farm labor, reproduced families and culture, and maintained the kin relationships that supported extended family settlement. These maps of extended family connections among AOA settlers also illustrate that gender must not be overlooked in the history of the AOA and other expansionist land policies. Although the ideal "settler" was nearly always understood as white and male, he was neither independent nor solitary but instead was supported by his immediate and extended family. As the congressmen believed, "families" were necessary to creating permanent settlements.

Most settlers, and a majority of the AOA settlers, came with extended families that consisted of white women, men, and children, and the wealthiest also included enslaved black families. Of 445 successful white AOA settlers, only 115 surnames appear only once in the land records, and these settlers likely intermarried with others. The remaining 330 AOA settlers came with at least 1 (and as many as 6) other settlers with the same surname. There are 82 distinct surnames among those 330 households. Map 5.3 shows where those 330 families settled.

Surnames are an imperfect measure of kinship. Not all those who shared a surname were necessarily related, and many people who did not share a surname were tied by blood and/or marriage. In the area around Chuko-chatty, for example, several female AOA settlers married men who also filed claims, but their kinship ties by marriage are not captured here because their maiden names were different from their married ones.[27] Of course, it is also possible and likely that neighbors and friends without family ties may also have migrated and settled together, supporting each other in the same way that extended families did. Ultimately, although shared surnames do not capture all kinship links, the number and proximity of settler families with the same surname suggest how interconnected these families were and provide a conservative estimate of how many of them were connected by kinship ties.[28]

The map of AOA settlers who shared a surname reveals that multiple kinship ties connected households within the four centers of dense population in this region, and between these regions. On top of Chukochatty, Peliklikaha, and Okahumpka, and stretching between Cuscowilla and Fort King, hundreds of families settled. In this rich agricultural region northeast of Tampa

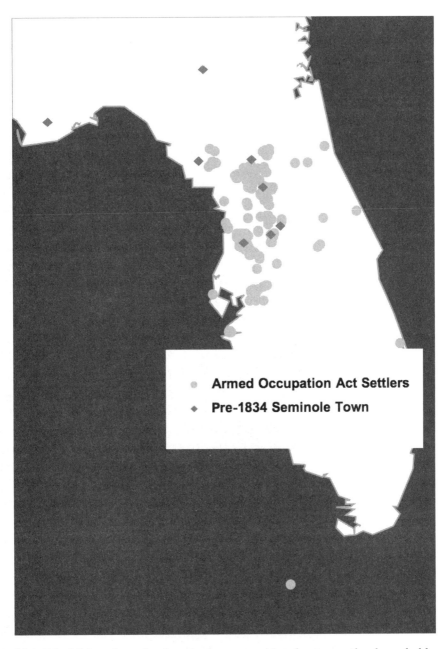

Map 5.3. AOA settlers who shared a surname with at least one other household of AOA settlers.

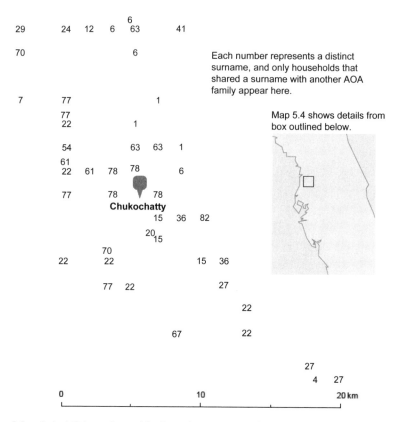

29   24 12   6   63   41

70   6   Each number represents a distinct
                                             surname, and only households that
                                             shared a surname with another AOA
                                             family appear here.

7   77   1
          77   Map 5.4 shows details from
          22   1   box outlined below.

          54   63   63   1
          61
          22   61   78   78   6

          77   78   78
                 Chukochatty
                         15   36   82
                      20
                        15
             70
22   22   15   36

          77   22   27

                                        22

             67   22

                                   27
                                 4   27

0   10   20 km

Map 5.4. AOA settlers with shared surnames who located near the site
of the Seminole town called Chukochatty.

Bay, where indigenous and black Seminole people had thrived for generations, white settlers came in and resettled in the same place in extended family
groups—ironically very much in the same fashion that matrilineal Native peoples had done before them.

The extended family settlement patterns within smaller regions allow one
to see these connections more clearly. Near Chukochatty, twenty-one settler
families shared a surname with at least one other family, and most of those
connections fell within the same county. The Garrisons (marked number 22
on map 5.4) settled seven AOA claims in this area, some of them so close
together that the markers cover each other up on a map at this scale. Most
others averaged two to three shared surname connections, and the map makes
it clear how frequently they settled in close proximity to each other and to the
former sites of Native towns. These families illustrate how important the labor

of extended kin groups was to the process of making permanent settlements. While most, but not all, of those who applied for AOA permits were adult white men, their households were peopled by women, children, and sometimes enslaved families as well.[29]

In all, 1,312 white householders, including forty single women, filed permits to settle approximately 210,000 acres of Florida land under the AOA in 1842 and 1843. The final bill had capped the total acreage that would be granted under the AOA at 200,000 acres. Only 445 (34 percent) of those who filed permits eventually succeeded in completing all the requirements of the law, thus claiming roughly 73,440 acres in Florida under the AOA. The act's impact on the population of Florida reached well beyond the 1,312 AOA permit applicants, however. Hearing of the opportunities for good farmland in Florida, many people migrated there following passage of the bill, often from upper Florida and neighboring states. Rather than pursuing land via the AOA, some purchased public land directly or else squatted on it and later preempted government land auctions, purchasing their farms for the base government price of $1.25 per acre. A set of generous, pro-settler national land policies followed the AOA. Land sales, including preemptions, continued in the 1840s and increased in the 1850s. The Military Bounty Land Act of 1850 (free land for veterans) and the 1854 Graduation Act (which reduced prices over time for any public lands that had not yet sold) added further to Florida's population of white settlers. After 1862, male and female householders also claimed public lands in Florida under the Homestead Act, which was modeled on the AOA.[30] These policies continued the colonization begun under the AOA, which had opened up central Florida to white settler families on the heels of war and Seminole removal.[31]

With inexpensive or even free land available, white settler families streamed into Florida in the 1840s. The total population of Florida, which achieved statehood in 1845, increased overall between 1840 and 1850, from 54,477 to 87,445. By 1860, Florida's population had risen to 140,424 people; 78,679 of them were free and white, while 61,745 were enslaved blacks.[32]

Aided by the AOA stipulation, most of the growth in Florida's population occurred south of existing settlements, where the increasing number of whites effectively rendered more of Florida under American control. In 1840, the population of the counties where AOA lands would become available was only 11,657. By 1850, their population reached 40,872, an increase of nearly 30,000 people, and 88 percent of the overall increase in the Florida population from 1840 to 1850. Map 5.5 shows the distribution and density of successful AOA settlers at the center point of each county in Florida (using modern county boundaries). As this demonstrates, most of the AOA settlers chose

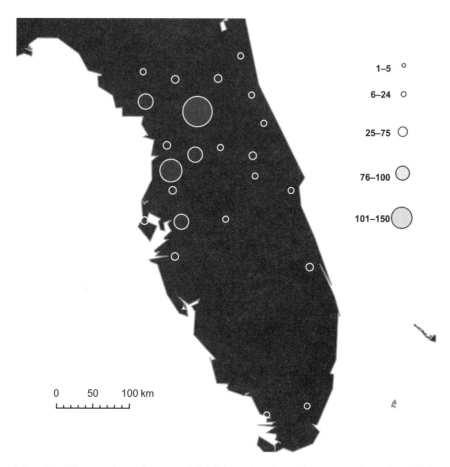

Map 5.5. The number of successful AOA settlers in each county where the AOA encouraged white settlement, 1842–1843.

lands in central Florida, but some ventured farther south. Perhaps many of them would have migrated into Florida without the land enticements offered by the government, but without some incentive to move that far south into the vicinity of former Seminole towns, it is likely most whites would have chosen to remain in the more densely populated parts of North Florida.[33]

NOT ALL FREE, NOT ALL WHITE

Finally, not all settlers brought into Florida by the AOA were white, and enslaved black people did not come willingly. This final section presents maps showing the increasing number of enslaved people in the region of Florida

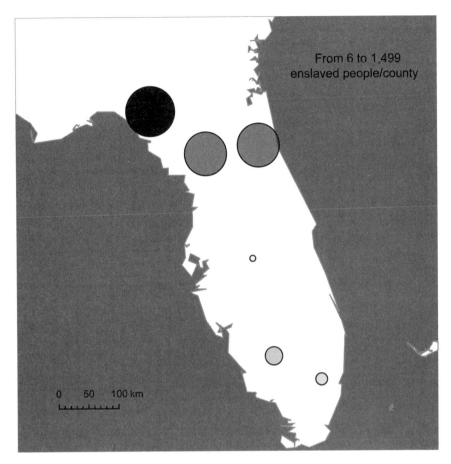

From 6 to 1,499
enslaved people/county

0   50   100 km

Map 5.6. The number of enslaved persons per county in 1840.

recently emptied of Native people and their free black allies and settled under the AOA between 1840 and 1860. These maps use disks of increasing size and opacity to indicate the number of AOA settlers and enslaved persons in each county (the circles are plotted at the center of each county). They clearly show how much the population of enslaved people increased over time from before the AOA in 1840 to after it brought thousands of whites farther south by 1860 (maps 5.6 and 5.7). The populations followed the same pattern: where more AOA settlers planted their families, the number of enslaved people also increased more quickly and in terms of absolute numbers. By combining the density of AOA settlers and the density of slaves over time (1850–1860), the final map (map 5.8) in this section joins the story of white settlement to the story of slavery's spread. These maps visually and geographically illustrate that the

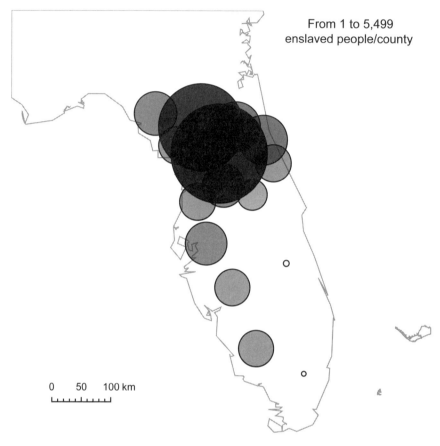

From 1 to 5,499
enslaved people/county

0   50   100 km

Map 5.7. The number of enslaved persons per county in 1860.

consequences of Indian Removal in Florida were terrible for indigenous people and also had devastating consequences for African Americans.[34]

As the white settlers who displaced Seminole families streamed into Florida in the 1830s and 1840s, they brought racial slavery, and its attendant miseries, with them. Note, for example, the large disks at the center of maps 5.7 and 5.8, which represent the number of AOA settlers and enslaved persons in Marion County. Overall, more AOA settlers claimed land there than in any other single county, and enslaved people in Marion County outnumbered the population in all the other counties as well. Thousands of enslaved people were forced to migrate or were sold south into Marion and other counties in Florida. They faced difficult traveling and working conditions, as well as the quotidian horrors of slavery. Of course, as among whites, not all of the

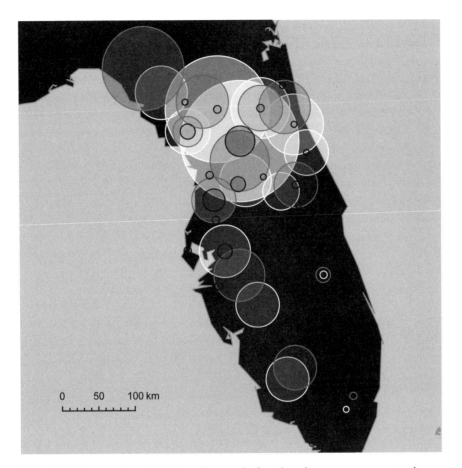

Map 5.8. The number of AOA settlers and of enslaved persons per county in 1850 and 1860.

enslaved black migrants coerced into aiding the colonization of Florida were male. Women and children shared in the backbreaking work. Due to the sexual economy of slavery, enslaved women also contributed (involuntarily) to the growth of the enslaved population.[35]

The fate of Peliklikaha, the former Black Seminole town resettled by the Mobley brothers and other whites in the 1840s, illustrates the effects of removal, war, and the AOA on people of African heritage particularly well. Sometimes called "Old Abraham's Town," Peliklikaha had been a Black Seminole town since the early 1810s. After fleeing enslavement in Pensacola, Abraham had made his way east to join the British-Native-African alliance during the War of 1812. He remained at the "Negro Fort" at Prospect Bluff at the end of the war with hundreds of other blacks who had joined the British in exchange for the promise of freedom. After US forces destroyed that fort in 1816, he and other survivors again migrated east, settling at Peliklikaha. There, he became a religious and military leader. In exchange for alliance and protection, Abraham served Micanopy as an interpreter at many diplomatic meetings with US representatives at various sites in Florida, in Oklahoma, and in Washington, DC. American military leaders understood his importance and his influence, and they hoped to capture or kill him when US forces invaded Peliklikaha in March 1836 and burned it to the ground. They did not find him, but Abraham eventually surrendered and worked for the United States as a scout and interpreter during the Second US-Seminole War, in exchange for the promise of freedom and safety for his family. He brought the terms of a peace agreement with the United States (which included freedom for Black Seminoles in exchange for their surrender) to other Black Seminoles in 1837 and 1838.[36]

Although Abraham and his people survived, Peliklikaha did not. By 1843, Robert Williams's family homestead stood directly on the site of the former Black Seminole town. Williams filed for this land under the AOA and received the title to it free and clear in 1850. Although Williams did not own any slaves, as did few of the AOA families, their presence in the region made it a much less risky place for slaveholders to settle. The presence of whites brought American race hierarchy to the region, eradicating not only independent Native and African American communities but also the potential for freedom they had offered to self-emancipated persons fleeing slavery. Changes in the region's population bear this out. By 1850, there were 1,269 enslaved persons, or 38 percent of the total population, in Marion County, the county in which Peliklikaha would have been included in 1850. By 1860, a *majority* (61.7 percent) of Marion County's population were enslaved people of African heritage. In 1860, Sumter County had been carved out of Marion County, and it included the site where Peliklikaha had existed from 1813 to 1836. Census takers counted a population of 1,549 souls, 65 percent free and white and 35 percent enslaved people. Peliklikaha, a place where indigenous and black migrants had found refuge before 1835, where they had built homes, enclosed fields and pastures, and cultivated a hundred acres, had been eradicated and replaced by white settlers and slaveholders.[37]

These maps demonstrate that slavery expanded southward by 1850. White population bubbles would also clearly show an increase across this region—but the numbers highlighted here aim to show the consequences that Indian Removal and the AOA had for nonwhites—those removed, and those forcibly relocated as enslaved laborers—not how whites took advantage of the opportunities for land in Florida. Significantly, the population of enslaved people followed the expansion of white settlers, who finally began to migrate south into central Florida after 1842, into the towns and farmlands where Native and free black people had lived before removal and war. In Florida overall, the number of enslaved people increased steadily from the eighteenth century until 1865. Overall, there were 25,717 enslaved persons in all of Florida in 1840; 39,310 in 1850; and 61,745 in 1860. Florida whites held, on average, almost as many enslaved people as the white population in older US slave states, such as South Carolina, and proportionately more than whites in other frontier states such as Georgia and Alabama.[38]

In the decades after the AOA, the number of enslaved persons and slaveholders in central and southern Florida changed especially dramatically. In the southern counties where the AOA granted nearly 75,000 acres of free land to white settlers, there were only 2,791 enslaved people in 1840. By 1850, the number of enslaved persons in AOA counties had increased by a factor of 2.82 to 7,882. By 1860, whites had moved 15,348 enslaved people to live and work in Florida's central and southern counties, an increase of a factor of 5.49 since 1840. Although there were still many fewer enslaved people in central Florida compared with its northern tier, where there were more large cotton plantations, these increases indicate that the AOA and other pro-white settler land policies also made thinly settled central Florida far more hospitable to racial slavery than it had been when Seminole and Black Seminole towns had dotted the landscape.[39]

As the number of white settlers, slaveholders, and enslaved blacks grew in the 1840s and 1850s, Florida's free black population dwindled. As people who might aid rebellious slaves and Seminoles, and whose freedom defied the association of African heritage with enslavement, free blacks were untenable under American legal and social norms. Lawmakers explicitly excluded them from making land claims under the AOA and also began to limit their freedom, a major loss for those who had exercised many rights under Spain. Many free blacks left Florida in this period. Some of those with family connections to powerful white families from the Spanish colonial period left for the urbanizing North. Under less voluntary circumstances, almost all of the Black Seminoles left Florida in the late 1830s, traveling to Indian Territory, Texas, and Mexico in hope of securing land and freedom.[40] In absolute numbers, the free black population remained very small in the 1840s and 1850s: it increased from 817 to 932 people between 1840 and 1850, and held steady at 932 in 1860.[41] Since the rest of the population—of free whites and enslaved blacks—expanded greatly in this period, free blacks increasingly made up a relatively tiny percentage of the total population.[42] As lawmakers hoped, white AOA settlers helped to install a new racial order in Florida, whether or not their families actually owned any slaves. Under that new racial order, free blacks lost rights and property, and those who could fled the state.

CONCLUSION

As the eight maps analyzed in this chapter show, the white settlers who arrived in Florida in the 1840s did not move into "virgin" land. They were the secondary wave of an American force following the military campaign aimed at pushing Native peoples off of land that they had settled and made agriculturally productive since the eighteenth century, and that indigenous and black refugees had fled to in the early nineteenth century. The US Army burned those people out of their homes, stole or destroyed their crops, killed many, and deported the survivors to Indian Territory (Oklahoma). Subsequently, US policies installed white families in those places to ensure that any remaining Seminoles and Black Seminoles could not rebuild there. Those white settlers came in families connected and supported by extended networks of kinship, especially those who eventually received title to AOA land. Hundreds of women and children came in these families and contributed to the resettlement of central Florida. Finally, whites did not do all the hard work of "carving civilization out of the wilderness" themselves. They forced thousands of people of African descent to migrate there, where they did the hardest labor of clearing, building and rebuilding, and establishing American social structures of inequality in Florida.

NOTES

1. Website, Sumter County, Florida (sumtercountyfl.gov).

2. Darrell G. Riley, "Marion County's Beginnings," *Ocala Star Banner*, April 25, 2008.

3. Jean M. O'Brien, *Firsting and Lasting: Writing Indians Out of Existence in New England* (Minneapolis: University of Minnesota Press), 2010.

4. Terrance M. Weik, "The Role of Ethnogenesis and Organization in the Development of African-Native American Settlements: An African Seminole Model," *International Journal of Historical Archaeology* 13, no. 2 (2009): 212, 214; Joe Knetsch, "Range War in the East: Conflict over Cattle and Land on the Georgia-Florida Borderlands," in *Proceedings of the 90th Annual Meeting of the Florida Historical Society* (Tampa: Florida Historical Society, 1992), 108–120.

5. There were other towns outside this area; Terrance Weik includes fourteen settlements in a map of early nineteenth-century Florida in "Role of Ethnogenesis and Organization," 213. Horatio M. Dexter, "Observations on the Seminole Indians, 1823,"

Letters received by the Office of the Secretary of War Relating to Indian Affairs, 1800–1823 (4 rolls, microfilm publication M271, Washington, DC: National Archives and Records Administration [hereafter cited as NARA]), roll 4, frames 505–519; Brent Richards Weisman, *Like Beads on a String: A Culture History of the Seminole Indians in North Peninsular Florida* (Tuscaloosa: University of Alabama Press, 1989), 67–69; Henry Prince, *Amidst a Storm of Bullets: The Diary of Lt. Henry Prince in Florida, 1836–1842*, ed. Frank Laumer (Tampa, FL: University of Tampa Press, 1998), 38, 70; Richard J. Stanaback, *A History of Hernando County, 1840–1976* (Brooksville, FL: Action '76 Steering Committee, 1976); Kenneth W. Porter, *The Black Seminoles: History of a Freedom-Seeking People*, revised and edited by Alcione M. Amos and Thomas P. Senter (Gainesville: University Press of Florida, 1996), 25–27; Virginia B. Peters, *The Florida Wars* (Hamden, CT: Archon Books, 1979), 30; Daniel F. Littlefield Jr., *Africans and Seminoles: From Removal to Emancipation* (Westport, CT: Greenwood Press, 1977), 3.

6. Weik, "Role of Ethnogenesis and Organization," 216.

7. Weik, 217.

8. Weiss is identified as Bird Clan, Brighton Reservation, Creek speaker, aged sixty-five. Mrs. H. M. Weiss oral history interview with Jean Chaudhuri, n.d. (transcript), 3–6, Samuel Proctor Oral History Program Collection, P. K. Yonge Library of Florida History, University of Florida (hereafter cited as SPOHP); Charlie Gopher oral history interview with Jean Chaudhuri, May 1971 (transcript), 5–7, SPOHP. See also Laurel Clark Shire, *The Threshold of Manifest Destiny: Gender and National Expansion in Florida* (Philadelphia: University of Pennsylvania Press, 2016), 31, 127–165.

9. On the families of John and William Mobley, and neighbors in the Hill and Whitton (also spelled Whidden) families, see Fifth Census of the United States, 1830 (201 rolls, microfilm publication [M19, NARA), roll 15; Sixth Census of the United States, 1840 (580 rolls, microfilm publication M704, NARA), roll 36; US Bureau of Land Management, *Florida Pre-1908 Homestead & Cash Entry Patents* (Springfield, VA: General Land Office Automated Records Project, 1993, CD-ROM) (hereafter cited as HCEP); Seventh Census of the United States, 1850 (1,009 rolls, microfilm publication M432, NARA), roll 59. On the families who settled Chukochatty (Benton/Hernando County), see Shire, *Threshold of Manifest Destiny*, 1–2, 186–190.

10. On the Armed Occupation Act, see Shire, *Threshold of Manifest Destiny*, 162–193; Eighth Census of the United States, 1860 (1,438 rolls, microfilm publication M653, NARA), rolls 109, 128; Ninth Census of the United States, 1870 (1,761 rolls, microfilm publication M593, NARA), rolls 132, 133; Florida State Census of 1885 (13 rolls, microfilm publication M845, NARA), roll 12.

11. In nearby Chukochatty, by 1850 there were 604 white people and 324 enslaved blacks. 1860 US Census, rolls 106–109; Prince, *Amidst a Storm of Bullets*, 38, 70; "An act to provide for the armed occupation and settlement of the unsettled part of the peninsula of East Florida," August 4, 1842, *U.S. Statutes at Large*, vol. 5, 27/2, chap. 122 (Boston: Little, Brown, 1856), 502–504; Thomas Hart Benton, January 7, 1840 "Armed Occupation of Florida: Debate in the Senate," *Appendix to the Congressional Globe* (26/1), 71–73; Stanaback, *History of Hernando County*; 1850 US Census, roll 58.

12. For examples of land records that reference indigenous land marks, see AOA permits, General Land Office Records, Title and Land Records Section, Division of State Lands, Department of Environmental Protection, Tallahassee, FL (hereafter cited as DEP), nos. 86, 177, 274, 330, 419, 811; HCEP, patent no. 347; entry for Thomas Alvaris in "Roll of Persons Forming New Settlements, Returning to Plantations, and Suffering Inhabitants," letters received by the Office of the Adjutant General Main Series 1822–1860 (636 rolls, microfilm publication M567, NARA), roll 262.

13. In order to map the locations of AOA settlers, I converted the original land record data, based on the original nineteenth-century surveys of Florida (on the Tallahassee meridian), to standard latitude and longitude. I did this by adding GIS shape files with the Tallahassee meridian land parcel data to ARCMap, joining an Excel spreadsheet with the locations of each AOA settler to that map, and then using ARC-Map to convert the old land description codes to latitude and longitude. I used the central point of each section as the point to locate on the map, so in subdivided sections there may be up to four AOA settlers mapped at that point (the AOA awarded a quarter section, or 160 acres, to each settler). The aliquot part or exact location of each settler's claim within the section (the northeast quarter of section 10, for example) is not indicated on these maps, as that level of detail is visible only on hyperlocal maps.

To plot the locations of former Seminole towns, I consulted archaeological and historical records. For example, in the case of Peliklikaha, an AOA settler's claim describes the parcel claimed as being located in the town, and so I used the latitude and longitude of that claim to estimate the central point of the town that existed there in 1823. Archaeologist Terrance Weik's work has been especially helpful in locating the pre-1836 towns. Weik, "Role of Ethnogenesis and Organization," and Terrance M. Weik, *The Archaeology of Antislavery Resistance* (Gainesville: University Press of Florida, 2012), 118–152.

14. Patricia Seed, *American Pentimento: The Invention of Indians and the Pursuit of Riches* (Minneapolis: University of Minnesota Press, 2001), 31–36; Theda Perdue, *Mixed Blood Indians: Racial Construction in the Early South* (Athens: University of Georgia Press, 2010), 63.

15. Weisman, *Like Beads on a String*, 67–69.

16. Theda Perdue and Michael D. Green, *The Cherokee Nation and the Trail of Tears* (New York: Viking, 2007), 20–41; Grant Foreman, *Indian Removal: The Removal of the Five Civilized Tribes*, 3rd ed. (Norman: University of Oklahoma Press, 1972), 13–14.

17. See for example, Jean Chaudhuri monologue (recollections of a conversation with a Seminole man she had seen carving out wood images), n.d., SPOHP (transcript).

18. Shire, *Threshold of Manifest Destiny*, 102–136; Transcript, Charlie Gopher oral history interview with Jean Chaudhuri, May 1971, 5–7, SPOHP.

19. See, for example, Chaudhuri monologue.

20. Betty Mae Tiger Jumper and Patsy West, *A Seminole Legend: The Life of Betty Mae Tiger Jumper* (Gainesville: University Press of Florida, 2001), 12; Paul N. Backhouse to Laurel Clark Shire, e-mail correspondence, September 2, 2015; Susan Micco Snow

and Susan Enns Stans, *Healing Plants: Medicine of the Florida Seminole Indians* (Gainesville: University Press of Florida, 2001), 13–15; Melinda Beth Micco, "'Blood and Money': The Case of Seminole Freedmen and Seminole Indians in Oklahoma," in *Crossing Waters, Crossing Worlds: The African Diaspora in Indian Country*, ed. Tiya Miles and Sharon Holland (Durham, NC: Duke University Press, 2006), 212–244; Jane Landers, "A Nation Divided? Blood Seminoles and Black Seminoles on the Florida Frontier," in *Coastal Encounters: The Transformation of the Gulf South in the Eighteenth Century*, ed. Richmond F. Brown (Lincoln: University of Nebraska Press, 2007), 99–116; Kevin Mulroy, "Behind the Rolls: Pompey Bruner Fixico," in *InDivisible: African-Native American Lives in the Americas*, ed. Gabrielle Tayac (Washington, DC: Smithsonian National Museum of the American Indian, 2009), 133–137.

21. 1840 US Census, roll 36; 1850 US Census, rolls 58, 59; Y. N. Kly, *The Invisible War: African-American Antislavery Resistance from the Stono Rebellion through the Seminole Wars* (Atlanta: Clarity Press, 2006); Patsy West, *The Enduring Seminoles: From Alligator Wrestling to Ecotourism* (Gainesville: University Press of Florida, 2008); Snow and Stans, *Healing Plants*, 13–15.

22. Shire, *Threshold of Manifest Destiny*, 181, 203–206.

23. Other southern frontier states had similar white gender patterns. See 1830–1860 census records for Arkansas, Mississippi, Alabama, South Carolina, Georgia, Virginia, and Florida prepared by Social Explorer (socialexplorer.com) (hereafter cited as SE).

24. "An act to provide for the armed occupation and settlement of the unsettled part of the peninsula of East Florida" (5 Stat 502); United States, General Land Office, *Report of the Commissioner of the General Land Office, Communicating an Abstract of Permits Granted under the Acts for the Armed Occupation of Florida* (Washington, DC, 1848).

25. The language of the final AOA bill made single or widowed women tacitly eligible for its benefits if they claimed to be "heads of families," and forty *single* women sought to claim free public land in Florida in 1842 and 1843. "An act to provide for the armed occupation and settlement of the unsettled part of the peninsula of East Florida" (5 Stat 502); James W. Covington, "The Armed Occupation Act of 1842," *Florida Historical Quarterly* 40 (July 1961): 45. An AOA permit was just the promise to settle on a land claim. A patent, the document granting the right to full title to the land claim, was awarded if the settler proved after five years that he or she had made an actual settlement on that claim. "Roll of Persons Forming New Settlements," roll 262; "An Act to secure Homesteads to actual Settlers on the Public Domain," May 20, 1862, in *United States Statutes at Large*, ed. George P. Sanger, vol. 12 (Boston: Little, Brown, 1863), 392–393; permits in DEP; patents in HCEP. Wives and daughters also inherited the AOA claims they had settled with men; at least twenty male AOA settlers who had died during the first five years of settlement left their estates to women and children. Five titles went to female heirs who were only partial heirs (shared title with siblings/others), seven titles went to widows of settlers who died before the five-year term of settlement was over, and another eight titles were issued jointly to "widow and heirs" of the deceased AOA permitee. Permits in DEP; patents in HCEP. On Barker

and Baker, see Papers Concerning Permits of Claims for Land under the Armed Occupation Act, Record Group 49, NARA, boxes 513A and 508. Twenty-three women filed AOA permits but did not ultimately receive patents. Seventeen women received patents for their AOA claims (or their heirs did if they were deceased by 1849). Permits in DEP; patents in HCEP.

26. Shire, *Threshold of Manifest Destiny*, 162–193; S.B. 120, 26th Cong. (January 3, 1840, amended January 10, 1840); S.B. 160, 25th Cong. (January 3, 1839, amended February 9, 1839); Appendix to Cong. Globe, 26th Cong., 1st Sess., 73–74 (1840).

27. For example, some female AOA settlers wed men with AOA claims near their own and thus created kin connections that surnames on AOA permits do not indicate. 1850 US Census, rolls 58, 59; patents in HCEP; Florida Compiled Marriages, 1822–1850 (ancestry.com).

28. AOA settlers who shared surnames included members of these families: Baker, Ballard, Barnes, Bates, Bleach/Blitch, Boyet/Boyett, Branch, Brooks, Brown, Carruthers, Cavass, Clark, Conyers, Crawford, Crum, Curry, Daniels, Davis, Durance, Eaton, Galbreath, Garrason/Garrison, Geiger, Gill, Goff/Gough, Hall, Harn, Harrell, Hart, Harvill/Harville, Hayman/Haymans, Hill, Hogan, Hollingsworth, Hooker, Hope, Jackson, Jernigan, Johnson, Kettles/Kittles, Knight, Lee, McLeod, McNeill, Miller, Mizell, Mobley, Monroe, Moody, Munden/Mundin, Parker, Pellicer, Pennington, Peterson, Piles, Potter, Priest, Reinhardt, Ridaught, Robertson, Russell, Saunders, Selph, Severy, Sherouse, Smith, Sparkman, Stephens, Sturges, Taylor, Tiner/Tyner, Tison, Tucker, Turner, Weeks, Whidden/Whitten/Whitton, White, Whitehurst, Wiggins, Wilkie, Williams, and Wilson.

29. Patents in HCEP. Richard, William, Joseph, Michael, Isaac, Mary Ann, and Seaborn Garrison, and their families, settled AOA claims near Chukochatty. Michael Garrison was a land surveyor who had scouted land for the extended family, and Isaac Garrison later served as courier for the family and community, taking many AOA applications and other documents to the land office at Newnansville in 1844 and 1849. In August 1849, Mary Ann, Isaac, Michael, and William Garrison all got their land patents (the title to their AOA claims) on the same day. In the vanguard of American expansion into this region of Florida, Isaac and his second wife, Laura, were also the proud parents of the "first white child" born in the county, a son named for Isaac whom Laura gave birth to in 1842. Isaac, Joseph, and Richard Garrason and their families were listed on the roll of Captain John Curry's party of settlers to the head of the Chocochattee Savanna, forty-six miles north of Tampa, "Roll of Persons Forming New Settlements," roll 262; patents in HCEP; 1840 US Census, roll 36; Covington, "Armed Occupation Act," 47; 1850 US Census, roll 58.

30. Michael E. Welsh, "Legislating a Homestead Bill: Thomas Hart Benton and the Second Seminole War," *Florida Historical Quarterly* 57 (October 1978): 157–172. The land offices in Florida recorded 459 patents (titles) to lands settled under the AOA. HCEP. Shire, *Threshold of Manifest Destiny*, 172–181.

31. All land entries are recorded in HCEP, but preemptions are not differentiated from other sales. The correspondence of the land offices contains many preemption

claims. Ledger of Monies Received, 1825–33, Tallahassee Land Office; letters regarding preemption laws in Commissioners Letters to Registers of Land Offices, Land Office Correspondence, Newnansville, vol. 1, 1821–1844, vol. 2, 1845–1845, vol. 4, 1847–1854, vol. 17, 1843–1851, DEP. See also Letters, Tallahassee Land Office, 1851–1854, vol. 3, DEP. At least 120 veterans of Florida wars received land bounties for their service, James W. Oberly, *Sixty Million Acres: American Veterans and the Public Lands before the Civil War* (Kent, OH: Kent State University Press, 1990), 17–19; Peter S. Genovese Jr., "The Graduation Act (1854)," in *The Louisiana Purchase: A Historical and Geographical Encyclopedia*, ed. Junius Rodriguez (Santa Barbara, CA: ABC-CLIO, 2002), 128–129. Homestead entries in Florida are recorded in HCEP; Alicia E. Rodriguez, "The Homestead Act (1862)," in Rodriguez, *Louisiana Purchase*, 140–142.

32. 1840 and 1850 census population figures in Florida from Historical Census Browser, University of Virginia, Geospatial and Statistical Data Center (2004) (map server.lib.virginia.edu). John K. Mahon provides Florida population figures circa 1835 when the total population of the Florida territory was 34,000 (18,000 whites and 16,000 slaves). Mahon, *History of the Second Seminole War, 1835–1842*, rev. ed. (Gainesville: University of Florida Press, 1985), 130.

33. The AOA required that eligible settlers had to claim land south of the existing "line of settlement," which the law stipulated existed between township lines 9 and 10, roughly south of Gainesville. This requirement encouraged settlers to move farther south than the more settled region of north Florida. In 1840, this land was in Alachua, Dade, Hillsborough, Monroe, and Orange/Mosquito Counties. By 1850, the same area had been further carved into the following counties: Alachua, Dade, Benton/Hernando, Hillsborough, Levy, Marion, Monroe, Orange/Mosquito, Putnam, and St. Lucie counties. I have included all of Alachua County in this number even though not all of it was available for armed occupation, but including it *over*estimates the 1840 (pre-AOA) population of the AOA-eligible area. Census Browser (http://mapserver .lib.virginia.edu). Some scholars estimate that only about two thousand people came to Florida as a direct result of the AOA, while two-thirds of the six thousand AOA settlers (this number includes an estimate of the number of family members who accompanied those who filed claims) were already Florida residents in 1842. Joe Knetsch, *Florida's Seminole Wars, 1817–1858* (Charleston, SC: Arcadia Press, 2003), 139–140; Daniel L. Schafer, "U.S. Territory and State," in *The New History of Florida*, ed. Michael Gannon, rev. ed. (Gainesville: University Press of Florida, 2013), 231.

34. In order to plot AOA settler and slave populations by county, I converted the land permit data (the locations of the AOA settlers) into county-level populations that I could compare with the census counts of slaves, which are available only at the county level, not to exact MTRS (meridian, township, range, and section) or latitude/longitude locations. To do that, I coded each AOA settler for the county he or she settled in based on modern Florida county boundaries, as well as the county each claim would have been in based on 1840, 1850, and 1860 county lines in Florida (they changed frequently in the nineteenth century as the American population increased (see mapof us.org/florida for details, including an interactive map). The resulting maps show the

number of AOA settlers in each county (only counties in which the AOA applied are included) and the number of slaves in each county in 1840, 1850, and 1860. I have located the colored disks representing settlers and enslaved persons—size and opacity indicating the relative number of settlers/enslaved persons in each county—at roughly the central point of each county. For the AOA settlers, I used modern county borders, which provides the most granular county-level data (as counties multiplied and got smaller over time). For each map of the number of enslaved person per county, I used the county lines that applied in that census year to find the rough centroid and plot the relative number of slaves. I then converted the AOA settlers to 1860 county boundaries and plotted those over the 1850 and 1860 slave populations to reveal how slavery followed the AOA. AOA patent information came from HCEP. Population of enslaved and free persons in the 1840, 1850, and 1860 US Censuses prepared by SE.

35. A former Florida slave recalled that his mother, Fannie Parish, was utilized by her owner as a "breeder" who produced and cared for children on the plantation. Enslaved women in Florida began bearing children early, sometimes as young as thirteen, and most bore their first child at age fifteen to sixteen. Larry Eugene Rivers, *Slavery in Florida: Territorial Days to Emancipation* (Gainesville: University Press of Florida, 2000), 86–87, 88–97, 105–123, 128; Adrienne Davis, "Don't Nobody Bother Yo' Principle: The Sexual Economy of American Slavery," in *Sister Circle: Black Women and Work*, ed. S. Harley (New Brunswick, NJ: Rutgers University Press, 2002), 103–127; Jennifer L. Morgan, *Laboring Women: Reproduction and Gender in New World Slavery* (Philadelphia: University of Pennsylvania Press, 2004); Edward E. Baptist, *Creating an Old South: Middle Florida's Plantation Frontier before the Civil War* (Chapel Hill: University of North Carolina Press, 2002), 48.

36. Mahon, *History of the Second Seminole War*, 237; Foreman, *Indian Removal*, 362; Porter, *Black Seminoles*, 96.

37. There were 3,338 people in Marion County in 1850; 27.5 percent of them (921) were white females. In 1860, 5,314 enslaved persons endured in Marion County, while 549 enslaved persons lived in the new Sumter County (carved out of Marion County in 1852). By 1860, the total population of Marion County had grown to 8,609, which included 1,498 white women and girls. So, 5,314 slaves were 61.7 percent of the population, while 1,498 white females were 17.4 percent of the total population. Aggregate county-level census figures are from Historical Census Browser, University of Virginia.

38. In 1830, 54.3 percent of the total South Carolina population was enslaved, compared with 42.1 percent in Georgia and 38 percent in Alabama. The number of whites and enslaved blacks continued to grow in antebellum Florida, reaching a combined total of 140,424 in 1860, when 44.95 percent of them were enslaved. 1830–1860 US Census data prepared by SE.

39. 1830–1860 US Census data prepared by SE.

40. Frank Marotti Jr. "Negotiating Freedom in St. Johns County, Florida, 1812–1862" (PhD diss., University of Hawaii, 2003), 204–205; Marotti, *Heaven's Soldiers: Free People of Color and the Spanish Legacy in Antebellum Florida* (Tuscaloosa: University of Alabama Press, 2013), 91–93; Kevin Mulroy, *Freedom on the Border: The Seminole Maroons*

in Florida, the Indian Territory, Coahuila, and Texas (Lubbock: Texas Tech University Press, 1993); Shirley Boteler Mock, *Dreaming with the Ancestors: Black Seminole Women in Texas and Mexico* (Norman: University of Oklahoma Press, 2010).

41. 1830–1860 US Census data prepared by SE.

42. Shire, *Threshold of Manifest Destiny*, 47–63; Marotti, "Negotiating Freedom in St. Johns County, Florida," 204–205; Marotti, *Heaven's Soldiers*, 91–93; Mulroy, *Freedom on the Border*; Mock, *Dreaming with the Ancestors*.

CHAPTER 6

Geographies of Expansion: Nineteenth-Century Women's Travel Writing

Susan L. Roberson

In the nineteenth century the idea of progress was complicated, connoting not only geographic expansion and a manifest destiny to "overspread the whole of the continent" but also technological advancement and personal self-cultivation. Because travelers both participated in the extension of boundaries and visited places under the pressure of expansion, recording its effects on people, institutions, transportation, technology, and geography, travel writing provides one way to gauge the meanings and effects of US expansionism. Travel writing follows the mobile narrator across the terrain and through the daily challenges that enable the journeyer to gain new experiences and knowledge of places and people. Because of these experiences, the traveler gains new insights not only of herself but of the social, economic, and political forces at work in the locations visited and in the nation as a whole. Terry Caesar has argued that nineteenth-century writing about travel abroad prompted writers to think about home, about the United States, and national identity. In similar ways, writing about travel to the West gave writers space to think about the nation and the direction it was taking in the nineteenth century. As travelers across the West that is now our Midwest at a time of rapid transformation, Caroline Kirkland, Margaret Fuller, Catharine Maria Sedgwick, and Constance Fenimore Woolson were poised to make firsthand observations from a woman's perspective of the settlement of the Old Northwest, the growth of cities into commercial and industrial hubs, and the increasing sophistication of transportation and communication technologies. Because a woman's standpoint originates in women's experiences of the everyday world, in what Judith Fetterley and Marjorie Pryse call the "poetics of detail" of women's lives, and advocates an ethos of accountability, women's views of expansionism in the Old Northwest fill a gap in the dominant ideologies of expansionism.[1] Tempering their faith in progress with ideals of Christian republicanism, community building, and thoughtful stewardship of the land, these writers were also poised to critique the consequences of expansion on the settlers, Native Americans, the environment, and the nation. Because these authors traveled to and through the Great Lakes region at different times during the nineteenth century, from 1836 to 1872, their travel narratives also show the progressive transformation of the region by the pressures of expansion as they both celebrate and critique the changes they witness.

For Caroline Kirkland, US expansionism was a personal, family affair. Having left New York to take posts at the newly established Detroit Female Seminary in 1835, she and her husband, William, began buying land so that by 1836 they owned more than thirteen hundred acres west of Detroit and had begun plotting out the village of Pinckney in hopes of capitalizing on the "great Michigan land fever," which brought "over a thousand new emigrants a day" to Detroit. Amy Kaplan has demonstrated how the rhetorics and ideologies of manifest destiny and domesticity were intertwined in antebellum rhetoric as the country expanded its borders. Coining the term "manifest domesticity," Kaplan argues that domesticity played "a major role in defining the contours of the nation" and domesticating or civilizing the other, the savage, the foreign. At the same time, then, that the Kirkland family moved west to improve their personal situation, they also participated in the larger national project of pushing the borders of the nation westward and conquering the wild, of turning the backwoods into farms and villages. A book about settlement and the domestication of the newly opened Michigan lands, Caroline Kirkland's *A New Home, Who'll Follow? Or Glimpses of Western Life* (1839) follows the fictional, pseudoautobiographical narrator, Mary Clavers, as she attempts to create a home in the Michigan frontier, an "American back-woods settlement."[2] It provides a woman's perspective on expansion, focusing on the domestic scene, the garden, and the community of women who populate her narrative, as well as sharp criticism of those who fraudulently speculated in land without the intention to build or improve the lives of the settlers.

From the beginning, Mrs. Clavers presents her journey to her new home from a woman's perspective, focusing on the lack of the comforts of travel, the domestic scene, the rustic quality of the earlier settlers, and her own efforts at establishing a home in the backwoods. She begins by recounting her misadventures as a traveler to the frontier region of Michigan, poking fun at her own romantic, flower-gathering idea of travel. The Michigan mud hole that requires sounding to find a spot to cross it, her dunking into a bog hole, and her overnight stays, first at a rural inn inhabited by a terrifying drunk and then at a "Hotel," which was really a "log-house" with a communal sleeping apartment in the roof space (*ANH* 9), speak to the conditions of travel in the backwoods of Michigan before modern transportation and the hospitality industry reached this remote region, when, as William Cullen Bryant expressed, "Every house on the great road in this country is a public house, and nobody hesitates to entertain the traveler or accept his money."[3]

Once arrived in Montacute (the fictional version of Pinckney), Clavers's husband, who had "purchased two hundred acres of wild land" (*ANH* 4), drew up a diagram of the new village with the other men, planning to build a mill, tavern, store, and other municipal improvements, while Mary Clavers focuses on the domestic scene. Attempting to bring her middle-class ideas of homemaking to the frontier, Clavers is dismayed by the unruliness of the Ketchum home in which they initially stayed. She remarks about that first night in Montacute, made uncomfortable by Mr. Ketchum's drunkenness, "every thing was so different from our ideas of comfort, or even decency" (*ANH* 37). When she finally moves into her own temporary log cabin home, she finds that the array of trunks and boxes "which we then in our greenness considered indispensible" were not suitable to log cabin living (*ANH* 32). As she says, "My ideas of comfort were by this time narrowed down to a well-swept room with a bed in one corner, and cooking-apparatus in another—and this in some fourteen days from the city!" (*ANH* 44). Even so, she records the things missing in the backwoods like milk, eggs, and vegetables, as well as the ways women improvise with the ingredients on hand, balancing lack against accommodation (*ANH* 33–34). Bringing "order out of chaos" (*ANH* 42) that her rustic home and superfluous belongings created, Clavers records the ways that domesticity tames the wild at the same time that she shows herself becoming acclimated to life in the backwoods. For Clavers, expansionism is a personal record of improved living conditions as she establishes her first home in the forest and then moves to a "'framed house,' a palace of some twenty by thirty feet, flanked by a shanty kitchen, and thatched with oak shingles" (*ANH* 145). The domestic spaces she occupies and the ways her conditions are improved reify the nation and the civilizing, progressive aspects of expansionism in her own version of manifest domesticity.

Mary Clavers's garden is another instance of the representation of the process of expansion by which the so-called wild is tamed, cultivated, and transformed. As she puts it, "As women feel sensibly the deficiencies of the 'salvage' state, so they are the first to attempt the refining process, the introduction of those important nothings on which so much depends" (*ANH* 147). In addition to improvements made indoors, Clavers attempts to refine the garden space by sowing seeds she brought from home and by transforming the natural Eden into a cultivated garden. Annette Kolodny has argued that women who moved to the frontiers "dreamed of transforming the wilderness" and "quite literally set about planting gardens in these wilderness places" as part of an "idealized domesticity" in which the garden figures "as domestic space." Clavers participates in this woman-driven impulse to break up the "grubs" or "gnarled roots of small trees and shrubs" that interfere with the productive use of the "incipient Eden" (*ANH* 78–79). One of the driving impulses of many women pioneers was the effort to re-create the old home in the new western location and to retain identities of domesticity as they attempt to refashion the new environment into a familiar shape.[4] Like other women, Clavers seeks to improve on the natural scene by refashioning it. On the verge of being a true Eden, of providing the aesthetic and culinary benefits she desires, Clavers's garden, like the village and the spaces of national expansion, must first be controlled, refined, improved so that, ironically, it resembles the home they left.

Creating a community of women through her digressive storytelling and her focus on the lives of women who must tend to children and make homes in the backwoods, Clavers indicates that a real community is composed of people and not just buildings and gardens. From satiric portraits of some of the early settlers like Mrs. Jennings, who drank the remains of green tea from the "spout of the tea-pot" (*ANH* 51), to sympathetic portrayals of women like Mrs. Rivers, her neighbor who shared her fondness for literature; from the critical exposure of Amelia Newland, whose sexual improprieties led to a botched abortion, to the tale of the dignified Mrs. Beckworth, settled finally with the love of her life, and the Indian woman who wanders by to "*swap*" whortleberries for flour (*ANH* 81), the narrative paints a gallery of the women of Montacute. Clavers introduces this range of women to suggest that the West is being populated by people from a diversity of regional and national origins as well as classes to form a community, and that women were an important element of community building. A true community, Clavers suggests, requires women, children, families—not just men. And it requires that women find space in which to be themselves. One of the problems with early settlements, as Kirkland and Margaret Fuller realize, is that women who follow the economic hopes of their husbands are frequently left alone, held captive by their cabins and chores while men are able to escape to work and to enjoy nature. Too often, Clavers comments, a young wife is left in the house "the

long, solitary, *wordless* day" without the "old familiar means and appliances"
of housekeeping. When the husband comes home after working out of doors,
"he finds the homebird drooping and disconsolate" (*ANH* 146). So, while the
conversion of the wilderness into a settlement requires the hand of women,
often the cost of expansion is too much to ask as they often bear the burden of
loneliness, or worse, in the domesticating process.

Once moved in to her cabin, Clavers watches the growth and improvements of Montacute, the "progress of the village," as buildings go up and
the niceties of civilization are introduced (*ANH* 58). Lawrence Buell writes
that in the nineteenth century the idea of progress connoted improvement,
"political liberalization and then . . . technological development."[5] Similarly,
Clavers enumerates the physical signs of the commercial and technological
progress that "Montacute, half-fledged as it is, affords"—a blacksmith, cooper,
chair maker, a "mantua-maker" and milliner—as she also sketches the political changes she witnesses (*ANH* 80). The addition of public worship services,
a library, the Montacute Female Beneficent Society, the new schoolhouse, and
a weekly mail service speaks to her of the "gigantic step in the march of improvement," of the civic institutions that transform the raw individualism of
the frontier into a cooperative society (*ANH* 178). Even the backwoods politics
that she satirizes in the form of Mr. Simeon Jenkins, "Justas of Piece," indicates to her "the progressive improvements in this model village of ours," as
the political liberalization and the "republican spirit" emerge out of the early
days of settlement (*ANH* 172, 177, 184). Calling herself "a denizen of the wild
woods" after three years in Pinckney, she ends the narrative by humorously
counting her own improvements: "Several of us have as many as three cows;
some few, carpets and shanty-kitchens; and one or two, piano-fortes and silver
tea-sets. I myself . . . have had secret thoughts of an astral lamp!" (*ANH* 187).
These are all signs to her of improvement and progress, the positive effects of
expansionism as the wilderness is converted into a scene with familiar accoutrements and definitions of womanhood and domesticity.

Even so, she critiques the greed and falseness of speculators who sold bad
bonds on land in the hopes of getting rich rather than forging new communities on the frontier. When American go-aheadism, a nineteenth-century
term for initiative with connotations of reckless selfishness, relied on credit
and trust, on advertisements that touted fortunes to be made, when sales were
seemingly supported by the usual instruments of trade, families looking for
a better life and men overtaken by greed were alike scammed. On the cusp
of the Panic of 1837, buying land must have seemed a safe bet for investors
like the Kirklands. Clavers understands the magic of the word "land" to the
"speculator of 1835–6" (*ANH* 26). But what she criticizes is the duplicity of

the sales, the "'tricksy spirit'" that defrauds naive buyers and the use of credit to purchase "property bought at five hundred dollars, [and] sold at once for twenty thousand" as part of get-rich-quick schemes of people who have no intention of settling in the West (*ANH* 31). Mr. Mazard, who had supposedly invested in Montacute, turns out to have "put large quantities of lumber" on Mr. Clavers's account, leaving him liable while Mazard "absconded; or, in Western language 'cleared'" (*ANH* 54). Mary Clavers warns her readers of "land sharks" (*ANH* 55) who promote towns like Tinkerville sight unseen, without the intention of actually building the towns they had laid out on paper.

The bankers who defraud buyers also come under fire. Using the language of black magic, Kirkland describes the "necromantic power" by which Mr. Rivers and other bankers converted land to paper money borrowed at "certain rates of interest" that turned out to be as "valueless as the ragged paper which wrapped them!" (*ANH* 121, 126). She uses the term "'Wild Cats'" to describe the "thirty banks or more" that grew suddenly from the "political hot-bed" of the 1830s banking practices without ever locating in the emerging Michigan communities. These she calls "cunning and stealthy blood-suckers" who make the most of fraudulent banking practices to enrich themselves at the expense of "small farmers" in Michigan (*ANH* 121, 126). Understanding the plight of the farmers, she writes, "Those who have seen only a city panic, can form no idea of the extent and severity of the sufferings on these occasions" (*ANH* 126). In her criticism of Mr. Rivers, Mr. Mazard, and the ways banks and speculators preyed on the small farmers of rural Michigan, Kirkland enters not only a national debate about banking that Jessica Lepler identifies, "the issues of how to balance security and risk, morality and sin, independent democracy and national improvement," but also a debate about the costs of expansionism.[6] Kirkland understands that expansion without capital or trust was not just a local problem but a financial, moral, and national problem. For Kirkland, the enterprise of making a new home on the frontier is not questioned; it is a given in the national ideology of expansion, progress, and domesticity. What she criticizes, as do the other women in this study, are the greed and materialism in the name of progress that damage and taint the process of nation building.

When Margaret Fuller visited the Great Lakes region a decade later in the summer of 1843, she saw it, according to Lance Newman, at a period of transition, "at the moment of its most breakneck settlement and development," when the natural environment and the ideas of freedom it connotes were being contested by the attempt to control and reshape it as more settlers poured

into the region; as towns like Cleveland, Milwaukee, and Chicago were becoming cities; and as Native Americans were being displaced and deracinated.
It was a period when the two dreams of the West, "one of a life in nature,
the other in machines," were grating against each other before the line of the
frontier moved farther on. It was a time when the "solitude" of the frontier
was becoming "enlivened" as homes were growing up from "the rich soil."[7]
Anticipating that she would not welcome the growth of cities in what to her
mind was still open territory, Fuller writes in *Summer on the Lakes, in 1843* (1844)
that she came to the West "prepared for the distaste I must experience in its
mushroom growth . . . , where 'go ahead' is the only motto." What she found
was at once a vibrant mix of cultures and a natural location that seemed to
promise an ideal of harmony and self-cultivation that prompted her to predict
that a "new order; a new poetry is to be evoked from this chaos" of expansion
(*SoL* 18). She hopes a new ethos of thoughtful cultivation will emerge from the
energy that brings this mix of people together, stitching as she does an ideology of material progress onto a theology of self-cultivation.

Journeying to Rock River, Illinois, Fuller maps the palimpsest of the geographic and social transitions traced on the terrain, as well as her conflicting
attitudes toward expansion, as she looks out over the broad landscape. She
describes the natural landscape, the river that flows between "high bluffs," the
swallows' nests "clustered among the crumbling rocks" (*SoL* 27). This natural
environment gives way to the manicured landscape of an "Irish gentleman"
who has built his home along the river, improving upon the scene with an
avenue to his house and a lawn with "the most graceful trees" (*SoL* 28). Here
humans and nature, the European and American, seem happily to coexist.
Although the owner lives in a large, commodious home, he had first inhabited
a log cabin, which he has preserved as "a very ornamental accessory," archi-
tecturally marking the transition from crude frontier to refined country estate
(*SoL* 28). While this gentleman's home illustrates for Fuller the transition to
"enlivened" living, other homes she sees belie the "spirit of the scene" because
of "the slovenliness" of their owners who "had no thought beyond satisfying
the grossest material wants" (*SoL* 29). The lower class of settlers, whom she
calls "Gothic" invaders, "obliterate[d] the natural expression of the country"
in their rush to conquer the landscape and its original inhabitants, the Native Americans (*SoL* 29). Though Black Hawk's band had been defeated and
displaced by the time Fuller visited, they still haunt the area, "the marks of
their tomahawks, the troughs in which they prepared their corn, their caches"
evident in the land (*SoL* 32–33). In some ways, the Rock River section encap-
sulates much of what Fuller thinks about the West and the changes it is undergoing, putting in close proximity the natural environment, settlements by

Figure 6.1. Sarah Clarke, *Log Cabin at Rock River*. From S. M. [Margaret] Fuller, *Summer on the Lakes, in 1843*. Boston: Charles C. Little and James Brown, 1844. Courtesy of the University of Illinois Press.

whites, whether the wise Irish gentleman or the slovenly, and the vanquished if not quite vanished Native American. The scene also foregrounds the conflict in the narrative between depictions of an ideal West of thoughtful settlement and a critique of materialistic expansionism.

Looking out at the prairie and the homes nestled upon it, Fuller hopes for a kind of harmony between humans and the environment that will lead to the positive cultivation of both. When she and her party venture out on the prairie, she describes "the blooming plain, unmarked by any road," in which the "friendly track of wheels" did not leave marks of their passing (*SoL* 25). Looking at the scene through a "magic glass" (*SoL* 1), she imagines the groves of trees to be "blue islands" floating in the distance. Even when she realizes they are not images of a fairyland, her descriptions are still infused with the romantic, as she sketches pastoral scenes of "fair parks" and "little log houses . . . with their curling smokes" in which the human "harmonized beautifully" with the natural scene (*SoL* 25). Taking her reader through the picturesque scene, from her host's home and over the "blooming plain" to a view of the "little log houses" (*SoL* 25) before coming at the end of the day to a cathedral-like stand of trees, Fuller draws her reader into a world where natural and human objects coexist, where the domestic and the natural complement each other.

A visit to the home of an English gentleman rounds out the possibilities of harmonious living with nature. His house is filled with books, and the woods that surround it "have a very picturesque and pleasing effect." Here Fuller finds a "mixture of culture and rudeness" that she reads as a "feeling of freedom, not of confusion," of an orderly and just relationship: "This habitation of man seemed like a nest in the grass, so thoroughly were the buildings and all objects of human care harmonized with what was natural" (*SoL* 24). For Fuller the ideal of living in the West is based on a mix of culture and a peaceful coexistence with the natural world, as if one's home were a "nest" built from and in the natural setting. This kind of living suggests to her freedom, "the liberty of law, not license; not indolence," informed by "genial and poetic influences" and self-cultivation in which "all should be fitted for freedom and an independence by his own resources" (*SoL* 66, 77). Here Fuller echoes the tenets of self-cultivation articulated by the Unitarian minister William Ellery Channing, who tethered self-cultivation, "the care which every man owes to himself, to the un-folding and perfecting of his nature," to progressive, forward movement and to power over an untamed self. Using the very words John O'Sullivan used to describe the nation's political and racial manifest destiny, Channing connects "growth, expansion," and "progress" to individual and social improvement: "The past and the present call on you to advance."[8] For Unitarians and many Americans, progress and self-cultivation were intertwined, both often charted by metaphors of linear movement that parallel the geographic expansion and technological improvements of the nation. Visiting Illinois at this period of rapid transformation, Fuller was positioned to witness these possibilities of progress and self-cultivation in the pastoral lifestyle the West promised.

Yet against these depictions of an ideal West where the potential of the individual can be nourished, Fuller also understands that "the great problem of the place and time" (*SoL* 65) is the need for a thoughtful stewardship of the natural and human resources. Thus, even as she extols the possibilities of a "new poetry," a new ethos of cultivation and improvement, she also sees expansionism's problems, the materialism that values use over care, a racism that denigrates and impoverishes the Native American, and the sexism that results in the pinched lives of pioneer women. So stark is the contrast between the ideal of the West and the damage caused by materialistic expansion on Native Americans and women that Lance Newman calls *Summer on the Lakes* "dystopian." Newman writes, "*Summer on the Lakes* is structured by the tension between a vision of a just society rooted in nature and the stark reality of America's westward expansion, between an abiding faith in the human potential to live up to the beauty of picturesque landscapes and a clear understanding of the cold social calculus of immediate profit."[9] Early in the narrative, when Fuller is visiting Niagara Falls, overwhelmed by the sublime images of "the full wonder of the scene," a man comes also to look at the falls. Instead of admiring the natural wonder, he looked about "with an air as if thinking how he could best appropriate it to his own use, [and] he spat into it," claiming and using the environment for his personal aims (*SoL* 4–5). Then at Cleveland, where she has a fine view of the lake in which "the waters presented kaleidoscopic varieties of hues," she describes her fellow steamboat passengers as "New Englanders, seeking their fortunes." They talked only of "what they should get in the new scene"; their minds are not on the natural or human view before them but on "accumulation." Rather than projecting hopes for freedom or self-cultivation, these immigrants, trained in "habits of calculation," see the West as an arena for appropriation, accumulation, and "material interests" (*SoL* 12). Fuller's hopes for the possibilities of thoughtful stewardship and cultivation of the self and the land grate against evidence of crude go-aheadism and selfishness.

While Fuller understands that these New England immigrants will need "the spirit of religion" to guide them, she also criticizes the religious hypocrite who "turns in loathing" from the rituals of the Indian, cheats them in trade, and degrades them with rum (*SoL* 12, 114). At her angriest moment in the book, she cries out, "Our people and our government have sinned alike against the first-born of the soil," calling out the hypocrisy of a Christian nation that practices slavery and corrupts the Native American (*SoL* 114). She resoundingly criticizes the racism and materialism that have shaped government policy, reminding one of Ralph Waldo Emerson's anger unleashed at a government that advocated the removal of the southern tribes to make way for whites in search of more land and the gold recently discovered in northern Georgia. In his open letter to President Martin Van Buren in 1838, Emerson calls the removal "a dereliction of all faith and virtue, such a denial of justice" that asks Americans to question the "*moral* character of the Government."[10] Having gained a clearer understanding of Native Americans during her visit, observing their domestic activities and going out among them, Fuller likewise speaks out against their mistreatment. Commenting on a scene of "gipsy charm" as the Indians gathered to receive their government annuities at Mackinac, she writes: "The men of these subjugated tribes, now accustomed to drunkenness and every way degraded, bear but a faint impress of the lost grandeur of the race" (*SoL* 113). Even if her understanding of the Indians is still informed by nineteenth-century rhetorics of the Native Americans that view them as both noble and doomed, she writes, "I feel that I have learnt a great deal of the Indians, from observing them even in this broken and degraded situation" (*SoL* 153), indicating the moral, political, and imaginative effects of her travel experiences and her understanding of the costs of expansionism.

Fuller also directs her criticism of the West to the situation of pioneer women. After idealizing the life of settlers, Fuller learns that the frontier was harder than her idyllic dream of plenty in which "nature still wore her motherly smile" had suggested. She recounts the reality of pioneer life for women, commenting on the unfitness of many for their situation: "The great drawback upon the lives of these settlers, at present, is the unfitness of the women for their new lot." Following their menfolk "for affection's sake," women find they have the hardest part of the enterprise, one for which "they are least fitted." Ill-equipped by their eastern educations and without "aid in domestic labor," these women are confined to the cabin and domestic chores without the resources men have "to ride, to drive, to row alone." The wives of the poorer settlers, overworked with hard labor, she writes, "very frequently become slatterns" (*SoL* 38–39). Fuller also ponders the place of Indian women in their society and their "habits of drudgery" and submission. Though she is charmed by the women she visits, who tease her about her "little sun-shade," she understands that "their place is certainly lower, and their share of the human inheritance less" than that allotted to white women (*SoL* 111). In these sections Fuller looks at women of different classes and races to make a point about the difficulty of their lives, to call attention to their place in patriarchal and racist societies and the effects of expansionism on them. Having just brought to press "The Great Lawsuit. Man *versus* Men. Woman *versus* Women" (1843), Fuller was primed to remark on the situation of women. In it she had observed that woman's "circle, if the duller, is not the quieter. If kept from excitement, she is not from drudgery" and compares the lot of middle-class women to that of the Indian woman who "carries the burdens of the camp." Her observations on the frontier validate what she earlier had written. As she did in "The Great Lawsuit" advocating that "every barrier" be "thrown down" and "every path laid open to woman as freely as to man," in *Summer on the Lakes* she turns her new knowledge of frontier life to a call for action—a more enlightened education for western girls that would prepare them for the actualities of pioneer living and enable them to participate in the self-cultivation that movement to the West promises.[11] Fuller's view of the Great Lakes evidences the mixed, conflicting views of the nineteenth century. She sees possibilities for self-cultivation with the material improvement of the land at the same time that she clearly critiques the reckless materialism and go-aheadism that ignored the costs of expansion.

By the time novelist Catharine Maria Sedgwick journeyed to the West, it was opening up to fashionable tourism. In 1854, Sedgwick was an invited guest on the Great Excursion to celebrate the "first railroad to unite the Atlantic with the Mississippi River." Described by historian William J. Peterson as "one of the more notable women to make the trip," Sedgwick wrote her impressions of the journey in a brief letter published in *Putnam's Monthly* in September 1854. Quite different from the challenges of travel that Kirkland relayed, Sedgwick describes how the twelve hundred excursionists first gathered at Chicago and then departed on "two trains of nine coaches each gaily decorated with flowers, flags, and streamers" for Rock Island, Illinois. There they transferred to steamboats to continue the journey up the Mississippi River to Minneapolis, where excursionists could take side trips to Minnehaha Falls, the Falls of St. Anthony, and Fort Snelling. Along the way, they were feted and treated to parades, fireworks, dancing, and speeches extolling the nation's "internal improvements and the Great West." Connecting the East to the West, the railroad coupled fashionable tourism with westward expansion at the same time that it signaled the nation's commercial and technological progress during the decade since Fuller's summer adventure. As a traveler, a tourist, Sedgwick enjoyed the comforts of the Great Excursion, the "ices, jellies, cakes, and pyramids . . . of candied sugar," but she also used her article to think about "America's imagination of itself as a nation."[12]

For Sedgwick, the extension of the railroad to the Mississippi River was more than a convenience; it was a cipher of the nation. Even as she looked out on the "rich prairie turf," the grass "brilliantly embroidered with flowers" along the river, she also extolled the conversion of the prairies into cultivated farms and cities, signs of the expansion of the nation (*GE* 323). As the railroad stretches "over the vast prairies," it joins the "Free West to the East in inevitable and indissoluble Union" (*GE* 320). The rail lines mark not only the "advancement of true civilization," the technological advances of midcentury, but also all that the term "*true* civilization" means for Sedgwick (*GE* 320, emphasis added). By joining geographic areas and extended populations into one united nation instead of feudal "*patches*" (*GE* 320), the rail line suggests to her ideals of unity, equality, democracy, and piety. At a time when the indissolubility of the nation was not as sure as it may have been, when debates about slavery and what Sedgwick called the "misfortune of Missouri" (*GE* 325) were becoming more divisive, the rails provided a kind of proof of the Union/union and the spirit of democracy. In his brief history of the excursion, Peterson speculates, "Slavery probably was the chief topic of conversation" as he reminds his 1934 readers of the Kansas-Nebraska Act of May 30, 1854, and the dash to California during the gold rush of 1849, the kind of materialism and speculation that Sedgwick critiques even as she praises the "enlightened industry" of the builders of the line, "our *fellow-sovereigns*" (*GE* 320).[13] Quoting the line from the Declaration of Independence, "That all men are created free and equal," she imagines a nation of equals joined together as one, symbolically enacted during the excursion by the ritual act of "mingling the water taken from the Atlantic . . . with the water of the Mississippi" (*GE* 321, 324). For her, the advances in transportation signal the possibilities of connecting the expanding nation despite the threats that would sunder it in less than a decade.

Announcing that this "land of promise" was "prepared for them by the universal Father" (*GE* 321), Sedgwick conflates technological change, geographic movement, ideas of nationhood, and religion. She wrote that travelers on the Great Excursion were able to see "the inappreciable riches and untold beauty of our own country—our own inalienable possessions; to have our piety and our patriotism kindled . . . by the first revelation to our senses of the capacity of our country, the first intimation of its possible glorious future" (*GE* 321). Seeing the "abounding vitality" in the growth of the West and the progress of a "democratic republic" evidenced by the "railroads, telegraphs, aqueducts, and gaslights," Sedgwick also insists on a principled nationalism founded on "intellectual and moral development" (*GE* 320–322). While she articulates a version of manifest destiny, that God had promised the continent to the descendants of the Puritans who came with "the Bible and the school-book," she also insists on the necessity of "improving morals" that will raise the nation "above the vortex of speculation and mere material acquisition" (*GE* 321). For her, the impulses of nationalism were tempered by Christianity, republicanism, and democracy. John Austin has defined the Christian republicanism that appears in Sedgwick's novels as "a belief in Christian virtue as a positive moral force that transcends party politics and factional interests." Deborah Gussman adds that Sedgwick advocates "the sacrifice of individual interests to the public good . . . the subordination of individual liberty to civil liberty, the rejection of luxury, and the exaltation of independence, reason, benevolence, and public virtue."[14] These versions of nationalism are also apparent in her descriptions of the West, where she extols the honor of labor, the establishment of schools and churches in the newly settled towns, the generosity of Henry Farnam and Joseph E. Sheffield, contractors for the construction of the Chicago and Rock Island Railroad, and the physical achievements that raise the standard of living. Indeed, the technological, commercial, and agricultural improvements were evidence to Sedgwick of the "advancement of *true* civilization" founded on an ethos of caring, community, and piety (*GE* 320, emphasis added).

Even so, her version of ethical expansion comes at a cost that she does not seem to recognize in this short letter about the excursion. Unlike Fuller, who decried the degradation of the Natives, Sedgwick seems to see their disappear-

Plate 1. Thomas Cole, *The Course of Empire: The Consummation of Empire*. 1835–1836. Oil on canvas (relined). 51-1/4 × 70 in. Luce Center, Obj. No. 1858.3. The New-York Historical Society, New York.

Plate 2. Thomas Cole, *The Course of Empire: Destruction*. 1836. Oil on canvas (no dimensions). Luce Center, Obj. No. 1858.4. The New-York Historical Society, New York.

Plate 3. Charles Bird King, *Kee-o-Kuck, First War Chief of the Sauks (Watchful Fox)*. 1825. Oil on wood. 19 × 15-1/4 in. Thomas Gilcrease Institute of American History and Culture, 0126.119. Gilcrease Museum, Tulsa, OK.

Plate 4. Charles Bird King, *Keokuk, the Watchful Fox*. 1829. Oil on canvas. 38-1/2 × 26-1/2 in. Private collection. Image courtesy of Gerald Peters Gallery, Santa Fe, NM.

KEE-O-KUCK OR THE WATCHING FOX

The present Chief of the Sauk tribe and Successor to Black Hawk.

Painted by J.O.Lewis at the great treaty of Peace, du Chien 1825.

Plate 5. James Otto Lewis, *Kee-O-Kuck, or the Watching Fox*. 1836. Hand-colored lithograph. 18-1/4 × 11-1/2 in. From Lewis, *Aboriginal Port-Folio*, folio 2, based on his own 1826 watercolor after an 1825 field sketch, both lost in 1865 in the Smithsonian fire. Beinecke Rare Book and Manuscript Library, Yale University, New Haven, CT.

Plate 6. Nicholas Hilliard, *George Clifford, 3rd Earl of Cumberland*. 1590. Watercolor and body color, gold and silver leaf, on vellum, laid on fruitwood panel. 10-1/8 × 7 in. MNT0193. National Maritime Museum, Greenwich, London.

PHILIP. *KING* of Mount Hope.

P Revere sc

Plate 7. Paul Revere, after John Simon, *Philip, King of Mount Hope* (1762). Line engraving, colored by hand. 6-13/16 × 4-3/16 in. Here from Thomas Church, *The Entertaining History of King Philip's War*. Newport, RI, 1772. Mabel Brady Garvan Collection, 1946.9.994. Yale University Art Gallery, New Haven, CT.

Plate 8. Junius Brutus Stearns. *Hannah Duston Killing the Indians*. 1847. Oil on canvas. 36-1/4 in. × 42-1/4 in. (92.08 cm × 107.32 cm). Colby College Museum of Art. Gift of R. Chase Lasbury and Sally Nan Lasbury. Accession number 1992.001.

ance as part of the inevitable march of progress, in some ways reminiscent of her treatment of the brave Magawisca, who, at the end of *Hope Leslie*, vanished in the West in the vanguard of European American advancement. And although education is an important element of Sedgwick's version of Christian republicanism, apparently she does not extend it to the Native American. When she celebrates the young missionary who comes to Minnesota to bring education, she notes that the New England woman "hired two Indian girls to row" her to her future charges, "two white families and eight white children" (*GE* 322). Here the Native girls actually service the advancement that will continue to displace them. When she catalogs the warehouses, shops, and "beautiful private residences" in St. Louis, "the social shouts of civilized men, at the warehouses and huge hotels," she reminds readers of Black Hawk's War (*GE* 324). Noting that "a few years since was heard only the yell of the savage . . . tomahawk in hand in quest of his foe," she again joins the disappearance of the Native with the advancement of the white and the conversion of the wild (*GE* 322).

A writer who habitually advocates equality and union, who insists on piety and morality, Sedgwick also evidences the paradoxical attitudes about the environment, the Native American, and expansionism that entangled the nineteenth century. While fashionable tourism, advanced transportation, and the luxuries of the built environment speak to her of national progress and the benefits of expansionism, she misses seeing the costs that the Native Americans and the environment will pay for even an enlightened manifest destiny. Unlike Woolson, who will criticize tourists and American consumerism at the end of the century, the sixty-five-year-old Sedgwick writes of a charming excursion and anticipates returning home to "our own Berkshire," avoiding the national debate on the Indian question and leaving the task of settling the West to the young who "go in troops and caravans" (*GE* 325).

Revisiting the haunts of her youth, Constance Fenimore Woolson infuses her Great Lakes travel narrative, "Round by Propeller" (1872), with nostalgia, a keen understanding of the ethos of place, and a biting critique of the national ethic of use that squandered lives and the environment for commercial and political gain. Largely forgotten today, Woolson was a popular writer in the waning decades of the nineteenth century, an important voice in the debate about woman's role as an artist, and a valued friend of the novelist Henry James Jr. Between 1840 and 1873, the period when she lived in Cleveland, the "Forest City," Woolson witnessed its transformation from a sylvan town of seven thousand into an industrial city of ninety-two thousand. Attracted

to Cleveland because it was an important transportation link between the resources of the West and the markets of the East, manufacturers like her father,
owner of the Woolson stove foundry, and John D. Rockefeller, owner of the
much larger Standard Oil Company of Ohio, contributed to the growth of
the city. But they also contributed to the pollution of the natural environment at a time when little thought was given to conservation. Before Woolson
turned thirty, the Cuyahoga River, which runs through Cleveland, "caught
fire for the first time, its banks crowded with smoke-belching iron mills and oil
refineries." Events like this and the heritage of her famous great-uncle, James
Fenimore Cooper, prompted Woolson to "fill her fiction with laments for the
disappearance of the wilderness" and to use her satiric and biting travel narrative to critique expansionism, capitalism, and consumerism.[15]

Blending fiction with travel writing, "Round by Propeller" follows the excursion of a band of tourists on board the steamship *Columbia* around the
Great Lakes. Woolson invents a first-person narrator, Aunt Ruth Varick (Aunt
Rue), who tells the story of the excursion and comments on the goings-on
of her fellow travelers and the destruction of the natural landscape from a
woman's perspective. Published in the same year that Yellowstone Park was
established as the first national park (1872) and three years before Mackinac
Island would be named the second national park (1875), "Round by Propeller" can be read as a "travel narrative cast as environmental jeremiad."[16] At a
time when the nation was just beginning to understand the need to set aside
parcels of wilderness for public enjoyment even as it promoted industrialization as a sign of progress, Woolson fuses the rhetoric of the jeremiad to her
travel writing to expose the damage to the natural environment and to critique
a national ethic of use.

When Woolson's tourists arrive in Cleveland after sailing all night from
Buffalo, they are greeted by "a cloud of smoke" produced by the "iron mills
and oil refineries" shrouding the city.[17] Rather than go out onto the prairies
to see the wildflowers as former travelers had done, these tourists are eager to
see the built and industrialized environment. Deciding to tour the oil refineries
rather than Euclid Avenue, the narrator and Major Archer, another tourist,
view firsthand the refining process and the pollution of the flats, the Cuyahoga
River, and the Ohio Canal. Compared to the cauldrons of hell, with its "chok-
ing odors," "sulphurous in origin," and shimmering "crude green petroleum,"
the refinery, marked by rows of stills and pipes, is a "parable" of the commercial destruction of the environment. The allusion to hell is continued as the
river itself is described, the pollution that has transformed the "clear stream"
of the Cuyahoga into a river that is "more petroleum than water" and that
earlier "took fire, and . . . fairly blazed as it flowed down to the lake." Even

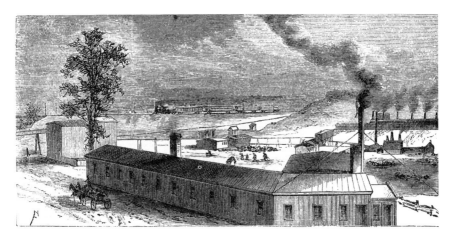

Figure 6.2. *Oil Refinery, Cleveland.* From Constance Fenimore Woolson, "Round by Propeller," *Harper's New Monthly Magazine* 45 (September 1872): 522.

though "the risk from fire and explosion is great," Major Archer explains that fortunes are being made from the oil business. With this comment, Woolson connects the degradation of the environment to American greed and expansionism. To punctuate her point, she has one of the travelers quote "Westward the star," a reference to the course of empire that has brought "civilization" to the west, figured ironically in the story by "A river on fire" (*RbP* 14–15).

Later, as the tourists sail through Lake Huron, they are told by the ship's mate about the fires of 1871 that destroyed much of the forests that had been clear-cut by settlers: "We couldn't see a thing for miles, the smoke was so thick." From Lake Michigan to Mackinac, it seemed "the hull country was afire" so that "the islanders thought the rest of the world must be having a judgment-day" (*RbP* 20). Woolson reads the destruction of the environment in biblical terms, with references to "judgment-day," hell's sulphurous cauldrons, and "original sin" (*RbP* 14). In jeremiadic fashion she figures the pollution as both a cosmic and a national problem. As Sacvan Bercovitch has pointed out, the American jeremiad joins politics, ideas of sacred and secular progress, and national identity to suggest an ideology of American exceptionalism. Woolson likewise fuses politics with the sacred, images of a biblical hell, in order to comment on national identity. But for her that identity is one not of exceptionalism but of promises broken. Understanding the "centrality of physical environment as a ground of personal and social identity," Woolson critiques a national identity polluted by imperialism and capitalism, by a landscape destroyed by politics. To drive home her point, she juxtaposes these scenes of environmental damage with views of the Detroit River, its "beautiful shores and islands" and the crisp, "delicious air" of the lakes reminders of what was and could have been (*RbP* 16).[18]

Not only has the landscape been changed over the years by industrialization, the growth of urban areas, and growing signs of affluence, the "large, costly houses" of Euclid Avenue (*RbP* 15), but the nature of tourism has changed as travelers seek cities, buildings, refineries, and social institutions as tourist sites rather than the natural landscape. Although Aunt Rue reminisces about old Detroit, "frontier life, and gay legends of the early French settlers," the tourists are guided to the new city hall, built after the "Italian order of architecture" (*RbP* 17). When they visit Milwaukee, "the best harbor on Lake Michigan," the tourists take in the courthouse, the opera house, the Plankinton Hotel, and the National Asylum for Disabled Soldiers as sites of the journey (*RbP* 26). The National Asylum, built for casualties of the Civil War, was "home" to six hundred men, "not a hospital, a prison, or a reform institution" but apparently a place where visitors thoughtlessly could poke their heads into the private lives of the nation's wounded (*RbP* 26–27). In Detroit, the "pale women" tourists shop in "search of new patterns for worsted," which they work on board the steamer rather than enjoy the natural views, and they dream of the "cheap goods of Canada . . . gloves, collars and ribbons," making the journey more about consumerism than enlightening experiences (*RbP* 16–17). Indeed, the women seem more concerned about the food they are served, the comforts of travel, and sexual conquests than in learning about the places they visit.

The America that these tourists represent is interested in the built environment and consumption, in viewing the damage to nature and the wounded soldiers, shopping, eating, and flirting. It is a society that ignores the costs of westward expansion, the disappearance of Native Americans like Chief Pontiac, and the costly Indian campaign west of the Mississippi River. Ending the narrative with a note that "the Burnt River stage was attacked last week by Indians, and the passengers killed," among them Major Archer, Woolson leaves readers with a final note on the costs of progress for both the Native Americans and the settlers. While Fuller goes out among the Indians, no Indians appear in Woolson's narrative. They exist as secondhand stories related to Aunt Rue, punctuating by their absence the disappearance of the Native American on the heels of the drive westward. If "Round by Propeller" is a satire of "the social customs of tourism," as Dennis Berthold contends, then it is also a satire of the social customs of middle-class America and the ideologies it supports.[19] More, it is an early example of ecofeminism that joins an ethos of environmental accountability to a critique of capitalism, racism, and a patriarchy that has converted women into thoughtless consumers.

Written over a span of five decades as the national boundary pushed west to the Old Northwest and beyond, these narratives not only indicate the changes to the region and the growing sophistication of travel but also offer critiques of expansionism from the perspective of women. At its best, expansionism for these women represents the domestic ideals of community building, uniting the nation, extending and nurturing the national family, and giving people the space in which to cultivate themselves. Yet even as the writers celebrate the ideals of growth and advancement, they are also critical of the toll of thoughtless expansion on the environment, women, and Native Americans, of the power of greed to undermine the ideals of piety, humanity, and domesticity in the rush to make and spend money. Speaking out against corruption, materialism, and prejudice, these women provide strong voices in debates about the nation and the direction it is taking during the nineteenth century. Together they would craft a "new poetry," a new ecology of expansion that would join community, stewardship, and piety in an ethos of caring and accountability, one that would enable Americans to exercise freedom and self-cultivation in the new territories of the West.

NOTES

1. John O'Sullivan, "Annexation," *United States Democratic Review* 17 (July and August 1845): 5; Terry Caesar, *Forgiving the Boundaries: Home as Abroad in American Travel Writing* (Athens: University of Georgia Press, 1995), 8; Judith Fetterley and Marjorie Pryse, *Writing Out of Place: Regionalism, Women, and American Literary Culture* (Urbana: University of Illinois Press, 2003), 259, 253.

2. Annette Kolodny, *The Land before Her: Fantasy and Experience of the American Frontiers, 1630–1860* (Chapel Hill: University of North Carolina Press, 1984), 131; Amy Kaplan, "Manifest Domesticity," *American Literature* 70, no. 3 (September 1998): 582; Caroline Kirkland, *A New Home, Who'll Follow? Or, Glimpses of Western Life* (1839; repr., New Brunswick, NJ: Rutgers University Press, 1990), 139 (hereafter cited parenthetically as *ANH*).

3. William Cullen Bryant, *Prose Writings of William Cullen Bryant*, vol. 2, *Travels, Addresses, and Comments*, ed. Parke Godwin (New York: Russell & Russell, 1964), 21.

4. Kolodny, *Land before Her*, xii–xiii; Susan Roberson, "'With the Wind Rocking the Wagon': Women's Narratives of the Way West," in *Women, America, and Movement: Narratives of Relocation*, ed. Susan Roberson (Columbia: University of Missouri Press, 1998), 228–229.

5. Lawrence Buell, *The Environmental Imagination: Thoreau, Nature Writing, and the Formation of American Culture* (Cambridge, MA: Belknap Press of Harvard University Press, 1995), 3.

6. Jessica M. Lepler, *The Many Panics of 1837: People, Politics, and the Creation of a Trans-atlantic Financial Crisis* (New York: Cambridge University Press, 2013), 19.

7. Lance Newman, "Margaret Fuller's *Summer on the Lakes, in 1843* and the Condition of America," *Transatlantic Romanticism* 38–39 (May 2005): 7 (erudit.org); Donald Worster, *Under Western Skies: Nature and History in the American West* (New York: Oxford University Press, 1992), 81; Margaret Fuller, *Summer on the Lakes, in 1843* (1844; repr., Urbana: University of Illinois Press, 1991), 75 (hereafter cited parenthetically as *SoL*).

8. William Ellery Channing, "Self-Culture," in *William Ellery Channing: Selected Writings*, ed. David Robinson (New York: Paulist Press, 1985), 226, 228, 264.

9. Newman, "Margaret Fuller's *Summer on the Lakes, in 1843*," 2.

10. Ralph Waldo Emerson, "Letter to Martin Van Buren (23 April 1838)," in *Transcendentalism: A Reader*, ed. Joel Myerson (New York: Oxford University Press, 2000), 228–229.

11. Margaret Fuller, "The Great Lawsuit. Man *versus* Men. Woman *versus* Women," in Myerson, *Transcendentalism*, 393–394.

12. William J. Peterson, "The Rock Island Railroad Excursion of 1854," *Minnesota History* 15 (December 1934): 405, 406, 409, 410; Catharine Maria Sedgwick, "The Great Excursion to the Falls of St. Anthony," *Putnam's Monthly Magazine of American Literature, Science and Art* 4 (September 1854): 320–325 (hereafter cited parenthetically as *GE*); Caesar, *Forgiving the Boundaries*, 8.

13. Peterson, "Rock Island Railroad Excursion of 1854," 412.

14. John Austin, "The Collection as Literary Form: Sedgwick's *Tales and Sketches* of 1835," in *Catharine Maria Sedgwick: Critical Perspectives*, ed. Lucinda L. Damon-Bach and Victoria Clements (Boston: Northeastern University Press, 2003), 165; Deborah Gussman, "'Equal to Either Fortune': Sedgwick's *Married or Single?* And Feminism," in Damon-Bach and Clements, *Catharine Maria Sedgwick*, 256.

15. Anne Boyd Rioux, *Constance Fenimore Woolson: Portrait of a Lady Novelist* (New York: W. W. Norton, 2016), 14.

16. Victoria Brehm, "Castle Somewhere: Constance Fenimore Woolson's Reconstructed Great Lakes," in *Constance Fenimore Woolson's Nineteenth Century: Essays*, ed. Victoria Brehm (Detroit: Wayne State University Press, 2001), 101.

17. Constance Fenimore Woolson, "Round by Propeller," in *Constance Fenimore Woolson: Selected Stories and Travel Narratives*, ed. Victoria Brehm and Sharon L. Dean (Knoxville: University of Tennessee Press, 2004), 11 (hereafter cited parenthetically as *RbP*). The essay originally appeared in *Harper's New Monthly Magazine* 45 (September 1872): 518–533.

18. Sacvan Bercovitch, *The American Jeremiad* (Madison: University of Wisconsin Press, 1978), xiii; Lawrence Buell, *Writing for an Endangered World: Literature, Culture, and Environment in the U.S. and Beyond* (Cambridge, MA: Harvard University Press, 2001), 18.

19. Dennis Berthold, "Miss Martha and Ms. Woolson: Persona in the Travel Sketches," in Brehm, *Constance Fenimore Woolson's Nineteenth Century*, 112.

CHAPTER 7

Revising Hannah Duston: Domesticity and the Frontier in Nineteenth-Century Retellings of the Duston Captivity

Chad A. Barbour

The reconciliation of domesticity and the frontier is an imperative of national expansion. White domesticity and its attendant protection emerge as a defining force of depicting expansion. The revisions of Hannah Duston's captivity narrative in the nineteenth century demonstrate the utilization of domesticity on the frontier as a means to channel expansionist desire into a productive and profitable force. Such revisions are representative of a larger force in US literature that advances claims of national exceptionalism, perpetuating and shaping the ideology of territorial acquisition with imaginings of the white settler's perseverance and courage in the face of obstacles both natural and human. The female presence on the frontier is a required component of expansion, necessitating the need for order and for "civilization" so as to facilitate the propagation of white domesticity. Duston's captivity narrative takes on a further valence of meaning when considering the nineteenth-century revisions and their proximity to the ideology and rhetoric that would become known as "manifest destiny." The protection and presence of the woman on the frontier become acknowledged as essential to expansion.

In her influential essay "Manifest Domesticity," Amy Kaplan establishes a link between domesticity and national expansion. She argues, "Domestic discourse both redresses and reenacts the contradictions of empire through its own double movement to expand female influence beyond the home and the nation while simultaneously contracting woman's sphere to police domestic boundaries against the threat of foreignness both within and without." In addition, according to Kaplan, "Domesticity makes manifest the destiny of the Anglo-Saxon race, while Manifest Destiny becomes in turn the condition for Anglo-Saxon domesticity." Significantly, Kaplan shows the centrality of white domesticity to national expansion. The wildness of the frontier must be domesticated, and in this logic that means the eradication of Native populations, the transformation of white frontiersmen into dedicated patriarchs, and the settlement of white women and children. This domestication would be viewed as a calming force on the chaos of the frontier. The reformulations of Duston's story during the nineteenth century illustrated the persuasive power of the domestic idea within the narratives of empire.[1]

Since its introduction into public life in a sermon by Cotton Mather in 1697, Hannah Duston's narrative largely conforms to a typical story of white conquest over Indians. Duston's murder of ten Abenakis, who were part of a family, was viewed as a justified and righteous act. Mather set this tone when he argued that "being where she had not her own Life secured by any Law unto her, she thought she was not forbidden by any Law to take away the Life of the Murderers, by whom her Child had been Butchered." Her heroic status in the local community can be attested to by the various markers and monuments that still stand today to commemorate her actions.[2]

Hannah Duston was taken captive on March 15, 1697, by a group of Abenakis in an attack on Haverhill, Massachusetts. Mary Neff, her nurse, was taken along with her. They joined Samuel Lennardson, a boy, who had previously been captured. Their destination was Canada, and on the way, Duston came into the company of an Abenaki family consisting of two men, three women, and seven children. Duston, with the aid of Neff and Lennardson, killed ten of the Abenakis, with two others escaping. After leaving the scene, they returned to retrieve the scalps as proof of their act—scalps that would be exchanged for bounties. These are the basic facts of Duston's experience; how they would be interpreted and translated by later writers is the focus of this chapter.

In the early nineteenth century, a revival of Duston's story occurs with a number of well-known writers telling it within a fifteen-year span: Timothy Dwight (1821), Sara Josepha Hale (1827), John Greenleaf Whittier (1831), and Nathaniel Hawthorne (1836). As well, notable artistic renderings during this time included the engraving *The Escape of the Duston Family* (1836) that is perhaps best known for its inclusion with Hawthorne's story although it was not exclusive to that appearance, and Junius Brutus Stearns's *Hannah Duston Killing the Indians* (1847).[3]

The details of Duston's story are mostly consistent in each retelling as each one relates her capture, her husband's rescue of their children, her infant's death, and her bloody escape. Variations occur in what elements of her story each writer includes or emphasizes and how each writer adjudicates the morality of her actions. Duston's murder of her captors, depending on the interlocutor, may receive approval, justification, or condemnation. At play as well in these retellings is the portrayal of gender roles and expectations. Her violation of or departure from perceived gender norms might be viewed as justified or excusable given the extraordinary circumstances. Her actions might also be condemned for their aggressiveness in contradiction to perceived womanly passivity. In some cases, she might even be barely present or excluded altogether as the writer or artist focuses on her husband and his supposed heroism in saving the Duston children (except for the newborn infant).

Two critics of note have identified significant threads in the nineteenth-century revisions. Ann-Marie Weis situates them in the context of Jacksonian ideology and its conception of family dynamics, especially in terms of a strong paternal leader, along with anxiety about changing economic and social conditions in the United States. According to Weis, Hawthorne, Whittier, and Hale sought to affirm the paternal-centered family as the social foundation for US society and culture. She concludes, "Attempting to reestablish paternal benevolence and condemning the suspicious entrepreneurship they saw lurking within Jackson's regime, Hawthorne and his contemporaries chose to revise Hannah Duston's story to portray an ideal father, who protects a family threatened to be shattered while chastising unjustified violence represented by a murderous mother." Barbara Cutter argues that the nineteenth-century revival of Duston's story facilitated a justification of American violence as innocent reprisal against attackers in service of US expansion; that, as she describes, "violence committed by the United States was, by definition, feminine, and therefore justified, innocent, defensive violence."[4]

Considering Weis and Cutter together constructs a picture of these nineteenth-century revisions as circulating within Jacksonian ideology of paternal leadership as it interacts with the absolution of violence in service of American expansion. My argument proceeds from this viewpoint to consider further how the nineteenth-century treatments of Duston's captivity incorporate domesticity in service of expansionist ideology. The nineteenth-century versions transform Hannah Duston's story from one of Puritan anti-Native propaganda to one that implements domestic elements that function to normalize national expansion as a natural extension of the family and home while addressing, explicitly or implicitly, moral ambiguity regarding the fate of Native peoples.

Nineteenth-century recollections of Duston's experience vary in how they depict her actions or whether she is even the focus of the account, but each one participates to some degree in domestic rhetoric. Hale extols the father's heroism in her poem while attending to the mother's actions in *Woman's Record*. Whittier frames Hannah's actions as necessary though they be brutal and not in accordance to a womanly ideal. Dwight's and Hawthorne's castigations of Hannah contrast with their sentimentalized view of Thomas. This domestic emphasis on Thomas Duston can also be seen in *The Escape of the Duston Family*. As well, the melodrama of *Hannah Duston Killing the Indians* illuminates the stakes of white domesticity on the frontier.

The nineteenth-century adaptations of Duston's story employ a domestic ideology that is frequently present in the sentimentalist texts of the period. Domesticity's association with order and civilization marks its space as one to be protected at all costs. Captivity narratives enact a disruption of the domestic space and the violation of whiteness: when the white wife and mother is taken away by "savages," the domestic center is removed. The white husband must regain his wife, freeing her from the potential contamination of Indianness. Captivity narratives dramatize the paranoia and fear embodied in the threat of captivity or Indian contact. This fear of the contamination of white domesticity can also be seen, for example, in such "Indian-fighting" texts as James Hall's "The Indian Hater" (1828) and Timothy Flint's "The Indian Fighter" (1830). Given these texts' proximity to the Duston stories examined in this chapter, they deserve further attention.

Hall's "The Indian Hater" demonstrates the interconnection between "Indian-fighting" and defense of white domesticity. This relationship is evident in Hall's story when Samuel Monson relates to the narrator his origins as an "Indian-hater." While sitting within the security of his home, he hears the yell of Indians and, looking at his wife, mother, and children, knows that, as he says, they "depended on me for protection." He runs to the door but is overwhelmed by "a gang of yelling savages [who] came pouring in at my door, like so many howling wolves." The "vile varmints" then set the house on fire, blocking the family from escape. Monson is finally able to escape the house but is caught and forced to watch his home burn, his family perishing inside. After escaping his captivity, Monson fashions himself "a scourge of the savage," being the "foremost in every fight" and unable to quench his bloodthirst for Indians.[5]

Less bloodthirsty and extreme, Timothy Flint's "The Indian Fighter" recounts the narrator's conversation with an unnamed "Indian Fighter" who tells his story of how he became known by that title. The "Indian Fighter" narrates how he had fallen in love with a girl, Emma. Their first romantic encounter occurs at a dance where they converse and begin to fall in love. Emma and her father leave, and the "Indian Fighter" decides to follow them due to "a mysterious intimation" that warns him of danger. He hears the sounds of attack and is able to rescue Emma and her father from death while killing his first Indian. Emma and the "Indian Fighter" are betrothed soon after. Then one night when the males of the settlement leave to help a "savage that we deemed friendly" bring in a deer, an ambush occurs on the settlement: "The yell of the savages, the dying groans of our neighbours, the sharp reports of the rifles, all ring in my ears as I think of the past. . . . The fathers and mothers, the brothers and sisters, the husbands and wives fell together. Savage knives spilled the blood of the young infants." Emma escapes the attack and is held captive. The "Indian Fighter" goes after her and finds the encampment of the captor Indians where they sleep and rescues Emma. The escape is not successful, however, as the Indians catch up with the rescue group, attacking and killing everyone except the "Indian Fighter," who is left for dead. Swearing revenge, the "Indian Fighter" leads raids on Indian villages, soon earning in the Indian's language "an appellation which imports Indian Fighter." He finally finds the band that killed his Emma and attacks their village. The massacre of those Indians that follows occurs at the hands of the Indians themselves: "Their warriors agreed to kill their women and children, and then dispatch each other. . . . All had fallen but the leader of the band. He fired the village, and came forth" to challenge the "Indian Fighter." The two fight, and the "Indian Fighter" kills his foe and gains his revenge. The conclusion takes up the trope of the vanishing American and utilizes it as divine vengeance on Indians. The "Indian Fighter" states, "That whole race is wasting away about me, like the ice in the vernal brooks."[6]

What is most notable in these stories for my argument is the significance of domesticity in them. Indians are completely antithetical to white domestic stability. Women, children, and even dogs are all the targets of what these stories convey as Indian hatred for the domestic. This fact receives further emphasis in Flint's narrative where the Indians kill their own women and children. In Robert Montgomery Bird's *Nick of the Woods* (1837), Nathan Slaughter's story participates in this same ideology of Indian hating in which Indians are condemned for their hatred of white domesticity. This maneuver is apparent in Bird's 1853 preface to *Nick* in which he argues that his "realistic" and hateful portrayal of Indians is justifiable because of "the single fact that he [the Indian] wages war—systematic war—upon beings incapable of resistance or defence,—upon women and children, whom all other races in the world, no matter how barbarous, consent to spare." The ideology of "Indian hating" found in these stories issues a call to protect white domesticity from the ravages of Indians. Defending white domesticity operates hand in hand with national expansion.[7]

In the Duston accounts by Hale and Whittier, protection of white domesticity operates through the figures of the father and mother, Thomas and Hannah. The complication in these depictions is that Hannah's actions diverge from those expected of a woman. While Thomas easily represents the heroic patriarch, evident in Hale's poem, the mother's murders must be negotiated into a domestic ideology that justifies and excuses her aberrant behavior. Hale's poem on Thomas Duston demonstrates the fulfillment of the male's obligation to protect his family, while her summary of Hannah Duston's captivity in *Woman's Record* reaffirms her heroic status. Whittier's account of Hannah Duston fixates upon the transformation of maternal love into fierce vengeance, a transformation made acceptable by the extenuating circumstances of Duston's captivity.

Hale's work in the context of my argument is best understood through the lens of Kaplan's "manifest domesticity." Kaplan addresses Hale directly in arguing, "Hale's conception of separate spheres . . . is predicated on the imperial expansion of the nation." Additionally, as Kaplan contends, "Hale's writing makes race central to woman's sphere not only by excluding nonwhites from domestic nationalism but also by seeing the capacity for domesticity as an innate, defining characteristic of the Anglo-Saxon race." This view of domesticity as a driving and defining force in expansion illuminates my reading of Hale's treatment of the Dustons in emphasizing the ideological force of their paternal and maternal figures in enacting a domestication of the frontier through both familial bonds and murderous violence.[8]

Hale's poem on Thomas Duston first appeared in *The Boston Lyceum* (1827). The poem then appeared in two anthologies during this time: Samuel Kettell's *Specimens of American Poetry* (1829) and Hale's *The Ladies Wreath: A Selection from the Female Poetic Writers of England and America* (1837). Notably for this chapter, in his *The History of Haverhill* (1832), Benjamin Mirick copies it from *The Boston Lyceum* for inclusion in his section on Duston.[9]

Hale includes a headnote in the *Lyceum* version, describing the poem's inspiration, with no mention of Hannah and her capture. Hale details how the father rescues his children from the attacking Indians, his choice being to leave no child behind: "He therefore determined to take his lot with them, and defend them from their murderers, or die by their side." He "keep[s] a resolute face to the enemy, and so effectually sheltered his charge." This explanatory note depicts Thomas Duston (though unnamed here) as the brave and heroic protector of his children, willing to leave none of them behind and, if needed, die with them rather than save himself.[10]

The poem itself progresses through typical sentimentalist tropes. For example, the cry of his children touches his heart: "When 'father!' burst from every voice, / And 'child!' his heart replied." Each of the next eight lines catalogs one of the children, assigning him or her a distinguishing trait, where the only mention of the mother exists in the reflection of two of the children: "And one that wears her mother's smile, / And one that bears her name." The rest of the poem describes the father's bravery in protecting his children against the attacking "savages." The Indian attackers are intimidated by the father's fierceness, "an ev'n that savage band / Lowered at his wrathful eye." In the face of the "hate [that] points the murderer's brand," the father remains resolute in his "love and duty" that "nerve the good man's hand." The father fights for his children, spurred on by his love for his offspring and his duty to protect them, and it is this dedication to his love and duty that strengthens him in striking down and outrunning his attackers.[11]

In all, this poem presents expected ideals of domesticity, the protective father who rescues his children from the murderous "savages." The father saves his charges, bound to them by love and duty, led by his heart to defend them even if it would cost him his own life. The poem is as notable for what it excludes as for what it includes. Hannah Duston's well-known story is present in its absence. While the poem refers to her only through her children, the actual context of the poem's events cannot be effaced. Hale's decision to focus on the father sets a precedent for some succeeding accounts in which the father receives emphasis and praise to the detriment of the mother.

Perhaps a factor in Hale's decision to focus only on the father, in addition to what many critics read as a gender bias, would be to maintain a focus on the domestic space of the home place. While the events of the poem occur outside the actual physical home (and, in fact, that home is invaded by the Indians), Hannah's experience takes her far afield of this domestic territory into the wilderness. In accord with Kaplan's concept of "manifest domesticity," Hale's emphasis in the poem would remain upon the defense of the domestic space and thus Thomas Duston's protection of his children on his land. Furthermore, if this domestic space is foundational for expansion, then the father's protection of it would supersede the mother's survival in the wilderness. A counterpoint here would be that Hannah's defeat of her captors represents the extension of maternal domesticity into the external world, and thus a force for expansion, and so Hale is ignoring or erasing that potential in her poem. If this poem were Hale's sole treatment of the Duston story, then that objection would be true. Hale does return to the story, though, and describes Hannah's side of it.

In *Woman's Record* (1853), Hale includes Duston in her massive encyclopedia of notable women throughout history from around the world. In this prose account, Hale identifies Hannah primarily as Thomas Duston's wife. Notably, Hale describes Duston's fellow captives as being useless in her murder of their captors: "The nurse, and an English boy, a prisoner, were apprised of her design, but were not of much use to her in the execution of it." Hale also keeps with the convention in many of these retellings of omitting reference to the children who were among the victims. Hale highlights, though, that Duston did not kill an Indian boy, attributing this mercy to her maternal and feminine nature: "For the avenger of blood was a woman and a mother, and could not deal a death-blow upon a helpless child." Upon her return, the people "found her as modest as brave," and Hale calls her "an American heroine."[12]

If domestic ideology underscores Hale's approach to the Duston story, then the father's actions fit more easily into those conventions. Thomas models the heroic father, connected to his family and willing to protect it. Hannah, on the other hand, does not so easily conform to domestic standards. On this point, Hannah's violent departure from feminine ideals is problematic.

Whereas for Hale we might view a justification of Hannah Duston's non-conformity to a womanly ideal through the logic of "manifest domesticity," Whittier provides another tactic to contain her nonfeminine behavior within a domestic ideology. His opening paragraph observes what is understood to be the qualities of women, that their "attributes are generally considered of a milder and purer character than those of man." The body of the paragraph catalogs those qualities associated with domestic, separate-spheres ideology. The complication here is that Hannah Duston's actions during her captivity do not conform to this way of thinking. Whittier explains that such departures occasionally occur: "Yet, there have been astonishing manifestations of female fortitude and power in the ruder and sterner trials of humanity; manifestations of a courage rising to almost a sublimity; the revelation of all those dark and terrible passions, which madden and distract the heart of manhood." Whittier then ruminates upon the demands placed on womanhood on the frontier, that the wife finds herself sometimes to be the protector and guardian of the home because of "the absent husband." Whittier identifies her motivation to violence as being born out of vengeance for the death of her child. He describes her transformation as follows:

> A new and terrible feeling came over her. It was the thirst of revenge; and from that moment her purpose was fixed. There was a thought of death at her heart—an insatiate longing for blood. An instantaneous change had been wrought in her very nature; the angel had become a demon,—and

she followed her captors, with a stern determination to embrace the earliest opportunity for a bloody retribution.

Duston's bloody purpose springs not from a primal savagery or a malicious
darkness but from what is cast here as a pure source of motherly revenge for
her infant's death. While Whittier acknowledges that transformation from domestic angel to violent demon, he casts her ensuing actions as "retribution."
This word choice is significant given its general meaning of being vengeance
for a criminal act. More important here would be the biblical usage of divine
punishment. Duston's actions are not mere bloodthirsty revenge but a divinely
ordained punishment meted out by the bereft mother. Whittier's omission of
the fact that seven of the victims are children keeps with his purpose of describing Duston's murderous act as appropriate. As with Hale, this omission
is highlighted by his attributing her sparing a boy to her maternal mercy as
he imagines her thinking, "It is a poor boy . . . a poor child, and perhaps he
has a mother!" Although Duston experiences a moment of savagery, she soon
reassumes her maternal self, practicing mercy for a child and returning home
to become a part of her community again. This sequence of violence in the
wilderness and return to the domestic space is an important feature of the
Duston story in general and represents a larger attempt to reconcile the utility
of frontier savagery with the maintenance of domestic stability.[13]

Whittier closes his account on an elegiac note, recalling a frontier past inhabited by "spirits of that stern race." Stories such as Duston's recount that
"twilight time," as Whittier calls it, whose events can call up "admiration and
horror." There is an element of the vanishing American here, but it is applied
not only to an imagined Indian disappearance but also to a disappearance
of an ancestral white American who endured the hardships and travails of
the frontier. Duston, then, represents a lost people of sterner stuff, it seems,
than Whittier's contemporaries. On this point, his account might also convey
a sense that the frontier was a place that truly tested the domestic obligations
of Americans, the duties of men and women to their families. In Whittier's
account, he demonstrates the fortitude of the mother in exceeding her womanly bounds so as to enact divine punishment upon those who would murder
infants and tear apart families. He calls his story of Duston "unvarnished,"
and his use of this term gains significance when connected to its common
appearance in slave narratives (including Whittier's own use of the term in
this context). While James Olney ascribes the use of "unvarnished" in slave
narratives to an evocation of Othello, which would not be relevant in this instance of Duston's story, Whittier's use of the term here (which predates many
of the slave narratives Olney examines) perhaps points toward its popularity

in conveying the authenticity of the story being told. With this gesture toward the authenticity of his account of Duston, Whittier argues for the importance of remembering this story, its "sacred legacy," to his contemporaries, preserving a frontier past in which the domestic ideology of family was upheld and sustained, protected to the point of violence when such violence was due and necessary.[14]

Hale and Whittier operate under an assumption that the parental violence as enacted by the Duston father and mother is justified and necessary. While Mather would have operated under an assumption of cultural and racial superiority that allowed for the violence of white settlers against their "savage" adversaries, such racialized hierarchy is not the sole driving factor for Hale and Whittier. Their description of the Dustons' actions is largely founded in a domestic ideology that allows for mother and father to fulfill their duty to home and family even through violence. Hale and Whittier do not question the ways in which this domestic ideology abets an expansionist one. On the other hand, Duston does not get a similar pass from other nineteenth-century writers such as Dwight and Hawthorne, who are particularly inimical to her actions.

Departing from the deference to Hannah Duston given by Hale and Whittier, Dwight and Hawthorne elevate Thomas Duston as the hero of the story and depreciate Hannah's actions as immoral. This shift demonizes Hannah so that, contrary to the typical captivity narrative role for white women, she symbolizes the "savagery" that threatens "civilized" values. Teresa A. Toulouse confirms this reading of Duston: her "aggressive female body becomes a major sign of what has fragmented and threatened that social body in the first place." While Toulouse's argument focuses on Mather's context, it remains an accurate statement of the threat that Duston poses in the retellings of Dwight and Hawthorne. Hale places Duston in a pantheon of great women. Whittier is willing to allow for Duston's aberrant behavior by interpreting it as the product of maternal anger, and thus keeping her within an acceptable ideological frame of domesticity. Dwight and Hawthorne resist such accommodations for Duston, criticizing her actions as despicable and abhorrent.[15]

In the early 1820s, Dwight published a four-volume travelogue, *Travels in New-England and New-York.* Dwight includes in his history and exploration of the New England countryside a short recounting of Hannah Duston's story. Preceding her murder of the Indians, Dwight offers a sympathetic view of Duston. In one instance, she is "feeble, sick, terrified beyond measure, partially clad, one of her feet bare" and at the hands of Indians who are "unfeeling, insolent, and revengeful," with murder their glory and torture their sport. The death of the infant inspires Dwight to wonder what she must have felt: "What were then the feelings of the mother?" This sympathetic attitude changes, though, after the Indians' deaths at the hands of Duston and her companions. Dwight observes that her actions might be viewed as immoral: "Whether all their sufferings, and all the danger of suffering anew, justified this slaughter may be probably questioned by you or some other exact moralist." Although not directly condemning Hannah's actions, Dwight introduces the potential of doubt toward a justification of those actions.[16]

With Thomas Duston, there is no such ambiguity. Dwight transitions from Hannah to her husband by claiming: "Whatever may be thought of the rectitude of *her* conduct, that of her husband is in every view honourable." There may be debate about whether or not Hannah was right in killing ten Indians, but there is no doubt that her husband was completely and unquestionably honorable in his protection of his children. While her situation raises tricky moral questions, her husband's situation is in the clear (as discussed earlier with Hale, Thomas's side of the story appears with more moral clarity than Hannah's and thus is easier to tell). Dwight introduces uncertainty about Hannah while asserting certainty regarding Thomas. When husband Duston engages in a gunfight with attacking Indians, he is such an "excellent marksman" that he had to be guided by Providence. Thomas's murder of Indians is ordained by a higher power; Dwight does not afford Hannah this righteous assurance. This rewarding of unquestionable honor to Thomas is equally evident in the following passage that foregrounds Thomas while marginalizing the female participants Hannah and the nurse:

> A finer succession of scenes for the pencil was hardly ever presented to the eye than is furnished by the efforts of this gallant man, with their *interesting appendages*. . . . In the *background* of some or other of these pictures might be exhibited, with powerful impression, the kindled dwelling, the sickly mother, the terrified nurse with the newborn infant in her arms, and the furious natives, surrounding them, driving them forward, and displaying the trophies of savage victory and the insolence of triumph. (emphasis added)

This passage demonstrates the bravado and eloquence with which Dwight presents the father's story (a focus that anticipates Hale's own treatment of the story). Thomas Duston rescues his children (who qualify for the whole "family," although his newborn and wife are not included). Dwight literally foregrounds the father's story, while placing the females and the infant in the background (their story is but an "interesting appendage"). Dwight, as will Hawthorne, emphasizes Thomas's gallantry and bravery as the white father against the savage foe.[17]

Story structure, too, places Thomas center stage as Dwight begins and ends with him. The reader first sees a party of Indians approaching "the house of a Mr. Dustin . . . abroad at his usual labor." Duston, a hardworking man, upon seeing the Indians, rushes to his house "with a hope of hurrying to a place of safety with his family." From hard worker to defender of his family, Thomas Duston shines in these opening lines. Then the choice: go with his fleeing seven children or stay with his lying-in wife and infant. He chooses the former, and this is how Dwight describes it:

> Her husband, despairing of rendering her any service, flew to the door, mounted his horse, and determined to snatch up the child with which he was unable to part when he should overtake the little flock. When he came up to them . . . , he was unable to make a choice, or to leave any one of the number. He therefore determined to take his lot with them and to defend them from their murderers, or die by their side.

And then ensues an intense firefight between the Indians and Thomas, who keeps "so resolute a face to his enemy" and "shelter[s] so effectually his terrified companions that he finally lodged them all, safe from the pursuing butchers, in a distant house." Dwight then attributes to Providence Thomas's boldness, marksmanship, and "the preservation of this family." Part of his family, at least; or the part that counts, the seven oldest children. Hannah and infant lie in bed, left for capture. The domestic language of the family here emphasizes the paternal role as defender and leader: he is a shepherd to a "little flock," he is willing to either defend or die with his children, and his actions here function to preserve his family, as ordained by God's will. Dwight establishes the paternal figure as *the* defender and center of the family. His acts of Indian killing are beyond reproach in his protection of his (partial) family.[18]

While Dwight presents an ambiguously tolerant view of Hannah in service to Thomas's glory, Hawthorne takes this interpretation further, more explicitly reviling Hannah and glorifying Thomas. In Hawthorne, the father and husband is the valiant hero, whereas Hannah Duston is the "awful woman," her murder of the Indians a despicable act. Appearing in the May 1836 issue of the *American Magazine of Useful and Entertaining Knowledge*, of which Hawthorne was editor at the time, "The Duston Family" relocates the centrality of the tale from "Mrs. Duston" to "Goodman Duston," raising him as the dutiful and brave husband and lowering Hannah as a "bloody old hag."[19]

According to B. Bernard Cohen, Hawthorne derived his account primarily from three sources: Mather's *Magnalia*, Samuel G. Goodrich's *Peter Parley's Method of Telling about the History of the World to Children* (1836), and Mirick's *The*

History of Haverhill. (If Hale's poem as it appears in Mirick is also included, then the number of Hawthorne's sources would actually be four.) The account in *Peter Parley's Method* is notable not only for its shaping some aspects of Hawthorne's story but also for how it affirms an expansionist ideology for an audience of children. Given that its intended audience is children, it elides the gorier aspects of the story and emphasizes the stability and security of family (Thomas goes back for his wife to find her gone, and after her escape she entertains her children with the story of her capture). With this particular rhetorical framing of the story for children in mind, its perpetuation of expansionist ideology possesses additional indoctrinating power. For example, the beginning of the attack is described in this way: "The yells of the savages, the smoke of the burning houses and the cries of the affrighted white people were the first warnings of danger." While such a dichotomy of "savages" versus "affrighted white people" is typical, its potency in shaping views of white expansion cannot be overlooked. Likewise, a detail such as "the savages had no pity" furthers the antagonistic depiction of the Native peoples. This account's resolution contains Duston's captivity to a story for her children: "She used often to tell them the story of her adventures, and they would listen with breathless interest as she gave an account of her journey, and described the wild manners of the savages." The classification of "savages" along with the softening of her captivity into something like a bedtime story works simultaneously to demonize and trivialize the Native peoples: they are uncivilized, yet easily vanquished and reduced to a subject of exotic adventure. While this account itself is perhaps most notable for being one of Hawthorne's sources (and, as Cohen shows, Hawthorne borrowed some language from it), its recitation of standard prejudices of the time in regard to Native peoples marks it as perpetuating the ideology of expansion that was dependent on the reduction of Native peoples to less than human. Given this backdrop of Hawthorne's account, one might be more attuned to how his story participates in that expansionist rhetoric.[20]

Hawthorne begins his tale, like Dwight, immediately foregrounding Thomas. "Goodman Duston" is the central figure and namesake, his wife's first name not appearing until three pages into the sketch. As with Hale and Dwight, "Goodman Duston" also gets an expanded role here, his two to three lines in Mather expanding to nearly three pages (half of the piece) of Hawthorne's account. Although "Goodman Duston" was publicly known for "rebellious and abusive behavior," in Hawthorne's telling Thomas is a valiant hero, but his heroism is defined by his fatherly defense of his children. When the attack begins, Thomas bids his children to flee, then goes in to see his wife, still in bed after giving birth. The Indian yell goes up again, and "Goodman Duston" chooses to leave his wife and follow their children: "At this terrible

instant, it appears that the thought of his children's danger rushed so power-
fully upon his heart, that he quite forgot the still more perilous situation of
his wife." Overwhelmed by feelings of fatherly love and protection, Thomas
leaves his wife to Indian capture. Hawthorne qualifies this action by assuring
the reader that Duston had "such knowledge of the good lady's character"
that he knew she "would hold her own, even in a contest with a whole tribe
of Indians." Thomas flies after his children with the impetus to save them,
"lest his whole race and generation should be blotted from the earth." This
depiction of "Goodman Duston" affirms him as the good father who ensures
the continuance of his bloodline. The preservation of his wife is relatively
less important than the preservation of his children; after all, he can remarry.
But, the loss of children, or the loss of so many (as opposed to the brutal
death of the single just-born child), presents a greater danger and threat than
the capture and loss of Hannah. Thomas not only prioritizes his children
above his wife but possesses tender feeling for them: "He felt his heart yearn
towards these seven poor helpless children, as if each were singly possessed
of his whole affections." In an echo of Hale's poem, Hawthorne provides a
detailed catalog of the children along with conjecture about their futures. This
conjecture strengthens the emphasis on the children as the future and continuance of the white family and, therefore, the necessity of Thomas to defend
them. Thomas Duston's *heart* leads him to protect his children, thus indicating
the domestic frame of Hawthorne's depiction of the father.[21]

The father's yearning heart contrasts sharply with the "hardened" heart
of "Mrs. Duston." Within the domestic paradigm, Thomas feels correctly,
his heart guiding him toward tender affection for his family, whereas Hannah
feels incorrectly, her heart not softening her actions against the Indian family.
In fact, Hawthorne's depiction of Hannah's captivity invokes sympathy for
her captors by emphasizing the domestic nature of that Indian family. Their
prayers, presented in Mather as some sort of child abuse or mistreatment, suggest to Hawthorne a domestic scene: "Yet what can be more touching than to
think of these wild Indians, in their loneliness and their wanderings, wherever
they went among the dark, mysterious woods, still keeping domestic worship,
with all the regularity of a household at its peaceful fireside." The wilderness takes on the feeling of the home and heart; these Indians transform the
"dark, mysterious woods" into a comfortable and warm domestic space. Hawthorne envisions this natural scene as a literal home, complete with "peaceful fireside." This family feeling continues to encompass the white captives:
"The barbarians sat down to what scanty food Providence had sent them, and
shared it with their prisoners, as if they had all been the children of one wig-
wam, and had grown up together on the margin of the same river within the

shadow of the forest." Hawthorne heightens the domestic unity of this group, a familial attachment that crosses racial and cultural lines: Duston, Neff, and Lennardson are siblings, children of the same family, to their Indian captors.[22]

And so, Hannah Duston's murderous act then reads as an act of betrayal and destruction of family attachment. Nature "wail[s] over her wild children" as Hannah prepares to murder them. As they commit their fatal acts, the white prisoners possess "in the doubtful gleam of the decaying fire . . . ghastly visages." Hawthorne emphasizes that children are among the victims: "little red skins" crying in sleep whose deaths are met with the narrator's protest: "But, Oh, the children!" Hawthorne then pleads with Hannah to spare them, "for the sake of the seven that have fed at your own breast." This plea sympathetically links the children that Hannah kills and the children that she nurses. Her murderous action provokes a nervous ambiguity about her power as a female. Following such merging of murderess and mother, Hawthorne unleashes his contempt for the woman: "the raging tigress" and "bloody old hag" who he wishes "had been drowned in crossing Contocook river." Hawthorne levels at Hannah such hatred and contempt, wishing that she had died to face her day of judgment, so that her story would have been lost to the world. Hawthorne sees her reward as an injustice, even into her older days when she supposedly received a pension, "as a further price of blood."[23]

Hawthorne's vitriol for Hannah continues into the concluding paragraph, where he places Hannah and her husband as polar opposites: she is the "awful woman," and he is the "tender hearted, yet valiant man." The final words further the difference between the two: "But how different is her renown from his!" Her renown is an infamy; she is a murderous woman who forsakes familial attachment for her own self-interest. "Goodman Duston," in contrast, represents kind and tender affection, as he protects and saves his children.[24]

Hawthorne's reaction to Hannah Duston has been explained in at least a couple of ways. Cynthia Brantley Johnson contends that he disparages Duston by way of rejecting "Cotton Mather as the shaper and promoter of this story and all it symbolizes." Johnson implies here that Hawthorne viewed Mather as competition for status as the mythmaker of the United States. Hawthorne's attachment to traditional gender norms has also been viewed as a rationale for his hostility toward Duston. In his analysis of *The Blithedale Romance*, T. Walter Herbert demonstrates Hawthorne's adherence to a view of womanhood as naturally passive. As Herbert contends, "Womanly aggression was pictured as a misplaced manly trait." Hannah Duston, then, violates Hawthorne's expectations for womanhood, and she upends the perceived natural order of gender roles with her aggressive actions. By this logic, Hannah goes "savage" not only in acting as an Indian in using the tomahawk but

Figure 7.1. *The Escape of the Duston Family*. Engraving from the *American Magazine of Useful and Entertaining Knowledge*, May 1836.

also in acting as a man in exhibiting aggression. Hannah's actions represent a double betrayal: she shirks both her nature as a white person and her nature as a woman.[25]

Accompanying Hawthorne's piece is the engraving *The Escape of the Duston Family* (fig. 7.1). If the painting that Dwight described were to be created, it would appear similarly to the illustration accompanying Hawthorne's "The Duston Family." Cohen shows that this engraving is based on an illustration that appears in *Peter Parley's Method*. This illustration is not exclusive to its appearance with Hawthorne, then, but for the purposes of this chapter, its significance derives greatly from its proximity to Hawthorne's account of the Dustons.[26]

In the foreground of this illustration, a group of children flee the attack, while behind them Thomas Duston, on horseback, faces backward shooting, the rifle with a cloud of gun smoke centering the picture. Farther down the road, on the right edge of the sketch, almost half the size of the fleeing children, a band of Indians stand, one among them with gun in firing position. Behind this group of Indians, a few paces back, the Duston house burns and three figures stand before it, one holding a rifle: possibly Hannah, Mary, or an Indian, but it is hard to tell. The size and proportion of the figures accentuate their relative importance in this image: the children and Thomas, appearing on the left, are much larger than the figures on the right, which are barely distinguishable. Like Dwight's imagined painting, this image emphasizes the prominence of Thomas Duston in this story, and, as I have discussed earlier, Hawthorne's essay follows suit.

This drawing echoes Hale's focus in her poem upon Thomas Duston as well. The father's figure dominates the scene, and thus his heroic protection of his children is the focus. The composition embodies visually the ideological bent of Hale, Dwight, and Hawthorne. There emerges in this scene the endowment of the father as the last and best defense of white domesticity on the frontier. His physical presence acts as a wall between the attacking Indians and the children, and thus illuminates his role as defender of the family. By erasing Hannah from the scene, this engraving, like Hale's poem and Dwight's and Hawthorne's essays, sidesteps the problematic presence of Hannah, whether it be for her nonconformity to gender roles or for her potentially showing up her husband in her fierceness to maintain her white domesticity.

While these depictions of Hannah Duston encounter her actions uneasily or with disdain, Junius Brutus Stearns's painting (plate 8) takes on her actions without flinching and portraying her as the heroic vanquisher of Indians. The painting stages a triangle between the three women with an Indian male between them, his attempt to stop Duston frozen in its futility. In this particular detail Stearns departs from the history and makes a similar divergence by including three white women instead of Duston and Neff and the boy, Lennardson. Linda Kim supposes that the inclusion of Lennardson "would have diluted the potency of Duston's agency" while also maintaining a gender symmetry between the captives and captors. Furthermore, no children are present, and all the victims depicted seem to be men. Duston's position is in the center of the painting, and her colors of yellow and white, her whiteness, even, glow in contrast to the darker hues of the Indians and the landscape.[27]

Lauren Lessing provides a powerful analysis of the painting, arguing that it "evokes a theatrical performance through the fanciful costumes and expressive poses of its figures, and through its lighting and composition." Her analysis poses a significant enhancement for my argument, as well, in her linkage of the painting to the popular melodramas of the time, especially such performances as Edwin Forrest's as Metamora in John Augustus Stone's 1829 play of the same name. As Lessing shows, the melodramatic element of this scene evokes the vanishing Indian in parallel to the victorious settler. This painting operates on two ideological planes, then: one is the evident depiction of the white settler overcoming Indian "savagery." Duston's murder of her captors reads as triumph over those foes who would stand in the way of a supposed Anglo-European inheritance of the American land. Parallel to this image is that of the death of the Indians. When this painting is viewed in concert with the melodramas of the noble Indian's last stand and the vanishing-Indian mythos of the early nineteenth century, the scene takes on a sorrowful tone regarding the perceived necessity of Native depopulation. Duston's act reads in this regard as a necessary evil; though these Indian deaths might invoke sympathy, ultimately the Natives' demise is viewed as a necessity for the westward progress of a white nation. If they had acquiesced and accepted the inevitable expansion, this line of thought goes, these Indians could have lived out the rest of their days in peace on some western reservation. The painting conveys this dual meaning perhaps more explicitly than the prose renderings of this scene.[28]

Hawthorne's sentimental histrionics in bewailing the death of the Indian children conjures sympathy toward Duston's victims, but this sympathy operates more toward supporting Hawthorne's attack on Duston rather than a genuine concern for the slain Indians. Stearns's painting, in contrast, depicts the sleeping Indians soon to be murdered yet also includes one of them awake, trying to stop Duston. The inclusion of this detail, which is not present in any telling of the story, adds the element of human agency and feeling in the Indian subjects. Stearns depicts this Indian as focusing on the tomahawk, his hands reaching for it. He aims to arrest Duston's swing of the weapon. Notably, this posture focuses him on the weapon but not on Duston herself. A different dynamic would be in effect if this Indian were to be reaching for Duston's body. Such a gesture, forecasting physical contact between an Indian male body and a white female body, would read as disturbing. Instead, his reaching for the weapon negates the potential unease of bodily contact between the two and focuses the viewer's attention on the Indian's struggle to survive. This positioning works more effectively to invoke sympathy for the Indian.

The dual depiction of aggrandizement of white victory and sympathy for the defeated Indian can also be seen in Horatio Greenough's *The Rescue* (1837–1853) (fig. 7.2), a sculpture that depicts a physical encounter between a white frontiersman and an Indian male. A woman and child cower on the side as the frontiersman successfully pins back the Indian's arms, the white male towering over his combatant, gripping the Indian's right wrist that holds a now ineffective tomahawk. The idealized body of the Indian evinces some

Figure 7.2. National Photo Company, *Rescue Statue*, ca. 1926. Glass negative. Photograph of Horatio Greenough's *The Rescue*. National Photo Company Collection, Library of Congress.

admiration in the audience, but his strength has been neutralized by the frontiersman. This sculpture, then, presents an admirable Indian male body posed in submission to an admirable white male body.[29]

The connections between Stearns's painting and Greenough's sculpture are compelling. For instance, these two pieces work inversely. In the painting, an Indian male unsuccessfully attempts to stop a white female from attacking his family with a tomahawk. In the sculpture, a white male successfully stops an Indian male from attacking his family with a tomahawk. Additionally, these two pieces interact on a thematic level in that both depict the triumph of white settlers over Indian foes. The titles as well deliver such a theme. Yet, the works' depiction of such triumph contains some ambiguity in the presentation of the Indian foes as sympathetic to some degree. Situating *Hannah Duston Killing the Indians* in concert with *The Rescue* illuminates a general ambiguity in the early nineteenth-century United States regarding national expansion and the plight of Native peoples. The dominant meaning of these pieces conveys the exceptionalist rhetoric of white superiority and the necessary vanquishing of Indians, but there lie within them glimmers of uncertainty, or at least hints of regret, regarding the course of national advancement.

As the United States expanded its borders, a tension would arise between the necessary wildness of the frontier and the desire for domestic stability. Although it would be necessary to venture into the wilderness, to attend to the pushing out of the borders of the nation, one always must return to the domestic space, reaffirming one's attachment to white domesticity. The perceived savagery of the frontier was seen to give way to domestication, and during the nineteenth century, this progression is reenacted in many texts. The early nineteenth-century accounts of Hannah Duston's captivity are no exception. These accounts seek to contain the brutality of Duston's actions (deemed as necessary for the success of expansion) by parsing her violence as maternal vengeance or outright condemning it. These two strategies are counterbalanced by the depiction of her husband as the heroic defender of white domesticity. The violence of the frontier represented by Duston's captivity is contained by the stability of white domesticity. Notably, this relationship is a reversal of the typical paradigm found in most other texts of this time. Usually the white frontiersman required the balance of a female counterpart. The feminine influence tempered the wildness of the male, bringing him back home and taming his baser impulses. Duston's captivity departs from this paradigm, and so these nineteenth-century accounts work to make sense of her experience and negotiate its terms to produce a domestic ideology that serves the needs of expansion.

The rhetorical power of Duston's story can further be seen in its reappearance more than one hundred years later in a *Wonder Woman* comic. A prose piece appears in issue number eighty-nine titled, "Fabulous Females." The piece opens with its premise: "Throughout history there have been women who deeply felt that whatever a man could do, they could do better." Duston is credited with beginning this "trend." The author attributes to Duston a feminist sensibility: "But Hannah fumed at this role of the weaker sex which was forced upon her. And she insisted all along that there was no reason why women couldn't make as good Indian fighters as the men." The piece goes on to describe her using a musket to shoot and skill "ten of the raiding red men," which "set a record." The alteration to the original story moves her location, it seems, to a home space that is being raided. Shooting the attackers rather than killing them with a tomahawk depicts her in a more "civilized" fashion. And her actions are framed as a demonstration of female competency relative to men. I close with this example so as to contrast the ideological terms of this piece from 1957 with those of the nineteenth-century accounts. The earlier accounts obviously aim to satisfy a different set of needs: abetting the desire for expansion while maintaining appropriate foundations in white domesticity. The *Wonder Woman* piece has no need for such rhetorical moves and thus takes on the question of female value and capability, arguing for the ability of women to perform as well as men. This twentieth-century account not only demonstrates the malleability of Duston's meaning but also highlights the expansionist ideology circulating in and around the nineteenth-century versions of her story.[30]

Hannah Duston's story represents the powerful pull of expansionist ideology, a pull most evident in the multiple revisions and retellings that emerge in the nineteenth century. Her murder of a group of Native persons echoes and embodies the larger push to rid the continent of the indigenous presence so as to make way for the imagined ordained advancement of a white nation. This national advancement couples with the domestic symbolism of Duston as a woman; her presence in the frontier space points to the importance of the feminine presence and its role in furthering that advancement. This facet is true of the captivity narrative in general, a story line that enacted threats to frontier womanhood and, usually, its survival in the face of such threats. Duston's story not only dramatizes the perseverance of the American female in the face of danger and death but also empowers her to carry out the bloody violence of US expansion while also being the dutiful mother and wife. While such coupling of these roles spurs some criticism, ultimately her story demonstrates a potent combination of the ideologies of "manifest destiny" and white domesticity.

NOTES

1. Amy Kaplan, "Manifest Domesticity," *American Literature* 70 (September 1998): 585, 587.

2. Cotton Mather, *Days of Humiliation: Times of Affliction and Disaster*, ed. George Harrison Orians (Gainesville, FL: Scholars' Facsimiles and Reprints, 1970), 185. On monuments of Duston, see Barbara Cutter, "The Female Indian Killer Memorialized: Hannah Duston and the Nineteenth-Century Feminization of American Violence," *Journal of Women's History* 20 (Summer 2008): 10–33.

3. This fifteen-year period includes significant developments of US expansion, especially with the Indian Removal Act of 1830. Henry David Thoreau's 1849 account of Duston in *A Week on the Concord and Merrimack Rivers* is worth noting but falls outside the scope of this analysis.

4. Ann-Marie Weis, "The Murderous Mother and the Solicitous Father: Violence, Jacksonian Family Values, and Hannah Duston's Captivity," *American Studies International* 36 (February 1998): 61; Cutter, "Female Indian Killer Memorialized," 26.

5. James Hall, *The Wilderness and the War Path* (1846; repr., New York: Garrett Press,

1969), 150, 151. For this story's publication history, see Richard Drinnon, *Facing West: The Metaphysics of Indian-Hating and Empire-Building* (Minneapolis: University of Minnesota Press, 1980), 204.

6. Timothy Flint, "The Indian Fighter," in *The First West: Writing from the American Frontier 1776–1860*, ed. Edward Watts and David Rachels (New York: Oxford University Press, 2002), 232–239.

7. Robert Montgomery Bird, *Nick of the Woods* (1837; repr., New York: American Book Company, 1939), 5.

8. Kaplan, "Manifest Domesticity," 592, 596.

9. Benjamin Mirick, *The History of Haverhill, Massachusetts* (Haverhill: A. W. Thayer, 1832), 93–95.

10. The headnote appears with the poem in *Specimens of American Poetry* (1829) and *The Ladies' Wreath* (1837), although in the latter one, she names the father but does so mistakenly as "Mr. Thurston." Sara Josepha Hale, "The Father's Choice," in *The Boston Lyceum*, 2 vols. (Boston: True and Greene, 1827), 1:85.

11. Hale, "Father's Choice."

12. Sara Josepha Hale, *Woman's Record, from the Creation to A.D. 1869*, 3rd ed. (New York: Harper and Brothers, 1876), 291, 292.

13. John Greenleaf Whittier, "The Mother's Revenge," in *American Voices, American Lives: A Documentary Reader*, ed. Wayne Franklin (New York: W. W. Norton, 1997), 120, 121, 122.

14. Whittier, 122; James Olney, "'I Was Born': Slave Narratives, Their Status as Autobiography and as Literature," *Callaloo* 20 (Winter 1984): 62–63.

15. Teresa A. Toulouse, "Hannah Duston's Bodies: Domestic Violence and Colonial Male Identity in Cotton Mather's *Decennium Luctuosum*," in *A Centre of Wonders*, ed. by Janet M. Lindman and Michele L. Tarter (Ithaca, NY: Cornell University Press, 2001), 194. For his characterization of the role of white women in captivity narratives as "symbolizing the values of civilization imperiled by savagery," see also Richard Slotkin, *Fatal Environment: The Myth of the Frontier in the Age of Industrialization, 1800–1890* (Norman: University of Oklahoma Press, 1985), 102.

16. Timothy Dwight, *Travels in New-England and New-York*, 4 vols. (New Haven, CT: Timothy Dwight, 1821), 1:412, 413.

17. Dwight, *Travels*, 1:414.

18. Dwight, *Travels*, 1:411.

19. Nathaniel Hawthorne, "The Duston Family," *American Magazine of Useful and Entertaining Knowledge* 2 (May 1836): 395–397

20. Samuel G. Goodrich, *Peter Parley's Method of Telling about the History of the World to Children* (Hartford, CT: F. J. Huntington, 1836), 37, 39; B. Bernard Cohen, "The Composition of Hawthorne's 'The Duston Family,'" *New England Quarterly* 21 (June 1948): 236–237, 238.

21. Hawthorne, "Duston Family," 395, 396; Gordon Sayre, *American Captivity Narratives* (Boston: Houghton Mifflin, 2000), 180. For information on Hannah Duston's sister, Elizabeth Emerson, who had been executed for killing her twin children, see

Laurel Thatcher Ulrich, *Good Wives: Image and Reality in the Lives of Women in Northern New England 1650–1750* (New York: Alfred A. Knopf, 1982), 184–185, 197, 235.

22. Hawthorne, "Duston Family," 396–397.

23. Hawthorne, 397.

24. Hawthorne, 397.

25. Cynthia Brantley Johnson, "Hawthorne's Hannah Dustan [*sic*] and Her Troubling American Myth," *Nathaniel Hawthorne Review* 27 (Spring 2001): 31; T. Walter Herbert, *Dearest Beloved: The Hawthornes and the Making of the Middle-Class Family* (Berkeley: University of California Press, 1993), 11.

26. Cohen, "Composition of Hawthorne's 'The Duston Family,'" 237.

27. Linda Kim, "Hannah Duston Killing the Indians," in *Art at Colby: Celebrating the Fiftieth Anniversary of the Colby College Museum of Art*, ed. Joseph N. Newland (Waterville, ME: Colby College Museum of Art, 2009), 86.

28. Lauren Lessing, "Theatrical Mayhem in Junius Brutus Stearns's *Hannah Duston Killing the Indians*," *American Art* 28 (Fall 2014): 85, 88, 89–90.

29. See also Chad A. Barbour, *From Daniel Boone to Captain America: Playing Indian in American Popular Culture* (Jackson: University Press of Mississippi, 2016), 45–47.

30. "Fabulous Females," in *Wonder Woman* 89 (April 1957).

CHAPTER 8

Autobiography across Borders: Reading John Dunn Hunter's Memoirs of a Captivity among the Indians of North America from Childhood to the Age of Nineteen

Andy Doolen

By the time John Dunn Hunter arrived in London in 1823, his *Memoirs of a Captivity among the Indians of North America from Childhood to the Age of Nineteen* was in its third edition, and Hunter was a celebrity.[1] The British gentry held lavish parties in his honor, marveled at his stories about growing up with the Kaws and the Osages, and lauded his seemingly natural sense of gentility and integrity. Hunter's book touted indigenous traditions, intelligence, and character and expressed his affection for the families who had adopted him and treated him as one of their own. Being raised so close to nature in the North American interior, and so far from the vices of modern society, made him a unique and beguiling figure. This was the age of British romanticism, after all, and the "American savage" seemed to have been transported magically from the primeval forests of North America to the industrial metropolis of London.[2]

Using the *Memoirs* to impugn the United States for its treatment of American Indians, British reviewers sparked a rancorous transatlantic debate about Hunter's credibility. Lewis Cass, the governor and superintendent of Indian affairs for the Michigan Territory, initiated a campaign to prove that Hunter was an imposter. Cass scoured the *Memoirs* for inaccuracies and falsehoods. He reviewed War Department reports on indigenous activity in Missouri, where Hunter claimed to have spent his childhood, solicited information from government officials and fur traders in the region, and consulted recognized experts on American Indians. Cass published his attack on Hunter in the *North American Review* in January 1826, just as Congress returned to debate a bill on Indian Removal. The timing was no accident. Cass and Jared Sparks, the editor of the *North American Review*, calculated that the article, written by one of the most powerful officials in the US West, would ease the bill's passage.[3]

The belief that Hunter was an imposter has remained remarkably consistent ever since the campaign to silence him in 1826 and 1827. He remains an obscure historical figure. Nearly fifty years ago, in the only book-length study of Hunter to date, Richard Drinnon established that the major charges against Hunter were flimsy, mostly either false or unprovable. Drinnon conceded that Hunter withheld some details about his past, as autobiographers are wont to do, and likely invented some others, but that did not make him a charlatan. However, Drinnon's exhaustive defense could not break the consensus formed back in 1826 and 1827: with few exceptions, historical scholarship describes Hunter as either an imposter or a suspicious character.[4] The roots of this problem are traceable back to that precarious moment of fact creation, when the allegations of imposture, introduced by his enemies, entered historical discourse as practically unopposed truths. In the production of national histories, as Michel-Rolph Trouillot reminds us, racial disparities and biases corrupt the creation of facts, inevitably forming a discursive process that silences the experiences of subjugated peoples.[5]

Hunter's "mixed" identity was one reason his adversaries viewed him as an imposter. Cross-cultural individuals like Hunter, who seemed both white and Indian, and who moved fluidly across borders, were very difficult to taxonomize in an era of ethnic cleansing. He challenged the settler nation's prevailing racial and cultural categories. Extending the doctrine of discovery into the nineteenth century, the United States rationalized the acquisition of indigenous lands by classifying who was, and was not, an "Indian." Definitions of Indianness—essentially, "savages" who roamed over lands they neither improved nor occupied—helped to do the work of territorial conquest. "Native peoples were held to be so different," Maureen Konkle writes, "an anachronistic relic of an early moment in the history of man locked in a state of nature without history and without a future, that they would rapidly disappear when confronted with the pinnacle of human civilization, the new United States."[6] The idea of a separate and doomed race of indigenous peoples articulated a logic of elimination that keyed the development of settler states worldwide.[7]

Hunter's *Memoirs* challenges that logic of elimination at a moment when the United States was rapidly expanding into the lands west of the Mississippi River. In writing his personal narrative, Hunter faced a fundamental problem of representation—there was no adequate textual form, certainly not captivity or conversion narratives, for relating his exceptional life story.[8] He was a white individual raised by sympathetic indigenous families, who adopted him and who cared for him like their own son. Despite being falsely billed as a captivity narrative, Hunter's *Memoirs* diverged sharply from the genre's imperial logic. He discarded the genre's key assumptions about savage and inferior Indians, embraced racial and cultural mixture and indeterminacy, and highlighted the ways American Indians were reconstituting themselves in the rapidly changing borderlands west of the Mississippi. In sum, he defied the settler nation's binary models of identity formation.

This chapter proposes that Hunter addressed these problems of representation by composing a dynamic border narrative, thereby eschewing a specific genre or any preconceived definitions of Indianness. Of that class of border literature that articulates alternatives to empire building, Hunter's *Memoirs* offers a history of contested North American lands, as seen through the eyes of an adopted indigenous son.[9] He challenges prevailing theories of vanishing indigenous cultures, calls attention to predatory settlers and officials, and evokes empathy for American Indians trapped in the path of expansion. Like many oppositional border narratives, Hunter's *Memoirs* did not valorize empire building or ignore its devastating effects on American Indians. The book inevitably provoked US officials and leading "Indian experts," particularly when British critics began using it as a political cudgel. As Robert Gunn recently put it, the *Memoirs* "represented a multipronged threat to their bid for narrative control of a program of westward expansion."[10] In contrast to Hunter, US officials claimed that American Indians were destined to disappear; characterized expansion as an orderly and fair process; praised the guiding light of laws, moral principles, and ethnological studies; and recommended Indian Removal as a humane strategy. Little wonder, then, that Lewis Cass and his allies rejected Hunter's *Memoirs* as a hoax.

This chapter begins by reconsidering the stigma of imposture that continues to shadow John Dunn Hunter. As an established authority on the US West, Cass possessed more than enough political and discursive power to discredit him. In the *North American Review*, he wrote with the supreme confidence of a colonial administrator with a bird's-eye view of the continental interior, whose position and expertise gave him the extraordinary power to locate the whereabouts of indigenous nations at all times. Demonstrating his clout, Cass accuses Hunter of inventing the most significant moment in his life—that

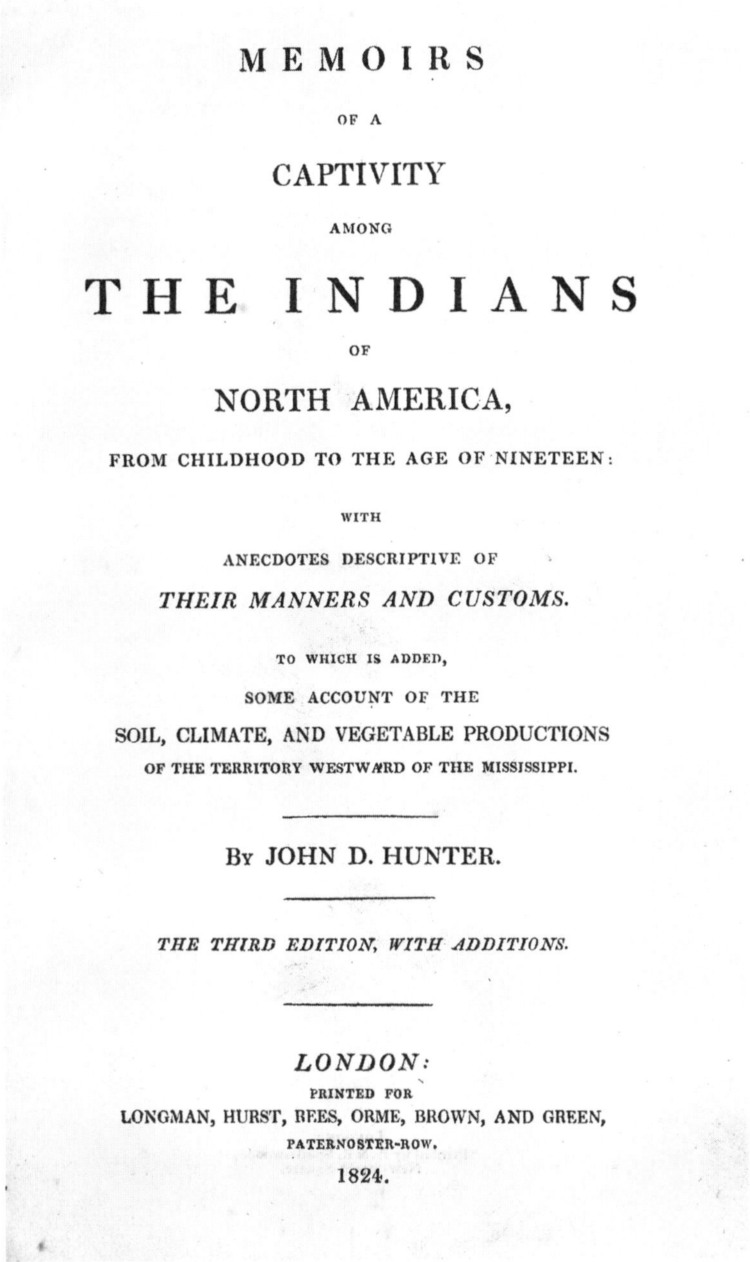

MEMOIRS

OF A

CAPTIVITY

AMONG

THE INDIANS

OF

NORTH AMERICA,

FROM CHILDHOOD TO THE AGE OF NINETEEN:

WITH

ANECDOTES DESCRIPTIVE OF

THEIR MANNERS AND CUSTOMS.

TO WHICH IS ADDED,

SOME ACCOUNT OF THE

SOIL, CLIMATE, AND VEGETABLE PRODUCTIONS

OF THE TERRITORY WESTWARD OF THE MISSISSIPPI.

By JOHN D. HUNTER.

THE THIRD EDITION, WITH ADDITIONS.

LONDON:
PRINTED FOR
LONGMAN, HURST, REES, ORME, BROWN, AND GREEN,
PATERNOSTER-ROW.
1824.

Figure 8.1. Title page. *Memoirs of a Captivity among the Indians of North America*, 3rd ed. London: Longman, Hurst, Rees, Orme, Brown, and Green, 1824.

Kickapoo raiders massacred Hunter's family on the Illinois frontier and then took him captive. Cass alleges it was pure fiction. Not only were there no reports of the Kickapoos living west of the river around 1800, but an authority no less than William Henry Harrison, governor of Indiana Territory at the time, also had informed Cass that the story must be bogus. If the Kickapoos had seized a white child on the Illinois border around 1800, Harrison said, the incident "would have electrified the whole country west of the [Appalachian] mountains."[11] Adding more evidence to his case, Cass states that he received the same report from both William Clark, the famed explorer and former governor of Missouri, and Pierre Choteau, a prominent St. Louis fur trader. Both men found it implausible that they would have been unaware of a white boy living with a tribe under their jurisdiction.

Cass's presumed dominion over indigenous space led him to charge Hunter with fabricating other moments of his life story, such as the time he witnessed Tecumseh deliver a rousing address to an Osage village. So much of Hunter's childhood could not be easily corroborated by historical records, but some information on Tecumseh's movements could be found in the War Department archives. Cass introduced a report that claimed the Shawnee warrior's travels never brought him near the Osages in Missouri: "No Shawnese [*sic*] had, in 1812, ever visited the Osage as a friend, nor was Tecumthe [*sic*] ever within many hundred miles of a party of that nation."[12] The power of his office gave Cass the opportunity to convert Hunter's memory into a highly controversial claim. Nevertheless, historical researchers have cited contemporaneous evidence from travelers, fur traders, and Indian agents that puts Tecumseh in Missouri, and near the Osages, around the same time.[13]

Cass was just as certain that no Osage or Kaw had ever crossed the Rocky Mountains, which called into question Hunter's amazing story about a journey to the Pacific Ocean in the company of an adventurous band of Osage and Kaw hunters. Perhaps the most damaging evidence that Cass introduced against Hunter was the testimony of a Missouri legislator named John Dunn—he denied ever meeting the young man who said that he had taken his mentor's name. (Even this evidence is flawed; as Drinnon points out, Cass may have misled John Dunn, pressured him to disavow Hunter, or simply found the wrong Dunn.) By the time Cass was through with him, Hunter's credibility was ruined. He appeared to be an imposter with no firsthand experience of a remote frontier that Cass and other officials professed to know in great detail. After the *North American Review* published the essay, a number of acknowledged authorities on American Indians, including William Clark, Jared Sparks, Henry Rowe Schoolcraft, Peter Stephen Duponceau, and Stephen Austin, dutifully attacked Hunter's legitimacy. They essentially repeated the allegations and evidence that Cass had provided in his essay.[14]

The repetition of accepted truths about Hunter, ongoing since 1826, has always glossed over a stubborn fact: some notable friends and supporters did not question his integrity or his identity. Thomas Jefferson corresponded with Hunter, and they visited at Monticello to discuss Hunter's plans for founding an indigenous settlement west of the Mississippi. The arctic explorer Sir John Franklin also knew Hunter; he praised Hunter's study of indigenous culture as one of the best he had ever read on the subject, and defended him against the charges of imposture.[15] George Catlin, the renowned painter and ethnologist, who lived intermittently with the Osages during the 1830s, verified Hunter's story of living with the Osages by consulting the chiefs mentioned in Hunter's book. Herman Mayo, a newspaper editor from Nacogdoches, accompanied Hunter to a Cherokee village and was regaled by stories about Hunter's time with the Osages. Richard Fields, the mixed-race Cherokee chief, regarded Hunter as a partner in their fight for a free homeland in the Red River valley in Mexican Texas. Finally, even a staunch enemy like the US novelist John Neal acknowledged that Hunter hailed from the western territory. The two authors had become friends in the London rooming house they shared, and Neal had witnessed the British gentry fawn over the "North American Crusoe." Even though Neal thought the captivity story was a hoax, he believed that Hunter was from the backcountry, very likely the child of an indigenous woman and a French or Anglo fur trader.[16]

The timeline of the attacks on Hunter is crucial to understanding and clarifying this murky history. During his time in England, there was no debate over his identity. He was recognized as an exotic American borderer on a humanitarian mission to establish a settlement for besieged American Indians west of the Mississippi. Hunter was seeking British backers for a settlement plan that was attached to the third edition of his *Memoirs*. He departed England in the spring of 1824 to pursue his project in North America. Traveling west in the company of Robert Owens, who was headed to New Harmony, Indiana, Hunter eventually made his own way down the Mississippi to New Orleans. By early 1825, he had reached Arkansas, but it was a very different Arkansas than the one he had left eight years earlier. The surge of white settlers, the seizures of tribal lands, the organization of government, and the expansion of the fur trade had devastated the foundations of indigenous life.[17] His plan to establish a free settlement had no chance of succeeding—it was clear that the settlers pouring into the region would never respect indigenous claims on the land. Driven from their villages and hunting grounds, American Indians migrated westward beyond the US boundary or southward into Mexican Texas. After failing to find his adopted Kaw and Osage families in Missouri, Hunter also decided to cross the border into Texas in search of a Quapaw band that he knew.

By March 1826, when Hunter reappeared on the international stage in Mexico City, there was still no debate over his identity. A member of a pan-Indian coalition in northeastern Texas, Hunter had been appointed its emissary to the Mexican government. In the capital, Hunter lobbied officials for a land grant on the northern border, pledging that the territory would be the home of thirty thousand Native peoples, who would be forever grateful and loyal to the new Mexican republic. Their presence on the border might stabilize the remote province and check US expansion; while this prospect intrigued Mexican officials, it alarmed the US envoy, Joel Poinsett. He believed that the United States could soon purchase Texas, as long as Mexico did not sanction any sovereign indigenous territories, so he pressured Mexico to reject the application.

The heated debate over Hunter's identity commenced a few weeks later, when Hunter had already returned to Texas. He was likely unaware of the debate, and he never had the opportunity to vindicate himself. After he informed his coalition's governing council about Mexico's refusal to give them a land grant, it abandoned any further diplomatic efforts and began preparing for direct action. In a fateful move, the coalition allied with a faction of disaffected Anglo settlers led by Benjamin and Haden Edwards. They debated the terms of their alliance, established a governing compact, and declared their independence in the name of the Red and White Republic of Fredonia. However, the fighters who were supposed to flock to its banner never materialized, the alliance splintered, and Mexican troops soon crushed the uprising. Hunter died on the plains outside of Nacogdoches, likely assassinated by Cherokee warriors, who had become enemies after Hunter and other members of the movement united with the Anglo faction.[18]

I have argued elsewhere that Hunter's activism in the Red River valley, if only we acknowledge it, challenges the conventional wisdom about his *Memoirs*.[19] Even if its publication predates the Fredonian Rebellion by three years, his book provides a rare perspective on the life of one of the movement's leaders and the possible origins of his political philosophy. In this light, his *Memoirs* hardly seems like a hoax. Hunter had been entrusted with the mission to Mexico City to acquire a land grant. When the strategy shifted to direct action, Hunter and the Cherokee chief Richard Fields traveled through the Red River valley in an effort to unify the confederacy and recruit fighters. Herman Mayo, who collaborated with Hunter on the Fredonian treaty, had witnessed

Hunter's activism in the valley. After Hunter was killed, Mayo wrote a eu-
logy that praised his character. In sum, Hunter's experience in the resistance
movement suggests that he was knowledgeable of indigenous ways of being in
and understanding the world, as Gunn affirms in his brilliant examination of
Hunter's use of Plains Indian sign language.[20]

If not for the fraud charges, Hunter's *Memoirs* would surely be grouped with
the life stories of his two contemporaries, Mary Jemison and John Tanner,
both of whom were taken captive as children, spent much of their lives as
adopted members of indigenous nations, absorbed their beliefs and traditions,
and constructed complex cross-cultural identities.[21] As a result, Jemison, Tanner, and Hunter did not write from the perspective of captives held against
their will and yearning to be reunited with their white countrymen, and so
their autobiographies subverted a textual form that was integral to nineteenth-
century discourse on the "Indian" and Indianness. Some traditional expectations define the captivity genre: the captive must survive a series of trials,
typically cultural, racial, or religious in nature, before being redeemed from
the "savages" and reassimilated into white society. The autobiographies by
Jemison, Tanner, and Hunter do not fulfill these expectations. In Hunter's
case, he neither demonizes American Indians nor ridicules their ancient traditions nor frets about "going Native." Hunter would eventually return to the
United States, but his *Memoirs* does not depict it as a victory over an inferior
culture. Perhaps this explains why the word "captivity" does not even appear
in the title of the first Philadelphia edition of the *Memoirs*. This edition emphasized Hunter's ethnographic study of indigenous cultures west of the Mississippi, which constitutes the bulk of the book. It was the London edition, and a
publisher looking to capitalize on the popular captivity genre, that released the
book under a new title—*Memoirs of a Captivity among the Indians of North America
from Childhood to the Age of Nineteen*.[22]

I believe that Hunter's *Memoirs* has more in common with nineteenth-
century Native American autobiography than with any other genre of written discourse. Authors such as Samson Occom (Mohegan), William Apess
(Pequot), George Copway (Ojibwe), and Black Hawk (Sauk) composed "bicultural documents" that drew from both indigenous and Anglo-American
autobiographical traditions.[23] These authors occupied precarious social spaces
in the United States—contact zones, as Mary Louise Pratt defines them,
where "peoples geographically and historically separated come into contact with each other and establish ongoing relations, usually involving conditions of coercion, radical inequality, and intractable conflict."[24] American
Indians during the nineteenth century composed autobiographies that were
the textual equivalent of contact zones. Their narratives negotiated cultural

differences and unequal power relations, interjected indigenous histories into settler national discourse, signified on settler histories of conquest, contested expansionist practices and policies, and envisioned geographic borderlands less defined by racial and ethnic absolutism.[25]

Conceiving of Native American autobiography as a border narrative complicates the controversial concept of authenticity that is integral to the genre. Philip Deloria outlines this imperfect standard for evaluating indigenous authors and texts. Scholars measure Indianness *in degrees* by factoring in the author's closeness to a combination of four variables: time (primitive past), space (frontier), culture (tribal traditions), and race (indigeneity).[26] As a result, the authenticity of some nineteenth-century figures seems obvious and uncomplicated. For instance, Black Hawk was a full-blooded Sauk warrior from a remote frontier, spoke no English, refused to assimilate, and took up arms against the United States. For good reason, then, nobody has ever questioned his authenticity. The problem arises when measuring the degrees of Indianness of someone like William Apess, one of the so-called Christian or civilized Indians of New England. Of mixed ancestry (Pequot, African, and white), Apess grew up in abject poverty in Rhode Island and was abused by his Pequot family members. The state eventually took custody of him and indentured him to several white families in New England. He learned how to read and write, joined the US military as a drummer boy in the War of 1812, and soon experienced a religious awakening. Practicing a Christian faith that did not discriminate based on skin color, Apess subsequently wrote the autobiography that certified him as a Methodist minister in 1829 and launched his remarkable, if brief, career as a writer and an activist.[27]

Until relatively recently, scholars attributed the least amount of authenticity to Apess, pigeonholing him as a Christian convert disconnected from American Indians and their cultures and concerns. Even his white readers at the time did not regard him as being sufficiently Indian; they preferred the "as-told-to" autobiography of Black Hawk, which appeared a few years later.[28] Even in translation, that text seems to promise the rare opportunity to hear a pure, timeless, authentic indigenous voice. As Susan Scheckel argues, "The real 'unadulterated' Indian is a wild Indian, and by definition wild Indians do not write. For an Indian, then, the only way the 'real' can be recorded and history preserved is through an act of representation performed by a white."[29] It was not only the fact that Apess wrote his autobiography that marked him as inauthentic. The critical decision, by scholars, to place *A Son of the Forest* within the genre of the Christian conversion narrative also inevitably narrowed our perspective on Apess's identity and obscured his complex narrative practices. Even the most astute scholars were slow to recognize that Apess actually had authored a multifaceted border narrative about his coming of age in New England during a period marked by the escalation of ethnic cleansing.[30]

Methods for measuring Indianness, flawed as they may be, are designed to subvert an exploitative American tradition of cultural misappropriation. Dating back to the costumed Indians at the Boston Tea Party and earlier, Anglo-Americans defined their sense of national character by imitating the stereotypes and myths about American Indians and their cultures. A settler nation of immigrants used Indianness to proclaim their unifying whiteness and Christianity, their spirit of independence, and their claim on the lands supposedly bequeathed to them.[31] During the subsequent Indian mania of the 1820s, when Hunter became an international celebrity, the settler nation's imaginary Indian circulated through a wide range of narratives, including the frontier romances of James Fenimore Cooper, Lydia Maria Child, and Catharine Maria Sedgwick, the stage dramas such as *Pocahontas* and *Metamora*, and captivity narratives. The figure of the dying Indian hero, and a white audience who wept over his vanishing into the atmosphere like melting snow, was an integral part of the politics and the ideology of Indian Removal.[32]

Given the long history of "playing Indian" in the United States, some evidence of legitimacy traceable back to indigenous ancestors and tribal membership seems like a reasonable rule for protecting the integrity of Native American literary history. At least, the rule seems reasonable until we encounter the autobiographies by Hunter, Tanner, and Jemison. Nowhere in *Playing Indian* does Deloria say exactly how we should evaluate the bicultural narratives of these acculturated white authors. Hunter's *Memoirs* is "historically entangled" within North American contact zones west of the Mississippi, to borrow Christopher Taylor's terminology, occupying a liminal space between indigenous and nonindigenous cultures at once unstable and fecund.[33] Hunter's white ancestry did not prevent him from also identifying with the Kaws and the Osages and engaging in an ongoing process of negotiation on the border. Hunter resisted racial and cultural categories of identity, raised awareness about settler violence and land rights, contested the authority of so-called Indian experts, and represented a western borderland that displaced American Indians were reshaping. As I see it, Hunter's *Memoirs* is a dialogic text marked by many voices and experiences.

In ways germane to Native American autobiographical traditions, Hunter envisioned a *communal* sense of self inextricably bound to indigenous families, cultures, traditions, and histories.[34] Indeed, the parts of Hunter's life story that his adversaries held up as proof of his imposture are perfectly intelligible within this wider social context. The most important example is Hunter's roundly mocked self-identification as an adopted son of the Kaws and the

Figure 8.2.
C. R. Leslie,
"John. D. Hunter."
From *Memoirs of
a Captivity among
the Indians of North
America*, 3rd ed.
London: Longman,
Hurst, Rees, Orme,
Brown, and Green,
1824.

Osages. By the ancient practice of ceremonial adoption, the surrogate may take the figurative place of a deceased or absent family member. This substitution is more than a symbolic gesture—both the family and the community accept the surrogate as actual kin. This process of "requickening" transforms both the surrogate and the people, thus mending a social fabric torn by displacement, suffering, and death.[35] For many indigenous peoples across history, the multidimensional practice of adoption has served a crucial sociopolitical function. Adoption incorporates outsiders into families, regulates civic membership, and enables communal growth and continuity.[36]

Hunter provides his readers with an ethnography of this phenomenon among the Kaws and the Osages. His adoption into Kaw society would not have been unusual during the years of his childhood, when the expansion of the fur trade led to an increase in intermarriage between Kaw women and foreign trappers. Adoption practices already had evolved so that these outsiders and their children of mixed ancestry could be formally incorporated into the community.[37] At the time, conceptions of identity and tribal belonging were not based in an objectified racial essence or in an Indian census roll.[38] Rather, to be known and accepted by the community: this was the only principle that really mattered in the days before the ascendancy of biological and legal definitions of identity.[39] These expanded kinship networks also helped American Indians to adapt to the drastic changes caused by an expanding United States. By adopting outsiders, indigenous nations could reverse demographic losses and strengthen the community; in the process, they might gain both political clout and better access to the lucrative fur trade, which the Kaws were attempting to accomplish during the early 1800s.[40] Indigenous nations often operated in stark contrast to the settler nation's practices of classifying and counting American Indians. These aimed, first and foremost, to reduce their numbers as a way of controlling, subjugating, and dispossessing them.

Hunter's sense of being transformed into a worthy Kaw son was at the core of his identity, even if his rebirth was inherently difficult to explain to skeptical and unsympathetic whites. Nevertheless, Hunter attempts to defend himself and his Kaw family in the eyes of his readers by adapting a traditional autobiographical tale that David Brumble calls the self-vindication narrative. While conceding that the impulse to answer accusations and falsehoods is "universally human," Brumble traces the self-vindication narrative, in indigenous cultures, back to its roots in ancient oral traditions. For instance, Black Hawk, Yellow Wolf, Black Elk, Geronimo, and Chief Joseph might have written down and published their autobiographical vindications for an Anglo-American audience, but they were "acting in a perfectly traditional manner" in trying to counter the charges of barbarism made against themselves and their people.[41]

In defending the Kaws, Osages, and other indigenous peoples in print, Hunter was very likely motivated by similar customs and storytelling practices. In the years following the Louisiana Purchase, there was a massive effort to acquire information about its indigenous inhabitants. Government officials, explorers, travelers, fur traders, Christian missionaries, and settlers reported on their encounters with American Indians west of the Mississippi River. At least four fur trade companies were based in St. Louis, and each hoped to monopolize the Kaw trade, exploit Kaw labor, and cultivate Kaw dependence.[42] The information they generated about the Kaws was marred by prejudices, errors, and myths about American Indians west of the Mississippi. The Missouri Fur Company provided a particularly "barbarous characterization" of the Kaws. As one official observed, they "rob, murder, and destroy when opportunity offers" and were the "terror of the neighboring Indians."[43] Henry Marie Brackenridge, in his well-known account of traveling up the Missouri

River, reinforced this one-sided and simplistic view of the Kaws. "A few years ago they were the greatest scoundrels of the Missouri," Brackenridge writes, "robbing traders, and ill-treating the whites." An officer at Fort Osage shares a dreadful story with him about a Kaw and Osage war party returning from a victorious battle against the Iowas. Displaying the scalps of women and children at the fort, they were "so elated with this exploit" that US troops were forced to flog one "defiant" warrior and threatened the rest with violence until they were subdued.[44] Both the Missouri statehood movement and Christian missionaries provided other negative reports on the Kaws. With their main village located at the mouth of the Kansas River, the Kaws were viewed as an obstacle to national expansion; consequently, the statehood movement explained Kaw persistence and defiance as the predictable actions of savages who stubbornly refused to accept the values of Western cultures. Dating back to the early 1700s, as William E. Unrau observes, the missionary activity of Catholic and Protestant missionaries fed false notions of cultural superiority, producing a particularly ugly discourse about the supposedly pagan, lewd, and inferior Kaw nation.[45] Missionary activity and fur trade capitalism were integral parts of US imperialism. "Missionaries contributed to the pacification of Indian nations," George Tinker writes in *Missionary Conquest* (1993), "thereby aiding and abetting the companies' exploitation of Indians, Indian lands, and Indian resources."[46]

By telling the poignant story of his adoption, Hunter hopes to vindicate the Kaws, and himself, from this ugly discourse on their savagery. After the Kaws rescued him from the Pawnees, the family of Keeneestah adopted him.[47] Hunter recalls fondly how his Kaw mother, who was mourning the death of her son, treated him with "great tenderness and affection," nurtured him, and mentored him in Kaw ways of life. Her accidental drowning, when he was around twelve years old, devastated him. His experience of adoption encourages readers to feel sympathy for American Indians, to discover the familiar feelings that they share as human beings, and, hopefully, to accept the possibilities of political and moral reform.[48] Hunter's outpouring of feelings for his Kaw mother was also a way to assert his authenticity as her Kaw son: "She was indeed a mother to me; and I feel my bosom dilate with gratitude at the recollection of her goodness, and care of me during this helpless period of my life. This, to those who have been bred in refinement and ease, under the fond and watchful guardianship of parents, may appear gross and incongruous."[49] He was a child alone in a foreign culture, "a thousand miles away from any white settlement," and Keeneestah and the Kaws cared for him like one of their own. "It will appear not only natural but rational," he claims, "that he should return such kindness with gratitude and affection. . . . I have no hope of seeing happier days than I experienced at this early period of my life."[50] Hunter stays true to the purpose of the self-vindication narrative. His memory of happier, kinder days with his Kaw family has the potential to transform the hearts and minds of readers. Perhaps they will be moved to feel genuine affection for the Kaws and to reconsider what they think they know about American Indians.

Hunter's self-vindication narrative thereby discloses a pointed critique of the 1820s United States. It was the inclusiveness of Kaw and Osage culture that made possible the happier days of his childhood. His white ancestry neither prohibited his incorporation into the community nor relegated him to a lower caste; he enjoyed the benefits and protections of being accepted by his Kaw and Osage families. He recalls his Kaw family reinforcing this principle, assuring their surrogate son that no phylogenetic racial barriers would impede him from developing his talents and pursuing his dreams: "I might become an expert hunter, brave warrior, wise counsellor, and possibly a distinguished chief of their nation."[51] Hunter's memory of an early lesson in natural rights theory both echoes the Cherokee chief John Ross and anticipates William Apess in shrewdly critiquing the way white racism was propelling ethnic cleansing and corrupting the settler nation's most cherished political values. By accepting Hunter and nurturing his *communal* sense of self, the Kaws and the Osages modeled a more enlightened and democratic approach to personhood and nationhood than the kind being modeled by the United States during the 1820s.[52] Not only rebutting the charges of barbarism made against American Indians, Hunter's self-vindication narrative also *reverses* those charges so that they at once expose the hypocrisy of the United States and reject the ideas and myths being used to oppress American Indians.

This dissident critique is commonly found in both Native American autobiographies and border narratives. Each has the tendency to express social and political alternatives, as Claudia Sadowski-Smith argues, that cut against the grain of empire and settler hegemony.[53] For Hunter, the practice of adoption inspired his vision of shared borders, of a contact zone in which affective similarities were the basis of belonging. Such sentimental scenes were ubiquitous in nineteenth-century autobiographies written or narrated by American Indians. Even if these scenes risked objectifying American Indians, the sentimental mode, as Arnold Krupat points out, also interjected indigenous voices and perspectives into national discourse and opened up possibilities of resistance.[54] Hunter's ability to generate emotional power, to bridge cultural differences with the expression of genuine feelings, is likely one reason the *Memoirs* was released in four editions and attracted an international audience. Moreover, Hunter's self-vindication narrative causes his *Memoirs* to diverge sharply from an autobiographical tradition defined by the canonical narratives of Benjamin Franklin, Thomas Jefferson, and John Adams. In contrast to those founders, Hunter's remarkable life did not embody the progress of a revolutionary re-public and its democratic attitudes and principles. Writing with a different didactic purpose in mind, Hunter challenged the underpinnings of American exceptionalism. He had grown up with the Kaws and the Osages—those na-tions and cultures, not the United States, had instilled in him the radical ideas of universal liberty, social equality, and national belonging.

This chapter has emphasized Hunter's adaptation of the self-vindication narrative, but other traditional autobiographical conventions also left their mark on his *Memoirs*. He includes versions of coup tales, war and hunting stories, self-examinations, vision quests, naming practices, and sacred land-scapes—the same autobiographical narratives, as David Brumble, Dawn Wong, Arnold Krupat, and other notable scholars have demonstrated, that indigenous authors modified and incorporated into a range of US discourses, including the spiritual autobiography, religious sermon, and missionary tract. There is more work to be done in itemizing and exploring all of Hunter's adap-tations of autobiographical modes. However, I wish to conclude by emphasiz-ing another intersection between his border narrative and nineteenth-century Native American literature more generally. Hunter's *Memoirs* was part of a print revolution sweeping Indian Country, a conceptual-geographic space that refers at once to specific tribal lands and their respective spheres of cultural production.[55] Personal narratives, historical writings, maps, oratory, laws, trea-ties, and art—by articulating structures of feeling and remembering—bound together indigenous peoples across Indian Country. Like these other texts, the *Memoirs* articulated cultural and political possibilities that were not tied to set-tler notions of race, place, or nationality. Above all else, Indian Country dis-course challenged the attempts by the United States and its citizens to define, exploit, and eliminate American Indians.[56]

A sense of solidarity with American Indians permeates Hunter's *Memoirs*, an oppositional text truly rare for its time. The adopted indigenous son nar-rates an alternative history of North America, of fragmented and dispersed indigenous nations surviving and remaking themselves within unstable contact zones. In the final pages of his *Memoirs*, Hunter returns to the United States, hopeful about his future. Based on what we know of his last years, he did not leave behind the communal sense of self that had been forged during his childhood with the Kaws and the Osages. Three years after the publication of his book, after being celebrated in London, Hunter returned to the border re-gion and made his way to the Red River valley, where he became a leader in a pan-Indian resistance movement, traveled on a diplomatic mission to Mexico

City, and helped to write the Declaration of Independence for the short-lived Red and White Republic of Fredonia.

At that moment, Hunter's critics in the eastern United States were accusing him of being a fraud. If we acknowledge the continuity between Hunter's *Memoirs* and his political activity in the Red River valley, then his controversial recollection of Tecumseh's visit to his Osage village takes on a new meaning. Recall that while Lewis Cass accused Hunter of fabricating the event, historical researchers have placed Tecumseh near the Osage village at that time.[57] Tecumseh's impassioned speech on the need for pan-Indian unity made a lasting impression on Hunter. He recalls the essence of Tecumseh's appeal: "*Brothers*—We are friends: we must assist each other to bear our burdens. The blood of many of our fathers and brothers has run like water on the ground, to satisfy the avarice of the white men. We, ourselves, are threatened with a great evil; nothing will pacify them but the destruction of all the red men."[58]

Traditional autobiographical narratives were often educational, as Brumble explains, and they were important tools for teaching and socializing indigenous children. On that day around 1811, Hunter listened intently as the Shawnee warrior implored the Osage to join the movement by appealing to their common ancestry as indigenous peoples, to their collective struggle against the white invaders, and to the necessity of uniting as one people against them. No archive has yet to give up the textual evidence to support Hunter's claim. But given his final days as a resistance fighter, Hunter seems to have been guided by this unforgettable lesson in indigenous resurgence.

NOTES

1. John Dunn Hunter, *Memoirs of a Captivity among the Indians of North America from Childhood to the Age of Nineteen*, ed. Richard Drinnon (New York: Schocken Books, 1973). Four editions of Hunter's memoirs were published in four countries during the decade: the US edition was published in Philadelphia in 1823; two English editions were published in London in 1823 and 1824; and German and Dutch editions appeared in 1824. Drinnon edited the version that I cite throughout, and his introduction offers a helpful summary of the text's publication history. Drinnon's *White Savage: The Case of John Dunn Hunter* (New York: Schocken Books, 1972) remains the only book-length study of Hunter's life and career.

2. On the British reception of Hunter, see Tim Fulford, *Romantic Indians: Native Americans, British Literature, and Transatlantic Culture, 1756–1830* (Oxford: Oxford University Press, 2006), 236–254.

3. Lewis Cass, "Manners and Customs of Several Indian Tribes, Located West of the Mississippi, Including Some Account of the Soil, Climate and Vegetable Productions; and the Indian Materia Medica; among Them by John D. Hunter; Historical

Notes Respecting the Indians of North America, with Remarks on the Attempts Made to Convert and Civilise Them," *North American Review* 22 (January 1826): 53–119.

4. Drinnon, *White Savage*. While many elements from Hunter's autobiography remain impossible to verify—not uncommon in the autobiographical tradition—Drinnon provides a detailed record of Hunter's movements after the publication of his book put him squarely in the public eye.

5. Michel-Rolph Trouillot, *Silencing the Past: Power and the Production of History* (Boston: Beacon, 1995).

6. Maureen Konkle, *Writing Indian Nations: Native Intellectuals and the Politics of Historiography, 1827–1863* (Chapel Hill: University of North Carolina Press, 2004), 4

7. See Patrick Wolfe, "Settler Colonialism and the Elimination of the Native," *Journal of Genocide Research* 8 (December 2006): 387–409; Chadwick Allen, *Blood Narrative: Indigenous Identity in American Indian and Maori Literary and Activist Texts* (Durham, NC: Duke University Press, 2002); Jodi A. Byrd, *The Transit of Empire: Indigenous Critiques of Colonialism* (Minneapolis: University of Minnesota Press, 2011).

8. Hilary Wyss first brought this problem of representation to my attention. See Hilary E. Wyss, "Captivity and Conversion: William Apess, Mary Jemison, and Narratives of Racial Identity," *American Indian Quarterly* 23 (Summer–Autumn 1999): 63–82.

9. On this aspect of border literature, see Claudia Sadowski-Smith, *Border Fictions: Globalization, Empire, and Writing at the Boundaries of the United States* (Charlottesville: University of Virginia Press, 2008).

10. Robert Lawrence Gunn, *Ethnology and Empire: Languages, Literature, and the Making of the North American Borderlands* (New York: New York University Press, 2015), 126. Joshua David Bellin also mentions the potential disruptive effects of Hunter's ideas on US expansionism in *The Demon of the Continent: Indians and the Shaping of American Literature* (Philadelphia: University of Pennsylvania Press, 2001), 184–185.

11. Cass, "Manners and Customs," 101. On the efforts of Cass and other US officials to control the intellectual discourse about American Indians, see Robert E. Bieder, *Science Encounters the Indian, 1820–1880: The Early Years of American Ethnology* (Norman: University of Oklahoma Press, 2003); Sean P Harvey, "'Must Not Their Languages Be Savage and Barbarous Like Them?': Philology, Indian Removal, and Race Science," *Journal of the Early Republic* 30 (Winter 2010): 505–532.

12. Cass, "Manners and Customs," 102.

13. In particular, consult John Sugden and his comprehensive biography of the Shawnee warrior. Sugden, *Tecumseh: A Life* (New York: Henry Holt and Company, 1998).

14. On the recycling of these attacks, see Drinnon, *White Savage*.

15. Drinnon, "Introduction," in Hunter, *Memoirs*, xx.

16. See John Neal, *London Magazine*, n.s., 5 (July 1, 1826): 317–343. On Neal's relationship with Hunter, see Jonathan Elmer, "John Neal and John Dunn Hunter," in *John Neal and Nineteenth-Century American Literature and Culture*, ed. Edward Watts and David J. Carlson (Lewisburg PA: Bucknell University Press, 2012).

17. Kathleen DuVal, *The Native Ground: Indians and Colonists in the Heart of the Continent* (Philadelphia: University of Pennsylvania Press, 2006).

18. My account of the Fredonian Rebellion draws from a range of sources, including Gary Clayton Anderson, *The Conquest of Texas: Ethnic Cleansing in the Promised Land, 1820–1875* (Norman: University of Oklahoma Press, 2005); Dianna Everett, *The Texas Cherokees: A People between Two Fires, 1819–1840* (Norman: University of Oklahoma Press, 1990); Andrés Reséndez, *Changing National Identities at the Frontier: Texas and New Mexico, 1800–1850* (New York: Cambridge University Press, 2005); James L. Haley, *Passionate Nation: The Epic History of Texas* (New York: Free Press, 2006); Jack Jackson, *Indian Agent: Peter Ellis Bean in Mexican Texas* (College Station: Texas A&M University Press, 2005); David J. Weber, *The Mexican Frontier, 1821–1846: The American Southwest under Mexico* (Albuquerque: University of New Mexico Press, 1982). The congressman, physician, and scientist Samuel Latham Mitchell had proposed changing the name of the United States to Fredonia in his 1804 Fourth of July address, believing that the name Fredonia would better define the country as a "Land of Freedom." His recommendation was never seriously considered, but Terence Martin points out that twelve states have towns named Fredonia. Martin, *Parables of Possibility: The American Need for Beginnings* (New York: Columbia University Press, 1995), 30.

19. See Andy Doolen, "Claiming Indigenous Space: John Dunn Hunter and the Fredonian Rebellion," *Early American Literature* 53 (November 2018): 685–713.

20. Gunn, *Ethnology and Empire*.

21. I am in dialogue here with Hilary Wyss (on Jemison and Apess), Gordon Sayre (on Tanner), Susan Walsh (on Jemison), and Kathleen Sands (on cross-cultural autobiographical texts). See Wyss, "Captivity and Conversion"; Gordon M. Sayre, "Abridging between Two Worlds: John Tanner as American Indian Autobiographer," *American Literary History* 11 (Autumn 1999): 480–499; Kathleen M. Sands, "Narrative Resistance: Native American Collaborative Autobiography," *Studies in American Indian Literatures* 10 (Spring 1998): 1–18. June Namias discusses the gender dynamics in Hunter's *Memoirs*, but the absence of historical context avoids the thorny issues of the controversy over Hunter's identity and his political activity. Namias, *White Captives: Gender and Ethnicity on the American Frontier* (Chapel Hill: University of North Carolina, 1993), 50–76.

22. Sayre claims that the absence of the word "captive" from the title of Mary Jemison's book suggests that she preferred Seneca life and identified as a Seneca woman until the day she died. Sayre, "Abridging between Two Worlds," 486.

23. H. David Brumble III, *American Indian Autobiography* (Berkeley: University of California Press, 1988). For seminal studies on the genre, see also Hertha Dawn Wong, *Sending My Heart Back across the Years: Tradition and Innovation in Native American Autobiography* (New York: Oxford University Press, 1992); Arnold Krupat, *The Voice in the Margin: Native American Literature and the Canon* (Berkeley: University of California Press, 1989).

24. Mary Louise Pratt, *Imperial Eyes: Travel Writing and Transculturation* (New York: Routledge, 1992), 7.

25. I am drawing on Pratt's key insight about ongoing colonialism in contact zones as a way to redefine Krupat's formulation of Native American autobiography as the "textual equivalent of the frontier." Arnold Krupat, "Introduction," in *Native American Autobiography: An Anthology*, ed. Arnold Krupat (Madison: University of Wisconsin Press,

2004), 4. Christopher Taylor's contact zone model is also useful for locating these border texts at the many intersections between Native American and settler cultures. See Taylor, "North America as Contact Zone: Native American Literary Nationalism and the Cross-Cultural Dilemma," *Studies in American Indian Literatures* 22 (Fall 2010): 26–44.

26. Philip J. Deloria, *Playing Indian* (New Haven, CT: Yale University Press, 1998).

27. David Murray made this important point about the link between speech and writing: for an Indian voice to sound authentic to white readers, it must sound primitive and unadulterated by Anglo civilization, hence the preference for Black Hawk's translated autobiography. See Murray, *Forked Tongues: Speech, Writing, and Representation in North American Indian Texts* (Bloomington: Indiana University Press, 1991). Building on Murray's argument, Susan Scheckel contrasts the reception of Black Hawk and Apess and cogently sums up the trap of "white representation" for American Indians: "The Indian is granted subject status only as he becomes subject to white representation. Indians, such as the Cherokees, who establish their own representative government or Indians, such as William Apess, who represent themselves through writing cannot be tolerated as Indians." Scheckel, *The Insistence of the Indian: Race and Nationalism in Nineteenth-Century American Culture* (Princeton, NJ: Princeton University Press, 1998), 124. While recent scholarship finds much to appreciate in Apess's hybridity and his cross-cultural narrative practices, the early position on his supposed inauthenticity must still be reckoned with.

28. See Krupat's classification of Apess in both *The Voice in the Margins* and *Native American Autobiography*.

29. Scheckel, *Insistence of the Indian*, 124.

30. William Apess, *On Our Own Ground: The Complete Writings of William Apess, a Pequot*, ed. Barry O'Connell (Amherst: University of Massachusetts Press, 1992).

31. In addition to Deloria, see David Waldstreicher, *In the Midst of Perpetual Fetes: The Making of American Nationalism, 1776–1820* (Chapel Hill: University of North Carolina Press, 1997); Jill Lepore, *The Name of War: King Philip's War and the Origins of American Identity* (New York: Alfred A. Knopf, 1998); Brian W. Dippie, *The Vanishing American: White Attitudes and U.S. Indian Policy* (Middletown, CT: Wesleyan University Press, 1982).

32. Lepore, *Name of War*; Dippie, *Vanishing American*.

33. Taylor, "North America as Contact Zone," 26.

34. This is fundamental to literary scholarship on Native American autobiography. See Lisa Brooks, *The Common Pot: The Recovery of Native Space in the Northeast* (Minneapolis: University of Minnesota Press, 2008); Brumble, *American Indian Autobiography*; Arnold Krupat, *For Those Who Came After: A Study of Native American Autobiography* (Berkeley: University of California Press, 1985); Sayre, "Abridging between Two Worlds"; Robert Allen Warrior, *The People and the Word: Reading Native Nonfiction* (Minneapolis: University of Minnesota Press, 2005); Wong, *Sending My Heart Back*; Wyss, "Captivity and Conversion."

35. On the phenomenon of "requickening," see Gordon M. Sayre, *Les Sauvages Américains: Representations of Native Americans in French and English Colonial Literature* (Chapel

Hill: University of North Carolina Press, 1997), 190–191; James Axtell, "The White Indians of Colonial America," *William and Mary Quarterly* 32 (January 1975): 55–88.

36. On this issue, see Eva Marie Garroutte, *Real Indians: Identity and the Survival of Native America* (Berkeley: University of California Press, 2003); Julia M Coates, "'This Sovereignty Thing': Nationality, Blood, and the Cherokee Resurgence," in Maximilian Christian Forte, ed., *Who Is an Indian? Race, Place, and the Politics of Indigeneity in the Americas* (Toronto: University of Toronto Press, 2013), 132.

37. William E. Unrau, *The Kansa Indians: A History of the Wind People, 1673–1873* (Norman: University of Oklahoma Press, 1986), 52–111

38. As Forte notes, indigenousness at the time "had little to do with race, biology, or ethnicity." See Forte, "Introduction: 'Who Is an Indian?': The Cultural Politics of a Bad Question," in Forte, *Who Is an Indian?*, 22.

39. This summary draws on Eva Marie Garroutte's and C. Matthew Snipp's excellent study, "The Canary in the Coal Mine: What Sociology Can Learn from Ethnic Identity Debates among American Indians," in Forte, *Who Is an Indian?*, 92–123. On the vexed issue of contemporary indigenous identity, see Eva Marie Garroutte, "The Racial Formation of American Indians: Negotiating Legitimate Identities within Tribal and Federal Law," *American Indian Quarterly* 25 (Spring 2001): 224–239; Bonita Lawrence, *"Real" Indians and Others: Mixed-Blood Urban Native Peoples and Indigenous Nationhood* (Lincoln: University of Nebraska Press, 2004). Pauline Turner Strong and Barrik Winkle, "'Indian Blood': Reflections on the Reckoning and Refiguring of Native North American Identity," *Cultural Anthropology* 11 (November 1996): 547–576; Hilary N. Weaver, "Indigenous Identity: What Is It and Who Really Has It?," *American Indian Quarterly* 25 (Spring 2001): 240–255.

40. Unrau, *Kansa Indians*.

41. Brumble, *American Indian Autobiography*, 22–23, 60.

42. Unrau, *Kansa Indians*, 84.

43. Quoted in Unrah, 84.

44. Henry Marie Brackenridge, *Views of Louisiana: Together with a Journal of a Voyage up the Missouri River, in 1811* (Chicago: Quadrangle Books, 1962), 75, 217–218.

45. Unrau, *Kansa Indians*, 112–138.

46. George E. Tinker, *Missionary Conquest: The Gospel and Native American Cultural Genocide* (Minneapolis: Fortress Press, 1993), 10.

47. In his study of John Tanner, Sayre notes that standard editorial practice in the nineteenth century was to print Indian names with hyphens, which more often than not reminds readers of Indian illiteracy rather than helping with pronunciation. Following his lead, I have omitted the hyphens in Indian names in Hunter's *Memoirs*, save in quotations. Sayre, "Abridging between Two Worlds."

48. Laura L. Mielke, *Moving Encounters: Sympathy and the Indian Question in Antebellum Literature* (Amherst: University of Massachusetts Press, 2008).

49. Hunter, *Memoirs*, 18.

50. Hunter, 19.

51. Hunter, 26. In her analysis of Mary Jemison's life narrative, Wyss observes that Jemison's "mixed" identity is more intelligible if understood within an indigenous context of identity formation characterized by fluid definitions of racial and cultural belonging. Wyss, "Captivity and Conversion," 65.

52. Hunter shares much in common with John Tanner. Both were adopted to replace a dead son; their indigenous mothers were both caregivers and teachers and were central to their respective stories; both boys navigated a rite of passage based in succeeding as hunters and warriors. The personal narratives of John Tanner and Mary Jemison also articulated this indigenous view of identity, which did not reflect the settler colonial imaginary, and which, as Sayre argues, continues to confound their critics. Sayre, "Abridging between Two Worlds," 481.

53. Sadowski-Smith, *Border Fictions*.

54. Krupat, *For Those Who Came After*.

55. I am building on Philip Round's formulation of Indian Country. He compares the conceptual and physical space of Indian Country to Paul Gilroy's black Atlantic, which also connected specific geographies of displacement and spheres of cultural production. See Phillip H. Round, *Removable Type: Histories of the Book in Indian Country, 1663–1880* (Chapel Hill: University of North Carolina Press, 2010), 5–19.

56. In American Indian studies, scholars have examined the complex role of print discourse in indigenous cultures. Their scholarship, often reconstructing tribal-specific literary histories, has collectively overturned the dated assumption that print literacy made American Indians less authentic and virtually erased their indigenous subjectivity. See Brooks, *Common Pot*; Warrior, *People and the Word*; Daniel Heath Justice, *Our Fire Survives the Storm: A Cherokee Literary History* (Minneapolis: University of Minnesota Press, 2006).

57. Sugden, *Tecumseh*.

58. Hunter, *Memoirs*, 30.

CHAPTER 9

The Lansford Hastings Imaginary: Visions of Democratic Patriarchy in the Americas, 1842–1867

Thomas Richards Jr.

Historians do not know quite what to do with Lansford Warren Hastings. Works that focus on Hastings specifically include a few scholarly articles and one dissertation, yet he deserves a biography. He published and promoted the influential book *The Emigrants' Guide to Oregon and California* in 1845, which historians have both credited for exponentially increasing American immigration to California in 1846 and blamed for leading the Donner Party on the "Hastings Cutoff" that ensured their terrible fate. In addition, Hastings secretly sought to create a California republic, in which Anglo-Americans would seize the territory from Mexico while simultaneously keeping it independent from the United States. Like many Anglo-Americans who expatriated themselves during the era of expansion, he did not see the West as a place simply awaiting US conquest but as a blank slate where he could enact his personal vision of the ideal society—a society this chapter defines as a "democratic patriarchy."

Originally a practicing lawyer from Ohio, at age twenty-three Hastings led an overland company to Oregon in 1842. There, John McLoughlin, the chief factor of the Hudson's Bay Company, hired him to settle a land claim. In 1845, Hastings worked to facilitate a Mormon colony in California. One year later he fought in the California Battalion in the US-Mexican War and in 1849 was elected as a delegate to the California Constitutional Convention, at which he made several influential contributions. In the mid-1850s, Hastings left California for Arizona, where he became a territorial judge. In 1861, he proposed to Brigham Young that the Mormons should settle the banks of the Colorado River to facilitate trade between Utah and the California coast. In 1863, he proposed to Jefferson Davis a scheme to secure Arizona and New Mexico for the Confederacy and was subsequently appointed as a major in the rebel army. Finally, in 1867, he promoted a Confederate colony in Brazil, writing *The Emigrants' Guide to Brazil* and embarking with more than one hundred immigrants for his chosen site in the Amazon region. This settlement would prove to be one of the most durable of all Confederado colonies in Brazil, but Hastings did not live to see its survival, dying of yellow fever in the Virgin Islands in 1867.[1]

Unfortunately for the scholar, little of Hastings's correspondence survives that might provide insight into his mercurial life. He remains shallowly enigmatic. To describe him as mysterious gives too much depth of thought to a person who seemingly possessed few obvious principles or a coherent ideology. Indeed, the few works that have focused on Hastings largely concentrate on his actions, and only superficially attempt to understand what motivated him. Yet, this superficiality and inconsistency mask his persistent talent for commanding the allegiances of his contemporaries. He was a persuasive promoter of California, twice an elected overland trail leader, an elected major in the California Battalion, an elected delegate to the constitutional convention, an Arizona judge, a major in the Confederate army, and a successful promoter of southern immigration to Brazil. While not everyone may have listened to Hastings's many schemes, a critical mass did. Significantly, the people who listened were always Anglo-American men.[2]

Why did Anglo-American men so often follow Hastings? What did he offer that no one else did? This chapter proposes to answer these questions through a careful reading of both emigrants' guides and Hastings's few surviving letters. In contrast to his apparent capriciousness, I argue that Hastings demonstrated a consistent ideology that blended the values of Jacksonian democracy—in particular, a reverence for the majority rule of white men—with those of a more traditional form of patriarchy he encountered in Mexican California. Unlike the ideal of the Jeffersonian yeoman farmer prevalent in much of the US North, West, and even parts of the slave-owning South, Hastings's vision of patriarchy rested on a male head of household owning vast tracts of land, commanding the allegiance of not just his nuclear family but also a wide array of nonwhite laborers. While these servants would live in conditions in many ways similar to slavery, they would not be officially termed slaves—a distinction that mattered to Hastings and the northerners who followed him. In his vision, the Anglo-American patriarch would act not as a farmer himself but

Figure 9.1. "Lansford Warren Hastings." From Lansford W. Hastings, *The Emigrants' Guide to Oregon and California*, edited by Charles Henry Carey. Princeton, NJ: Princeton University Press, 1932. Beinecke Rare Book and Manuscript Library, Yale University, New Haven, CT.

as a local ruler. His "work" would be administrative rather than physical, as he managed his vast estate as his own private fiefdom. Moreover, while the patriarch would hold sway over his vast lands and numerous dependents, his rule would be inherently benevolent. Yet, while in the home the patriarch would operate on autocratic yet benign rule, society beyond it would operate on democratic principles, in which these male patriarchs would elect government officials based on the principles of Jacksonian democracy. In short, Hastings's worldview combined the democratic values he learned in Ohio with the patriarchy evidenced by the Californio elite in California, in a worldview I term "democratic patriarchy."[3]

In his idealization of democratic patriarchy, Hastings was not alone among Anglo-American men. On the contrary, it was his espousal of such a vision in *The Emigrants' Guide to Oregon and California* and likely in person that made so many Anglo-American men follow Hastings's lead in the mid-1840s. Moreover, Hastings was opposed to slavery, but nevertheless his ideas mirrored the planter class of the US South in regard to the economic power and social clout the upper tier of white men should possess. Thus, it was no coincidence that Hastings eventually turned to the Confederacy as the Republican Party's yeoman ideal of "free soil" and "free labor" came to dominate California and most northern states in the 1850s. Ultimately, while Hastings's vision was not the majority view among Anglo-American men in the United States, it was hardly exceptional, as many of these men did indeed hope to become democratic patriarchs.[4]

Yet, while Hastings's ideology may not have been exceptional, his temperament was. For all of his celebration of democratic patriarchy, he was unable to settle into this lifestyle himself. Instead, he traveled from place to place and from audience to audience, hoping to translate his various political schemes into lasting political power. Time and again, if Hastings lost his influence in one place, he tried to regain it somewhere else. Thus, while most of the men with whom he interacted and collaborated remained in Oregon, California, Arizona, and the US South until their deaths, Hastings moved on; they died in their homes, while he died of yellow fever in the Caribbean in his final attempt to become the leader of a democratic patriarchal society in Brazil's Amazonia.

As an actual guide to navigating the overland trail, Hastings's *Emigrants' Guide to Oregon and California* left much to be desired. Both his contemporaries and later historians have criticized its frequently shoddy geographic information and lack of attention to detail, which has helped solidify the assumption that Hastings was largely responsible for the fate of the Donner Party. As a piece of literature, *The Emigrants' Guide* is slightly better, as it is at least entertaining in certain places. However, when compared with similar works, such as Richard Henry Dana's memoir *Two Years before the Mast* (1840), which until *The Emigrants' Guide* was likely the most popular western travelogue, Hastings's book is uneven, repetitive, and frequently plodding. Part of the reason for this difference, of course, is that, unlike Dana, Hastings wrote for the purpose of guiding more US citizens west, and thus his immensely detailed, and therefore tedious, descriptions of geographic features constitute a large portion of the work. Embedded within this geographic detail, however, are some entertaining scenes and interesting, albeit frequently racist, sociological descriptions of the peoples whom he encountered on his journey. These interspersions provide the basis for understanding Hastings's underlying ideology.[5]

In the very first pages of *The Emigrants' Guide*, Hastings established the importance of democracy, describing how the overland party with which he traveled coalesced into a mobile "elected republic." Soon after setting out from Missouri, the hundred-some people in Hastings's overland party were unable make unified decisions. As Hastings described the problem, "But we had only proceeded a few days of travel, from our native land of order and security, when the 'American Character' was fully exhibited. All appeared to be determined to govern, not to be governed." Subsequently the men in the party discussed enacting a code of laws, but they quickly voted this down for the "moral code . . . found recorded in the breast of every man" would prove sufficient. Yet it soon became clear that this "moral code" was not enough, as disorder continued to plague the party. Disagreements erupted over various issues—a stolen horse, an idea to shoot all dogs accompanying the party (some believed their barking would give the party's position away to Indians), and, most crucially, the leadership of trail leader Elijah White. After various delays, a majority of the men in the overland party worried about reaching Oregon before winter. To them, White had already evidenced few leadership abilities. As one member of the party described him, White possessed "no particular force of character and no administrative ability." Subsequently, the men in the party decided to vote on a new leader. The stage was set for the most formative moment in young Lansford Hastings's thus far uneventful life.[6]

The majority of the company elected Hastings their new trail guide. We have no information about why a majority chose him, or whether he or his opponents performed any electioneering before the vote. Considering the members of the company were entrusting him with their lives, he must have evidenced leadership abilities in the weeks before and after departing Missouri. While Hastings never described his personal feelings explicitly, it is clear that he was intoxicated with his election. In *The Emigrants' Guide*, he wrote, "An election was held, which resulted in the election of myself to the first, and Mr. Lovejoy to the second office of our infant *republic*." This was the second time Hastings deemed the overland party a "republic," but the first time he had used the phrase as a sarcastic term to denote the chaos on the trail. Now it was an official government—as, perhaps, the italics emphasized—over which he held elected control. He chose to place his election on the title page of *The Emigrants' Guide*, writing "Leader of the Oregon and California Emigrants of 1842" below his name. From this moment on, whenever Hastings encountered a group of Anglo-American men, he sought to gain leadership through democratic means—as a trail leader, potential California president, delegate to the California Constitutional Convention, Arizona judge, Confederate general, and leader of ex-Confederates in Brazil. From 1842 to the end of his life, Hastings continuously demonstrated that he believed he could lead Anglo-American men—and they would willingly follow him.[7]

In an important sense, there is nothing exceptional about Hastings's political behavior that did not stem from his background as a white American man growing up in the 1830s and 1840s. On the contrary, his actions were positively Jacksonian. In that world, white men sought political power by actively gaining the support of other white men, and this was a perfectly honorable and legitimate practice to follow. Hastings had almost certainly supported democracy before leaving Ohio, because that ideology pervaded all aspects of US society, and now this support was more firmly buttressed with his election. What Hastings would praise in *The Emigrants' Guide* as "genuine *republicanism*, and unsophisticated *democracy*" (emphasis in original) had provided him with a position of leadership and influence, validating both the perfect egalitarianism of the overland company and Hastings's belief that he was uniquely suited to be elevated as its leader. The use of the word "unsophisticated," along with the small and localized nature of this democracy, points to an additional component of his worldview. Beginning with his election—and perhaps fully entrenched because of it—Hastings supported versions of democracy that were parochial in nature, and thus echoed aspects of his overland trail "infant republic." His preference for both local democracy and his own power within that democracy explains why he sought to make California an independent republic in 1845—his unsaid purpose in writing *The Emigrants' Guide*. Moreover, it should come as no surprise that, following California's conquest by the United States, when there is evidence of Hastings's national political leanings, it shows that he voted for Democrats, the party that consistently supported localist democracy and—at least rhetorically—states' rights.[8]

And yet, for all his localist democratic leanings, Hastings established some quite exceptional political affiliations in 1842 and 1843, particularly in regard to the relationships he forged on his overland journey. His two most important and lasting connections were with the two most *un*democratic personalities in the North American West: in Oregon, John McLoughlin, the chief factor of the Hudson's Bay Company (HBC), and, in California, Swiss emigrant John Sutter. Hastings spent only a few months in Oregon, but in that time, he was almost completely occupied as McLoughlin's lawyer, working to secure his client's land claim in Oregon City against a countersuit from Methodist missionaries. During this time Hastings and McLoughlin clearly developed fondness for one another—a relationship that was at odds with the latter's tense relationship with many other American settlers in Oregon. While Hastings was in Oregon, sixty-five Americans sent a petition to the US Congress that attacked McLoughlin for threatening their economic interests through his extensive land claims and HBC trade connections, which allowed him to undersell all competition from his general store. In a letter to McLoughlin—by now a friend of sorts—Hastings vehemently disagreed with the petition, describing it as "most rediculous most scandalous" and exclaiming, "how ungenerous, how exaggerated how false." A few years later, when penning *The Emigrants' Guide*, Hastings continued to gush that McLoughlin was "courteous, intelligent, and companionable, and a more kind, hospitable, and liberal gentleman, the world never saw." He then described how McLoughlin treated all his guests with "kindness and hospitality," housing them in a refined "bachelor's hall." When they left, McLoughlin sent them off in fine style in a "cart with servants." This would not be the last time in *The Emigrants' Guide* that Hastings would admire the use of servant labor. Ostensibly dedicated to "unsophisticated democracy," Hastings found affinity with a man who at one point ruled the Willamette Valley as a private fiefdom.[9]

This pattern continued after Hastings left Oregon for California. Once there, he encountered John Sutter. In temperament and purpose, Sutter was far different from McLoughlin. While the sober-minded McLoughlin had worked diligently for decades to advance the interests of the HBC, Sutter was the supreme confidence man of the Far West, employing his gregariousness and false assertions of personal wealth to acquire vast tracts of land in northern California. In their day-to-day operations, however, the two men were quite similar. Like McLoughlin at Fort Vancouver, Sutter wielded significant economic and political power, and he administered the lands around his fort of New Helvetia as his own private fiefdom. Like McLoughlin, his power was based on Indian labor, although his workers were much more akin to slaves than the HBC's Indian and métis voluntary employees. As he had been with McLoughlin, Hastings was drawn to Sutter's personality and power, referring to him with almost the same words he used to describe the HBC factor: "A more kind and hospitable gentleman, it has seldom been my fortune to meet. Such is his treatment of all foreigners, who visit him, that when they leave him, they are compelled to do so, with much regret, and under many obligations, for his continued, untiring, and gentlemanly affections." This praise followed two pages in which Hastings described Sutter's "invincible" military and economic power on the California frontier. Clearly, in Hastings's eyes, Sutter's local autocratic rule did not diminish his standing.[10]

For an overlander from the United States, Hastings's attraction to first McLoughlin and then Sutter was, to put it simply, not normal. To be sure, many other Americans voiced respect for both men, and many also praised both for their generosity to incoming migrants, but most migrants frequently coupled respect for both McLoughlin and Sutter with an acute level of distrust. The former was an agent of the British Empire and was tasked with maintaining its predominance over the Oregon country. The latter was an agent only to himself, a fact that an increasing number of American immigrants learned in the mid-1840s when he persuaded them to take the side of the Mexican government in suppressing a Californio rebellion. By the end of its participation in this venture, Sutter's American contingent had come to realize he was unreliable and cared little for their personal well-being. Yet Hastings exhibited no such distrust in either McLoughlin or Sutter. Although he penned *The Emigrants' Guide* before Sutter's fallout with his Anglo-American neighbors, Hastings continued his close relationship with the discredited Swiss once he arrived back in California in the fall of 1845. He even partnered with Sutter in his attempt to found "Sutterville" in the 1850s, which both men hoped would surpass Sacramento as the economic capital of the gold rush. To Hastings, that these men were quite hostile to democracy was no deterrent to doing business with them and ultimately befriending them.[11]

Hastings's respective relationships with McLoughlin and Sutter illuminate his ideology, one that may have only fully formed after he met them and became taken with how they operated. Hastings was committed to democracy for both intellectual and self-interested reasons, but he was also undeniably captivated by McLoughlin's and Sutter's power, influence, and lifestyle. Both men evidenced their power by showing Hastings immense hospitality, which was a quality for which he voiced admiration at other places in *The Emigrants' Guide*. Notable, too, were his descriptions of how both of these men commanded a population of laborers—métis under McLoughlin, and particularly Indians under Sutter—whom he understood as the backbone of each man's economic and military power. Indeed, it was Indian soldiers whom Hastings credited with Sutter's "invincible" power on the northern California frontier. Needless to say, these laborers did the actual work to make Hastings feel so welcome in each man's company. He identified cheap Indian labor as one of the best qualities of living in California. "Indians are readily employed, and, in any numbers," he wrote, "for the trifling expense of merely furnishing them with such clothing, as a course [*sic*] tow shirt, and a pair of pantaloons of similar cloth, and for such food as meat alone," but the employer need not feel guilty about this treatment because "any thing, which you might feel disposed to provide them, would be preferable to the crickets and grasshoppers, upon which they have formerly subsisted." Thus, to Hastings, the use of Indian labor was doubly attractive, for it yielded power and prosperity to the Indians' "employer," while costing the employer very little money or time. Indian labor was both lucrative and effortless.[12]

McLoughlin and Sutter were not the only men whom Hastings encountered on his overland journey who displayed patriarchal power. In California he also met an entire class of people whom scholars have also deemed landed patriarchs: the small contingent of wealthy Californio men. These few dozens out of a population of seven thousand owned vast landed estates and ruled over their families and employees—both Indian and Californio—with the power of local despots. Like McLoughlin and especially Sutter, they utilized their prosperity to display immense hospitality to their guests. Hastings, however, exhibited typical Anglo-American racism, and he punctuated *The Emigrants' Guide* with insults for both the Indians and the Californios he encountered. The "Mexicans"—his term for the Californios—"differ, in every particular, from the foreigners [European and American]; ignorance and its concomitant, superstition, together with superstition and superciliousness, constitute the chief ingredients, of the Mexican character. More indomitable ignorance does not prevail, among any people who make the least pretentions of civilization." He explained that these qualities likely stemmed from the Californios' prior willingness to propagate with Indians. At another point, Hastings explained their work traditions: "Inherent indolence forbids any course which requires any active exertion. A Mexican always pursues that method of doing things, which requires the least physical or mental exercise, unless it involves some danger, in which case, he always adopts some other method." To Hastings, an industrious Anglo-American population in California would correct such lazy economic habits.[13]

Yet, Hastings expressed some sympathy for the Californios—or at least to their way of life. At one point, he described how they were excessively generous, writing that if you stopped by a Californio residence "you would not only be received kindly, but you would also be annoyed with continued proffers, of all the luxuries which they possess." Thus, the virtues of McLoughlin and Sutter became the vices of the Californios, a dissonance that Hastings did not attempt to resolve. On the contrary, later in the same paragraph in which he criticized their excessive hospitality, he reverted to praising it, writing, "All classes of Mexicans are unusually kind and hospitable to foreigners, as far as it relates to their reception and treatment as guests. Whatever attention and kindness you may receive at their hands, while guests, and however long you remain with them, they will receive no compensation." Thus, his inherent racism mandated that he condemn wealthy Californios, but his actual experience mitigated it only a page later. Moreover, later in his life, he would marry a woman whose mother came from Venezuela, suggesting that his bias against people of Spanish descent was at least somewhat fungible.[14]

This about-face is even more revealing in how Hastings waxed about the benefits of California. As he tried to sell the region to potential migrants, he settled on two strategies. First, he praised the climate and fertility, which he contrasted favorably with that of Oregon. Second, he extolled the lifestyle one could achieve. He noted how the land could accommodate "immense herds" of cattle "with little, or no expense." He described how Indian laborers would protect the cattle, negating the need to build fences, and how they would do additional work if only they were provided with food and clothes. They would perform the forced labor of black slaves in the US South, but their "employer" had no need to exhibit a paternalist ideology, in which he would need to care for them as his family. While California settlers could exhibit benevolence to passersby, they could treat their Indian laborers solely as workers. In essence, potential landholders could reap the benefits of slaveholding without its supposed burdens. Moreover, in addition to cheap Indian labor, land was readily available, up to "eleven leagues" that could be either granted by the Mexican government or simply taken due to the lack of oversight. Between the use of Indian labor and the ease of raising cattle, Hastings consistently stated that life in California was remarkably effortless, yielding "prosperous circumstances . . . with very little labor or expense." Indeed, each California estate was self-sustaining. As he noted, every rancho was "supplied with all the means of subsistence within [itself]." While a market did exist for trade, it was "certain and uniform," and not subject to the "fluctuations" that plagued the US economy—a statement that many potential migrants would have understood all too well during the depression that followed the Panics of 1837 and 1839. In sum, for migrants, California could be a paradise of little work and much wealth.[15]

Hastings described the potential lives for Anglo-American migrants in California in remarkably similar ways as he described the lives of the current wealthy Californios who occupied the land. What he pronounced as a life of "very little labor and expense" for Anglo-Americans became an example of "indolence" displayed by the Californios. His differing treatment of the two groups may have stemmed from an ingrained racist stance he had toward the peoples of Mexican descent. Yet it also served his greater purpose in writing *The Emigrants' Guide* to portray the Californios as lazy, at the same time as he enticed Anglo-American migrants to mimic their lifestyle. Hastings needed to justify his desire to seize the territory, and part of his justification lay in the fact that its idle inhabitants did not get full use of the land. In this rhetoric, he followed the example of generations of Anglo-Americans, who had used similar terms to justify the confiscation of Indian land throughout eastern and central North America. If Anglo-Americans filled the region, he believed California could become a land of "continuous improvement, universal enterprise, and unparalleled commerce," but until then it was "sparsely" populated by an "indolent" race.[16]

To be sure, Hastings also employed several other rhetorical strategies to justify American immigration and eventual conquest. In particular, he spent several pages detailing the "oppressions" of the Graham Affair of 1840, in which California governor Juan Alvarado suspected American mountain man Isaac Graham of leading a rebellion of American and British immigrants and imprisoned several dozen of them without adequate food or water.[17] Yet Hastings admitted that, by the time of his writing in 1844, Californio leaders feared the power of the increasing numbers of migrants and now treated them with "utmost respect, kindness, and hospitality." Ultimately the goal of this migration was not to avenge Graham and his comrades but to populate California and eventually bring it under Anglo-American governance that would assume the economic, social, and political position previously occupied by the wealthy Californios. Anglo-Americans would, in essence, become California's new patriarchs.[18]

Hastings's affinity for patriarchy explains his differing stances toward California and Oregon. By the time he published in 1845, most overland literature in the United States favored the latter. "Oregon Fever," rather than "California Fever," engulfed the Old Northwest and Upper South, regions that provided the bulk of the migrant population in the first half of the 1840s. Migrants favored Oregon because the United States and Great Britain officially shared territory, and thus American migrants believed they had a legal right to occupy the land. California, however, remained Mexican territory. More important for the purposes of this chapter, many Anglo-Americans perceived Oregon as a yeoman's paradise. Upon their arrival there, men could claim 640 acres of land for free, as long as they erected improvements on the land within six months. That amount was four times more land than the United States offered under the 1841 Preemption Act that also required a fee of $1.25 per acre. Moreover, 640 acres was enough to fulfill the desire of fathers to pass on land to their multiple sons, particularly when it was situated in the fertile Willamette Valley. No wonder it enticed more than six thousand American migrants by 1846. In describing Oregon society, Hastings praised the migrants for their "industriousness" and described how most of them lived frugally, erecting simple log cabins, growing wheat and raising cattle, and generally mimicking the lives of small farmers in the "western states." Their attention to their "individual interests" meant that they had little time to devote to roads and other internal improvements, which he described as scarcely existing. Oregon may have been a yeoman's paradise, but to Hastings, a yeoman's life was *hard*. In describing the industriousness of Oregon settlers, he essentially damned the region with faint praise, in contrast to the easygoing life he described as there for the taking in California.[19]

For many Oregon migrants, gender was a crucial factor in the decision to travel west. In the aftermath of the Panic of 1837, and amid the growing market economy more generally, American yeomen and would-be yeomen found it increasingly difficult to provide for their families, and thus their ideal of republican masculinity was under threat. Under the liberal Oregon land law, they could become independent landholders and thereby provide for their nuclear families, fulfilling the American ideal of the homestead. Tellingly, however, Hastings had almost nothing to say about families in *The Emigrants' Guide*. Women and children were practically invisible throughout the entire book. Their absence, coupled with the author's personal life, helps explain his preference for a more distant patriarchy in which the male head of household acted more as ruler than father and husband of the domestic family. Hastings was a bachelor until 1848, when he married Charlotte Toler, the daughter of Hopeful Toler, a Virginian and former diplomat to Venezuela, and his Venezuelan bride whom he had met during his ambassadorship. The father moved his family to California a year prior to his daughter's marriage to Hastings. Over the next seven years, Charlotte gave birth to three children. The little information about his wife and children that survives provides a small glimpse of how Hastings treated them. The *California Star and Californian* reported that Hastings left Charlotte for the gold fields almost immediately after their marriage, a point upon which the writer remarked, "Let us hope that Mr. Hastings will soon acquire his *pile*, and . . . return to the bosom of domestic felicity, where we shall expect some day to take a seat beside his hospitable fire." At a time when so many men left their families in search of gold, Hastings's rapid abandonment of his wife for the gold fields was something the *Californian* deemed noteworthy. It seems he had little time for "domestic felicity."[20]

Even more telling was Hastings's treatment of his children. Charlotte died in 1862, at which point Hastings promptly abandoned his family in California, choosing to travel to Mexico and eventually Richmond, where he would pitch to Jefferson Davis his scheme of seizing the Far West for the Confederacy. He left his daughter Isabel in a Dominican convent in Benicia, California, and arranged for his other two children to be provided for, although the records do not reveal the manner of their care. Although the evidence does not confirm Hastings as an uncaring father, it suggests that he was not committed to the ideal of the yeoman family. He left his wife to get rich and left his children to

achieve power and fame. Thus, it is no wonder that the lifestyle of Sutter and
the Californios captivated him in the early 1840s in a way that of Oregon
nuclear families did not.[21]

Ultimately, then, Hastings hoped Anglo-American migration to California
would create a society that molded the ideals of Jacksonian democracy with
the daily life practiced by the Californios. At various points in *The Emigrants'
Guide*, he described this society as he envisioned it, and as it was currently exhibited by the several hundred Anglo-American and European immigrants in
California. The "foreigners" in California—read: *male* foreigners—Hastings
believed, possessed "industry, enterprise, and bravery," combined with "extraordinary kindness, courtesy, and hospitality." These traits created a society
that was "united by silken trains of friendship, exerting every energy, and doing everything in their power, to promote the individual and general welfare."
Their desire to "vie with each other" over their generosity and hospitality to
passersby demonstrated that this class had ample resources to devote to others,
which was predicated on the fact that each migrant possessed "one to eleven
square leagues of land," and sometimes up to "thirty leagues." With each
league equivalent to almost forty-five hundred acres, this meant that present
California immigrants did, and future California immigrants could, possess *at
the minimum* seven times the land they would in Oregon, and twenty-eight times
more land than available under the US Preemption Act of 1841. Presiding
over such estates, upon which lived their families and Indian laborers, American patriarchs in California could "afford all the enjoyment and luxuries,
of civilized life." Hastings concluded his work by looking forward to a time
in California in which "genuine *republicanism* and unsophisticated *democracy*,
shall be reared up, and tower aloft, even upon the wild shores of the great Pacific; where they shall stand forth, as enduring monuments, to the increasing
wisdom of *man*, and the infinite kindness and protection, of an all-wise and
overruling *Providence*."[22]

With the understanding that Hastings desired a society of democratic patriarchs, the rest of his life—a life that was punctuated by seemingly mercurial decisions—falls into place. First, he constantly exhibited a dedication to
local democracy and, just as important, an acute desire to lead it. He began
this quest modestly by becoming an elected trail leader to a small group of
overlanders in 1845. His long-term goal, however, was much more grandiose: founding a California republic, which he would presumably lead. This
plan was not as improbable as it seems in retrospect, for the US-Mexican
War had not yet erupted, and California's future remained ambiguous. For
the purposes of Hastings's ideology, moreover, an Anglo-American California
republic made sense, for it preserved local democracy and enshrined local

rule, as well as his predilection for patriarchy. And, of course, as someone who desired power through democratic means, he would have much better electoral prospects in this republic than in a US territory governed from distant Washington. Hastings's plan to populate California with the Mormons also fits into this ideology. With no firsthand knowledge of their religion or culture, he neither shared the prejudices of other Americans nor understood actual Mormon intentions in the West. As a result, he found their power, unity, and autonomy attractive. The Mormons would become a larger, more powerful emigrant company over which Hastings could gain leadership.[23]

Once he arrived back in California in the fall of 1846, Hastings discovered that his plan to create an independent California republic was permanently sidetracked. The Bear Flag Rebellion had erupted in June, and for a month the rebels claimed that they had created an independent California, although limited to the boundaries of the Sacramento Valley. Whether Hastings would have supported this rebellion is questionable, as he believed many more immigrants were needed to successfully conquer the territory. This question, however, was moot, for the Bear Flag Rebellion was preempted by news that the United States and Mexico were at war. As soon as he learned of this, Hastings once again sought a leadership position, becoming an elected captain of Company F of the California Battalion. Three years later he was elected as a representative from the Sacramento Valley to the California Constitutional Convention, where he made his presence known by arguing against enlarged California borders that would extend as far east as the Mormon settlements in the Salt Lake Valley. Hastings identified two problems with such large borders. First, as an advocate of local democracy, he believed inhabitants living east of the Sierra Nevadas "could not be fairly represented" in the state legislature, particularly because many of them were Mormons who wanted a state government of their own. Second, he believed such large borders would complicate the question of slavery in California then being debated in the US Congress, which would prevent statehood for the foreseeable future. Both rationales stemmed from Hastings's desire to promptly and efficiently preserve local power in California.[24]

Yet, in 1849, Hastings curiously rejected his election as the local alcalde, and for several years he disappeared from the political scene. His refusal and subsequent political decline likely stemmed from his growing notoriety among settlers in northern California. Circumstantial evidence suggests that a number of people started to blame his faulty *Emigrants' Guide* for the Donner Party tragedy—a reputation that continues to this day. He had become disliked among his peers. Hastings, however, still aspired to a political career. A few years later, he moved to Arizona City in the territory of New Mexico, what would eventually become the town of Yuma. His only surviving letter from these years finds him requesting information from the territorial governor on how to conduct local elections, for no one in Arizona City could find a copy of the laws of New Mexico. He also asked to be appointed a notary public to administer oaths, for no one in the town was empowered to do so. Once again he was attempting to both create and lead local government.[25]

Dedicated to local democracy, Hastings was also committed to the patriarchal society that he praised to such an extent in *The Emigrants' Guide*. Unlike his ability to gain the trust of fellow Anglo-Americans, however, he was much less successful gaining the economic prosperity necessary to become a landed patriarch. Part of the problem stemmed from his background: a trained lawyer from Ohio, Hastings likely had little knowledge of how to acquire and then manage one of the vast landed estates he so admired in California. Thus, in the late 1840s, he fell back on what he knew and resumed practicing law in San Francisco, but tellingly he did not give up his desire to gain great wealth. He attempted a series of failed business ventures, including gold prospecting and the founding of Sutterville. Not only was his political career dead due to his reputation as the Donner Party villain, but so too were his economic prospects. It is therefore not a surprise that Hastings chose to move to the tiny frontier settlement of Arizona City—after all, the Sacramento Valley had once been a tiny frontier settlement in its own right, and it was this fledgling society that spawned the most successful years of Hastings's life. Perhaps in Arizona City he could rebuild his political prospects and find the economic success that previously eluded him.[26]

Hastings devotion to democratic patriarchy also explains his three final ventures: an attempt to contract with Brigham Young to establish trade from San Francisco to Utah by seizing the banks of the Colorado River in 1861, an attempt to conquer the Southwest for the Confederacy during the Civil War, and finally his successful creation of a slaveholding colony of ex-Confederates in Brazil after the war's conclusion. All three plans were in many ways desperate schemes concocted by a man whose most influential moments were behind him, as Hastings inadvertently acknowledged by introducing himself in letters by citing events almost two decades in the past: "I am the person who raised a large company of Emigrants, in 1842." Yet each of these schemes would empower local government alongside a patriarchal social and economic system, at least in Hastings's eyes.[27]

Hastings's Mormon plan ostensibly does not to fit this pattern, until we read his vision of the future settlement as he described it to Brigham Young. Along the "rich fertile valleys on either side of the river," he claimed he would secure land grants for the Mormons, which would then yield "the very finest sugar, rice, cotton, and tobacco." Soon the Colorado River would become the "Mississippi of the Pacific." In regard to the Mormons' "peculiar" religion, Hastings argued that "the government has nothing to do with religion," which is why he claimed he always defended "the rights of your people." Young, of course, had no desire to create such a society, even if he believed Hastings could deliver on his promises, which is unlikely. He had a far better knowledge of western geography than Hastings, and he knew intuitively that the swift-moving Colorado and its arid banks would not become the next Mississippi River Valley. No wonder Young completely ignored Hastings.[28]

Hastings's citation of the Mississippi River and the planting of cash crops in his letter to Brigham Young foreshadows his support for the Confederacy during the Civil War a year later, and his seemingly newfound support for slaveholding more generally. As a lawyer from Ohio, and then a delegate who voted to keep slavery out of California in the 1849 constitutional convention, his shifting loyalties have been portrayed as the outlandish, self-serving plots of a desperate man—which, in many ways, they were. Indeed, it seems likely that Jefferson Davis's willingness to commission Hastings as a major and authorize his plan to seize Arizona stemmed from his belief not that the idea would succeed but that it would get this fanatical schemer out of Richmond, and Davis ultimately had nothing to lose in giving the go-ahead. Yet Hastings's affinity for the Confederacy also makes sense ideologically. He was devoted to local democracy and local autonomy, and from his writings about Indian labor in California, he fully supported forced servitude. Just as southern Californios' economic and social practices caused them to ally with southern slaveholders in California in the 1850s to create the political alliance known as the "Chivalry" or "Chivs," so too did his ideology of labor and politics lead him to support the Confederacy. Additionally, his worldview mirrored that of many northerners—particularly butternut Ohioans—who believed the North had no right to keep the South in the Union by force. In this belief, he echoed people like his fellow Ohioan and notorious Copperhead Clement Vallandingham and Joseph Lane, the Oregon senator who ran as the vice presidential candidate as a southern Democrat on the Breckinridge ticket in 1860. While Hastings came to support the Confederacy through a geographically anomalous route in which he rarely set foot in the South itself, ultimately his ideological affinities aligned to a much greater extent with the Confederacy than with a Republican United States, its constituency of yeomen farmers, and their support for a stronger national government.[29]

And, with the Confederacy's final defeat, Hastings's ideology of democratic patriarchy, and just as important his desire to be a leader of this society, made it quite logical that he would attempt to create a colony of ex-Confederate slaveholders in Brazil. Once again, he planned to lead a body of emigrants to create a colony of landed patriarchs—in essence, he would re-create the most successful part of his life in the early 1840s, when he wrote *The Emigrants' Guide to Oregon and California* and led two overland partics west. That Hastings was attempting to re-create his glory days was abundantly apparent when he published *The Emigrants' Guide to Brazil*, a work that mirrored the former in many ways, despite the vast differences that separated California in the 1840s from Brazil in the 1860s. In Brazil, Hastings described how the land was so fertile that it was possible to have a "livelihood with little or no labor," as the "usual incentives to labor, energy and enterprise are greatly diminished." However, this fertility presented an opportunity for immigrants, for "the industrious . . . who retain their energy, can, with these powerful aids, in a very few years, amass wealth and accumulate fortunes, which, in less favorable climes, would require a whole lifetime of incessant toil." He praised the hospitality and generosity of the Brazilian people and contrasted the personal safety he felt there with the thievery of New York City. Finally, in perhaps the most eloquent passage in either of the emigrants' guides, Hastings described a scene of solitude and bliss that he experienced while falling asleep on a boat through the Amazon:

> Night throws her mantle over the external world, still the happy groups and occupants of the hammocks remain at their respective posts, fanned by the refreshing trade winds, gazing upon the starry heavens, until the rising moon pours forth her mellow light, in cloudless majesty, unveiling a night scene, peculiar alone to the tropical climes; upon which, American emigrants gaze with ecstasies of delight, forgetting the past, in contemplating the beauties of the present, and in anticipation of the peaceful, glorious future of the New World.

If a former Confederate was contemplating remaking himself in Brazil, this passage would help sell him.[30]

As he did in the early 1840s, Hastings employed his endurance for travel, journeying more than nineteen thousand miles to and around Brazil to scout out his colony. Once again, his guidebook and promotional abilities proved successful, as he embarked with more than one hundred settlers from Mobile in late 1866. Once again, it seems Hastings also possessed grandiose dreams of empire, hoping to enlarge his colony to incorporate the Caribbean and the Gulf of Mexico. And, once again, Hastings possessed shoddy geographic knowledge, setting up his colony in Santarém in the Amazon region—a decision that would lead to much suffering of the colonists. Yet, despite Hastings's poor selection of a site, his colony was the only one of the various Confederate colonies in Brazil to persist for decades after initial settlement, whereas the other "Confederados" either relocated to established towns or returned to the United States. Unluckily for Hastings, he would not live to see his colony survive, dying of yellow fever in St. Thomas on his return to Brazil.[31]

While Hastings's decisions can be understood through his ideological affinity for democratic patriarchy, this ideology also helps us to understand why so many Anglo-American men chose to follow him during the several decades of his adult life. The pages of *The Emigrants' Guide to Oregon and California* described a world of "unsophisticated democracy" that was seamlessly attuned to the Jacksonian democratic ideology of these men, but combined it with a potential world of power, wealth, luxury, and leisure that did not exist in the northern United States where he promoted his guidebook. He offered northerners a way to live the seemingly easygoing life of southern planters, but without the moral baggage and supposed paternalist burdens of black chattel slavery. It remains impossible to pinpoint exactly why hundreds of Americans chose California over Oregon in 1846, the only year before the gold rush when California migrants outnumbered those to Oregon. Surely the very existence of *The Emigrants' Guide* had a large effect, yet in all likelihood its depiction of the idyllic lives of California landowners sold overlanders. Perhaps, too, it was this idyllic life that Hastings described in person on the overland trail, which turned even more from Oregon to California. While the yeoman ideal had taken hold among a wide swath of the US population—and, in the North, would soon be solidified with the dominance of the Republican Party—some wanted more land, more power, and more leisure than could be obtained with the life of a simple farmer. Would-be Sutters and would-be McLoughlins may have not constituted significant numbers in the early 1840s, but Hastings's success reveals that they existed.[32]

The reverse statement also holds true: the existence of, and desire for, a society of democratic patriarchs helps explain Hastings's personal achievements. His successful selling of California over Oregon meant that he tapped into a market in which some men did not want to remain or become yeomen farmers, but instead powerful patriarchs. His ability to sway men on the overland trail itself likely demonstrated the same thing. We do not know what Hastings said to become elected as a major in the California Battalion in 1846, or elected to the California Constitutional Convention in 1849, but clearly, he was able to speak to the dreams and possibilities Americans held for their lives in California. Finally, after a series of economic and political failures in the 1850s, Hastings was once again able to speak to a similar idea of democratic patriarchy when he found an audience with the Confederate government in

1864, and when he gathered more than a hundred settlers for Brazil in 1866. Even Brigham Young's snubbing of Hastings shows the same point: unlike some American overlanders, California residents, Confederate politicians, and ex-Confederate inhabitants, Young had no desire to create a society of Mormon democratic patriarchs that mirrored that of slaveholders along the Mississippi.

In the end, Hastings's writings and his larger ideology captured a worldview that has often been overlooked by historians of Jacksonian America, particularly when concentrating on the North and the West. Hastings did not ascribe to the Jeffersonian ideal of the yeoman farmer; to him, this figure worked too hard and possessed too little economic and social power. Nor did he find affinity with commercialism and fledgling industrialization of US cities and towns. He desired local democracy combined with landed patriarchy—a society that did not exist in the US North or West and existed in less than desirable form (in the eyes of northerners) in the US South. It is no coincidence that Hastings chose to leave the United States in order to realize this society. He found portions of this vision in the fiefdoms of John McLoughlin and John Sutter, in the vast ranchos of the Californios, and eventually in the plantocracy of the US South. With the triumph of the Republican Party in the United States, and its vision of yeoman farms, transcontinental railroads, and industrialized cities, Hastings's vision was no longer tenable, and both he and the societies that he admired disappeared into memory.

NOTES

1. Works on Hastings specifically include Will Bagley, "Lansford Warren Hastings: Scoundrel or Visionary?," *Overland Journal* 12 (Spring 1994): 12–26; John Cumming, "Lansford Hastings' Michigan Connection," *Overland Journal* 16 (Fall 1998): 17–28; Thomas Franklin Andrews, "The Controversial Career of Lansford Warren Hastings: Pioneer California Promoter and Emigrant Guide" (PhD diss., University of Southern California, 1970); Andrews, "The Ambitions of Lansford W. Hastings: A Study in Western Myth-Making," *Pacific Historical Review* 39 (November 1970): 473–491; Andrews, "Lansford W. Hastings and the Promotion of the Salt Lake Desert Cutoff: A Reappraisal," *Western Historical Quarterly* 4 (April 1973): 133–150. Historiography on Hastings generally revolves around whether he deserves his infamous status. Andrews argues that he did not deserve blame for the Donner Party disaster, and his scheme to seize California did not exist. Bagley counters that Hastings deserves his poor reputation, and he was a "scoundrel." This chapter is an attempt to ask a different question and is not concerned with whether Hastings was, in Bagley's words, a "scoundrel or a visionary." See also Will Bagley, *So Rugged and Mountainous: Blazing the Trails to Oregon and California, 1812–1848* (Norman: University of Oklahoma Press, 2010), 131–133,

168–171, 180–183, 187–188, 248–254, 304–314; Eugene C. Harter, *The Lost Colony of the Confederacy* (Jackson: University Press of Mississippi, 1985), 25–30; Cyrus B. Dawsey and James M. Dawsey, eds., *The Confederados: Old South Immigrants in Brazil* (Tuscaloosa: University of Alabama Press, 1995), 62–64; Dale Morgan, "Introduction," in *Overland in 1846: Diaries and Letters of the California-Oregon Trail*, ed. Dale Morgan, 2 vols. (Georgetown, CA: Talisman Press, 1963), 36–41.

2. Much of Hastings's correspondence sunk during his 1845 voyage to California. See Andrews, "Controversial Career," 194–195.

3. Florencia Mallon coined the expression "democratic patriarchy" in her description of the caudillos of early Mexico. Mallon, *Peasant and Nation: The Making of Mexico and Peru* (Berkeley: University of California Press, 1995), 74–88. While I subscribe to much of Mallon's definition, I argue that Hastings's democratic patriarchy had a distinctly Jacksonian and Anglo-American flavor. I have also drawn on the works of Louise Pubols on California and Andrew Cayton on Texas. See Pubols, *The Father of All: The de la Guerra Family, Power, and Patriarchy in Mexican California* (Berkeley: University of California Press, 2009); Cayton, "Continental Politics: Continentalism, Nationalism, and the Appeal of Texas in the 1820s," in *Beyond the Founders: New Approaches to the Political History of the Early Republic*, ed. Jeffrey L. Pasley, Andrew W. Robertson, and David Waldstreicher (Chapel Hill: University of North Carolina Press, 2004), 303–324.

4. For an analysis of the rapid Republican political takeover of California, see Glenna Matthews, *The Golden State in the Civil War: Thomas Starr King, the Republican Party, and the Birth of Modern California* (New York: Cambridge University Press, 2012), 64–83. The classic on Republican ideology remains Eric Foner, *Free Soil, Free Labor, Free Men: The Ideology of the Republican Party before the Civil War* (New York: Oxford University Press, 1970).

5. On Hastings's responsibility for the Donner Party tragedy, see Bagley, *So Rugged and Mountainous*, 132–133, 248–249. For a rebuttal, see Thomas F. Andrews, "The Controversial Hastings Overland Guide: A Reassessment," *Pacific Historical Review* 37 (February 1968): 21–34.

6. Lansford W. Hastings, *The Emigrants' Guide to Oregon and California* (1845; repr., Princeton, NJ: Princeton University Press, 1932), 5–9; Sydney Moss describing Elijah White, quoted in Andrews, "Controversial Career," 12.

7. Hastings, *Emigrants' Guide to Oregon and California*, 9.

8. Hastings, 150. For Hastings's support for Democrats, see Hastings to Abraham Rencher, July 11, 1858, William Gillett Ritch Papers, Huntington Library, San Marino, CA; David Alan Johnson, *Founding the Far West: California, Oregon, and Nevada, 1840–1890* (Berkeley: University of California Press, 1993), 111–113, 135–136. For the egalitarianism and individualism present in overland companies, see Jimmy L. Bryan Jr., *The American Elsewhere: Adventure and Manliness in the Age of Expansion* (Lawrence: University Press of Kansas, 2017), 222–229.

9. Hastings to McLoughlin, April 8, 1843, in *McLoughlin's Fort Vancouver Letters, Third Series, 1844–1846*, ed. E. E. Rich (Toronto: Champlain Society, 1944), 252; Hastings, *Emigrants' Guide to Oregon and California*, 51. On John McLoughlin, see Dorothy Nafus

Morrison, *Outpost: John McLoughlin and the Far Northwest* (Portland, OR: Portland Historical Society Press, 1999); Anne F. Hyde, *Empires, Nations, and Families: A New History of the North American West* (Lincoln: University of Nebraska Press, 2012), 89–146. For a full text of the anti-McLoughlin petition, see W. H. Gray, *A History of Oregon, 1792–1849, Drawn from Personal Observation and Authentic Information* (Portland, OR: Harris and Holman, 1870), 292–296. Bagley asserts that McLoughlin may have continued to employ Hastings after his departure from Oregon, paying him to divert American overlanders from Oregon to California (thereby preserving the HBC's power in Oregon). While this may have been wholly or partially true, there were many other reasons for Hastings to support immigration to California over Oregon. Bagley, "Lansford Warren Hastings," 17.

10. Hastings, *Emigrants' Guide to Oregon and California*, 103, 104. On Sutter, see Albert L. Hurtado, *John Sutter: A Life on the North American Frontier* (Norman: University of Oklahoma Press, 2006). For Indian slavery in California, see Stacey Smith, *Freedom's Frontier: California and the Struggle over Unfree Labor, Emancipation, and Reconstruction* (Chapel Hill: University of North Carolina Press, 2014), 15–24; Andrés Reséndez, *The Other Slavery: The Uncovered Story of Indian Slavery in America* (Boston: Houghton Mifflin Harcourt, 2016), 250–265; Michael F. Magliari, "Free Soil, Unfree Labor: Cave Johnson Coutts and the Binding of Indian Workers in California, 1850–1867," *Pacific Historical Review* 73 (August 2004): 349–389; Magliari, "Free State Slavery: Bound Indian Labor and Slave Trafficking in California's Sacramento Valley, 1850–1864," *Pacific Historical Review* 81 (May 2012): 155–192. For McLoughlin's métis workers, see Melinda Marie Jetté, *At the Hearth of the Crossed Races: A French-Indian Community in Nineteenth-Century Oregon, 1812–1859* (Corvallis: Oregon State University Press, 2015), 42–67, 121–126.

11. As I have argued elsewhere, opinions of McLoughlin shifted depending on the strength of the American community in Oregon. In the early 1840s, when HBC employees enjoyed a majority of the population and McLoughlin held sway, Americans feared his power. By 1845, when they constituted 90 percent of the population, they regarded McLoughlin with much greater affection. For this discussion and for US opinions of Sutter and the California rebellion, see Thomas Richards Jr., "Farewell to America: The Expatriation Politics of Overland Migration, 1841–1846," *Pacific Historical Review* 86 (February 2017): 134–137, 142, 146–147. See also Hurtado, *John Sutter*, 138–150, 240–241, 245–246, 343–344.

12. Hastings, *Emigrants' Guide to Oregon and California*, 113, 132.

13. Hastings, 93–94, 113. On the patriarchal power of wealthy California, see especially Pubols, *The Father of All*. For the California seigneurial system of land, labor, and dependency, see Douglas Monroy, *Thrown among Strangers: The Making of Mexican Culture in Frontier California* (Berkeley: University of California Press, 1990).

14. Hastings, *Emigrants' Guide to Oregon and California*, 125–126.

15. Hastings, 22, 33–42, 69–80, 85, 92, 110–111, 123, 132. For a discussion of patriarchy versus paternalism in California and an analysis of the historiography surrounding both, see Daniel Lynch, "Southern California Chivalry: The Convergence of Southerners and Californios in the Far Southwest, 1846–1866" (PhD diss., Uni-

versity of Southern California, 2015), 8–11. The classic on southern paternalism is Eugene Genovese, *Roll Jordan Roll: The World the Slaves Made* (New York: Vintage Books, 1976). Although this work has received much criticism in the past few decades, it is helpful for identifying what California Indian slavery was *not*.

16. Hastings, *Emigrants' Guide to Oregon and California*, 151, 133. Other travelogues from these years include Richard Henry Dana Jr., *Two Years Before the Mast* (New York: Harper & Brothers, 1840), 99–122, 216; Thomas J. Farnham, *Travels in California, and Scenes of the Pacific* (New York: Saxton & Miles, 1844), especially chap. 5. For a discussion on the anti-Mexican portrayals within US expansionist literatures, see Raymund A. Paredes, "The Mexican Image in American Travel Literature, 1831–1869," *New Mexico Historical Review* 52 (January 1977): 5–29; David Weber, "'Scarce More Than Apes': Historical Roots of Anglo-American Stereotypes of Mexicans," in *New Spain's Far Northern Frontier: Essays on Spain in the American West, 1540–1821*, ed. David Weber (Albuquerque: University of New Mexico Press, 1979), 293–307; Antonia Castañeda, "The Political Economy of Nineteenth-Century Stereotypes of Californianas," in *Between Borders: Essays on Mexicanas/Chicana History*, ed. Adelaida del Castillo (Encino, CA: Floricanto Press, 1990), 213–236.

17. For the story of Graham, see Doyce Nunis, *The Trials of Isaac Graham* (Los Angeles: Dawson's Book Shop, 1967).

18. Hastings, *Emigrants' Guide to Oregon and California*, 123.

19. Hastings, 55–57; "Law of Land Claims," in La Fayette Grover, comm., *The Oregon Archives, Including the Journals, Governors' Messages, and Public Papers of Oregon* (Salem, OR: Asahel Bush, 1853), 35. On the desire of Anglo-American men to bequeath their sons with land, see Kathleen Neils Conzen, "A Saga of Families," in *The Oxford History of the American West*, ed. Clyde A. Milner II, Carol A. O'Connor, and Martha A. Sandweiss (New York: Oxford University Press, 1994), 315–358.

20. *California Star and Californian* (San Francisco), December 9, 1848. On the threat of the market revolution to American manhood, see Joshua R. Greenberg, *Advocating the Man: Masculinity, Organized Labor, and the Household in New York, 1800–1840* (New York: Columbia University Press, 2008), 49–118; Amy S. Greenberg, *Manifest Manhood and the Antebellum American Empire* (New York: Cambridge University Press, 2005), 5–13; David Pugh, *Sons of Liberty: The Masculine Mind in Nineteenth-Century America* (Westport, CT: Greenwood Press, 1984), 3–44; E. Anthony Rotundo, *American Manhood: Transformations in Masculinity from the Revolution to the Modern Era* (New York: Basic Books, 1993), 167–221. For the desire for manly independence, see Richards, "Farewell to America," 118–121. For Hastings's family, see Hubert Howe Bancroft, *History of California*, 5 vols. (San Francisco: History Company Publishers, 1886), 5:749; *Californian* (Monterey), September 30, 1848; Joseph Eugene Baker, *Past and Present of Alameda County of California*, 2 vols. (Chicago: S. J. Clark Publishing, 1914), 2:465–466. For a gendered analysis of overland families, see John Mack Faragher, *Women and Men on the Overland Trail* (New Haven, CT: Yale University Press, 1979). For the motivations of overlanders, see John D. Unruh, *The Plains Across: The Overland Emigrants and the Trans-Mississippi West* (Urbana: University of Illinois Press, 1979), chap. 3.

21. Andrews, "Controversial Career," 216–217. Andrews cites a letter from Lansford to Isabel, dated April 10, 1863, and only listed it as "in private possession," with no other information provided. I have been unable to locate this letter.

22. Hastings, *Emigrants' Guide to Oregon and California*, xxix, 112 113, 123, 152.

23. Andrews, "Controversial Career," 172–184. Andrews disputes that Hastings sought a California republic, but the evidence suggests otherwise, and it remains consistent with his later schemes. See Lansford Hastings to Thomas Marsh, March 26, 1846, Marsh Family Papers; John Bidwell, *Echoes of the Past* (New York: Citadel Press, 1962), 92–94; Charles Putnam to Joseph Putnam, July 11, 1846, in *Overland in 1846: Diaries and Letters of the California-Oregon Trail*, ed. Dale Morgan, 2 vols. (Georgetown, CA: Talisman Press), 2:603; Ben E. Green to John C. Calhoun, April 11, 1844, in *The Papers of John Calhoun*, vol. 18, *1844*, ed. Clyde N. Wilson (Columbia: University of South Carolina Press, 1989), 203–204. For more on the contingency of western expansion, see Andrew C. Isenberg and Thomas Richards Jr., "Alternative Wests: Rethinking Manifest Destiny," *Pacific Historical Review* 86 (February 2017): 4–17. In the famed article in which he coined the term "manifest destiny," John L. O'Sullivan himself stated that he believed California would join the Union in one hundred years. O'Sullivan [attributed], "Annexation," *United States Magazine and Democratic Review* 17 (July and August 1845): 10. For the western hatred of territorial status, see Patricia Limerick, *The Legacy of Conquest: The Unbroken Past of the American West* (New York: W. W. Norton, 1987), 44–48. Hastings's contact with the Mormons was Samuel Brannan, who had been appointed by Brigham Young to oversee Mormon migration from the United States to Mexican California, from where these eastern Mormons would travel to the Salt Lake Valley. Brannan, however, hoped to get rich himself, disagreed with Young about going to the Salt Lake Valley, and hoped to keep the Mormons in California. He abandoned Mormonism for the wealth of the gold fields. Needless to say, he would probably not have given Hastings a reliable account of Mormonism or the Mormons' intentions. Will Bagley, ed., *Scoundrel's Tale: The Samuel Brannan Papers* (Spokane, WA: Arthur H. Clark, 1999), 75–130.

24. J. Ross Browne, *Report on the Debates on the Convention of California* (Washington, DC: John T. Towers, 1850), 123, 173; Andrews, "Controversial Career," 186; Johnson, *Founding the Far West*, 136–137.

25. Bagley, "Lansford Warren Hastings," 19–20; William C. Griggs, "Migration of the McMullan Colonists and Evolution of the Colonies in Brazil," in *The Confederados*, ed. Cyrus B. Dawsey and James M. Dawsey (Tuscaloosa: University of Alabama Press, 1995), 62; Eliza P. Donner Houghton, *The Expedition of the Donner Party and Its Tragic Fate* (Los Angeles: Grafton Publishing, 1920), 43; George R. Stewart, *The California Trail: An Epic with Many Heroes* (New York: McGraw-Hill, 1962), 182–183; Andrews, "Lansford W. Hastings," 473–474, 478n17. For Hastings in New Mexico, see Hastings to Rencher, July 11, 1858, Ritch Papers, Huntington Library.

26. Andrews, "Controversial Career," 213; Bagley, "Lansford Warren Hastings," 22; Hurtado, *John Sutter*, 245–250.

27. Lansford Hastings to Brigham Young, June 30, 1861, Brigham Young Office Files, Latter-Day Saints Church History Library, Salt Lake City, UT.

28. For an analysis of Hastings's faulty geographic knowledge, see Bagley, "Lansford Warren Hastings," 22–23.

29. Hastings to Jefferson Davis, January 11, 1864, reprinted in Andrews, "Controversial Career," 246–251; Lynch, "Southern California Chivalry"; Matthews, *Golden State in the Civil War*, 15–40.

30. Lansford Hastings, *The Emigrants' Guide to Brazil* (n.p., ca. 1867), 29, 32, 87–88, 101.

31. Hastings's embarkation in 1866 was actually his fourth journey. Griggs, "Migration of the McMullan Colonists," and John C. Dawsey, "Constructing Identity: Defining the American Descendants in Brazil," in Dawsey and Dawsey, *Confederados*, 62–65, 172.

32. For a discussion of why migrants chose Oregon or California, see Dorothy Johansen, "A Working Hypothesis for the Study of Migration," *Pacific Historical Review* 36 (February 1967): 1–12; Richards, "Farewell to America," 125–127.

CHAPTER 10

Safely "Beyond the Limits of the United States": The Mormon Expulsion and US Expansion

Gerrit Dirkmaat

Sometime in early April 1844, one of the more unusual exchanges occurred in the history of US expansion. Samuel Houston, president of the Republic of Texas, held several secret meetings with a foreign emissary. Houston had not expected the encounter, but the possibilities offered by the stranger were too enticing to reject outright.

The embattled president had been driven by desperation to seek any possible means to remedy the precarious situation of his country. Mexico had never recognized the nascent republic's independence. Indeed, several times in the preceding years Mexican forces had invaded the republic, capturing San Antonio and the infamous Alamo, causing both alarm and embarrassment in light of the Texan claim to national sovereignty. In addition, the republic's debts seemed insurmountable. Texas had never recovered from the economic catastrophe incident to the Panic of 1837, a financial position exacerbated by expensive military campaigns undertaken against both American Indian groups and Mexico. Houston had been elected to the presidency for the second time in 1841 when the economic catastrophe was still unfolding. His certitude of the precarious position his country was in had even led him to send commissioners to Mexico to seek an "armistice." Mexico had only agreed to the terms by inserting language into the document that asserted Texas was still a "department" of Mexico, challenging on paper, at least, the Texan claim to independence.[1]

Houston understood that the only thing preventing Mexico from militarily reasserting its control over the renegade "department" was the political instability inside Mexico itself. If that were ever remedied, Texas, with less than 10 percent the population of its former sovereign, would face a dire crisis. He had negotiated with French, German, British, and US governmental and nongovernmental actors, seeking foreign recognition, loans, and immigrants to bolster the position of Texas vis-à-vis Mexico. Houston's greatest hopes, however, lay with desperate efforts his ministers in Washington, DC, were making to bring about a US annexation of Texas. In short, he sought to save his beloved republic by dissolving it. For Houston, US expansion was the only viable answer to the Texan problem.

His counterpart in the negotiations that day was Lucien Woodworth, an elder in the Church of Jesus Christ of Latter-day Saints, whose members were commonly referred to as Mormons. Unlike most traveling Mormon elders, Woodworth was not there to proselytize Houston. In fact, when the president asked for some of the Mormon religious books, Woodworth had none to offer but promised to send some later. He explained to Houston, "I did not come to treat with [you] on religion." He was not on a mission to save souls but had instead been dispatched by the Mormon leader, Joseph Smith, to engage Houston on the possibility of saving the religious community, moving it out of its besieged enclave at Nauvoo in western Illinois to the Republic of Texas, en masse.[2]

The prospect of thousands of Mormon immigrants, potentially tens of thousands in the years to come, intrigued Houston. The Mormon population in the area surrounding Nauvoo alone was estimated to be near twenty thousand in 1844, or 20 percent of the population of the Republic of Texas. Newspapers often wildly exaggerated the number of Mormons, making such an arrangement all the more tempting as a last-ditch effort to save the territorial integrity of the republic.[3] In fact, while Woodworth and Houston spoke in Galveston of the possible immigration, Texas supporters in Washington, DC, had succeeded in pushing an annexation bill to the floor of the Congress, but it would be handily defeated weeks later, causing the republic further angst and despair. Reports of stiff US opposition to annexation were already circulating in Texas papers.[4]

The amicable talks between Houston and Woodworth resulted in the former's offer to press the issue of Mormon migration to Texas. Yet the two men, both hailing originally from the United States, could not have been further

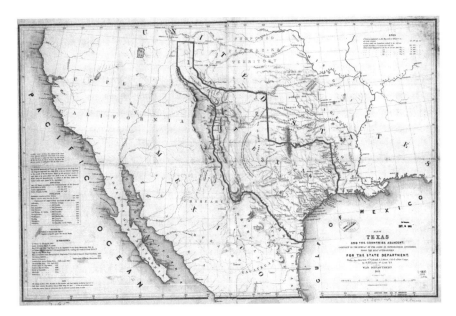

Figure 10.1. Anticipating the annexation of Texas, the US Senate commissioned this map that depicts that republic's expansive boundary claims. In addition, the label "Upper California" extends from the Pacific to the Great Basin. The Library of Congress copy includes a hand-drawn border for the Republic of Texas; this figure shows a digitally enhanced border. William H. Emory, *Map of Texas and the Countries Adjacent.* Washington, DC: US Senate, 1844. Library of Congress, Washington, DC.

apart in their view of US sovereignty. For Houston, annexation by the United States meant safety, security, stability, and economic relief. Ardent slaveholders of the republic also championed annexation as a way of saving their institution. For them, annexation would guarantee that slavery was defended from both the intrigues of British abolitionists and Mexican emancipationist laws. For the Mormons, the only reason they were considering the nearly thousand-mile trek to Texas was precisely because it was outside of the boundaries of the United States.

The Mormon views of sovereignty and expansion present a singular example of the limits of US nationalism and identity in the mid-nineteenth century. Though the vast majority of Mormons were US citizens, by the fall and winter of 1843, Joseph Smith and other Mormon leaders had concluded that American democracy was a failure, at least in their case. The US government had refused to intervene in the bloody expulsion of Mormons from Missouri, refused to force the state to grant them back their confiscated lands and properties, and even refused to acknowledge the gross violations of both personal and property rights in what was often termed the "Mormon War." Indeed, the governor of Missouri, Lilburn Boggs, had during that conflict signed an order that called for indiscriminate violence on the part of the forces of the state: "The Mormons must be treated as enemies and must be exterminated or driven from the State if necessary for the public peace; their outrages are beyond all description."[5]

While the history of US expansionism provides many examples of citizens striking out into disputed and foreign territories as they looked forward hopefully to the day of eventual US sovereignty and power encompassing them, the Mormons present a stark contrast.[6] By 1844, Mormon leaders were deliberately looking for a way to settle somewhere outside of US control. To that end, Joseph Smith formed a secret council, the Council of Fifty, whose mission it was to seek out a place somewhere in western North America where the thousands of harried Mormons could find peace, and ultimately establish their own kingdom. They envisioned a theocratically based democracy, one that, unlike the US federal and state governments, would allow them to gather together as a people with neither the subsequent fallout from their political and economic power nor the ire of their neighbors for what were almost universally deemed blasphemous alterations to traditional Protestantism. The minutes of the Council of Fifty meetings were until 2017 closed to academic research, but now scholars can gain a new understanding of how and why Mormons sought to find refuge outside of the United States and its territory.

Organized anti-Mormon committees, denunciatory religious and newspaper attacks, and even occasional mob violence escalated precipitously in Missouri in 1838 when the religious group attempted to vote in elections, leading to a brawl that ignited widespread violence of the Mormon War. While accusations of perfidy abounded on both sides, local county militias, under the auspices of the state, conducted a campaign of terror against Mormon settlements. The worst violence occurred at Hawn's (also Haun's) Mill, where the Missouri state militia from Livingston County had indiscriminately fired on men and women, killing seventeen and wounding more than a dozen others. Among the dead were two young boys aged nine and ten. Smith and other Mormon leaders were lured out of their headquarters in Far West to what they thought was a peace conference only to be arrested. Though one Missouri militia commander ordered that Smith be summarily executed, that order was delayed and instead the Mormon leader was imprisoned for months.[7]

Bolstered by the sweeping extermination order issued by Governor Boggs, the unrestrained Missouri militiamen then entered the largest Mormon settlement in Caldwell County, Far West. There they ravaged and looted the town, committing unspeakable depredations, including violent sexual assaults. Hyrum Smith, the brother of Joseph and likewise incarcerated, described the horrific reports that he and the others had at first greeted incredulously as they awaited one of their trials in prison:

> The grand Jury that was empaneled were all at the Massacre at Haun's Mills and lively actors in that awful, solemn and disgraceful cool blooded murder and all the pretense they made of excuse was "they had done it because the Governor ordered them to do it." This same Jury sat as Jury in the day time and were placed over us as a guard in the night time; they tantalized and boasted over us of their great achievements at Haun's Mills and other places, telling us, "how many houses they had burned and how many sheep cattle and hogs they had driven off belonging to the Mormons and how many rapes they had committed, and what squealing and kicking there was amongst the damned bitches"—Saying that "they lashed one woman upon one of the damned Mormon meeting benches, tying her hands and her feet fast and sixteen of them abused her as much as they had a mind to and then left her bound and exposed in that distressed condition." These fiends of the lower regions boasted of these acts of barbarity and tantalized our feelings with them for ten days. We had heard of these acts of cruelty previous to this time, but we were slow to believe that such acts of cruelty had been perpetrated, [but] the lady who was the subject of their brutality, did not recover her health, to be able to keep herself for more than three months afterwards.[8]

Despite such horrific scenes of violence and the misery and the scars that accompanied their expulsion from Missouri, the Mormons for several years continued to maintain their devotion to the United States and its institutions in their newly established city in Nauvoo, Illinois. While Smith and his followers were continually frustrated at the unwillingness of the federal government at the judicial, legislative, and executive levels to intervene on their behalf, their criticisms of the United States focused on its elected officers, like President Martin Van Buren, rather than its institutions.[9]

In 1841, three years after the horrifying ordeal in Missouri and with their love of the United States apparently undimmed, thousands of Mormons lined the streets of Nauvoo, Illinois, to celebrate the Fourth of July. According to one account, Joseph Smith "strongly testified of his regard for our national welfare, and his willingness to lay down his life in defense of his country—and closed with these remarkable words, 'I would ask no greater boon than to lay down my life for my country.'"[10]

But the rapidly growing city with its booming population quickly began to chafe the non-Mormon residents of western Illinois. By 1843, Nauvoo had become an economic and political power broker in the western portion of the state. Worse, the radical sect's followers tended to vote in blocs, which led to allegations of blind allegiance to Joseph Smith at best and outright vote simony to the highest bidder at worst. Local citizens also feared the large city militia Nauvoo had been granted in its organizational charter, especially so because the charismatic Smith was the commanding general, combining religious authority and martial power in a way that seemed antithetical to American democracy, whether Smith abused such power or not.

One newspaper at the time opined of the Mormon troubles, "All may be remedied, if the Mormons, as a religious body, will but eschew politics and amalgamate with our citizens." If the Mormons wanted peace in the United States, they would need to conform. Even then, this writer reflected an ominous foreboding: "We fear it is too late to do even that."[11] Of course, Mormon votes were deemed most offensive when they were cast for the opposition party. The *Quincy Whig* lamented that the Whig candidate for the Sixth Illinois Congressional District lost by "a few hundred votes" despite the fact that nearly the entire district favored the Whigs. The Mormons had voted for the Democratic candidate and single-handedly "settled the question in this district." Whig turnout was high, but nothing could "offsct the heavy Mormon vote."[12]

Another politically charged newspaper declared that Mormons' willingness to shift their allegiance between the two parties was proof of their depravity. When the Mormons switched from supporting a Whig candidate to his Democratic opponent, this Whig paper declared the election results to be clear evidence of Mormon immorality: "They are without principle, political or moral, and . . . treachery and deception constitute one of the principle attributes of their nature." Politically scorned, the Whig writer explained that the Mormons were incapable of having "feelings in common with men of integrity and honor."[13]

Such feelings appeared widespread even before the 1843 congressional elections. An Alton, Illinois, paper editorially lamented of Joseph Smith and Mormons:

> Their blasphemies, their violations of law, their utter disregard of all the social relations of life, are permitted to progress with impunity. We therefore regard it as the most unfortunate affair that ever befell the State of Illinois, when Joe Smith selected this State as the theatre of his actions, to carry out his blasphemous, corrupt, and irreligious designs. It speaks but poorly in favor of the advancement of Christianity or even civilization.[14]

When Illinois governor Thomas Ford reflected on the violence that ultimately forced a Mormon expulsion from his state, he too placed the blame primarily on Mormons' political power. "It is indeed unfortunate," he wrote, "for their peace that they do not divide in elections according to their individual preferences or political principles, like other people."[15]

Of course, like many minority groups, Mormons had a shared sense of what mattered most politically. They called for the recovery of thousands of acres of land confiscated from them by Missouri, as well as governmental guarantees that renewed mob violence would be snuffed out by authorities. The Mormons shifted their vote between the Whig and Democrat parties readily in pursuit of those ends. In any case, storm clouds were appearing on Nauvoo's horizon.

By late 1843, the situation in Illinois was becoming more precarious. Anti-Mormon conventions were frequently held in the surrounding non-Mormon communities. They passed a variety of resolutions and at times rejected the political authority of any Mormon elected to office or any official who was seen as trucking in Mormon votes. Under the ominous headline "Threatened Destruction of the Mormons," an Indiana paper reported on the "excitement" of non-Mormon residents of Illinois against the sect, "Many of the most violent are demanding the complete extermination of the Mormons from the country; and to effect this object, the aid of 20,000 Missourians is evidently expected."[16]

With the impending 1844 presidential campaign, Joseph Smith wrote letters to the presumed candidates from the Whig and Democratic Parties, asking if they would lend their support to protect the Mormons and help them get their confiscated land back from Missouri if they were elected. Lewis Cass, John C. Calhoun, Richard Mentor Johnson, and Henry Clay all refused to commit themselves to the Mormon cause. As a result, the Mormons were left with few viable options. Anti-Mormon threats and antagonism were growing on the local and state levels, and federal officials were now on record as refusing to help them remunerate the loss of their Missouri properties or defend them from such attacks in the future.[17]

In addition, Smith's radical teachings had expanded still further beyond the traditional Christian boundaries, extending to limits that even some of his closest followers could no longer stomach. Though not declared publicly to the parishioners in Nauvoo, Smith had begun teaching a small group of his closest followers not only that marriages could be "sealed," and therefore the couple could continue in the marriage relationship forever in heaven, but that they should reinstitute the Old Testament practice of plural marriage.[18] Smith had begun the practice of having other women "married or sealed" to him in

Nauvoo as early as 1841. Dozens of women consented to these polygamous marriage relationships with Smith and other male members. Some Mormon leaders like William Law, one of Smith's counselors, utterly rejected the practice of plural marriage as an aberrant evil, thus raising the specter of a schism.

While appalled at plural marriage teachings, Law seemed to be nearly as offended by another of Smith's radical teachings: the progression of God and the plurality of gods. While this idea had been fulminating for years, Smith dictated a revelation that declared not only that marriage was essential for exaltation in the highest glory of heaven, but that those who were faithful would become like God in the eternities: "Then Shall they be Gods, because they have no end. Therefore, Shall they be from everlasting to Everlasting because they Continue[.] Then Shall they be above all because all things are subject unto them. Then Shall they be Gods because they have all power and the angels are subject unto them."[19]

While mortals could be granted by the deity the godlike powers he held, Smith further declared in a public meeting that God himself was once a man on another earth and progressed to his position of power:

> I want you to understand God and how he comes to be God. We suppose that God was God from Eternity, I will refute that Idea, or I will do away or take away the veil so you may see. It is the first principle to know that we may convers with him and that he once was a man like us, and the Father was once on an earth like us . . . how consoling to the mourner when they part with a friend to know that though they lay down this body it will rise & dwell with everlasting burnings to be an heir of God & joint heir with Jesus Christ enjoying the same rise exhaltation & glory untill you arive at the station of a God.[20]

While these doctrines were embraced wholeheartedly by most Mormons, some, like William Law, recoiled in horror. He left the church and founded his own on Mormon principles, but with the claim that Joseph Smith had indeed once been a prophet before excesses led to his fall.[21]

Internal schisms and external political and economic frustrations combined to make a stew toxic to Mormon peace. By early 1844, anti-Mormon antagonism was so palpable that even the most hostile newspaper from nearby Warsaw, Illinois, remarked with at least feigned concern, "We see no use in attempting to disguise the fact, that many in our midst contemplate a total extermination of that people; that the thousands of defenseless women and children, aged and infirm, who are congregated at Nauvoo, must be driven out—aye, DRIVEN—SCATTERED—like the leaves before the Autumn blast!"[22]

In response, Smith made two sweeping decisions. In the short term, he declared himself a candidate for US president, hoping to use Mormon political leverage to bring attention to the continued plight of his people. Second, he began actively planning the Mormon exodus from the United States. His diary recorded on February 20, 1844, that he had met with the ruling leadership of the church, the Quorum of the Twelve Apostles, and instructed them "to send out a delegation & investigate the locations of California and Oregon to find a good location where we can remove after the Temple is completed & build a city in a day and have a government of our own—in a healthy climate."[23] Joseph Smith was not just exercising idle rhetoric. Three days later, in another meeting, he called for men to go on what was being termed "the Oregon Expedition." He wanted "an exposition of all that country."[24]

Just over two weeks after these meetings, letters from church leaders cutting wood in Wisconsin Territory for use in building the Nauvoo temple spurred an even more organized discussion about leaving the confines of the United States. These leaders suggested that once their logging was completed they should leave the United States behind and move to the Republic of Texas to establish another gathering place for Mormons. After a preliminary discussion on the night of March 10, 1844, another meeting was convened the next morning during which Joseph Smith organized a special council, later termed the Council of Fifty. This Council was primarily tasked with planning and undertaking the removal of Mormons from the United States. The minutes of those meetings reflected that all of the men "agreed to look to some place where we can go and establish a Theocracy either in Texas or Oregon or somewhere in California."[25]

California was the name regularly applied to the vast northern department of Mexico. The boundaries of the territory were ill-defined, in part because Mexican control of the eastern reaches of northern Mexico was less than nominal. By the Mexican constitution of 1824, Alta (upper) California encompassed all of present-day California, Utah, and Nevada and portions of Colorado. Many US maps showed an upper California that encompassed not only that area but also even larger swaths incorporating present-day Arizona and much of present-day New Mexico as well (fig. 10.2). To say the area was sparsely populated would be a dramatic understatement. The entire white population (including both Hispanic and non-Hispanic whites) of Mexican California (including Mexicans and US settlers) was estimated to be less than ten thousand.[26] The Mexican settlements were almost entirely clustered along a narrow strip on the Pacific coast. The largest of these was Los Angeles, boasting a population of around fifteen hundred mixed between Mexicans and Indians.[27] Though claimed by Mexico, much of this enormous expanse

Figure 10.2. Samuel Augustus Mitchell produced this map at the height of the "manifest destiny" debate and on the eve of the US-Mexican War. He shows the Republic of Texas and its Rio Grande claims as well as a boldly delineated Great Salt Lake region contained within the bounds of "Upper or New California." S. Augustus Mitchell, *A New Map of Texas, Oregon, and California*. Philadelphia: S. Augustus Mitchell, 1846. Library of Congress, Washington, DC.

was simply bereft of any settlements, let alone any semblance of military or practical control. Of course, tens of thousands of American Indians lived in California in hundreds of tribal groups of varying sizes, but neither Mexico nor the United States fully recognized their claims to the land.[28]

The Mormons considered pouring into this vacuum precisely because so few whites lived there. It was beyond the limits of US control and appeared to be beyond the limits of practical Mexican control. Anywhere the Mormons chose to settle in Mexican California, they would dwarf any existing white population. And this is precisely what made California such an attractive option. In most of the expansive territory there simply was no white population. Having time and again settled as a minority in various states, the Mormons had concluded that minority status anywhere in the United States was, at best, a certain prelude to antagonistic and vitriolic sentiment echoed in newspapers and local government; at worst, it allowed for the possibility of violent mobbings, theft of property, sexual and otherwise violent assault, and even indiscriminate murder.

Oregon Territory was also outside the realm of total US control. The joint occupation treaty between the United States and Great Britain allowed both nations to exploit and settle the area, with final boundaries to be determined at a later time. Despite increasing interest in the Northwest, by 1845, there were still fewer than six thousand white settlers in the whole of it, US or British. Once again, the Mormons perceived their superior population might allow them to secure a portion of the territory for themselves while playing off the two empires against one another. At any rate, their migration would double or triple the existing white population of the disputed territory and place the Mormons in a good position to secure favorable terms from either empire to protect their religious and property rights.

The proposed locale that gained early traction in these discussions was the Republic of Texas, and most of these early Council of Fifty meetings revolved around that nation as a potential landing spot for the Saints. It was these early council meetings that had determined to send Lucien Woodworth on the aforementioned journey to negotiate with Texas president Samuel Houston. Woodworth returned with favorable reports of both Houston and Texas. He explained to the Council of Fifty that he had "made a proposition to General Houston to give or sell us a tract of land on the Rio Grande."[29]

Aside from seeking out a place to settle, Woodworth had tried to lobby Houston to abandon any efforts at annexation by the United States, explaining to the council that he "did all he could to have Houston go against annexation."[30] This represented the fruition of the Mormon belief that they could no longer hope for equal treatment inside the United States. The last thing they wanted was to relocate to another nation with promises of protection only to find that nation dissolved into the larger United States. There, they could not be protected.

As annexation efforts were approaching their lowest point in 1844, no doubt Houston wanted to at least entertain the Mormon proposal as a contingency plan. In fact, after Joseph Smith's murder in the summer of 1844, Houston himself reached out to a prominent Mormon in Washington, DC, James Arlington Bennet. Bennet related back to Mormon leaders in Nauvoo that Houston had "assured me that if the Saints were in Texas then their religious & Civil rights should have the most ample protection. If occasion requires he assures me that he would receive the 'Mormon Legion' in Texas as armed Emigrants, with open Arms." Perhaps most impressive was the pronouncement Houston had made in the letter: "I am no bigot."[31]

While negotiations with Texas were pending and plans to explore other options in Mexico or Oregon were being considered, the long-simmering frustrations between the Mormon and non-Mormon residents in western Illinois exploded into bloody violence. The Mormons believed that their city charter granted them the right to remove the upstart and antagonistic press of former leader William Law as a public nuisance, accounting it libelous. The press was destroyed. But this step simply affirmed in the minds of antagonists the corrupt power Smith and the Mormons possessed. The outraged editor of the *Warsaw Signal*, long an enemy of growing Mormon power in the county, advocated the very extermination of Mormons from Illinois for which he had once feigned horror: "We have only to state, that this is sufficient! War and extermination is inevitable! Citizens ARISE, ONE and ALL!!! Can you stand by, and suffer such INFERNAL DEVILS!! to ROB men of their property and RIGHTS, without avenging them. We have no time for comment, every man will make his own. LET IT BE MADE WITH POWDER AND BALL!!!"[32] Governor Ford later explained that these anti-Mormons hoped to foment a popular mob that "would result in the expulsion or extermination of the Mormon voters. For this purpose public meetings had been called; inflammatory speeches had been made; [and] exaggerated reports and rumors had been extensively circulated." A public meeting in Warsaw had even passed resolutions determined to "exterminate the Mormon population."[33]

Ford ordered Smith to surrender himself to state authorities for trial outside of Nauvoo. The governor, having received affidavits on the destruction of the press, determined that Smith and the Nauvoo City Council had exceeded their power and needed to be tried outside of Nauvoo in order to allay public sentiment. He requested that the accused come to Carthage to stand trial. He promised that he would protect them if they came.[34]

Joseph Smith hesitated. The Mormons had once before surrendered to a state militia at the behest of a governor under a flag of truce, only to have Smith and other leaders imprisoned for months without being brought to trial as those state forces ransacked and robbed homes and properties, destroyed crops, and committed brutal assaults. Anti-Mormon antagonists were calling for his blood, and Smith took them at his word. He wrote back to the governor that he was willing to stand trial again for the destruction of the press, as the governor wanted, but they feared for their own lives. Joseph flatly stated in the letter, "We dare not come."[35]

Ultimately, after giving up on the idea of fleeing west himself to avoid the mob violence he thought would be incident to prosecution outside of Nauvoo, Joseph Smith and his brother Hyrum surrendered to the state authorities and were taken to a jail in Carthage. On June 27, 1844, after Governor Ford took most of his forces to Nauvoo, ostensibly to allay any possible Mormon retaliation for the arrest, a mob of men with painted faces stormed the jail and murdered Joseph and Hyrum Smith, and left apostle John Taylor riddled with bullet holes, though he would survive the encounter.[36]

The horrified Mormon community reacted with an outpouring of grief. The murders of Joseph and Hyrum Smith did not dissipate their determination to get outside of the boundaries of the United States. Rather, the fact that state authorities had allowed such violence to occur and appeared unlikely to bring anyone to justice for those deaths only further solidified in the minds of Mormon leaders that they would be safer among the American Indians than they would be among corrupt leaders and populations of the United States. Indeed, without many political allies left, the Illinois legislature passed a measure rescinding the Nauvoo city charter, thereby leaving the largest city in the state incapable of holding elections for public offices, maintain a city police force, pass ordinances, levy taxes, and all other administrative functions.

By January 1845, Mormon bitterness toward the United States for its lack of help, the murders of Joseph and Hyrum Smith, and the repeal of the Nauvoo city charter reached a boiling point. In these circumstances, whatever devotion to the United States and its laws that had once burned bright among Mormon leaders had been considerably dimmed. Brigham Young, the president of the Quorum of the Twelve Apostles and new leader of the church, bitterly explained of the continuing hostility following the Smith murders, "The nation has severed us from them in every respect, and made us a distinct nation just as much as the Lamanites, and it is my prayer that we may soon find a place where we can have a home and live in peace according to the Law of God."[37] He would later record in his journal, "I hope to find a place, where no self-righteous Neighbors can say that we are obnoxious to them."[38]

The Mormons thought of themselves as members of the House of Israel and referred to all non-Mormon Americans or Europeans with the term "gentile." Contrarily, they believed the American Indians to be Lamanites, members of the lost tribes of Israel, and consequently, God would help the Mormons negotiate and live among them. Young declared:

> The gentiles have rejected the gospel; they have killed the prophets, and those who have not taken an active part in the murder all rejoice in it and say amen to it, and that is saying that they are willing the blood of the prophets should be shed. The gentiles have rejected the gospel, and where shall we go to preach. We cannot go any where but to the house of Israel [in other words, among the American Indians]. We cant get salvation without it. We cant get salvation any where else.

A last-ditch effort had been made to send letters to every governor in the United States, begging for a place of Mormon refuge to be created in their respective states, but Young flatly stated that he knew "they will do nothing for us."[39] He reiterated to the Council of Fifty that the Mormons needed to "get out of the jurisdiction of the United States."[40]

In a Council of Fifty meeting on March 18, 1845, Brigham Young explained his view on leaving US territory in terms of safety. While they did not know precisely where they were going to move, Young asserted, "If we can get one hundred miles beyond the jurisdiction of the United States we are safe, for the present, and that is all we ask."[41] He further opined of Mexican California, "We want to get between some of those Mountains where we can fortify ourselves and erect the standard of liberty on one of the highest mountains we can find." In the Mormon view, the blessings of liberty were not secured by American sovereignty; in fact, they could only be obtained outside of the United States.[42]

This dichotomy in comparison to other settlers headed into the western portion of the continent could not be more pronounced. Several proposals were made by the gathered Mormon leadership to possibly settle among the Comanche Indians, at least temporarily, in their vast empire in what is today Texas and New Mexico. Rather than object to this plan because of fear of their Indian landlords, one of the primary oppositions was voiced by Brigham Young's son Brigham Young Jr. on the basis that it was too close to or within US sovereignty. "They are within the limits of the United States," he asserted, "and we should be in as great jeopardy there as here. . . . When we make a move from this place we want to go where we can be out of the reach of this government, where we can erect the standard in peace. Any where east of the rocky mountains we are within the reach of these governments."[43]

John Taylor, an apostle who had witnessed the murders of Joseph and Hyrum Smith a year earlier and whose body bore the scars of multiple bullet wounds received at the Carthage jail, similarly had enough of the United States. He had seen the Smiths murdered under the auspices of the law that was either so corrupt it refused to protect them or so inept it simply could not protect them. In frustration he said, "In regard to the situation of the world as it now exists I don't care a damn because they are as corrupt as the devil. We have no benifit from the laws of the land, and the only reason why they dont cut our throats is because they dare not." Responding to the concern that a more strident relationship with the United States might cause even greater persecution, Taylor scoffed, "They cannot lie about us, nor persecute us worse than they have done."

For Taylor, US democracy had proved to be a failure. The government was too easily corrupted, especially on a local level, and the rights of minorities were rarely protected and defended by the states or the federal government. Taylor explained:

> We know we have no more justice here . . . than we could get at the gates of hell, and the only thing we have got to do is to take care of ourselves. We have been excluded from all our rights as other citizens and we have a right to make law for ourselves and put them in force. . . . I go in for a company being sent out to find out place where we can establish the kingdom, erect the standard and dwell in peace, and have our own laws.[44]

This feeling of alienation from the United States extended beyond just Mormon men in the ruling hierarchy. One popular expression of frustration came on Independence Day. The Mormon community had traditionally celebrated the US holiday with parades and feasts, pomp, and public expressions of patriotic devotion. But on July 4, 1845, the streets of Nauvoo were silent. There were no parades. The Nauvoo Legion, which had been the martial expression of Mormon nationalism on such occasions, had ceased to exist with the dissolution of the city charter, along with all other municipal functions.

Irene Haskell, a married nineteen-year-old Mormon woman living in Nauvoo, juxtaposed the lack of celebration there against the rest of the nation. She wrote her parents in Massachusetts, "The fourth of July is just past. I suppose there were balls, teaparties and the like in the east, but here there were nothing of the kind. The Mormons think the liberty and independence of the United States has been too long trampled upon to be celebrated."[45] Zina Jacobs similarly lamented in her diary of Independence Day, "A day long to be remembered. O liberty how ha[s]t thou falen O Lord wilt thou restore thy People to trew liberty, even to keeping thy selestial [celestial] law. Forgive me all my sins that I may be free indeed."[46]

As the year progressed, this growing alienation was only exacerbated by political machinations and anti-Mormon violence. By the fall, organized anti-Mormon resistance had begun attacking outlying Mormon settlements in Illinois and systematically burning houses, barns, and crops to the ground. As one St. Louis newspaperman who had traveled to Illinois to witness the events explained, the anti-Mormons had "determined to drive the Mormons out of the county." They had been "out burning the Mormon houses, barns, stacks, etc. In this war of extermination, they include not only the Mormons, but all who are suspected of favoring the Mormon cause or harboring Mormons about them."[47] Zina Jacobs reflected the growing fear and alienation of the Mormon population over such attacks, writing in her journal, "When I cast mine eyes out, what do I behold, evry brother armed, his gun uppon his shoulder to protect his family and Bretheren from the violence of the furious Mob who are now burning all that falls into their way round about the Country. Ah Liberty, thou art fled. When the wicked rule the People mourn."[48] The Mormons made known to both Illinois politicians and the local anti-Mormon groups that they intended to leave the country in the coming spring for somewhere in the West. They asked for and hoped to gain a respite from violence, but such truces were only temporary.[49]

Despite the general lack of sympathy for the Mormon cause, as violent rhetoric became commonplace and the Mormon decision to abandon the country became clear, some at least posited concerns over the long-term implications for US democracy. For instance, as attacks on Mormon settlements continued in the fall of 1845 even after the Mormons made clear their intentions to leave the nation, one newspaper opined that the actions of the lawless mobs against the Mormons would "tear down the fabric of society . . . in violation of all private rights."[50] The *New York Sun* at first expressed shock and outrage at the continued mob violence and the demand that the Mormons leave the country:

> A whole community of the people banished! Driven violently from their homes, their farms, and their Church; their blood shed by lawless adventures of Illinois and the State, either unable or unwilling to protect them! How arc we as a nation to explain to a civilized world this dire calamity, this desecration of all that is free in our Government? Was it the religion of the Mormons to which objections were made? We have no right to interfere with the religion of any person, if the pursuit of that religion interferes with no man's rights or property. Were the Mormons a rascally, lying, thieving race of people, as alleged? Then enforce the laws against all offenders. But to drive them, their wives and children beyond the Rocky Mountains, beyond the barriers of civilization, to take lawless possession

of their farms and property, exceeds in iniquity everything that has been done in any country since the reign of the Goths and Vandals![51]

But such sentiments, welcome as they were to the harried Mormons in Nauvoo, were both sporadic and fleeting. The same *New York Sun* that had so damningly condemned the violence against the Mormons on October 18 was already backtracking by October 27. Perhaps due to an unfavorable public response, now the editor asserted that the Mormons themselves were primarily to blame for the violence enacted upon them. This was not a case of religious bigotry, because residents of Illinois claimed Mormon beliefs were not the reason for the violence, but the character of the people themselves. Tying Mormonism to another religion US citizens could not be expected to peacefully coexist with, the *Sun* now concluded:

We find a dangerous feature in Mormonism, requiring the active interference of state and national sovereignty, which has been entirely overlooked. It aims at nationality, conquest by the sword, and the temporal as well as spiritual subjugation of other governments, systems and churches. Constant warfare is the natural result, and unless the Mormons conceal these principles until they become strong enough to conquer their neighbors, as the Mahometans did, they will be received at the point of the bayonet whenever they attempt to settle among those who have the power and the will to protect existing institutions."[52]

Anti-Mormon sentiment and violence had ceased being evidence of society collapsing into barbarian incivility; now that very violence was lauded as a means of protecting American culture.

In any case, there was no groundswell of public support aimed at aiding the Mormons. If they wanted respite, they needed to leave the nation. To expedite their exodus, Governor Thomas Ford informed Mormon officials that he had intelligence that the federal government planned to intervene militarily and arrest their leaders, break up their community, and prevent them from moving to British or Mexican territory. If they waited until spring, Ford warned, it may be too late to leave.[53] In his later book chronicling the events in Illinois during his tenure as governor, Ford admitted that his claim to such intelligence was an outright fabrication. "With a view to hasten their removal," he bragged, "they were made to believe that the President would order the regular army to Nauvoo as soon as the navigation opened in the spring. This had the desired effect; the twelve, with about two thousand of their followers immediately crossed the Mississippi before the breaking up of the ice."[54] Ford's machinations caused a panicked state of affairs in Nauvoo and led to the brutal winter exodus of many thousands of Mormons months before they had intended. Many would perish in the elements.

Ford's dishonesty would probably not have carried as much weight with the Mormons had not Brigham Young just received a letter from a prominent Mormon authority in Washington, DC, who also warned of a coming military intervention. Samuel Brannan, president of the Eastern States Mission, wrote Young that he had learned some disturbing news. Brannan had been told that the "secretary of war and other members of the cabinet were laying plans" to prevent the Mormons from moving out of the country. He explained, "They say it will not do to let the Mormons go to California nor Oregon, neither will it do to let them tarry in the states, and they must be obliterated from the face of the earth."[55]

Illinois newspapers similarly reported on the expected federal intervention against the Mormons' exodus. The *Chicago Journal* reported that it expected the government to intervene to prevent the Mormons from moving to Mexico, citing sources in Washington, DC, who believed it was the "duty of the General Government to look in season to the expected removal of the Mormons, in order to prevent a hostile force, numbering many thousands, from taking a position which prove seriously detrimental to American interests in that quarter."[56]

Brigham Young himself had written to President James K. Polk hoping that, unlike his predecessors who had eschewed the political nightmare of intervening on the side of the universally despised sect, this executive would intercede. But now news reports, Samuel Brannan's letters, and especially Governor Ford's calculated subterfuge had convinced Young that his people could not wait until spring. Young now had corroborating reports, albeit false ones, that the United States had abandoned the position of passive observer of the murders and despoliation of Mormon property only to become an active participant in the violence. Young had once hoped a federal army would end disparate anti-Mormon violence and perhaps even restore the Mormons to their lands that they believed to be sacred in western Missouri. But these reports, combined with local anti-Mormon violence, convinced him that his people not only needed to leave the confines of the United States but needed to do so quickly.

As the Mormons prepared for their now-hastened exodus, their determination that peace existed only outside of the United States grew. A young Mormon man, John Needham, wrote to his parents of this impending expulsion and his disgust for his fellow Americans, "They will not let us live in peace, and so we must go elsewhere, at least they say we must, or they will drive us. This has hastened the move; but whether they did so or not we intend to go away for a time, and leave this abominable people of blood." Needham did not even know where he was going, but he knew it would be out of US territory. He explained, "We leave Nauvoo and the United States next Spring for some remote place, where, exactly, I don't know."[57]

The Mormon hierarchy shared Needham's views of the United States and its sovereignty. Apostle John Taylor had already declared, "We owe the United States nothing. We go out by force, as exiles from freedom. The government and people owe us millions for the destruction of life and property in Missouri and in Illinois. The blood of our best men will preserve it till God comes out of his hiding place, and gives this nation a hotter place than he did Sodom and Gomorrah."[58] Even more stridently, his fellow apostle Orson Pratt published his own diatribe against the United States for the expulsion:

> The time is at hand for me to take a long and lasting farewell to these Eastern countries, being included with my family, among the tens of thousands of American citizens who have the choice of DEATH or BANISH-MENT beyond the Rocky Mountains. I have preferred the latter. It is with the greatest of joy that I forsake this Republic: and all the saints have abundant reasons to rejoice that they are counted worthy to be cast out as exiles from this wicked nation; for we have received nothing but one continual scene of the most horrid and unrelenting persecutions at their hands for the last sixteen years. If our heavenly father will preserve us, and deliver us out of the hands of the blood-thirsty Christians of these United States, and not suffer any more of us to be martyred to gratify their holy piety, I for one shall be very thankful. Perhaps we may have to suffer much in the land of our exile, but our sufferings will be from another cause—there will be no Christian banditti to afflict us all the day long—no holy pious priests to murder us by scores—no editors to urge on house burning, devastation and death. If we die in the dens and caves of the Rocky Mountains, we shall die where freedom reigns triumphantly. Liberty in a solitary place, and in a desert, is far more preferable than martyrdom in these pious States.[59]

For Pratt and the Mormons, unlike other US settlers in Texas, California, and Oregon, freedom and security were to be found outside of the sovereignty of the United States rather than within it. Brigham Young told the Council of Fifty in one of its final meetings before the Mormons began to cross the frozen Mississippi in their flight, "When we leave here [my] mind is to go just beyond the Rocky mountains, somewhere on the Mexican claim and the United

States will have no business to come there and if they do we will treat them as enemies." While Samuel Houston and others saw the expansion of US sovereignty as the guarantor of the rights they held most precious, Young now saw the nation as his enemy and wanted the removal plans to include scouting the Mexican territory for "suitable places where we can locate and fortify ourselves so as to bid defiance to the enemy."[60] Earlier he had stated the matter more succinctly, "When we start we will move in a solid body untill we get beyond the limits of the United States so that we could protect ourselves."[61]

Prior to the California gold rush following the US-Mexican War and the cession of territory in the Treaty of Guadalupe Hidalgo (1848), the Mormon migration to the Salt Lake Valley was the largest movement of Americans into the vast reaches of the West and Southwest, outside of Houston's beloved Texas. Yet the Mormon view of "manifest destiny" had ceased being one that included US sovereignty. Alienated by years of antagonistic rhetoric and violence, horrified by the failure of US democracy to defend their rights as a minority, the Mormons believed they were embarking on a westward movement that would find them illegally settling on land nominally controlled by Mexico, but that would be safely outside the United States. Yet, the US empire expanded as quickly as the Mormons could run from it, again encompassing them inside its dominion. Over the course of the next half century, the Mormons would variously attempt to defy, embrace, bargain with, and mitigate the effects of that sovereignty. The United States demanded Mormon cessation of religious practices deemed too foreign, such as polygamy, and political participation that held the specter of theocracy as the requisite price for an uneasy reintegration into the union. After decades of resistance, Mormons in the twentieth century would come to embrace rather than reject US sovereignty.

The Mormons' alienation from the United States demonstrates both the zealous nature of the fervency in their religious beliefs and the limits of American identity and nationalism in the face of unmitigated persecution and unrelenting disregard for the rights of their singular and radical minority religious group. Not all who went out from under the eagle's wings were happy when that shadow again rested upon them. US expansion frustrated Mormon dreams and desires in the nineteenth century rather than fulfilling them.

NOTES

1. Andrew J. Torget, *Seeds of Empire: Cotton, Slavery, and the Transformation of the Texas Borderlands, 1800–1850* (Chapel Hill: University of North Carolina Press, 2015), 220–235; Randolph B. Campbell, *Gone to Texas: A History of the Lone Star State* (Oxford:

Oxford University Press, 2003), 182–184. For a detailed examination of the military vulnerability of Texas during Samuel Houston's presidency, see Sam W. Haynes, *Soldiers of Misfortune: The Somervell and Meir Expeditions* (Austin: University of Texas Press, 1990).

2. Council of Fifty record books 1844–1846 (hereafter cited as COFRB), May 3, 1844, MS 30055, box 1, folder 1, LDS Church History Library (hereafter cited as CHL). The subject of the Mormon negotiations with the Republic of Texas was very ably examined by Michael Scott Van Wagenen; however, at the time his book was published, historians did not have access to the Council of Fifty Minutes at the LDS Church History Library. These minutes detail the reasons for the negotiations and the discussions surrounding them that Van Wagenen could not have known or incorporated at the time. In preparing this chapter, I also used other unique sources beyond those minutes that shed further light on these negotiations. Van Wagenen still provides an excellent overview of the Mormon engagement with the Republic of Texas. See Michael Scott Van Wagenen, *The Texas Republic and the Mormon Kingdom of God* (College Station: Texas A&M University Press, 2002).

3. A Natchez, Mississippi, newspaper, for instance, reported that there were fifty thousand Mormons and twenty-five thousand living in the Nauvoo area alone. *Baltimore Sun*, February 17, 1844; "City of Ohio," *Cincinnati Enquirer*, July 10, 1843; "Nauvoo," *Mississippi Free Trader*, March 29, 1843.

4. *Telegraph and Texas Register* (Houston), March 20, 1844.

5. Governor Lilburn Boggs to General John B. Clark, October 20, 1838, Mormon War Papers, 1837–1841, Office of Secretary of State, Record Group 5, Missouri State Archives, Jefferson City, MO.

6. For example, see Tom Chaffin, *Pathfinder: John Charles Frémont and the Course of American Empire* (Norman: University of Oklahoma Press, 2014), 290–294.

7. For more details on the Mormon War in Missouri, see Alex Baugh, "A Call to Arms: The 1838 Mormon Defense of Northern Missouri" (PhD diss., Brigham Young University, 2000).

8. Hyrum Smith, Testimony Before the Municipal Court of the City of Nauvoo, July 1, 1843, MS 16800, CHL. Joseph Smith wrote bitterly from his prison cell in Missouri about the crimes committed against his people in that state: "the unrelenting hand the inhumanity and murderous disposition of this people it shocks all nature it beggers and defies all discription. it is a tail of wo a lamentable tail yea a sorrifull tail too much to tell too much for contemplation too much to think of for a moment too much for human beings it cannot be found among the hethans it cannot be found among the nations where Kings and tyrants are inthroned it cannot be found among the savages of the wilderness yea and I think it cannot be found among the wild and ferocious beasts of the forist that a man should be mangled for sport women be violated rob[b]ed of all that they have their last morsel for subsistance and then be violated to gratify the hellish desires of the mob and finally left to perish with their helpless ofspring clinging around their necks but this is not all after a man is dead he must be dug up from his grave and mangled to peaces for no other purpose than to gratify their

splean against the religeon of god." Joseph Smith to Edward Partridge, March 20, 1839, Revelations Collection, MS 4583, CHL.

9. Joseph Smith to Hyrum Smith, December 5, 1839, MS 155, CHL.

10. Nauvoo Legion Records, July 3, 1841, MS 3430, CHL.

11. *Saint Louis New Era* as reprinted in the *Madison City Express* (WI), October 12, 1843.

12. "The Election," *Quincy Whig* (IL), August 23, 1843.

13. "The Mormons," *Alton Telegraph and Democratic Review* (IL), August 26, 1843.

14. "Joe Smith," *Alton Telegraph and Democratic Review*, July 15, 1843.

15. Thomas Ford, *A History of Illinois: From Commencement as a State in 1818 to 1847* (Chicago: S. C. Griggs, 1854), 231.

16. "Threatened Destruction of the Mormons," *Indiana Statesman* as reprinted in *Paoli True American* (IN), October 5, 1843.

17. For more details on these letters and refusals, see Gerrit Dirkmaat, "Enemies Foreign and Domestic: US Relations with Mormons in the US Empire in North America" (PhD diss., University of Colorado, 2010), 42–46.

18. William Clayton, Journal, May 16, 1843, CHL.

19. Revelation, July 12, 1843, Revelations Collection, CHL.

20. Wilford Woodruff, Diary, April 7, 1844, CHL.

21. Law and his followers founded a newspaper, the *Nauvoo Expositor*, which denounced Smith's teachings on plurality of wives and the plurality of gods. See *Nauvoo Expositor* (IL), June 7, 1844.

22. "Remarks on the Above," *Warsaw Message* (IL), January 17, 1844.

23. Joseph Smith, Journal, February 20, 1844, Joseph Smith Collection, MS 155, box 1, folder 7, 276.

24. Smith, Journal, February 23, 1844,

25. COFRB, March 11, 1844.

26. David J. Weber has placed the number at considerably lower than that seventy-three hundred. Although population estimates vary, the planned Mormon migration was larger, and perhaps considerably larger than the entire existing California population by at least five thousand people. See David J. Weber, *The Mexican Frontier, 1821–1846: The American Southwest under Mexico* (Albuquerque: University of New Mexico Press, 1982), 206.

27. Daniel J. Garr, "Los Angeles and the Challenge of Growth, 1835–1849," *Southern California Quarterly* 61 (Summer 1979): 154.

28. Historian Benjamin Madley has estimated there were as many as five hundred separate tribal groups in the area that later became the state of California alone, not including the portions of Nevada and Utah considered part of Upper California. Madley, *An American Genocide: The United States and the California Indian Catastrophe* (New Haven, CT: Yale University Press, 2016), 9. For more on the tenuous hold Mexico exercised over these American Indian lands, see Brian Delay, *War of a Thousand Deserts* (New Haven, CT: Yale University Press, 2009).

29. COFRB, May 3, 1844.

30. COFRB, May 3, 1844.

31. James Arlington Bennet to Willard Richards and Brigham Young, June 4, 1845, Willard Richards Papers, MS 1490, CHL.

32. *Warsaw Signal* (IL), June 11, 1844.

33. Ford, *History of Illinois*, 330.

34. Thomas Ford to Joseph Smith, June 22, 1844, Joseph Smith Collection, MS 155, box 3, folder 8, 97–101, CHL.

35. Joseph Smith to Thomas Ford, June 22, 1844, Joseph Smith Collection, MS 155, box 2, folder 8, 58, CHL.

36. For more details on the assassination of Joseph Smith, see Richard Bushman, *Joseph Smith: Rough Stone Rolling* (New York: Alfred A. Knopf, 2005), 537–552; and Joseph Smith, *Joseph Smith Papers, Administrative Records, Council of Fifty, Minutes, March 1844–January 1846*, ed. Ronald K. Esplin, Matthew J. Grow, Mark Ashurst-McGee, Gerrit J. Dirkmaat, and Jeffrey D. Mahas (Salt Lake City: Church Historian's Press, 2016), 190–204.

37. William Clayton, Journal, January 26, 1845, *Joseph Smith Papers*, 258.

38. Brigham Young, Journal, January 24, 1846, MS 1234 1, CHL.

39. COFRB, March 1, 1845.

40. COFRB, March 11, 1845.

41. COFRB, March 18, 1845.

42. COFRB, March 18, 1845.

43. COFRB, March 11, 1845.

44. COFRB, March 1, 1845.

45. Irene Haskell to her parents, July 6, 1845, Irene Haskell Papers, Library of Congress.

46. Zina Diantha Huntington Jacobs, "'All Things Move in Order in the City': The Nauvoo Diary of Zina Diantha Huntington Jacobs," ed. Maureen Ursenbach Beecher, *BYU Studies* 19 (1979): 291–320.

47. "Mormon War," *Indiana Palladium* (Richmond), October 4, 1845.

48. Jacobs, "All Things Move,'" 30.

49. "Exodus of the Mormons," *New York Sun*, October 27, 1845.

50. *Zanesville Weekly Courier* (OH), September 12, 1846.

51. "Flight of the Mormons from Illinois," *New York Sun*, October 18, 1845.

52. "Exodus of the Mormons," *New York Sun*, October 27, 1845.

53. Thomas Ford to Sheriff J. B. Backenstos, December 29, 1845, CR 1234 1, CHL.

54. Ford, *History of Illinois*, 291.

55. Manuscript History of the Church, Samuel Brannan to Brigham Young, December 11, 1845, CHL, vol. 14, 284. For more on the deliberate attempts to deceive and thereby defraud the Mormons in relation to the US government's intended actions, see Dirkmaat, "Enemies Foreign and Domestic," 87–103.

56. "Removal of the Mormons," *Chicago Journal* as reprinted in *Janesville Gazette* (WI), December 12, 1845 (emphasis in original).

57. John Needham to parents, November 17, 1845, *Latter-Day Saints' Millennial Star* 7 (February 3, 1846).

58. "To Our Patrons," *Nauvoo Neighbor* (IL), October 29, 1845.

59. Orson Pratt, "Farewell Message of Orson Pratt," *Times and Seasons* (Nauvoo, IL), December 31, 1845.

60. COFRB, January 11, 1846.

61. COFRB, March 18, 1845.

CHAPTER 11

At the Center of Southern Empire:
The Role of Gulf South Communities
in Antebellum Territorial Expansion

Maria Angela Diaz

In 1859, the *Yazoo Democrat* proclaimed its support for any Democrat who supported Cuban annexation during the state and national conventions. The paper stated that "under the auspices of Jefferson, the Democracy acquired Louisiana. Under [James] Monroe they acquired Florida. Under Jas. K. Polk, Texas was given to the Union and California, with all their golden treasures, and the Territories of Utah and New Mexico."[1] At the heart of all of these prior expansionist projects and many others was the Gulf of Mexico, a region that tied together the US South, the US West, Latin American nations, and the Atlantic World.[2]

This chapter examines the central role that the port communities in the Gulf South played during antebellum southern expansion, and considers how that process affected them. The history of southern imperialism has enjoyed a resurgence in recent years, with many volumes detailing southern political leaders' interests in the acquisition of territory in the West and in parts of Mexico and the Caribbean.[3] This chapter shifts this discussion away from a sole preoccupation with the efforts of the top tier of southern society and focuses instead on how public discourse on these issues evolved in the southern borderlands of the Gulf Coast. It unites the larger regional story of imperialism with the very local story of people living at a point on the map where multiple worlds collided. Antebellum efforts to acquire territory produced a highly racialized language by which that conquest was justified. Both the efforts and the ideas had an impact on US coastal communities, as well as on how they sought to shape the story to their own benefit.[4]

Most often US expansion is described as the acquisition and extension of national authority over additional territory on the continent. Yet, southern interest in new land is usually described as a kind of imperialism. In more recent years the boundaries between these concepts—expansion and imperialism—have broken down, and territorial expansion is understood by many as part of a much longer trajectory of US imperialism throughout the nineteenth and twentieth centuries. Many historians of southern expansionism prior to the 1830s emphasize the extent to which slavery's expansion into the Gulf South was a national project in that the central government was used by many pro-slavery politicians and presidents to seize land from Native American nations and European colonizers. Southern historians studying the expansion of slavery in the antebellum era note the similarities between the planter classes in the United States and other slaveholding regimes in the Americas. Yet, it was not so much that southerners saw themselves as part of a cosmopolitan hemispheric master class or as having common interests with elites in the societies of the Caribbean and South America. Through an examination of discourse and the localized experience of expansion, it becomes evident that this solidarity was packaged and understood less as solidarity and more as justification for violent conquest and future acquisition. White southerners consumed ideas in newspapers and journals that placed their society far above the rest and showed them a picture of themselves as the future and rightful inheritors of territory far beyond the bounds of the United States and, in an echo of the racialized superiority of European colonizers, the only race capable of protecting and guiding slave societies in the Western Hemisphere. The Gulf South was a key space in which white southern expansionists worked out the highly racialized imaginary of southern imperialism and launched their efforts. For their part, boosters and citizens of the Gulf South imagined themselves at the very center of that growing empire.[5]

By the antebellum period the populations of Gulf South coastal communities tended to be more diverse than their counterparts on the Atlantic coast or in the southern interior. The Gulf South consisted of a series of communities that ranged in size from the 150,00 living in New Orleans, Louisiana, to the 5,000 living in Pensacola, Florida. Populations such as black and white Creoles created traditions of cultural, political, and economic connections that drew the Gulf South into the Caribbean and Latin American worlds. The burgeoning cotton trade that was such a central part of the Deep South's earlier history of US expansion mingled with the growing sugar trade of the

Gulf Coast and the social life of the ports during the antebellum period. The prospect of economic boom times often masked the instability inherent in such a diverse region; a number of wars and conflicts erupted in the Gulf South throughout the first half of the nineteenth century. The Gulf South witnessed several US armed expeditions to Spanish-held Florida, Coahuila y Tejas, and Mexico during the early nineteenth century. The nation's largest slave rebellion happened in Louisiana in 1811; the Battle of New Orleans was the most spectacular battle of the already-over War of 1812, but it was also tied to beginnings of the Creek and Seminole Wars in Florida; and the Texas War of Independence created a largely Anglo-American-controlled independent republic out of a former Mexican state in 1836. When we look at the entirety of the Gulf of Mexico, the conflicts on the mainland join others in the Caribbean such as the Haitian Revolution and rebellions in the Yucatán and Cuba. All of these conflicts transformed the Western Hemisphere. It is no surprise, then, that Gulf Coast expansionists welcomed the army and the navy and adopted a militaristic rhetoric well into the nineteenth century. The convergence of both national and local expansionist discourses developed out of Gulf South desires to defend their region's economy and social structures against threatening internal and external forces. By 1844, expansionists in the Gulf South looked forward to the annexation of Texas, what many considered to be an inevitability.

Announcing Texas's possible inclusion in the United States, the *New Orleans Picayune* proclaimed the "broad banner of Washington may be unfurled in glory on our Western border, and the burnished arms of American troops will be reflected from the sparkling waters of the Nueces. 'Westward! The star of empire takes its way!'" While in New Orleans, Rice Ballard, a Virginia-based slave trader often active in Louisiana, wrote to his friend and business associate Albert Sidney Johnston, former secretary of war for the Republic of Texas and future Confederate general, concerning the excitement over the prospect of annexation that existed in the nation. He felt "both North and South are interested to have Texas annexed to our country . . . we shall in this respect suffer a small diminution in the price of cotton, but we are compelled to have it annexed, or abandon our slaves if it is to be a British Colony of abolitionism."[6]

When James K. Polk became president in 1845, he had renewed the Texan and US hopes for annexation that stalled under two previous administrations. However, due to the slow pace, Albert Sidney Johnston, like many Texans who had hoped for a speedy route to statehood, had become wary of US presidents' promises regarding annexation. Johnston felt a strong sense of loyalty toward Texas, which emerged from his family's connection to the territory and the Lower South and its long history of expansion. In his youth, Johnston encountered US citizens migrating to Texas while he lived in Alexandria, Louisiana, a border town. Several of his siblings took part in the 1813 Gutierrez-Magee expedition, an early joint Mexican and Anglo-American filibustering expedition that aimed to wrest colonial Texas from the Spanish at the start of the Mexican War of Independence. Johnston's eldest son recalled that his father claimed that despite these familial connections with Anglo expansion into Texas, his real reason for going there was to help bring it into the Union. He wanted to "add another star to the American constellation." James Love, perhaps the most outspoken of Johnston's friends, wrote to him regularly, giving him updates on the proceedings of the Texas congress during the careful negotiations concerning annexation. In a letter of March 30, 1845, he wrote that if the Texas president, Anson Jones, refused to "call congress and take the mandatory steps to ascertain the will of the people, we will take the matter in our own hands, have a convention unseat him, and hang him if necessary." Militarism and military men were important to Texans' conceptions of themselves, and the process of annexation took on an immediacy for those who supported it in a way that the War of Independence once did.[7]

Newspapers in New Orleans kept careful tabs on reports of Texans' feelings over annexation throughout the final years on the path toward statehood. As efforts continued, George Wilkins Kendall, editor of the *Picayune*, claimed that passengers aboard the steamship *New York* who had come from Galveston said that "a large majority of the people of Texas are warmly in favor of annexation, and entertain strong hopes that a bill to that effect will pass before our present Congress closes its session." From their reading of the Texas papers, Kendall and the *Picayune* claimed that the Texas congress, however, objected to conditions in the bill that emphasized negotiation with Mexico over Texas's borders, and were anxious over the laws concerning slavery.[8] Despite reports between friends over the possibility that President Jones might be hanged if he dragged his feet on annexation, he put the resolution before Congress in June and framed it as a choice between Mexican-recognized independence, which involved Great Britain's backing and the possibility of emancipation, and annexation to the United States as a slave state. The prospect of emancipation haunted many throughout the Gulf South, and any mention of England sparked images of a giant door to freedom sitting on the South's southern border.[9]

Many changes rocked the region after Texas annexation. The US-Mexican War, for example, initiated a feverish drive for new territory. During the war, the Gulf South communities within Texas, Louisiana, and Florida became the major staging grounds for the army and navy. Louisiana troops were among the first to show up in the disputed territory in Texas, answering a premature call from Zachary Taylor. President Polk sent soldiers under the command of Taylor to the territory when it came under dispute between the United States and Mexico. Taylor's troops set up camp on a small island south of Galveston, Texas's principal port community. The camp quickly became a site of trade as local residents from the area aimed to make money off of the soldiers. It also became a site in which Anglo-American soldiers came into contact with the diverse population of Texas. A correspondent for the *Picayune* reported back that Texas's many "natural curiosities" included the Mexicans and Indians who traded in the camp regularly—Mexican Texans trading in horses and mules and Indians trading in animal skins. "No wonder an organized government cannot exist among the Mexicans! What a rag-tail and bob-tail, thievish, cut-throat set of cowards they must be, according to some of the specimens I have seen," scoffed the correspondent. Armed forces in the Gulf South were a part of the militaristic side of southern imperialism and national manifest destiny, as was the highly racialized language that became so central to the promotion of the US-Mexican War.[10]

Almost every soldier who wound up on the battlefronts of central Mexico journeyed through New Orleans. Many were part of the invasion of central Mexico under General Winfield Scott. Their experience was somewhat different in that they landed in Vera Cruz, Mexico's largest port city, and marched through the valley of Mexico rather than down through the arid mountains of northern Mexico. Albert Johnston had gone to war with the first invasion of northern Mexico, but his nephew, William Preston, was part of this second invading army. Preston sailed from New Orleans with the Fourth Kentucky Volunteers on November 11, 1847, where his regiment stayed only a night before heading downriver and reaching the Gulf of Mexico. For the Kentuckian Preston, the trip to Vera Cruz was the first time that he had ever seen the Gulf. Like many soldiers who had come from other parts of the South, the trip through New Orleans or Mobile was just as surprising and intriguing as was the experience of a foreign country. Of the Gulf, Preston wrote, "When they are at rest & only agitatedly slight winds, the sapphire sky, the light, fleecy, clouds drifting before the winds, the clear waves and delightful breeze, create a pleasant languor, which renders you careless of everything save the scene around you." When his regiment landed at Vera Cruz, it was a conquered city. He noted the remnants of the siege and battle surrounded them as they camped on a plain between the city and the sea where General Scott's troops had marched ten months earlier. Preston recorded the scene: "The trenches are still there & the fragments of the shells and round shot scattered over the plain still show the range and direction of the Mexican batteries." By 1847, the army had already won several battles, and the war was coming to a close.

Discharged soldiers made their way back through the Gulf ports, and as they did, the *Civilian and Galveston Gazette* reported that land speculators were waiting for them and the land scrip that many received when they were discharged from the service. New Orleans speculators, however, had been "sadly bitten" due to the fact that soldiers were not allowed to transfer their claims for other land or stock. As the nation had focused its attention on the war of conquest, the economics of that enterprise did not cease, and soldiers were as much a part of that form of expansion in the Gulf as they were a part of the violent pursuit of subjugation of the US-Mexican War.[11]

In addition to the consequences concerning land speculation already evident in the months after the surrender of Mexico's capital city, the war shaped the developing rhetoric of both Mexican people and African Americans in the United States. By the 1850s, southern politicians and intellectuals promoted the pro-slavery argument as a fight against the growing opposition of abolitionists, and this argument intermingled with the militant expansionism present in the region after the war. Southerners like Raphael Semmes, a veteran naval officer who participated in the Gulf blockade of the Mexican ports and the landing at Vera Cruz, described the division between elite and impoverished Mexicans in his memoir on the war in the same way that he did poor whites and free blacks—those individuals who could not find a place in the highly structured world of the slave South. Semmes stated:

> There is no more sympathy or affinity between these two great fractions of the eight millions of Mexico, than there is between the slaves of the southern part of the United States and their masters—indeed, not so much; as the closer relation which exists between master and slave with us, begets more or less of mutual regard; the master bestowing upon his slave the kindly feeling which is naturally inspired by those who are dependent upon us, and the slave, in return, regarding himself as a member of his master's family, and more or less identified with his interests.

Semmes regarded Mexicans as less intelligent than African American slaves, and he even went so far as to consider the Mexican people of northern Mexico as far less sophisticated than those of central Mexico near the capital. These individuals, Semmes believed, were condemned to a life of degradation. In similar fashion to the New Orleans correspondent observing trade between Mexicans and Anglo-American soldiers in Texas, Semmes described working-class Mexicans as "mixing with the Indians, and both of them mixing, again, with the white man, have produced the present abject and miserable race which constitutes so large a portion of the Mexican population."

In his reaction to the complex racial past of Mexico, Semmes revealed the strength of southern imaginings concerning their own ideas about race and class. Miscegenation was ever present on the plantations of the US South. Yet, in the Mexican population, Semmes found a nightmare scenario kept at bay by the hierarchies of the American system. Writers producing racialized discourse obsessed over this racial mixing, and so did Semmes, stating, "The negroes, as a separate race, have disappeared from among them, and one discovers but slight traces of their blood in this mongrel stock—nor have the whites mixed with them to any very great extent."[12]

Semmes's comments also reflected the messiness that followed the US-Mexican War in the Gulf South as the war changed back into an unorganized series of border conflicts. Although the Treaty of Guadalupe Hidalgo was ratified in 1848, the actual end of the war mirrored the ragged ending of the Civil War years later in that it too unleashed continued conflict between Anglo-Americans, Mexicans, and Native Americans. Pro-expansionists sought to solidify their hold on the Texas economy and its land. They hoped to knit together the rich and fertile cotton districts with the coastal trading centers and the growing river trade along the Rio Grande. To do this, the Texas interior would have to be settled, and, more important, Anglo southerners would have to assert their dominance over the seemingly unruly borders of the state.

Three years after the end of the war, a local incident between Mexican soldiers and Anglos became framed as a border war in miniature between Anglo-Americans and Mexican citizens. On May 13, 1851, several newspapers in cities such as San Antonio and Galveston received word of an altercation in the small border town of Roma, Texas. Mexican families living near Roma held a ball, and a party of eight individuals boarded a boat to attend the dance. It is difficult to piece together the exact series of events, but many reported that Mexican troops opened fire on the partygoers, wounding two of the people in the boat. While one letter stated that Mexican troops fired on Roma merchants for exporting cowhides to Mexico, another from Brownsville claimed that Roma citizens crossing the border to attend a dance in the town across the river were fired upon by the Mexican guard.

The party that had been fired on promptly returned to Roma and armed themselves to return to the Mexican dance. Yet they found no troops waiting for them. Ultimately, the incident itself was defused with no additional bloodshed, but the manner in which the "difficulty at Roma" came to be discussed in the public discourse revealed much about the Anglo-American vision of the border in the years after the US-Mexican War. The *Texas State Gazette* worried that such altercations would engender feelings of ill will between US citizens and Mexicans, and that if these incidents continued, they would lead to the "bathing of the banks of both sides of the river with blood." The Brownsville letter claimed that Mexicans were quickly forgetting "their thrashings," and a feeling of "envy and malice, is growing up in the breast of every low peon or highwayman, which, by the better class, is not at all partaken of which will soon have to be rooted out of them, and the sooner it is done the better." What would be their solution? Extending the border farther and annexing yet more Mexican territory because the "Rio Grande cannot remain the boundary and peace be preserved. Geographically and politically, it is the wrong boundary."[13] The only answer, then, according to this letter, was more imperialism, a continued movement south. Further subjugation of the Mexican people was the only way to keep the peace.

Although the Rio Grande was several hundred miles from the larger communities of East Texas, many there worried over the state's borders and continued to believe that a military presence would secure their ability to expand into the region. Throughout this period, southerners fought to reinforce their superiority and maintain the narrative of expansion into Latin America even as slaves, Mexicans, and Native Americans continued to call this discourse into question. If slaves did manage to escape, they often aimed for freedom across the Rio Grande, where Mexico was described in one newspaper article as "the Negro's promised land." The 1858 *Texas Almanac* warned new settlers that the counties along the Rio Grande desperately wanted slave labor, but "many slaves escape, every year, into Mexico."[14] It is difficult to know the exact number of enslaved African Americans who gained freedom by crossing the Rio Grande, but the possibility that it could happen enhanced the uncertainty of the border and made many Anglos believe that it required military control.[15]

In its aftermath, the US-Mexican War, with its spectacular victory over a Latin American people and the acquisition of new territory that came along with it, became both a driving cause and a symbol for a wave of armed expeditions to Latin American countries in efforts to take them over. Typically, this story focuses on the West and the US-Mexico border, which continued to be a space of violent contestation throughout the 1850s as Anglo-Americans, Mexicans, and Native Americans vied for control of it. Among the most spectacular of these were the Narciso López expeditions in 1851 and 1852, in which López and his crew attempted to rouse the Cuban people to overthrow the Spanish. Yet fascination with Cuba and the notion that annexation of that territory would protect the Gulf South ports also became framed by the victory of the US-Mexican War and dependent on an already strong connection between the crescent city and the jewel of the Antilles.[16]

Figure 11.1. Detail of Samuel Augustus Mitchell, *Mitchell's New National Map Exhibiting the United States with the North American British Provinces, Sandwich Islands, Mexico and Central America, together with Cuba and Other West India Islands.* Philadelphia: S. Augustus Mitchell, 1858. The David Rumsey Map Collection, Cartography Associates, San Francisco, CA.

It was the Gulf Coast communities that knit these two massive projects of conquest together, and New Orleans was the central launching pad for forays back into the Caribbean as it had been for the US-Mexican War, when thousands of soldiers filtered through the city bound for Vera Cruz. By the 1850s, a neighborhood of Cuban exiles emerged within the city, making New Orleans and the Gulf Coast an alternate site of political struggle between Cuba, the United States, and the last vestiges of Spanish colonial authority in the Western Hemisphere. Fears concerning the security of the US-Mexico borderlands and the fate of slavery in Cuba combined to create a potent mixture of borderland conflict that shaped the imagery and the actual events during these filibuster expeditions. Several years prior to the expeditions, a court case involving the kidnapping of a Cuban exile caused an uproar in the city that signaled the ways that New Orleanians thought about issues such as US dominance within the continent and its expansion.

Morro Castle stood guard over Havana Bay for more than two hundred years. The Spanish had intended for it to be seen from miles around, a formidable structure against all enemies to Spain's colonial authority. In 1848, it held prisoners, Creoles accused of plotting against that authority. Juan Garcia Rey worked as a turnkey, guarding several of the prisoners, yet in early 1849, Garcia decided to join the prisoners and reject his position as guard. He opened the dungeon cell door and allowed two of the prisoners, one of them being the revolutionary Cirilo Villaverde, to escape. Both Garcia and Villaverde slipped out of Havana, sailing for New Orleans, where they took shelter in various boardinghouses throughout the city. Once in New Orleans, Juan Garcia Rey became Juan Francisco Rey, and the pair split, quickly blending into the city's exile community. Garcia eventually came to live in the house of a cigar shop owner named José Morante, who was introduced to him through an acquaintance. Morante later claimed that he had reason to believe the young man was in danger for his life and agreed to hide him. As fate would have it, Garcia was indeed in danger of being sent back to Cuba and executed.

Carlos de España, the Spanish consul in New Orleans, eventually learned that the escaped jailer was hiding in the city. On July 5, his agents found Garcia and removed him to a waiting schooner, the *Mary Ellen*, for transport back to Havana and eventual execution. Garcia's abduction would have remained only a minor event had it not been for Morante, who alerted authorities in the city that his charge had been assaulted and forcibly abducted. When Garcia arrived in Havana, the ship he was on was quarantined. Garcia's execution was thus stayed by the fear of sickness aboard the *Mary Ellen*.[17]

In the meantime, upon hearing of the arrest, possible assault, and abduction of Garcia, Mayor Abdiel Crossman promptly wrote de España, requesting more information. De España responded with two letters. The first was a cordial note that invited the mayor to his home for a private discussion of the matter. The second, sent a day later, was a lengthy letter accusing the mayor of putting de España's career in jeopardy and insulting his honor by implying his involvement in the arrest of Garcia. Eventually, de España was arrested on charges of abduction. The altercation quickly gained the status of an international incident when the mayor arrested the Spanish consul. As a result of de España's acquittal, and Garcia's published story, the city's newspapermen treated the trial as another example of Spain denigrating US authority.[18]

The Cuban exile newspapers, along with US newspapers in New Orleans, launched into a flurry of action, covering the evolving case as a serious transgression of US sovereignty by a scheming representative of an equally scheming "old world" power. Cuban annexationists used the case as another example of the threat of Spain's colonial presence so close to US borders, and its burdensome rule over the island's Creole class, which they began to imagine as a white racialized class similar to the planter class of the South. Reviewing the recent history of diplomatic relations and Spain's actions in Cuba, the New Orleans correspondent for the *New York Times* recalled the efforts of Cuban Creoles on the island to "throw off the shackles of Spain." The *Times* correspondent accused the US government of allowing Spanish spies to infiltrate the New Orleans's Cuban exile community, which was what led to the abduction of Juan Garcia.[19] The *New Orleans Daily True Delta* called the outcome of the trial an "insult to the community." It also lambasted the choice of men for the jury, arguing that several were close friends of de España. In the newspaper's eyes it only proved that the trial was a travesty of justice.[20] New Orleanians questioned the jurors' ties to Havana industry and trade just as much as their ties to de España himself. The irony here was that scarcely half a year later, pro-annexationist news organs would support a militarized expedition to conquer Cuba, and ties with Havana would be celebrated in the city.

The de España case occurred in the midst of what many in the city had come to see as a series of instances in which the Spanish government, often depicted as inherently effeminate, conniving, and weak, had triumphed over the United States. Newspapers in New Orleans used the case as an example of Spain's trampling over US sovereignty. In addition to challenging the sovereignty of the United Sates, the *Delta* believed that the national government had also overstepped its boundaries by interfering with what the newspaper considered a city matter, not a federal issue. These events would help shape the depiction of Cubans and the Spanish, as well as further widening the divide between the Union and the South.

While many southerners thought they could solve the South's racial and economic issues through territorial conquest, for many Cubans the issue of US imperialism left several possibilities and questions. Many Cuban exiles, including a revolutionary junta operating in both New York City and New Orleans, lobbied vigorously for intervention and generally supported filibustering. There were, however, many others within Cuba, as well as in the exile community, who believed that total independence would not come with US annexation. Cubans, interested in independence from Spain, thought that encouraging US zeal for territory in Latin American might help in their cause, and that even if it meant becoming a state rather than an independent country, at least they would be a part of a nation based on republican ideals. Others viewed US interest in Cuba as an immediate threat, and an exchange from one colonial power to another.[21]

The de España case coincided with yet another Creole exile's efforts to wrest Cuba from Spain. As the de España controversy died down, Narciso López arrived in New Orleans to plan his second expedition. It is likely that López and Garcia never met, but they both existed within a larger power struggle of Cuban nationalism, US interests in annexation, an anxious southern slave society, and Spanish colonial rule, as well as the shifting space of Cuban Creoles within New Orleans.

Cuban annexation fever took many shapes in the 1850s, but none as spectacular as the filibuster movement. While filibustering in Cuba and other Latin American nations captured the public's attention in the United States during the early 1850s, men conducted several filibuster-style invasions under the banner of US expansion as far back as the early nineteenth century.[22] Within the Gulf South, the complex relations between southern whites and the transnational Creole community, as well as the US-Mexican war, shaped both the filibustering expeditions that sought to wrest Cuba from Spanish authority. The narrative of victory in the US-Mexican War further bolstered the idea of white southerners as rescuers and rehabilitators of transnational Creole spaces and people.

Ideas about race were as central to Cuba annexation as they had been to the US-Mexican War. However, instead of portraying Cubans as inferior due to miscegenation and, therefore, in need of conquest, pro-annexationists constructed ideas about Cuban Creoles as a class similar to themselves and in need of help. Instead of the Cubans, it was the Spanish who needed conquering. Before the first major effort to conquer Cuba in 1850, López's abortive attempt at setting sail from Mississippi was described in the context of this longer trajectory of southern imperialism that included the US-Mexican War. After this failed first attempt, the *Jackson Mississippian* proclaimed that the Spanish rulers of Cuba belonged to the same race as the Mexican *federales* who had murdered "Crockett, Bowie, and their companions in Texas."[23]

Expansionists valued Mexico for its land, but not necessarily for its people. Cuba was valued for its land, its crops, its slaves, its trade relations, and, to an extent, its Creole slaveholders. In 1851, Alexander Jones, a journalist and strong advocate of Cuban annexation, published a book on the island of Cuba detailing its current state and the efforts of the filibusters to free it from Spain's grasp. He estimated that roughly $114 million in exports per year—the majority leaving from New Orleans—made its way through the Gulf of Mexico. Jones estimated that the entire extent of trade in imports and exports from the Mississippi and California was $200 million. The majority of that trade was in exports of sugar and cotton from the Mississippi. Jones feared that this trade would be put in serious jeopardy "in the event of war with a strong maritime power." He reasoned, "Should the enemy occupy Havana on one side, and Yucatan on the other, he could do much towards destroying the trade of New Orleans." Annexing Cuba would solve these problems and put an end to the threats to New Orleans's commerce.[24]

Almost as soon as the first abortive attempt was over, López set about planning for the second. During the early months of preparation for the expedition, men interested in taking part traveled to New Orleans to meet with López and join the volunteer army quickly taking shape. Francis Calvin Boggess, an overseer from Alabama, arrived in the city and enlisted with a Louisiana regiment. Boggess, like many of the men who were attracted to the expeditions, had participated in other armed conflicts in the region such as the US-Mexican War, or they had missed out on the war and were eager to stake their claim of martial prowess through the expedition. They were looking for something. Boggess's father had been involved in the Second Seminole War, and his grandfather before that fought at the Battle of New Orleans. Calvin, as he referred to himself, enlisted with an Alabama company in the final months of the US-Mexican War. Boggess never saw significant action, however, participating in a small skirmish with guerrilla fighters in which the company lost two men.

Through the expeditions, López encouraged the commitment of his soldiers by promising them success and that they would remain in charge of the expeditions and their Creole accomplices. According to Boggess's memoirs, López assured the filibusters that the men involved "were to be put in charge of the Cubans and all to be perfect in military tactics," once the revolution began in Cuba.[25] This played both on the filibusters' expectation of riches and on their understandings of race. Cubans were treated as white to a certain extent, but the project of winning Cuban independence, once it involved Anglo-Americans, would be headed by Anglo-Americans. They would play the starring role in the story of Cuba's independence, thereby securing for the United States a new state brought into the nation by southern white men. Cuba would repeat the accomplishments of other Latin American spaces in North America that had been obtained by Anglos such as Texas and the Mexican cession. The *Picayune* announced that it had received letters from the nation's wealthy merchants, who claimed that all of Cuba was in favor of independence and annexation. These US observers assumed that the oppressed Cuban natives would rise up in rebellion as soon as the filibusters landed and lit the fire they needed to push for revolution.[26]

Throughout both expeditions, supporters and filibusters would intone the battles of the US-Mexican War in filibuster propaganda like a spell or a prayer, hoping to capture the magic of that war and transfer it to their own.[27] In May 1850, López addressed his fellow filibusters with a proclamation outlining their mission. He referred to the filibusters as the men of the "field of Palo Alto and Churubusco" and assured those who were not veterans of the war that they were the "brethren and worthy peers of the men of those immortal victories." López went on to predict that the Cubans would rise up once they saw a "legion of choice spirits amply powerful to deal Buena-Vista fashion with any force" that the Spanish government could muster against them. Echoing both López's and Boggess's references to the US-Mexican War veterans, the *New Orleans True Delta* surmised that three-fourths of the filibusters who set sail with López "served with distinction in Mexico." Linking the filibusters with the soldiers of the US-Mexican War gave the expeditions an air of legitimacy even when they had none. The expedition to Cuba was not sanctioned by the US government and violated its neutrality laws. The filibusters were condemned by the Spanish as little better than villainous pirates. In addition to legitimacy, the linkages between filibusters and US-Mexican war soldiers also recalled the success of the war and gave the expeditions an expected outcome of ecstatic revolution and conquest.

The expected outcomes did not happen as predicted. In the end, both expeditions were abject failures. The second expedition, in 1851, ended in the execution of many of the filibusters, López included, by the Spanish colonial government they attempted to overthrow. Rumors spread throughout New Orleans that the Spanish consul refused to hand over the filibusters' final letters, and the Spanish newspaper *La Union* printed articles defaming them. A resident of the city reported the details of the end of the expedition and the reaction of New Orleanians. Admitting that it was difficult to know the exact details of the events of the last few days, the author denounced the Spanish as acting inhumanely toward the filibusters. He claimed that "it appears that not satisfied with shooting them through the back at three paces those that were not killed on the spot were beaten on the head with the butt end of the musket, others were disemboweled, their private parts cut out and exposed to the pubic gaze." Public outrage exploded into outright violence and targeted destruction as mobs rioted in the streets. On the afternoon of August 21, New Orleanians gathered in the streets and marched to the offices of *La Union* in Exchange Alley just below Conti Street. The small streets of the Old Quarter became clogged with angry demonstrators who stormed the newspaper's printing room, destroyed the presses, and threw the metal type into the street. The crowd then tore down the Spanish flag and consulate sign, carried them to Lafayette Square, and proceeded to burn them. It continued marching through the streets, arriving in the Second Municipality, where many Spanish and Cuban businesses were located. The crowd destroyed some forty Spanish-owned coffeehouses and cigar shops. In an effort to protect the Cuban community from any kind of punishment from US or Spanish authorities and maintain favorable relations between Cuban Creoles and Anglo southerners, the *Picayune* stressed that Cubans did not take part in the riot and that no Cuban-owned businesses were harmed.[28]

Despite the failure of the López expeditions, Cuba continued to play a central role in expansionists' goals during the latter half of the decade. Yet, by the mid-1850s, internal division over the question of slavery's expansion forced Gulf Coast southerners to again worry about England's continued efforts to stop the slave trade. Persistent Anglo-American and Mexican conflict on the US-Mexico border made the Gulf South appear even more vulnerable against the backdrop of events such as Bleeding Kansas and John Brown's raid on Harpers Ferry. Whether they were pro-secessionist or antisecessionist, Gulf southerners used these same issues to voice their opinions on their region's best course of action. What would secure their continued expansion into Latin America? Would the region continue to be at the vanguard of the United States' pursuit of territory? Or would it become the threatened coastline of a new nation? In 1854, many of these questions had not yet been fully formed, but as they took shape. the residents of the Gulf South remembered the struggles of its past and wondered about its future.

NOTES

1. *Yazoo Democrat* (MS), March 23, 1859.

2. Joseph C. G. Kennedy, *Population of the U.S. in 1860*, cited in Tommy W. Rogers, "Migration Patterns of Alabama's Population, 1850 to 1860," *American Historical Quarterly* 28 (Spring–Summer 1966): 603; Ira Berlin, *Many Thousands Gone: The First Two Centuries of Slavery in North America* (Cambridge, MA: Belknap Press, 2000), 288–289, 325–365; Gwendolyn Midlo Hall, *Africans in Colonial Louisiana: The Development of Afro-Creole Culture in the Eighteenth Century* (Baton Rouge: Louisiana State University Press, 1992); Walter Johnston, *Soul by Soul: Life in the Antebellum Slave Market* (Cambridge, MA: Harvard University Press, 1999), 135–162; Adam Rothman, *Slave Country: American Expansion and the Origins of the Deep South* (Cambridge, MA: Harvard University Press, 2005), x–xi, 165–216.

3. Walter Johnson, *River of Dark Dreams: Slavery and Empire in the Cotton Kingdom* (Cambridge, MA; Belknap Press, 2013); Matthew Pratt Guterl, *American Mediterranean: Southern Slaveholders in the Age of Emancipation* (Cambridge, MA: Harvard University Press, 2008); Matthew Karp, *This Vast Southern Empire: Slaveholders at the Helm of American Foreign Policy* (Cambridge, MA: Harvard University Press, 2016).

4. Brian DeLay, *War of a Thousand Deserts: Indian Raids and the U.S.-Mexican War* (New Haven, CT: Yale University Press, 2008), xiv–xviii; Sam W. Haynes and Christopher Morris, eds., *Manifest Destiny and Empire: American Antebellum Expansionism* (College Station: Texas A&M University Press, 1997); Andrés Reséndez, *Changing National Identities at the Frontier: Texas and New Mexico, 1800–1850* (New York: Cambridge University Press, 2005).

5. Anthony Kaye, "Second Slavery: Modernity in the Nineteenth-Century South and the Atlantic World," *Journal of Southern History* 75 (August 2009): 627; Deborah Cohen, "The South and the Caribbean: A Review Essay," *Southern Quarterly* 42 (Spring 2004): 155–156; Jessica Adams, Michael P. Bibler, and Cécile Accilien, *Just Below South: Intercultural Performance in the Caribbean and the U.S. South* (Charlottesville: University of Virginia Press, 2007), 2–6; Nathalie Dessens, *Myths of the Plantation Society: Slavery in the American South and the West Indies* (Gainesville: University Press of Florida, 2003); Sam W. Haynes, *Unfinished Revolution: The Early American Republic in a British World* (Charlottesville: University of Virginia Press, 2010), 1–2.

6. *New Orleans Daily Picayune*, February 14, 1844; Rice Ballard to Albert Sidney Johnston, April 17, 1844, Albert Sidney and William Preston Johnston Papers, Louisiana Research Collection, Howard-Tilton Memorial Library, Tulane University, New Orleans.

7. William Preston Johnston, *The Life of General Albert Sidney Johnston* (New York: D. Appleton and Company, 1878), 67–68; H. Clay Davis to Albert Sidney Johnston, March 27, 1844, J .S. Mayfield to Johnston, March 8, 1845, and James Love to Johnston, March 30, 1845, Johnston Papers.

8. *New Orleans Daily Picayune*, April 11, 1844, and January 10, 1845.

9. Herbert Pickens Gambrell, *Anson Jones: The Last President of Texas* (Garden City, NY: Doubleday, 1948).

10. *New Orleans Daily Picayune*, January 18, 1846; Charles G. Bryant to Johnston, July 10, 1846, Johnston Papers; Kent Barnett Germany, "Patriotism and Protest: Louisiana and General Edmund Pendleton Gaines's Army of Mexican-American War Volunteers, 1845–1847," *Louisiana History* 37 (Summer 1996): 325–335.

11. William Preston, Diary, November 1, 7, and 14, 1847, Johnston Papers; *Civilian and Galveston Gazette*, July 15, 1847.

12. Raphael Semmes, *Service Afloat and Ashore during the Mexican War* (Cincinnati: Wm. H. Moore & Co., 1851).

13. *Galveston Weekly News*, May 13, 1851; "More Difficulties," *Texas State Gazette* (Austin), May 13 and 24, 1851; David Montejano, *Anglos and Mexicans in the Making of Texas, 1836–1986* (Austin: University of Texas Press, 1987).

14. *Galveston Weekly News*, October 7, 1856; *The Texas Almanac for 1858* (Galveston: Richardson & Co., 1857), 92–93; Sean Kelley, "'Mexico in His Head': Slavery and the Texas-Mexico Border, 1810–1860," *Journal of Social History* 38 (Spring 2004): 709–710, 717.

15. James David Nichols, *The Limits of Liberty: Mobility and Making of the Eastern U.S.-Mexico Border* (Lincoln: University of Nebraska Press, 2018).

16. Tom Chaffin, *Fatal Glory: Narciso López and the First Clandestine U.S. War against Cuba* (Charlottesville: University Press of Virginia, 1996).

17. Juan Rey Garcia, *Abduction of Juan Francisco Rey: Narrative of Events from His Own Lips*, trans. Daniel Scully (New Orleans: New Orleans True Delta Office, 1844), 8–12.

18. Phillip Thomas Tucker, *Cubans in the Confederacy: José Agustín Quintero, Ambrosio José Gonzales, and Loreta Janeta Velazquez* (Jefferson, NC: McFarland, 2002), 20–21.

19. "The South; Cuban Affairs—Lieut. Marcy—Mr. Bradford—News from Havana—The Cotton Crops, &c.," *New York Times*, August 30, 1852.

20. *New Orleans Daily True Delta*, December 16, 1849.

21. Rodrigo Lazo, *Writing to Cuba: Filibustering and Cuban Exiles in the United States* (Chapel Hill: University of North Carolina Press, 2005); Johnson, *River of Dark Dreams*, 330–366.

22. Robert E. May, *The Southern Dream of a Caribbean Empire, 1845–1861*, 2nd ed. (Gainesville: University Press of Florida, 2002), 4–6; May, *Manifest Destiny's Underworld: Filibustering in Antebellum America* (Chapel Hill: University of North Carolina Press, 2002); John Hope Franklin, *The Militant South, 1800–1861* (Cambridge, MA: Harvard University Press, 1970), 105–115; Charles H. Brown, *Agents of Manifest Destiny: The Lives and Times of Filibusters* (Chapel Hill: University of North Carolina, 1980); Amy S. Greenberg, *Manifest Manhood and the Antebellum American Empire* (New York: Cambridge University Press, 2005), 31–32, 148–151; Guterl, *American Mediterranean*, 85–86, 90–113.

23. *Jackson Mississippian*, September 14, November 9, and December 12, 1849.

24. Laird W. Bergad, Fe Iglesias Garcia, and Maria del Carmen Barica, *The Cuban Slave Market, 1790–1880* (New York: Cambridge University Press, 1995), 146–149; Alexander Jones, *Cuba in 1851* (New York: Stringer & Townsend, 1851), 154.

25. Francis Calvin Morgan Boggess, *A Veteran of Four Wars, The Autobiography of F. C. M. Boggess: A Record of Pioneer Life and Adventure, And Heretofore Unwritten History of the Florida Seminole Indian Wars* (Arcadia, FL: Champion Job Rooms, 1900), 20.

26. *New Orleans Daily True Delta*, April 13, 1850; *New Orleans Daily Picayune*, May 1, 1850.

27. Chaffin, *Fatal Glory*, 110–113.

28. *New Orleans Daily Picayune*, August 22, 1851; *Alabama Daily Journal*, August 25, 1851; John Kendall, *History of New Orleans* (New York: Lewis Publishing Company, 1922), 171–172.

CHAPTER 12

Inventing a National Past: Archaeological Investigation in the Southwest in the Aftermath of the US-Mexican War, 1851–1879

Matthew N. Johnston

In the spring of 1851, the new commissioner of the US-Mexican Boundary Survey, John Russell Bartlett, examined some curious pictographs in the vicinity of El Paso, Texas (fig. 12.1). Only a few months earlier he had met with his Mexican counterpart, General Pedro García Conde, and had fatefully determined the physical location where the new border between the two countries would proceed west from the Rio Grande. The Treaty of Guadalupe Hidalgo (1848), which concluded the US-Mexican War, had stipulated that this portion of the new border would begin near the town of El Paso, but it had given inaccurate coordinates for the town, and the two commissioners had resolved this dilemma by deciding to adopt the coordinates that were given in the treaty. Unfortunately for Bartlett, this resolution placed the border substantially north of the town of El Paso, earning him the ire of critics who claimed that he had needlessly given away what was rightfully American soil, ultimately leading to his ouster from the Boundary Commission. That ignominious dismissal would color much of his account of the Boundary Survey, his *Personal Narrative of Explorations and Incidents in Texas, New Mexico, California, Sonora, and Chihuahua* (1854), which was published by the commercial firm D. Appleton & Company (as opposed to the Government Printing Office), since

246

feet in length, by ten in width. Its entire surface is covered with paintings, one laid on over the other; so that it is difficult to make out those which belong to

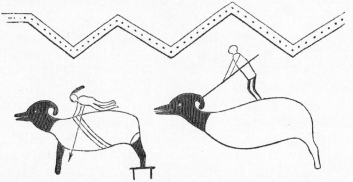

the aborigines. I copied a portion of these figures, about which there can be no doubt as to the origin. They represent Indians with shields and bows, painted

with a brownish earth; horses with their riders; uncouth looking animals; and a huge rattlesnake. Similar devices cover the rock in every part, but are much defaced. Over these are figures of late travel-

Figure 12.1. Indian pictographs at the Hueco Tanks, Texas. Illustration from John Russell Bartlett, *Personal Narrative of Explorations*, vol. 1. New York: D. Appleton, 1854.

it was not the official survey report, that document being produced by his successor and former nominal subordinate, William H. Emory.[1]

However, those events still lay some distance in the future when Bartlett took advantage of a delay in survey operations to explore the rock inscriptions near the Sierra Waco, a mountain chain east of El Paso, in March 1851. These drawings, although "mere peckings with a sharp instrument, just below the surface of the rock," offer multiple perspectives on the Boundary Survey's larger project of defining a new national territory, in particular in terms of the relationships among its inhabitants, white American, Indian, and Mexican. In the text, Bartlett characterizes the pictographs as a kind of palimpsest, even as the interleaved illustrations attempt to isolate a set of marks that are both ethnically and chronologically distinct:

> Hundreds of similar ones are painted on the rocks at this place; some of them, evidently of great antiquity, had been partly defaced to make room for more recent devices. . . . The overhanging rock seemed to have been a favorite place of resort for the Indians, as it is at the present day for all passing travelers. . . . Its entire surface is covered with paintings; one laid over the other; so that it is difficult to make out those which belong to the aborigines.[2]

These observations, despite the cleaning up taking place in the illustration, emphasize three qualities. First, it is difficult to distinguish Indian from non-Indian signs. Second, the successive layering of signs merges past and present, although some signs clearly have "been partly defaced to make room for more recent devices." Third, the process of marking the stone surface is ongoing "for the Indians" and "at the present day for all passing travelers." Transposed onto the shifting political and demographic conditions of the Southwest in the aftermath of war, Bartlett's description suggests a model for the newly acquired national territory that acknowledges both a multiethnic population and an unbroken historical continuum.[3]

This chapter examines the role of archaeology in normalizing the acquisition of territory and people after the US-Mexican War, in particular how textual and pictorial narratives were used conjointly to situate these new lands and their inhabitants in relation to American national history. The development of more professionalized archaeological science in the second half of the century (marked by university programs, national academic organizations, and government-funded institutions) largely coincided with the more systematic examination of substantial built remains in the Southwest, such as Casas Grandes, Arizona (Hohokam), and Mesa Verde, Chaco Canyon, and Canyon de Chelly (Ancestral Puebloan). This chapter investigates the degree to which archaeological conclusions about those remains, especially those that involved the analysis and presentation of visual evidence, were oriented toward integrating the Southwest both culturally and historically. Studies of the development of archaeology in the United States have noted how the discipline was gradually subsumed within anthropological science in the late 1800s, adopting an evolutionary perspective toward past and present indigenous societies that—unlike Bartlett's pictographs—excluded the Indian from contemporary white American society, helping to justify the removal of tribes and the acquisition of Native lands.[4] This chapter focuses on the role of illustrations and visual interpretation in effecting this disciplinary shift, but it also seeks to complicate the kinds of historical experience that were arguably shaped by it, comparing Bartlett's midcentury *Personal Narrative* with Frederic Ward Putnam's *Reports upon Archaeological and Ethnological Collections from Vicinity of Santa Barbara, California, and from Ruined Pueblos of Arizona and New Mexico* (1879), published some three decades later.[5] Briefly, in Bartlett's report, narrative form and its relation to images of landscape reinforce a sense of history unfolding, even of the present accelerating into the past, in part supporting a critical attitude toward the process of annexing the Southwest that doubtless arose from his professional disappointments connected with the Boundary Survey. In contrast, in Putnam's report, text and image fix attention on the present while simultaneously denying ownership of specifically Indian history to either the Indian subject or the report's principal, governmental audience. In a sense, as will be shown, both writers absolve the reader of agency or responsibility regarding the fate of the Indian (and, it is important to note, the Mexican), but Bartlett does so by positing that history can only be experienced, not shaped or bent to one's will, while Putnam does so by asserting that any tangible connection with the indigenous past is an impossibility outside the nonspecialist's experience.

In *History's Shadow: Native Americans and Historical Consciousness in the Nineteenth Century* (2004), Stephen Conn traces the way Americans' emerging sense of historical exceptionalism hinged on an evolving understanding of Native American history, or more precisely how that history could or could not be seen as essentially distinct from the nation's history itself. As he writes, "The change of American historical consciousness across the stretch of the nineteenth century meshed with attempts to figure out exactly where and how Indians fit into 'history,' as it was pursued and understood. . . . More importantly, could 'their' history be seen as part of ours?"[6] The development of archaeology over the course of the nineteenth century was certainly fixated on the question of Indian origins, in part because it threatened a perception of the uniquely favored status of the country as a blank slate granted for the creation of a more perfect society. Thus, the earliest conjectures about Native American history, going back to the colonial period, were religion- and text-based and hypothesized the descent of indigenous populations from Old World cultures found in written history, helping to preserve a providential framing of colonization. Religious assumptions also continued to influence more secular efforts in the early republican period to find a common basis for the multitude of Native dialects and thence to reconstruct a history of migrations to account for their differences.[7]

However, these approaches became increasingly inadequate as expansion accelerated in the years leading up to the Civil War and evidence mounted that pointed to the antiquity of human settlement in the New World, perhaps most especially the numerous Mound Builder sites found in the Ohio River Valley. In particular, earlier theories of Indian history had supported a notion of Indian cultural inferiority that helped to justify the displacement of Native Americans, but that perception was difficult to square with proliferating signs of a history of more sophisticated cultural achievement. Nonetheless, the two dominant schools of thought regarding Indian history at the time both attempted to assert a condition of cultural inferiority that was innate as opposed to being the result of a history of colonial occupation: monogenism, a belief in a common origin for humanity, posited various forms of cultural stagnation occurring prior to the arrival of Europeans, while polygenism put forward the idea of separate human races and the possibility of earlier, more advanced cultures succumbing to the ancestors of contemporary Native Americans. American archaeological science became more professionalized in the second half of the century, including the founding of the Peabody Museum of Archaeology and Ethnology in 1866 and the Bureau of American Ethnology in 1869. It also adapted key European advances in the field to a home context in ways that sought to preserve indigenous cultural inferiority. These advances included a notion of "prehistory" that substantially expanded the time frame of the archaeological past and a model of "evolutionary archaeology" that productively periodized cultural development in terms of social and technological stages.[8] Thus, ethnological research among living Native Americans came to constitute a method by which to shed light on "prehistoric" cultural entities, while, conversely, archaeological research enabled the reconstruction of what contemporary Native American societies would look like without the corrupting influences of the modern world, merging archaeology and anthropology.

For some historians of American archaeology, like Conn, this shift to "evolutionary archaeology" and the complementary relationship between archaeology and anthropology essentially removed Native Americans from history altogether: "Unlike European archaeology, which pushed the idea of linear progress backward in time and helped unify the history of the recent past with that of ancient times, American archaeology reinforced the idea that only Europeans had a history, as defined in these progressive terms." However, this position is not without its critics, and historians have pointed to, among other things, the Bureau of American Ethnology's preoccupation with the project of reconstructing tribal movements after European contact, an essentially histori- cal undertaking.[9] What seems clear, though, is that earlier archaeology had en- tertained the possibility of seeing Indian history as a part of national history in a way that ceased to be really prevalent after midcentury. Such appropriative gestures were often admittedly predicated on an archaizing attitude toward indigenous populations. For example, Henry Rowe Schoolcraft, in the first volume of the first federally funded, comprehensive study of Native Ameri- cans, writes:

> It is but the other day, as it were, that we began to look around the north- ern parts of the continent for objects of antiquarian interest. Every thing [*sic*] in our own history and institutions is so new and so well known . . . it appears refreshing to light on any class of facts which promises to lend a ray of antiquity to our history. The Indian race is, indeed, the oldest thing in American antiquity, and they bid fair to take the place of the inscribed shaft and undeciphered medal of the old world.

Schoolcraft in a sense anticipates an Indian subject who is precisely no longer present, but he nevertheless includes that subject in a joint national history. This anticipatory and appropriative attitude is echoed in Bartlett's *Personal Narrative*, albeit in relation to both Native Americans and Mexicans, when he observes "a large collection of old Spanish documents" in the county clerk's office in San Antonio and speculates that "their careful perusal by some persevering antiquary would develope [*sic*] many interesting facts connected with the early history of the country."[10]

In thinking about the ways that archaeological science construed Indian history over the period 1850–1870, rather than seeing the discipline as solely arriving at the point of outright denying that history, it might be more con- structive to come back to archaeology's role in justifying expansion. In *A History of Archaeological Thought* (2006), Bruce Trigger writes, "No archaeologist in the late nineteenth century seems to have been prepared to believe that in prehis- toric times indigenous North Americans might have evolved cultures that were more complex than those observed in the seventeenth century." Trigger cor- relates this disbelief with the clearly reduced state of Native communities after centuries of European-introduced epidemics and violence. In other words, the denial of cultural sophistication is linked with a denial of complicity in suppressing Indian societies. A similar shunning of complicity is advocated by Putnam's superior, George M. Wheeler, when he asserts the following in the first volume of the survey reports (published in 1889; although published earlier, in 1879, Putnam's report is the seventh volume, last in the series):

> The history, yet to be written, of the contact of American civilization with the aboriginals, the subjection of the latter, the appropriation of the lands, through conquest and "treaty," the gradual apparent decimation of these races, their amalgamation in part, and the hastening of their final extinction, furnish food for thought for the ethnologist and the philosopher, but scarcely for the practical man of affairs.[11]

It may be that with much of the continent still untouched in 1851, Schoolcraft could indulge in an anticipatory fantasy of an Indian subject existing entirely in the past, as a future event that might be inevitable but that could also be blamed on a future party. By 1889, however, with the conclusion of the Plains Indian wars and Native populations entirely contained within a fully mapped national territory, ownership over the history that would result in "their final extinction" could only be avoided by "the practical man of affairs." In what follows, this chapter explores how text and image frame Indian history but also, critically, the degree to which that framing encourages or fends off an awareness of complicity.

BARTLETT'S *PERSONAL NARRATIVE*: ACCELERATING PROGRESS, ACCELERATING ANTIQUITY

Despite the fact that Bartlett had been dismissed as commissioner of the Boundary Survey and Congress had elected not to publish his narrative as part of the official report on the survey (even with Samuel Houston, then serving as senator from Texas, introducing the measure), Bartlett was very much interested in defining and promoting a sense of national identity. Before embarking on the survey, he wrote a popular reference work on distinctive American expressions, his *Dictionary of Americanisms* (1848), which continued to be an authoritative work on the development of the American language into the twentieth century. Although the survey was charged principally with practical matters like marking the boundary, looking for mineral deposits and a viable transportation route to California, encouraging trade with Mexico, Bartlett's *Personal Narrative* is also notable for its wide-ranging discussion of the

Figure 12.2. John Russell Bartlett, *Ruins at Casas Grandes, Chihuahua.* Plate from John Russell Bartlett, *Personal Narrative of Explorations*, vol. 2. New York: D. Appleton, 1854.

region's flora and fauna, local customs, and especially history. As an index of his interest in specifically antiquarian materials, it is significant that so many of the illustrations in his report, including the frontispiece to the second volume (fig. 12.2), are devoted to archaeological subjects, not just Native American ruins and petroglyphs, but also the remains of the more recent Spanish and Mexican colonial past, such as abandoned missions, haciendas, and presidios (fig. 12.3). Indeed, although many of the illustrations in his report are prints of drawings by the artist Henry C. Pratt, many are also based on his own watercolor sketches (including the frontispiece). If Bartlett strove to familiarize his audience with the distinctive plants, animals, and people of the Southwest, as new components of an expanding nation, he was equally concerned to acquaint them with its history.

That being said, throughout the *Personal Narrative*, Bartlett may be perpetually drawn to history, but he also just as consistently struggles to convey it fully or coherently. As Thomas Gunn makes clear in two recent articles that address Bartlett's involvement in the Boundary Survey and his promotion of ethnological publications as a publisher and bookseller in New York, Bartlett had been involved in ethnological circles for some time before assuming his post as commissioner. Gunn shows that Bartlett's mentor, Albert Gallatin, the politician and renowned philologist of Native American dialects, used his political influence and contacts within the Bureau of Indian Affairs to help Bartlett

Figure 12.3. *Presidio of San Eleazario*. Illustration from John Russell Bartlett, *Personal Narrative of Explorations*, vol. 1. New York: D. Appleton, 1854.

secure his appointment, in part to place someone with ethnological training in a portion of the North American continent that was still a lacuna in Gallatin's mapping of Native American languages. In different places throughout his report, Bartlett refers to the potential of philological research to clarify relations between indigenous tribes as well as their various migrations over time, as when he states about the Apaches that "it is only by a comparison of their languages that their ethnological position can be accurately determined." Nonetheless, his only major ethnological publication before departing for the Southwest was *The Progress of Ethnology, an Account of Recent Archaeological, Philological and Geographical Researches* (1847), which was a summary of others' work. If Gallatin had hoped that the philological data Bartlett collected on the Boundary Survey (basically vocabularies) would aid in clarifying the relationship between the native dialects in New Mexico and Arizona and those of the rest of the continent, Bartlett himself, in his report, is notably frustrated in presenting anything like a coherent chronology of linguistic dispersal and development (for example, the precise "ethnological position" of the Apaches is never fully made clear). In his preface, while he stresses that he was able to "obtain vocabularies of more than twenty aboriginal languages . . . all taken down by myself, with great care, and according to one system," he also admits that "I have also incidentally spoken of the tribes through whose countries I passed, without entering into any detail," explaining that time constraints prevented him from offering a more complete picture.[12]

However, Bartlett's difficulties in presenting substantive ethnological conclusions about indigenous populations in the Southwest are not just the result of a relative lack of experience in fieldwork and the survey's demands on his time. Gunn focuses on the way Bartlett's compromised position as narrator, recounting the Boundary Survey's activities while no longer being its official head, parallels the uneasy codependency between empire making and knowledge creation embodied in his dual roles as boundary marker and ethnologist and that this "fractured embodiment of national authority . . . is most keenly legible in discussions of racial and national difference."[13] This split authorial subject also arguably impacts on his difficulties presenting a coherent history, whether national or ethnological. In particular, in his capacity as commissioner, motivated to convey the sense of a new territory successfully being integrated with the rest of the nation, Bartlett will at times portray Progress as proceeding apace, as almost unavoidable. At other times, however, and reflecting both his frustrations with being unable to perform that role fully and his struggles to fashion a coherent history, that sense of Progress as inevitable reads instead as history out of control.

Instances where Bartlett portrays Progress as well under way also notably occur more frequently in the opening chapters, before the challenges of both the physical traversal of largely unmapped desert terrain and the process of collecting and synthesizing largely unknown ethnological data actually begin. As the expedition moves inland from the Gulf Coast, he notes with approval towns that are plainly growing and prospering. In Goliad, traces of bloodshed during the Texas Revolution are fast disappearing as former battlefields are converted to cropland, so that "the sword has truly given place to the ploughshare." In San Antonio, the larger number of buildings there makes Progress visible as new construction and changes in architectural style, reflecting an upsurge in American newcomers whom he sees as more attuned to what he later terms "this steam and lightning age." As he writes, "The town is a strange mixture of massive old Spanish buildings and recent American structures. But upon the plaza the modern buildings have for the most part superseded the ancient." Although "some few of the Mexicans have the good sense to fall in with the spirit of progress," "the great majority draw back before it, and live upon the outskirts of the town in the primitive style of their forefathers."[14] There is no speculation on preferential treatment of Americans over Mexicans; Progress is visibly occurring, and the relative success of the former compared with the latter is reduced to an ethnic affinity for the modern era.

As the expedition moves farther into the interior, though, leaving Texas and entering lands that had only recently belonged to Mexico, Progress is still manifestly happening, but it is no longer clearly "smart-looking," as Bartlett registers a rapid and chaotic process of new American settlers crowding out former Mexican citizens and new laws and institutions being put precariously in place. Particularly striking is his description of a frontier murder trial, in which both American and Mexican participants seem "more characteristic of feudal times than of the nineteenth century":

> In the court room, therefore, where one of the most solemn scenes of human experience was enacting, all were armed save the prisoners. There sat the judge, with a pistol lying on the table before him; the clerks and attorneys wore revolvers at their sides; and the jurors were either armed with similar weapons, or carried with them the unerring rifle. . . . The fair but sunburnt complexion of the American portion of the jury, with their weapons resting against their shoulders, and pipes in their mouths, presented a striking contrast to the swarthy features of the Mexicans, muffled in checkered *serapes*, holding their broad-brimmed glazed hats in their hands, and delicate cigarritos in their lips.

It is also in the later portions of the *Personal Narrative* that Bartlett takes on a more openly critical stance toward the processes involved in extracting wealth from the new territory. The expedition is plagued by other incidents of murder, including one of Bartlett's favorite officers, Colonel Louis S. Craig, and on multiple occasions they retrieve hostages from the Apaches, in the midst of an astonishingly harsh desert environment, leading him to ask, "Is this the land which we have purchased . . . and keep at such a cost?" In the vicinity of Doña Ana near where Bartlett and García Conde located their contentious boundary marker, Bartlett notes the recent creation of the town of Mesilla on the opposite side of the Rio Grande, populated by Mexicans who had been evicted from their homes in Doña Ana through the granting of "Texas head-rights" to American settlers, a practice all along the river. He also reports the mistreatment of Mexicans and their property by emigrants imposing on them for food and shelter, without giving payment, en route to California. Finally, although "Indian depredations" occur constantly (in particular the theft of horses), Bartlett is clear that hostile relations with Native American tribes are mainly the result of a similar history of unfair dealing with them:

"It is the conduct of unprincipled traders and emigrants, who sow the seeds of intemperance and vice among them, which has created most of the difficulties before experienced. These men defraud them of their property, and, on the slightest pretense, take their lives." In view of the past Mexican atrocities committed against Native Americans that he mentions, Progress becomes instead a history of abuse uniting older Mexicans and newer Americans. It is important to note that Bartlett is not critical of Progress per se but rather of how it is unfolding through existing laws governing the acquisition of property, measures to provide security, and, as well, his own surveying enterprise. Scholarship on these survey reports, in general, often highlights the way writers will stress elements of danger to convince a congressional audience of the need for, precisely, more surveying activity; what makes Bartlett's report somewhat unique is that, because he has already failed to secure congressional backing, what might otherwise read as a dire situation in need of further professional attention reads instead as a dire situation only.[15]

This sense of Progress or historical change out of control is most forcefully conveyed, though, by the conjunction of narrative form and illustration, in three key ways: first, the correlation between physical and historical progress, supported by the kinds of landscape illustrations commonly used in the report; second, an essential confusion as to how ancient different kinds of "ruins" are, whether Indian or Mexican; and third, an emphasis on the rapid creation of ruins, a kind of accelerated antiquity, that is likewise supported by landscape views. Regarding the first effect of text and image, the first-person narration naturally invites the imaginative participation of the reader in Bartlett's journeys, a drawing in of the reader that is reinforced by one of the dominant types of illustrations featured in the report, a modified picturesque view that exaggerates the pull from foreground to background. For example, in *Approach to Mule Spring. Picacho de Mimbres*, the repoussoir, or foreground landscape feature that serves as an entry point for the viewer, forms the initial point of a dotted line composed of the Boundary Commission's wagon train that curves into the distance, disappearing at the horizon line (fig. 12.4; see also fig. 12.5). However, to the extent that Bartlett's observations about the signs of Progress shift from ordered ("smart-looking") to chaotic as the expedition proceeds west from the Rio Grande, that visceral pull along the track of their progress renders that increasingly disordered flow of history equally unstoppable. The proliferating negative signs of Progress that Bartlett notes are also accompanied by increasing incidents temporarily checking the expedition's movement or, rather, not wholly fixing them in place but forcing changes of direction, dividing them into subgroups moving at different rates of speed, making them lose their way. The equation between physical and historical progress that is

Figure 12.4. *Approach to Mule Spring. Picacho de Mimbres.* Illustration from John Russell Bartlett, *Personal Narrative of Explorations*, vol. 1. New York: D. Appleton, 1854.

produced becomes a kind of negative variation on Thomas Gast's *American Progress* (1872).

Although Gast's famous image was painted almost two decades later, the correlation between the viewer's imagined movement and historical time was already an established convention in American landscape painting at the time of Bartlett's involvement with the Boundary Commission. In *The Empire of the Eye: Landscape Representation and American Cultural Politics, 1825–1875* (1993), Angela Miller analyzes Asher Durand's *Progress (The Advance of Civilization)* (1853) as a paradigmatic example of landscape paintings, after Thomas Cole, that used this correlation to instill confidence in manifest destiny, noting in particular that, within the painting, "specific temporal correlates were assigned to the organizing planes within the image, embedding historical meaning in the very structure of space itself."[16] It was not just that Durand showed different "stages of civilization" (as one's eye moves back into the painting, one sees a log cabin, then a village, then a busy seaport); it was the ordered manner in which these visual way stations were encountered, showing a clear and measured progression. In the liminal space of the Southwest, there are certainly signs of past habitation, but their chronological relations become increasingly uncertain the farther Bartlett travels into the interior. Early discussions of de-

Figure 12.5. Henry C. Pratt, *Basin of the Gila*. Illustration from John Russell Bartlett, *Personal Narrative of Explorations*, vol. 2. New York: D. Appleton, 1854.

caying Spanish missions and haciendas can be tied to events in written histories, but just as the philological relations between Apaches, Navajos, Pimas, and other southwestern indigenous dialects are difficult to parse, so is it a challenge to distinguish between Native American settlements that are ancient and those that were more recently abandoned, especially given that his principal tools are linguistic and historical.[17] However near or far in time, though, the illustrations that show past remains present them according to more or less identical picturesque landscape conventions, confirming an impression of hoary old age onto all dilapidated structures, whether Indian or Mexican. Characteristic is the middle-ground positioning of the structure, the broken outline, and the inclusion of modern-day staffage figures (cattle, shepherds, even members of the expedition), typically unaware of the historical significance of the ruin behind them in order to amplify the sense of a time long gone (see figs. 12.2 and 12.3).

Finally, the sense of being immersed in but lacking control over historical change is buttressed by the different ways that text and image suggest that the extreme (social as well as ecological) environment of the Southwest accelerates antiquity, jeopardizing the forward-looking orientation of Progress and bringing the diverse cultures of the Southwest together in history. As with Bartlett's allusions to the positive and negative signs of Progress, here too the impression of accelerated antiquity reads as a good thing earlier in the *Personal Narrative*, especially in Texas, in the sense that traces of the recent conflict with Mexico are fast disappearing. Later on, however, in particular as the expedition finds evidence of the Apache raids that dogged the northern frontier of Mexico in the decades leading up to the US-Mexican War, and which are continuing in Bartlett's time, accelerated antiquity points rather to the precariousness of "civilization" in the region.[18] The chronological confusion of Mexican versus older or more recent Native American ruins merely underlines this point of view, as do the frequent landscape illustrations that exaggerate distance and the pull from foreground to background (see figs. 12.4 and 12.5). The lines of wagons and troops diminish rapidly in size, vanishing in front of the viewer's eyes, as if they are entering a land lost to time. The way that the specific depiction of pictorial depth in these landscape views suggests a skewing of time is buttressed in the text by an ongoing theme of distorted vision, in which landscape features consistently appear much closer than they actually are. Objects that are closer are effectively more "recent" in the sense that it takes less time to reach them; in effect, assorted mesas, buttes, and ridges seem close, but they end up being "older" than they appear. In the end, the desert seems like nothing so much as an immense charnal field, littered with the bleached bones of people and structures, Indian, Mexican, and American—irrespective of chronology, equally ancient-seeming. Wandering near the Salinas River, Bartlett writes, "From the summit of the principal heap [or ruin] . . . there may be seen in all directions similar heaps." While in the vicinity of Casa Grande, Arizona, he observes, "In every direction as far as the eye can reach, are seen heaps of ruined edifices."[19]

PUTNAM'S *REPORTS UPON ARCHAEOLOGICAL AND ETHNOLOGICAL COLLECTIONS*: OWNING THE ARCHAEOLOGICAL PAST

Whereas Bartlett uses picturesque conventions to collapse pre-Columbian, colonial, and more recent events into a uniform antiquity, Frederic Ward Putnam's work enforces an irretrievable separation between past and present. Putnam's *Reports upon Archaeological and Ethnological Collections* was also a distinctly different kind of narrative. American archaeological science was much more sophisticated and institutionally supported at the time of its publication. Putnam himself was a leading figure of American archaeology at the end of the century, chief curator of the prestigious Peabody Museum of Archaeology and Ethnology at Harvard University, lead organizer of the Anthropology Department at the Chicago World's Fair of 1893, and mentor to Franz Boas, who established anthropology as a respected academic field in the United States. Then, too, it was just one part of a larger apparatus of publications, some seven volumes of data and analysis accumulated over the course of George M. Wheeler's *Report upon United States Geographical Surveys West of the One Hundredth Meridian* and covering, respectively, geography, astronomical and elevation data, geology, paleontology, zoology, botany, and archaeology. Finally, as a government publication, it employs a kind of official-speak and is more of a collection of documents than a single text. Historian Robert Hine's remarks on the actual official report on the Boundary Survey apply equally to Putnam's report: "Emory's narrative had little of the verve of Bartlett's. It did not flow with a paced series of events."[20] These differences in organization and writing style, however, as well as changes in the kinds of images used as evidence, facilitate conveying a changed model of history for its Native American subject.

The first volume of Wheeler's seven-volume report focuses on geography and contains an overview of the areas surveyed, an abbreviated account of the expedition's ascent of the Colorado River, innumerable tables of surveying data, and, in the penultimate section, an outline of Native American tribes living there. The preface to this volume begins by giving a data-driven description of the terrain of the West as a whole—lowest and highest points of elevation, lengths of rivers, principal direction of mountain passes, distribution and size of different land categories and their definitions—laying out for the reader the pure physical dimensions of the region exclusive of time or history, what is "there." The preface then acknowledges history by noting that "the geologist has ample room to reduce to a system the rock exposures as well as their origin and history" and, within the same paragraph, introducing the subject of indigenous peoples by stating that "the student of antiquity of the ancient races and their ruins and the present aboriginals has a horizon the value of which is but just dawning on the public mind." The proximity of geological time has the effect of emphasizing the past as the proper "horizon" to be explored in investigations of Native cultures. This sequence could characterize the temporal orientation of the entire series of volumes, and certainly Putnam's work in volume 7. Overall, there is an emphasis on physical location, the present, and measurement, while access to history is belated and takes on a curious form as detached from the present, available only to specialists, whether geologists, historians, or archaeologists/ethnologists. The preference for physical location, the present, and measurement is manifested in the overall structure of the series of volumes, as collections of field reports with assorted appendixes of tables of numerical data. Indeed, any sustained narrative text (or "paced series of events," to use Hines's phrasing) often carries with it some sort of justification or is understood to be a form of evidence in itself (as in "exhibit A" in a trial proceeding). The narrated account of the ascent of the Colorado River, for example, opens by excusing its "itinerary form."[21]

In terms of how the Wheeler reports approach Native American societies, the insertion of "present aboriginals" at the end of a list of topics of interest to "student[s]" (or specialists) inaugurates the report's archaizing perspective on Native Americans, in which the "authentic Indian" is understood to be a past entity that is available principally to professionals with the training to find and study them. Although the passage mentions "present aboriginals," it also concludes by stating that the chief object of interest is "the nature of pre-aboriginals." In this same volume's later section giving an overview of the expedition's observations of Native American tribes, this interest in "pre-aboriginals" is explained in terms of the exigencies of settling the region and making it economically productive. The section opens with a calculation of land allotted per Native American individual and asserts that, once agriculture is more widely adopted by Native Americans, such an amount of land will be superfluous, and hence much of it should be available for white American settlement. Native Americans as a whole are here further divided into three categories: "civilized," "partly civilized," and "'blanket Indians'" or "nomads," the latter of which were Native Americans still living beyond the confines of the recently introduced reservation system.[22] The section concludes by observing that these "nomads" "are now being ethnologically considered and it is hoped that the types of this remnant of a former population will have been secured before they have become absorbed, or at least have assimilated certain arts of civilization."[23] In other words, this "type" has no future and is properly (or "ethnologically") considered a "remnant of a former population"; it speaks instead to a cultural entity whose time is essentially in the past. This orientation toward the past as the appropriate context in which to find and describe the "authentic Indian" is exemplified in Putnam's contribution to the Wheeler series by its overwhelming focus on archaeological material. The first part is devoted to portable objects found primarily in burials and shell heaps and the second part to "the Pueblo ruins and the interior tribes."

The idea that the "authentic Indian" would soon disappear was by no means new at the time that Putnam and Wheeler were writing. George Catlin is a familiar earlier example of this perception among the protoethnographers of the first part of the century, as when he infamously explained the value of his "Indian Gallery," his collection of paintings and artifacts, on the grounds that "I have flown to their rescue—not of their lives or of their race (for they are '*doomed*' and must perish), but to the rescue of their looks and their modes . . . phoenix-like, they may rise from the 'stain on a painter's palette.'"[24] What is new in Putnam's work is the extent to which archaeology-as-ethnology is systemized, specifically according to Lewis Henry Morgan's adaptation of European notions of "prehistory" in *Ancient Society: or, Researches in the Lines of Human Progress from Savagery through Barbarism to Civilization* (1877). The notion of prehistory was a recent component of American archaeology, a blanket term that described past cultures without written records, but also more controversially understood in some circles to apply to contemporary cultures of equivalent technical sophistication. John Lubbock, the English writer who was largely responsible for introducing the term, wrote in *Pre-historic Times as Illustrated by Ancient Remains and the Manners and Customs of Modern Savages* (1865) that "if we wish to understand the antiquities of Europe, we must compare them with the rude implements and weapons still, or until lately, used by the savage races in other parts of the world." Morgan developed an evolutionary model of successive stages of social complexity (moving from "savagery" to "barbarism" to "civilization," with each stage in turn subdivided into three phases) and applied them to North American indigenous groups, matching them up with his version of European archaeological stages of prehistory (the familiar Paleolithic, Mesolithic, and Neolithic). The Morgan system is used extensively throughout *Reports upon Archaeological and Ethnological Collections*, and Morgan's "comprehensive work" is singled out for praise in Putnam's introduction.[25]

Moreover, the organization of the report treats past and present material together, with the latter examined primarily to the extent that it sheds light on the former. For Putnam, the present-day Native American was only a degraded version of the prehistoric and more authentic ancestor. For example, he describes the technical skill of contemporary California tribes by quoting another author, Stephen Powers, to the effect that "'the few and simple stone implements used by the California Indians resemble, in their main purpose and design, those of the extinct races exhumed in the shell-mounds, only they are conspicuously ruder and simpler.'" Notably, Putnam avoids accounting for this deterioration, stating only at the very beginning of his report that "it can hardly be questioned that it is in great part owing to [the Jesuits'] endeavoring to 'save the souls of the savages' regardless of the body, that the deluded Indians . . . owe their rapid and almost unresisted extermination." Furthermore, this pristine prehistoric Indian is understood to be a uniform entity over time in terms of cultural innovation. Referring to implements discovered at grave sites in New Mexico, he writes that "so far as the testimony of the graves is concerned, there was . . . no advance in any of the arts by which we are wont to estimate the progress of a people in civilization." Putnam's sense of the authentic Indian is consequently doubly disengaged from considerations of recent history: as prehistoric, but also as essentially unchanging.[26]

Putnam's concentration on the prehistoric Indian is reinforced by the way the illustrations in the report's first section (portable objects from Southern California) shore up a sense of the specimen as disconnected from its original, social context. First an account is given of some of the sites investigated, including an attempt to match these locations up with places mentioned in historical sources, in particular the narrative of Juan Rodríguez Cabrillo, who explored the coastline in the early sixteenth century. What then follows is an analysis by category of objects amassed by the expedition, some of which were obtained at these sites, some elsewhere in Southern California, and some with uncertain provenance. Whereas much of the impact of Bartlett's presentation of Native American remains depended on their being embedded in a particular kind of landscape, the picturesque view, Putnam's report shifts attention to the provenance of artifacts or, more precisely, the retrieval and assembly of artifacts in a collection as the place for their proper examination and understanding. The sources for objects consist of a spatial location alone, while their new context, their relations of size and shape that suggest their grouping with other like objects, assumes greater importance. Moreover, as much as possible these assorted celts, arrowheads, and pestles are startlingly convincing: the heliotype is quasi-photographic, and the objects are actual size and oriented flat to the page—indeed, the page itself seems like a drawer in a collector's cabinet (fig. 12.6). They are coextensive with the page, less a "figure" and more like tangible objects resting on the page and on occasion requiring the text to be blocked out to make room for them. Finally, this emphasis on the reality of the collection is underscored by Putnam's statistical, tabular mode of analyzing artifacts and remains. The presentation of objects as arranged on a table-like surface, actual size and therefore measurable, resonates with the assorted tables of measurements scattered throughout the report, such as craniological data.

This emphasis on physical location (the sources of objects), the present (the tangible reality of objects in a collection, rendered almost coextensive with the report's tables of data), and measurement is also present in the use of illustrations in the report's second section on the pueblos and cliff dwellings of New Mexico and Arizona. Curiously, there are no illustrations here; the reader is instead referred to images included in earlier preliminary reports and appendixes, which in fact often contain the entire texts inserted as field reports in this section of Putnam's report. In addition, many of the sites explored were photographed by the survey photographers Timothy O'Sullivan and William

Figure 12.6. *Implements of Stone, California.* Plate from Frederic Ward Putnam, *Reports upon Archaeological and Ethnological Collections.* Washington, DC: Government Printing Office, 1879.

Bell, and these pictures would have been available to view as well.[27] In *Archive Style: Photographs and Illustrations for U.S. Surveys, 1850–1890* (2007), Robin Kelsey explains the distinctive style of O'Sullivan's survey work—its starkness, its flatness, its tendency toward self-reflexivity (commenting on the process of taking pictures within the picture)—in terms of the photographer imitating, or rather imitating the effect of, the maps and diagrams used in the reports to efficiently communicate actionable data for the purpose of developing the West economically (fig. 12.7). As he writes: "The photographer evidently began to work a middle ground to exploit the compelling rhetoric of graphic codes. O'Sullivan, in other words, learned to harness the power of the cartographic or diagrammatic gaze as a fiction, to signify through pictorial choices the distillation, organization, and uniformity at the core of a new economy of images."[28] What Kelsey describes here as a visual style is in essence what drives the presentation of objects in part 1 of Putnam's report—extracting archaeological data, in this case, and laying it out in tabular form in order to maximize a certain kind of analysis of size and shape based on precise measurement—but it is present in the use of illustrations in part 2 as well, if dispersed across the larger apparatus of the survey publications as a whole.

For example, one of the field reports, written by Edward Drinker Cope, paleontologist, describes ruins found near the Gallinas River in New Mexico. Perhaps owing to his particular training, the report situates the ruins in terms of the geological formations in which they are found and also comments on the flora found in their vicinity. In other words, the description is almost entirely physical, as opposed to containing any cultural speculations, an orientation matched by illustrations that reduce the structure to the two-dimensional space of the page, such as plan and elevation views of *Ground-Plan of Houses Nos. 4 and 5* (fig. 12.8). The elimination of pictorial illusion (present as well in the illustrations of objects in part 1 of Putnam's report) is a central component of what Kelsey terms "the rhetoric of graphic codes." The one heliotype illustration of a pueblo structure, *Ruin in the Pueblo San Juan* (found earlier in the same appendix), shares similar features (fig. 12.9). There are field reports in this section of Putnam's report that address cultural practices and even historical traditions, when the subject is a still-inhabited pueblo, but they are notably less numerous and, perhaps more significant, they lack illustrations (even in the earlier preliminary reports and appendixes).[29] Moreover, Putnam tends to dismiss local traditions as myths and stories brought from Mexico by the Spanish missionaries (such as tales featuring the so-called Spirit of Guadalupe and Montezuma). It is as if the reality offered by currently practiced rituals and currently narrated histories is less tangible, or less illustratable according to the prevailing "graphic codes" of the survey reports, than the abandoned ruins.

Figure 12.7. Timothy H. O'Sullivan, *Ancient Ruins in the Cañon de Chelle, In a Niche Fifty Feet above Present Cañon Bed*. 1873. Albumen silver print. The J. Paul Getty Museum, Los Angeles. Digital image courtesy of the Getty's Open Content Program.

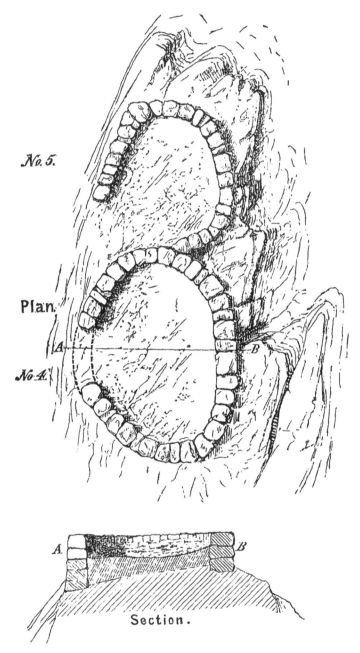

Figure 12.8. *Ground-Plan of Houses Nos. 4 and 5 and Profile of No. 4.* Illustration from George M. Wheeler, *Annual Report upon the Geographical Explorations and Surveys*, app. LL. Washington, DC: Government Printing Office, 1875.

Figure 12.9. *Ruin in the Pueblo San Juan, Showing Walls of Room in Third Story.* Plate from George M. Wheeler, *Annual Report upon the Geographical Explorations and Surveys*, app. LL. Washington, DC: Government Printing Office, 1875.

A final aspect of the illustrations within Putnam's report underscores its opposite orientation to Native history compared with Bartlett's work. Within the mass of photographs produced for the survey, there also are several pictures of Native Americans, principally Apaches, Zunis, and Mojaves. In *Archive Style*, Kelsey discusses how O'Sullivan's photographs place Indian subjects within various framing devices or in a shallow space in a manner suggestive of "an allegedly necessary confinement with a tenuous security."[30] Other examples not discussed by Kelsey are quite similar in effect, for example, a series that shows Zuni Indians posed against a timber structure akin to a terrace that juts forward from an adobe complex (fig. 12.10). However, one could also relate this visual "containment" with the decontextualizing operations found in Putnam's *Reports upon Archaeological and Ethnological Collections* in the sense that these figures, despite their distinctive architectural backdrop, are detached from their environment in a fashion entirely opposite to the spatial logic of illustrations in Bartlett's *Personal Narrative*. There, immersion in history was evoked by movement into depth within a larger landscape image. The kinds of picturesque views used in Bartlett's report provided a means by which the reader could vicariously participate in the expedition's travels and were a mainstay of survey illustration practice before the Civil War. In Bartlett's report, they were modified to facilitate a sense of subjection to history, whereas here there

Figure 12.10. Timothy O'Sullivan, *Group of Zuni Indians, with Albino Boy in Foreground.* 1873. Stereocard. Library of Congress Prints and Photographs Division.

is literally no place (or time) for the Indian subject (or the viewer) to go. Indigenous history would be crafted elsewhere, specifically in Putnam's report, with its object-based, collections-based reconstruction of prehistory.

NOTES

1. For the particulars of Bartlett's participation in the US-Mexican Boundary Survey, see Robert V. Hine, *Bartlett's West: Drawing the Mexican Boundary* (New Haven, CT: Yale University Press, 1968); Robert Gunn, "John Russell Bartlett's Literary Borderlands: Ethnology, War, and the United States Boundary Survey," *Western American Literature* 46 (Winter 2012): 349–380. For an overview of the various surveys connected with western expansion over the course of the nineteenth century, see William H. Goetzmann, *Exploration and Empire: The Explorer and the Scientist in the Winning of the American West* (New York: Alfred A. Knopf, 1966).

2. John Russell Bartlett, *Personal Narrative of Explorations and Incidents in Texas, New Mexico, California, Sonora, and Chihuahua, Connected with the United States and Mexican Boundary Commission, during the Years 1850, '51, '52, and '53*, 2 vols. (New York: D. Appleton & Company, 1854), 1:170–172.

3. This is not to claim that Bartlett advances this model intentionally, although it is perhaps significant that this episode occurs just after the Boundary Commission's agreement about the border's starting point and just before the actual process of physically marking the border begins.

4. See in particular Stephen Conn, *History's Shadow: Native Americans and Historical Consciousness in the Nineteenth Century* (Chicago: University of Chicago Press, 2004); Curtis M. Hinsley Jr., *Savages and Scientists: The Smithsonian Institution and the Development of American Archaeology, 1846–1910* (Washington, DC: Smithsonian Institution Press, 1981); and Bruce Trigger, *A History of Archaeological Thought*, 2nd ed. (New York: Cambridge University Press, 2006). These studies complement critiques of anthropological practice generally, such as James Clifford, *The Predicament of Culture: Twentieth-Century Ethnography, Literature, and Art* (Cambridge, MA: Harvard University Press, 1988); Johannes Fabian, *Time and the Other: How Anthropology Makes Its Object* (New York: Columbia University Press, 1983); and Clifford Geertz, *The Interpretation of Cultures: Selected Essays* (New York: Basic Books, 1973).

5. Frederic Ward Putnam, *Reports upon Archaeological and Ethnological Collections from Vicinity of Santa Barbara, California, and from Ruined Pueblos of Arizona and New Mexico* (Washington, DC: Government Printing Office, 1879).

6. Conn, *History's Shadow*, 6.

7. See Trigger, *History of Archaeological Thought*, chap. 3; Hinsley, *Savages and Scientists*, chap. 1. The philological reconstruction of tribal movements, pioneered by Peter Stephen Duponceau and Albert Gallatin, was shaped by Enlightenment assumptions about the essential unity of humanity that echoed earlier religiously informed views on Indian origins. Bartlett was one of Gallatin's protégés.

8. See Trigger, *History of Archaeological Thought*, chap. 4; Hinsley, *Savages and Scientists*, chap. 5. Although he did not coin the term, the notion of "prehistory" was most fully elaborated by John Lubbock in *Pre-historic Times as Illustrated by Ancient Remains and the Manners and Customs of Modern Savages* (London: Williams and Norgate, 1865). Lewis Henry Morgan's *Ancient Society: or, Researches in the Lines of Human Progress from Savagery through Barbarism to Civilization* (New York: Henry Holt & Co., 1877) was a pivotal work for American archaeology in modeling how to apply evolution to theories of social development.

9. Conn, *History's Shadow*, 144. Hinsley, for one, writes in his review of *History's Shadow* that while Conn's "argument is straightforward and consistent . . . it is fundamentally wrong." Hinsley review of Conn, *Pacific Historical Review* 76 (May 2007): 292.

10. Henry Rowe Schoolcraft, *Historical and Statistical Information Respecting the History, Condition and Prospects of the Indian Tribes of the United States*, 6 vols. (Philadelphia: Lippincott, Grambo & Co., 1851–1857), 1:109. Bartlett, *Personal Narrative*, 1:41.

11. Trigger, *History of Archaeological Thought*, 185; George M. Wheeler, *Report upon United States Geographical Surveys West of the One Hundredth Meridian*, 7 vols. (Washington, DC: Government Printing Office, 1875–1889), 1:219.

12. Thomas Gunn, "John Russell Bartlett's Literary Borderlands" and "The Ethnologist's Bookshop: Bartlett & Welford in 1840s New York," *Wordsworth Circle* 41 (Summer 2010): 159–163. Bartlett was also a cofounder of the American Ethnological Society in New York. Bartlett, *Personal Narrative*, 1:vi, 325.

13. Gunn, "John Russell Bartlett's Literary Borderlands," 351.

14. Bartlett, *Personal Narrative*, 1:28, 38–40.

15. Bartlett, 1:161, 247, 321. The issue of landownership was exacerbated by Texas's claims on parts of what is now New Mexico. Mark Stegmaier, *Texas, New Mexico, and the Compromise of 1850: Boundary Dispute and Sectional Crisis* (Kent, OH: Kent State University Press, 1996). "Filibustering bands," such as the one headed by William Walker, also made spurious land claims (south of the border) as advance agents of anticipated US expansionism. See Rachel St. John, *Line in the Sand: A History of the Western U.S.-Mexico Border* (Princeton, NJ: Princeton University Press, 2011), chap. 2. On survey report writers' emphasis on danger to encourage further government support, see Goetzmann, *Exploration and Empire*; Joel Snyder, "Territorial Photography," in *Landscape and Power*, ed. W. J. T. Mitchell (Chicago: University of Chicago Press, 1994), 175–201.

16. Angela Miller, *The Empire of the Eye: Landscape Representation and American Cultural Politics, 1825–1875* (Ithaca, NY: Cornell University Press, 1993), 4, 154–160, 163–165.

17. For example, Bartlett is unsure what relationship exists between modern-day Pima-Maricopa Indians living near the site of Casa Grande, Arizona, and its original inhabitants. His historical sources, specifically a travel account written by the Franciscan missionary Pedro Font in the eighteenth century, speculate that the occupants were ancestors of the Aztecs, but as Bartlett correctly writes, "People have got too much in the way of ascribing all ancient remains to the Aztecs." *Personal Narrative*, 1:283. Late Hohokam occupation of the site would be in the date range 1350–1600 C.E. Lacking any more modern archaeological tools for establishing chronology, though, Bartlett also tends to reduce southwestern historical complexity.

18. The second half of volume 1 is littered with mentions of abandoned rancheros and haciendas: San Bernardino ("the frequent attacks of the Apaches led to the abandonment of this place"), Fronteras (recently resettled, but "like most of the military colonies, [it] fell into decay, chiefly from the neglect of the central government to properly provide for the soldiery"), and so on. *Personal Narrative*, 1:255, 266. Bartlett will also often wax poetic about how an abandoned site might once have appeared. As noted, this emphasis on danger is a frequent feature of survey reports generally.

19. Bartlett, *Personal Narrative*, 2:247, 275.

20. The Wheeler survey was one of four major expeditions conducted after the Civil War, primarily to locate a viable railroad route to California, and was focused on the Southwest. Putnam's report is volume 7 of the Wheeler survey reports. Hine, *Bartlett's West*, 89.

21. Wheeler, *United States Geographical Surveys*, 1:18, 156. The emphasis on the present and on measurement in the Wheeler series has been explored at length in relation to the use of photographs by Robin Kelsey in *Archive Style: Photographs and Illustrations for U.S. Surveys, 1850–1890* (Berkeley: University of California Press, 2007) and is discussed in more detail later in this chapter.

22. The Indian Appropriations Act of 1851 authorized the creation of reservations for Native American tribes, principally in Oklahoma Territory; however, stepped-up relocation of tribes onto reservation lands occurred under the "Peace Plan" of President Ulysses S. Grant in 1869.

23. Wheeler, *United States Geographical Surveys*, 1:218, 219.

24. George Catlin, *Illustrations of the Manners, Customs, and Condition of the North American Indians* (1848; London: Henry G. Bohn, 1851), 16. On the fantasy of a *"doomed race,"* see especially Brian Dippie, *The Vanishing American: White Attitudes and U.S. Indian Policy* (Middleton, CT: Wesleyan University Press, 1982).

25. Lubbock, *Pre-historic Times*, 430; Putnam, *Reports upon Archaeological and Ethnological Collections*, 7, in reference specifically to shedding light on the question of whether Native Americans were autochthonous or had migrated from Asia.

26. Putnam, *Reports upon Archaeological and Ethnological Collections*, 4, 1, 279.

27. Putnam refers primarily to *Annual Report upon the Geographical Explorations and Surveys West of the One Hundredth Meridian, in California, Nevada, Nebraska, Utah, Colorado, New Mexico, Wyoming, and Montana: Being Appendix LL of the Annual Report of the Chief of Engineers for 1875* (Washington, DC: Government Printing Office, 1875).

28. Kelsey, *Archive Style*, 88. If one looks closely at O'Sullivan's photograph of the Cañon de Chelle, one can see members of the expedition posed on top of the ruined buildings both above and below the cliff.

29. The exception is the frontispiece to Putnam's report, a depiction of "The Cachina (a Sacred Dance) at the Zuni Pueblo."

30. Kelsey, *Archive Style*, 114.

Contributors

Chad A. Barbour is associate professor of English at Lake Superior State University. He is the author of *From Daniel Boone to Captain America: Playing Indian in American Popular Culture* (2016). His articles have appeared in the *Journal of Popular Culture* and the *International Journal of Comic Art*. His current research focuses on depictions and interpretations of US history in underground comix.

Jimmy L. Bryan Jr. is associate professor of history at Lamar University. He is the author of *The American Elsewhere: Adventure and Manliness in the Age of Expansion* (2017) and *More Zeal Than Discretion: The Westward Adventures of Walter P. Lane* (2008). He is also the editor of *The Martial Imagination: Cultural Aspects of American Warfare* (2013). His article "Unquestionable Geographies: The Empirical and the Romantic in U.S. Expansionist Cartography, 1810–1848" was published in the *Pacific Historical Review* (2018). Bryan's next book will investigate how early nineteenth-century Gothic authors and artists subverted the project of US expansion. Visit his website at www.jimmylbryanjr.net.

Daniel J. Burge is an instructor of history at the University of Alabama. His research focuses on opposition to manifest destiny during the nineteenth century. His article "Manifest Mirth: The Humorous Critique of Manifest Destiny, 1846–1858" appeared in the *Western Historical Quarterly* (2016). He is currently working on a book-length manuscript on the opponents of manifest destiny.

Maria Angela Diaz is assistant professor of history at Utah State University. She published "To Conquer the Coast: Pensacola, the Gulf of Mexico, and the Construction of American Imperialism, 1820–1848," in the *Florida Histor-*

ical Quarterly (2016). She is working on a book entitled *Saving the Southern Empire: Territorial Expansion in the Gulf South and Latin America, 1845–1865.*

Gerrit Dirkmaat is an assistant professor of church history and doctrine at Brigham Young University. He has worked with the Joseph Smith Papers Project since 2010, serving as a historian/volume editor on four separate volumes. He currently serves as editor of the academic journal *Mormon Historical Studies*, published by the Mormon Historic Sites Foundation. In addition to multiple articles, he is the coauthor, along with Michael Hubbard MacKay, of *From Darkness unto Light: Joseph Smith's Translation and Publication of the Book of Mormon* (2015).

Andy Doolen is a professor of American literature at the University of Kentucky. His books include *Territories of Empire: U.S. Writing from the Louisiana Purchase to Mexican Independence* (2014) and *Fugitive Empire: Locating Early American Imperialism* (2005). His current research focuses on John Dunn Hunter and Native self-determination in Mexican Texas.

Kenneth Haltman is H. Russell Pitman Professor of Art History at the University of Oklahoma. Among other accolades, he received fellowships from the Fulbright-Hays Program, the Andrew W. Mellon Foundation, and the Henry C. Luce Foundation. He is the author of *Looking Close and Seeing Far: Samuel Seymour, Titian Ramsay Peale, and the Art of the Long Expedition, 1818–1823* (2008). With Jules David Prown, he edited *American Artifacts: Essays in Material Culture* (2000) and has translated and edited French works by Gaston Bachelard, including *Earth and Reveries of Will* (2002) and *Fragments of a Poetics of Fire* (1997), and by René Brimo, *The Evolution of Taste in American Collecting* (2016). He is currently working on a collection of essays, *Artists and Hunters: Figures of Predatory Looking in Nineteenth-Century American Art*, and an edited volume with Richard Read, *Colonization and Wilderness in Nineteenth-Century Australian and American Landscape.*

Matthew N. Johnston is an associate professor in art history and chair of the Art Department at Lewis and Clark College. He is the author of *Narrating the Landscape: Print Culture and American Expansion in the Nineteenth Century* (2016). His article "Hamlin Garland's Detour into Art Criticism: Forecasting the Triumph of Popular Culture over Populism at the End of the Frontier" appeared in the *Journal of American Culture* (2011).

Elana Krischer is a PhD candidate and graduate assistant at the University at Albany, SUNY. Her research focuses on the Senecas, western expansion, and settler colonialism. Her work has appeared in *Iroquoia: The Journal of the Conference on Iroquois Research*. She was a Gest Fellow at the Haverford College Quaker and Special Collections and received the Larry J. Hackman Research Residency Award from the New York State Archives.

Thomas Richards Jr. was named the 2017–2018 David J. Weber Fellow for the Study of Southwestern America at the Clements Center for Southwest Studies, Southern Methodist University. He previously served as 2015–2016 Dissertation Fellow at the McNeil Center for Early American Studies. His article "'Farewell to America': The Expatriation Politics of Overland Migration, 1841–1846," which appeared in a special issue of the *Pacific Historical Review* (2017), won the Michael P. Malone Award from the Western History Association. He also coauthored the introduction to that issue. He is currently at work on a book that examines breakaway republics during the era of US expansion that is forthcoming from Johns Hopkins University Press.

Susan L. Roberson is a professor of English and director of the Women and Gender Studies Program at Texas A&M University-Kingsville. She has published two books, *Antebellum American Women Writers and the Road: American Mobilities* (2010) and *Emerson in His Sermons: A Man-Made Self* (1995). In addition, she has edited four collections of essays, including *Women, America, and Movement: Narratives of Relocation* (1998) and *Defining Travel: Diverse Visions* (2007). She has received two Humanities Initiatives Grants from the National Endowment for the Humanities (2009, 2017). She is currently working on a project that examines nineteenth-century American travel writers who reflect on their country to get at a sense of how some of the keenest observers commented on transportation, as well as geographic, economic, and political changes during the long nineteenth century.

Laurel Clark Shire is associate professor of history and codirector of the Digital History Lab at Western University in London, Ontario, Canada. The maps that she created for this volume developed out of research conducted for her monograph *The Threshold of Manifest Destiny: Gender and National Expansion in Florida* (2016). She thanks Steve Marti, Bill Turkel, and the rest of the DH Lab Group for introducing her to the wonders of historical GIS and Wolfram Mathematica.

Index